HELLENIC STUDIES 32

The Politics of Ethnicity and
the Crisis of the Peloponnesian League

T0339175

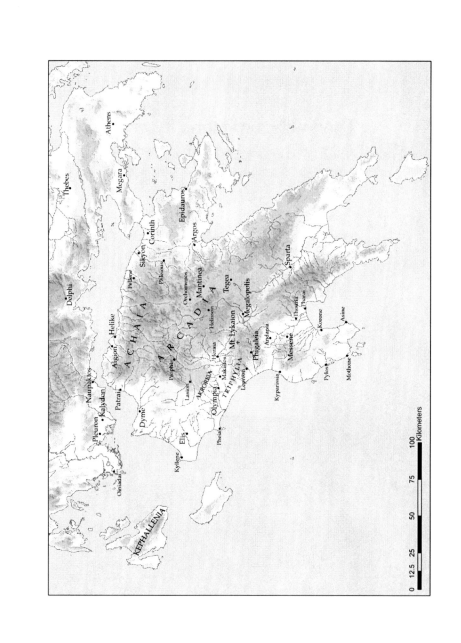

Kilometers
0 12.5 25   50   75   100

The Politics of Ethnicity and
the Crisis of the Peloponnesian League

Edited by
Peter Funke and Nino Luraghi

CENTER FOR HELLENIC STUDIES
Trustees for Harvard University
Washington, DC
Distributed by Harvard University Press
Cambridge, Massachusetts and London, England
2009

The Politics of Ethnicity and the Crisis of the Peloponnesian League
Edited by Peter Funke and Nino Luraghi
Copyright © 2009 Center for Hellenic Studies, Trustees for Harvard University
All Rights Reserved.
Published by Center for Hellenic Studies, Trustees for Harvard University,
    Washington, DC.
Distributed by Harvard University Press, Cambridge, Massachusetts
    and London, England

LIBRARY OF CONGRESS CATALOGING-IN-PUBLICATION DATA
The politics of ethnicity and the crisis of the Peloponnesian League : textual and
philosophical issues / edited by Peter Funke and Nino Luraghi.
    p. cm. -- (Hellenic studies ; 32)
 Includes bibliographical references and index.
 ISBN 978-0-674-03199-9 (alk. paper)
1. Peloponnesus (Greece)--Politics and government. 2. Peloponnesian League.
3. Ethnicity--Political aspects--Greece--Peloponnesus--History. 4. Regionalism--
Political aspects--Greece--Peloponnesus--Case studies. 5. Peloponnesus (Greece)--
History. 6. Peloponnesus (Greece)--Antiquities. 7. Ethnology--Greece--Peloponnesus.
8. Sparta (Greece)--History. 9. Sparta (Greece)--Politics and government. I. Funke,
Peter, 1950- II. Luraghi, Nino. III. Title. IV. Series.
 DF261.P3P65 2009
 938'.606--dc22
                                                                    2009015260

Contents

Acknowledgements

MOST OF THE CONTRIBUTIONS COLLECTED in this book were first submitted as papers at the conference "Ethnizität als Argument. Der Untergang des Peloponnesischen Bundes," held at the Westfälische Wilhelms-Universität of Münster (Germany) on November 14th-16th, 2003. The editors wish to acknowledge the generous financial support of the Gerda-Henkel-Stiftung, which made the conference possible. In Münster, Dr. Matthias Haake and Ms Annedore Wessels contributed in a most selfless way to the smooth progress of the event: to them goes the heartfelt gratitude of the editors. Turning a number of papers written in various languages into the chapters of this book would not have been possible without the help of Clare M. Gillis and Richard Short (both Harvard), who worked on translating and fine-tuning texts in foreign languages or written in English by non-native speakers, and Maša Ćulumović and John Tully (both Harvard), who did editorial work on footnotes and bibliographies. Rose McLean (Princeton) did invaluable work on the index. They all deserve the warmest thanks from the editors. The Loeb Fund of the Department of the Classics of Harvard University provided welcome financial support for most of such work. In its final stages, the Magee Fund of the Department of Classics of Princeton University added its crucial contribution. In the end, the anonymous referee for Harvard University Press contributed a most careful and perceptive reading and much food for thought to the contributors. The editors wish to acknowledge his especially selfless contribution.

Peter Funke and Nino Luraghi

Abbreviations

CEG   P. A. Hansen (ed.), *Carmina epigraphica Graeca saeculorum VIII-V a.Chr. n.*, Berlin and New York 1983.

DGE   E. Schwyzer (ed.), *Dialectorum Graecarum exempla epigraphica potiora*, Leipzig 1923.

FdD   *Fouilles de Delphes*, III, *Les Inscriptions*, Paris 1909-

FGH   F. Jacoby (ed.), *Fragmente der griechischen Historiker*, Berlin, then Leiden, 1923-1964.

Fowler   R. L. Fowler (ed.), *Early Greek Mythography*, I, *Text and Introduction*, Oxford 2000.

I. Delos   *Inscriptions de Délos*, Paris 1926-.

I. Ephes.   C. Börker, H. Engelmann, D. Knibbe, R. Meriç, J. Nollé, S. Sahin (eds.), *Inschriften von Ephesos*, Bonn 1979-1984.

IG   *Inscriptiones Graecae consilio et auctoritate Academiae Scientiarum Berolinensis et Brandenburgensis editae*, Berlin 1873-

IKRP   W. Blümel (ed.), *Inschriften der rhodischen Peraia*, Bonn 1991.

I. Lindos C. Blinkenberg (ed.), *Lindos. Fouilles de l'acropole 1902-1914*, II, *Inscriptions*, Berlin and Copenhagen 1941.

I. Magnesia am Sipylos
          T. Ihnken (ed.), *Inschriften von Magnesia am Sipylos*, Bonn 1978.

I. Mylasa W. Blümel (ed.), *Inschriften von Mylasa*, Bonn 1987.

IPArk   G. Thür, Gerhard and H. Taeuber (eds.), *Prozessrechtliche Inschriften der griechischen Poleis: Arkadien*, Vienna 1994.

I. Smyrna G. Petzl (ed.), *Inschriften von Smyrna*, Bonn 1982-1987.

IvO   W. Dittenberger and K. Purgold (eds.), *Inschriften von Olympia*, Berlin 1896.

LIMC   *Lexicon iconographicum mythologiae classicae*, Zurich 1981-1999.

LSCG   F. Sokolowski (ed.), *Les lois sacrées des cites grecques*, Paris 1969.

LSJ   H. G. Liddell, R. Scott, H. S. Jones et al. (eds.), *Greek-English Lexicon*, revised edition, Oxford 1996.

LSS   F. Sokolowski (ed.), *Les lois sacrées des cites grecques. Supplément*, Paris 1962.

Milet   *Milet. Ergebnisse der Ausgrabungen und Untersuchungen seit dem Jahre 1899*, Berlin 1908-1935.

ML   R. Meiggs and D. Lewis (eds.), *A Selection of Greek Historical Inscriptions to the End of the Fifth Century BC*, Revised edition, Oxford 1988.

OGIS   W. Dittenberger (ed.), *Orientis Graeci inscriptiones selectae*, Leipzig 1903-1905.

RO   P. Rhodes and R. Osborne (eds.), *Greek Historical Inscriptions, 404-323 BC*, Oxford 2003.

RE   A. F. Pauly, G. Wissowa, W. Kroll et al. (eds.), *Realencyclopädie der klassischen Altertumswissenschaft*, Stuttgart, then Munich, 1894-1980.

SEG   *Supplementum epigraphicum Graecum*, Amsterdam 1923-

SGDI   F. Collitz and H. Bechtel (ed.), *Sammlung der griechischen Dialekt-Inschriften*, Göttingen 1884-1915.

Syll.[3]   W. Dittenberger (ed.), *Sylloge inscriptionum Graecarum*, third edition revised by F. Hiller von Gaertringen, Leipzig 1915-1924.

Staatsverträge
    Die Staatsverträge des Altertums, Munich 1969-

I

Between Mantinea and Leuctra

The Political World of the Peloponnese in a Time of Upheaval

Peter Funke

THE AIM OF THE REFLECTIONS that follow is to define the historical and political framework in which to locate the central topic of the conference whose results are presented here. In other words, my contribution has an introductory function and will try to sketch a background of sorts for the volume.[1] It will summarize the political prerequisites and conditions of the crisis of the Peloponnesian League and of the political upheaval in the Peloponnese after the battle of Leuctra, in an attempt to free the evaluation of these events from a one-sided perspective that is still widespread in scholarship. Thereby the complexity of the political configuration from which the new system of polities in the Peloponnese emerged in the late seventies and early sixties of the fourth century will appear with greater clarity.

1. Thebes and the Effects of the Battle of Leuctra (371 BCE)

An inscription from Thebes commemorates three men who clearly had distinguished themselves in the battle of Leuctra.[2] Their names—Xenokrates, Theopompos and Mnasilaos—are followed by this epigram:

> When the Spartan spear was dominant, then Xenocrates took by
> lot the task of offering a trophy to Zeus, not fearing the host from

---

[1] I thank K. Freitag and M. Haake for their critical reading of my manuscript, as well as all participants in the conference for suggestions and stimuli, and especially N. Luraghi and R. Short, who have also translated the text of my contribution.
[2] IG VII 2462; CEG 632; Rhodes and Osborne 2003:150–151 (= Nr. 30); references to further editions in Beister 1973:65fn3a.

the Eurotas or the Spartan shield. "Thebans are superior in war," proclaims the trophy won through victory/bringing victory by the spear at Leuctra; nor did we run second to Epaminondas.[3]

The monument appears to have been erected immediately after the battle.[4] Ever since the inscription was published,[5] scholars have tried to connect the text to passages from ancient authors that mention the fact that, before the battle, the oracle of Trophonios in Lebadeia emphatically encouraged the Thebans to fight against the Spartans. Besides shorter references by Callisthenes (FGH 124 F 22a = Cicero *On divination* 1.74), Diodorus (15.53.4), and Polyaenus (2.3.8), a passage from Pausanias (4.32.4–6) deserves special attention. According to Pausanias, Epaminondas had asked Xenokrates, in accordance with an oracle, to fetch the shield of Aristomenes, a legendary hero presumably from the time of the Second Messenian War, that was kept in the temple of Trophonios in Lebadeia, and use it to decorate a victory monument erected before the battle, for all the Spartans to see.

Hartmut Beister (1973) and Christopher Tuplin offer the most recent extensive discussions of these texts, revising previous interpretations in the attempt to clarify possible connections between the inscription and the literary tradition. They come to very different conclusions, which cannot be discussed in detail here, especially since it seems impossible to reach a final decision.[6] However, they agree that the story of the shield of Aristomenes reported by Pausanias has to be considered an invention of the Messenian historiography of the fourth century BCE.[7] This integration of the hero of Messenian freedom into Theban traditions about the battle of Leuctra certainly goes back to the attempt by the Messenians to consolidate their identity in the years after 370/69;[8] but it also reveals something about the

---

[3] Translation from Rhodes and Osborne 2003:151.

[4] For the date see the commentary of W. Dittenberger to IG VII 2462; see also Tuplin 1987:94f.

[5] The inscription was first published on May 17th, 1877 by S. A. Kumanudis in the Athenian newspaper *Palingenesia* and immediately generated lively reactions; see Beister 1973:65n1 and 2.

[6] See also the commentary by Rhodes and Osborne 2003:151f.

[7] Beister 1973:79–81; Tuplin 1987:101–103; Ogden 2004:134–138; see already Kiechle 1959:126f. On the person of Aristomenes, around whom many legends obviously grew after the liberation of Messenia by the Boeotians, see now Ogden 2004.

[8] However, the relationship to Boeotia, which was also displayed in, for example, the iconographic program of the statuary in the sanctuary of Asklepios and in the *hierothysion* at Messene (Pausanias 4.31.10–32.1), is only one component of this effort; on this, see also the fundamental treatments of Figueira 1999; Luraghi 2002; Luraghi, this volume.

way in which Thebes, the new dominant power in the Greek world, if for a short time, depicted itself in historiography. For the Thebans, it was obviously very important to show their newly acquired hegemony in the best light and to underpin it with ideology.[9] Of course, the Thebans did unquestionably play a decisive role in the liberation of Messenia. The foundation of the city at Mount Ithome and the creation of a new Messenian state that accompanied it were doubtless consequences of the first Theban expedition in the winter of 370/69; Epaminondas' initiative and commitment clearly deserve credit for this.[10] It is also beyond question that the battle of Leuctra laid the foundations for the dissolution of Spartan hegemony over the Peloponnese. From this point of view, it can be said that the (fictive) participation of Aristomenes in the outcome of the battle of Leuctra was perfectly justified on the level of ideology.

However, the Thebans' attempt to set themselves up as the champions of all the political upheavals in the Peloponnese and to take exclusive credit for all these profound transformations is much more controversial. Already the statue of Epaminondas, erected by the Thebans after his death, was allegedly accompanied by the following epigram:

> By our counsels was Sparta shorn of her glory, and holy Messene received at last her children. With Thebes' arms Megalopolis was surrounded with walls, and all Greece won independence and freedom.[11]

Pausanias and Plutarch—and before them, presumably, already the Boeotian or Theban local historiography of the Hellenistic age—have contributed to overemphasizing the role of Thebes in such processes of political transformation.[12] It is the Thebans who decide after Leuctra to bring back the Mantineans to their city (Pausanias 8.8.10), and Epaminondas in particular is depicted not only as the founder of Messene, but also as being responsible for the Mantineans' return and for the unification of Arcadia and the foundation of Megalopolis (Pausanias 9.14.4; Plutarch *Pelopidas* 24).

This Theban viewpoint has had a long-lasting influence and its traces can still be seen in modern scholarship. In the nineteenth century, Ernst

---

[9] See also Ogden 2004:138–142.

[10] See Roebuck 1941:27–41; Meyer 1978:263–266; Buckler 1980:70–90; Buckler 2003:308–310; Grandjean 2003:49–53, 65–70; Shipley 2004:562f.

[11] Pausanias 9.15.6; translation from Beck 2000:341f; cf. also Luraghi, this volume.

[12] A brief overview of the development of Boeotian historiography is offered by F. Jacoby in FGH IIIb:151–153; see also Shrimpton 1971; Sordi 1974; Buckler 1980:263–277; Tuplin 1984.

Curtius wrote in his *Griechische Geschichte*: "Considering that Epaminondas, in such a short time and with his limited resources, founded or contributed to the foundation of Mantinea, Messene, Megalopolis, ... one will not want to deny him the honor of having been the predecessor of Alexander and his successors in the royal art of city-founding."[13] The depiction of Thebes as the force that propelled and shaped everything, that single-handedly ignited the political upheaval in the Peloponnese, and that left its imprint on the emerging new political world by transmitting to it its own constitutional model, is still present in the most recent scholarship. The underlying assumption is that the basic federal structure of the Boeotian League, in its reformed state after 379, can be identified as the model for the new political formations of the Peloponnese. Hartmut Beister writes: "As is generally known, the tendency to replicate and disseminate its own political model is characteristic of Theban foreign policy after Leuctra."[14] And Simon Hornblower observes: "One of the most permanent legacies (of the Theban hegemony) was the export of the federal principle."[15]

Admittedly, it is indeed noticeable that most of the new or reformed polities that emerged in the Peloponnese did not follow the "classical" model of the Greek *polis*, but rather showed a basic federal structure, more or less pronounced in each case, or at any rate were characterized by peculiar forms of political participation for the various groups of populations that formed the several polities.[16] But only a very superficial analysis could lead one to interpret this as the result of the export by the Thebans of their federal principle. Such an interpretation misunderstands the character of the Boeotian κοινόν after its re-foundation in 379 BCE, as Hans Beck has recently insisted.[17] With his detailed analysis of the institutional structure of the Boeotian League, Beck has shown that in the form it took after 379 BCE it could not be considered a true federal state any more, but should rather be seen "as a highly centralized or as a unitary state."[18] It is not necessary

---

[13] Curtius 1889:383: "Bedenkt man, wie Epameinondas mit seinen geringen Mitteln und in so kurzer Frist Mantineia, Messene, Megalopolis gründete oder gründen half, ... so wird man dem Epameinondas nicht die Ehre streitig machen dürfen, dass er in der königlichen Kunst der Stadtgründungen Alexanders und seiner Nachfolger Vorgänger gewesen ist."

[14] Beister 1989:151: "Kennzeichnend ... für die thebanische Außenpolitik nach Leuktra ist bekanntlich die Reproduktion und Verbreitung des eigenen politischen Modells."

[15] Hornblower 2002:200; see also 258f.

[16] For an overview of these political developments, with references to sources and bibliography, see Beck 1997; Funke 1998; Lehmann 2001.

[17] Beck 2000.

[18] Beck 2000:338.

to repeat Beck's arguments in detail. For present purposes, it will suffice to note that he has shown convincingly that Thebes was able to use the correlation between κοινόν and συντέλεια as an instrument to consolidate its grip over the whole of Boeotia. Therefore at that point the Boeotian constitution can hardly have functioned as an immediate model for the new states emerging in the Peloponnese.[19]

The constitutional character of the Boeotian League, which had undergone fundamental transformations with respect to the regime in force until 386,[20] is not the only argument against overestimating the influence of Thebes on the political developments in the Peloponnese. As George Grote clearly showed,[21] a critical analysis of the sources, comparing the aforementioned statements by Plutarch and Pausanias with, in particular, the relevant narratives by Xenophon and Diodorus, leaves no doubt that foundations had already been laid in the Peloponnese before the first Theban expedition. The συνοικισμός of Mantinea and the foundation of the Arcadian League had already taken place, and it seems that even the foundation of Megalopolis had already been decided upon in the summer of 370.[22] Furthermore, the diplomatic maneuvers of Arcadians, Eleians, and Argives in the summer of 370 show that, in spite of the success of Leuctra, Thebes was not necessarily the first choice of ally for the Peloponnesians. On the contrary, the Athenians were the first to be approached, and only after their refusal did the three Peloponnesian states turn to Thebes and conclude an alliance with the Thebans.[23]

It is not my intention to throw out the baby with the bath water and to suggest that Thebes could not have had any influence whatsoever on the political developments in the Peloponnese. What my contribution criticizes is the overestimation of the role of Thebes in the political reorganization of the Peloponnese, because it promotes a distorted assessment of the complexity of the situation. There is no doubt that the outcome of the battle of Leuctra was a fundamental and necessary precursor to the thorough-going transfor-

---

[19] Contrary to what I previously thought, see Funke 1998:63 on the Arcadian League.
[20] See most recently, with further bibliography, Lehmann 2001:25–33; Behrwald 2005:119f. Notice that the system of the συντέλεια of single member-states already functioned as an instrument of power before 386.
[21] Grote 1888 v.8:194–196.
[22] Συνοικισμός of Mantinea: Moggi 1976:251–256 (= Nr. 40); foundation of the Arcadian League: Dušanić 1970; Nielsen 2002:474–499; foundation of Megalopolis: Moggi 1976:93–325 (= Nr. 45); Hornblower 1990; Nielsen 2002:414–455.
[23] On this, with references to sources and bibliography, Hornblower 2002:247–249; Buckler 2003:302–310.

mation of the power balance in the Peloponnese—fundamental and necessary, but not sufficient. By the same token, it is beyond question that Thebes
played an active role in the liberation of Messene and in the creation of the
Messenian state. Theban ambitions and their clash with Spartan hegemony
corresponded to the interests of most Peloponnesian states—but only temporarily, as shown by the admonition of Lykomedes of Mantinea, who as early
as 368 warned his fellow Arcadians against the danger of rashly granting
the Thebans the dominant position formerly occupied by the Spartans
(Xenophon *Hellenica* 7.1.24).

2. Sparta and the Consequences of the Battle of Mantinea (418 BCE)

No attempt to explain the events in the Peloponnese in those years that sees
the battle of Leuctra as the single cause of everything can do justice to the
facts. Rather, it is necessary to recognize that the Peloponnesian states had
their own dynamics that certainly received new and decisive impetus from
the Theban victory, but that had displayed their effectiveness already before
that event. In what follows, I intend to investigate whether it is possible to see
in Peloponnesian politics before 371 significant points that can contribute to
a better understanding of the events after 371, and, if so, where these may be
found. To this end it is necessary to look closely at the conditions of the first
decades of the fourth century and to the already precarious situation of the
Peloponnesian League. However, since my observations are intended only to
provide a framework for further reflection, I will confine myself to a rather
general outline, considering only one case study more closely.[24]

In the immediate aftermath of the Peloponnesian War, burgeoning
resistance amongst their former allies, which had sprung up suddenly,
was already creating difficulties for the Spartans.[25] Disappointed by the
limited readiness of the Spartans to allow for their allies' interests in the
rearrangement of the political balance, some states, especially Boeotia and
Corinth, famously turned their backs to the Spartan alliance and eventually,
together with Athens and Argos, openly declared their hostility to Sparta
in 395/4. The Corinthian War that followed, which soon sucked in the whole
Greek world, destabilized Sparta's hegemonic position, increasingly endan-

---

[24] A more comprehensive discussion of the διοικισμός of Mantinea, here taken as case study, can be found in Funke 2004.

[25] On what follows, see the relevant discussions e.g. in Hamilton 1979; Funke 1980; Hamilton 1991; Tuplin 1993; Buckler 2003.

gering even the cohesion of the core area of the Peloponnesian League. Only in 386 were the Spartans able to emerge as προστάται of the King's Peace and to exploit this position in order to consolidate their wavering hegemony. The fact that in these circumstances Sparta treated its own allies in the Peloponnese particularly harshly shows how tense the situation within the Spartan alliance had become. With targeted punitive measures the Spartans tried to re-establish their authority over the Peloponnese and to prevent any further disloyal behavior on the part of their allies (Xenophon, *Hellenica* 5.2.1). At first, in 385/4, they made of Mantinea an example that cannot have failed to impress the other allies. Since the Mantineans had rejected the request of the Spartan envoys to pull down their city-walls as a token of loyalty to the Peloponnesian League, the Spartans started a siege that ended up with the conquest of Mantinea and the διοικισμός of the city.[26]

What makes the treatment the Spartans meted out to Mantinea particularly telling about the political situation in the Peloponnese is its extraordinary brutality, perceived as such also by contemporaries. After the city surrendered, the Spartans were not content with destroying the fortifications and putting in place a regime favorable to themselves, but insisted on the dissolution of the urban center.[27] The Mantineans were compelled to give up their houses in the city and to move back to the four or five villages from whose union the city of Mantinea had originated, in the first half of the fifth or already around the middle of the sixth century BCE.[28]

What motivated the Spartans in 385/4 to such a harsh course of action against Mantinea, and to such a blatant violation of the conditions of the King's Peace?[29] I intend to pursue this question in what follows, because this case makes it possible to show that the Spartan system of alliances in the Peloponnese was already fragile in the decades before the battle of Leuctra. At the same time, it is possible to point to the broad increase in autonomy that the individual *poleis* were striving for already in those years—always within the limits of what was politically feasible.

---

[26] Moggi 1976:151–153 with overview of the sources.

[27] The destruction of the city-walls was part of the normal repertoire of Greek power politics; cf. e.g. the measures taken by the Athenians against Poteidaia (Thucydides 1.56.2), Thasos (1.101.3), or Chios (4.51.1), by the Thebans against Thespiai (4.133.1), and by the Spartans themselves in previous years against Argos (5.83.2), Athens (Xenophon *Hellenica* 2.2.20; 2.2.23) and Elis (Xenophon *Hellenica* 3.2.30). By comparison, the διοικισμός was extraordinarily harsh.

[28] Xenophon *Hellenica* 5.2.5–7; Ephoros FGH 70 F 79; Diodorus 15.5.4;15.12.2; Strabo 8.3.2.

[29] On the question to what extent the treatment of Mantinea equalled a violation of the King's Peace see Funke 2004:429.

Xenophon mentions some reasons that are supposed to explain the behavior of the Spartans. However, the list of complaints that the Spartan envoys issued to the Mantineans before the opening of the hostilities, pointing to their disloyal behavior during the Corinthian War (*Hellenica* 5.2.2), is relatively vague and offers little explanation for the particularly harsh actions of the Spartans. Neither the Mantineans' secret dealings with the Argives, nor the fact that they contributed their contingent of troops only reluctantly, offer a really satisfactory justification for the brutal demolition of the urban settlement of the city, which was not only coupled with the shift from a democratic to an oligarchic-timocratic constitution, but possibly involved a radical transformation of the unitary constitution of the *polis*.[30]

In this connection, Xenophon's reference to the fact that the treaty between Sparta and Mantinea, concluded after the dissolution of the anti-Spartan alliance of 418/7 and agreed to last thirty years,[31] had just expired (*Hellenica* 5.2.2) may be more important. The conclusion of this treaty for a limited period of time shows in itself that the structure of the Spartan system of alliances we call the Peloponnesian League was decidedly more complex than we often tend to think. Clearly not all the bilateral treaties that formed it replicated the model of the treaty between Sparta and the Aetolian Erxadieis,[32] but rather, they adapted to concrete political needs and possi-

---

[30] On the institutional form of the constitution of Mantinea in the years between 384 and 370 the sources offer hardly any useful evidence. According to a note in Xenophon *Hellenica* 5.2.7, from 384 onwards it was no longer the *polis* of Mantinea that had to contribute its contingent of troops, but each of the four or five villages by itself, each under the control of one Spartan *xenagos*. This regulation suggests that in all likelihood the very unity of the *polis* was at least to some extent dissolved. It is questionable whether this dissolution implies that each of the components of the former *polis* of Mantinea now had its own oligarchic constitution, as suggested by Gehrke 1985:104f; cf. e.g. Hodkinson and Hodkinson 1981:287f. In any case, this rearrangement could not be very effective, since clearly the vast majority of the population of Mantinea opposed it. The extraordinarily smooth and resolute implementation of the second synoecism (see Moggi 1976:251–256 [=Nr. 40]; Gehrke 1985:105) shows that even fifteen years later the cohesion of the civic body had not suffered lasting damage.

[31] *Staatsverträge* II² 195.

[32] The interpretation advanced by Gschnitzer 1978 (= SEG 28.408; also SEG 49.392) for the treaty originally published by Peek 1974 (= SEG 26.461) still seems to me convincing, both as regards the date (first half of the fifth century BCE) and in the interpretation (treaty between Sparta and a hitherto unknown Peloponnesian polity). Every attempt to date the treaty later and to connect it with the Aetolians of Central Greece (see the overview of the different suggestions in Yates 2005:66n4) is undermined by a consideration of the historical circumstances that this would imply; see now also SEG 51.449.

bilities, and the Spartans must have accepted this situation as inevitable. The expiration of the peace treaty between Sparta and Mantinea in 387 must have made the continuing membership of Mantinea in the Peloponnesian League seem precarious, and correspondingly it must have conjured up at Sparta the fear that the relationship to Mantinea, tense as it was, but at least so far stabilized by the peace treaty, could once again, as it had done before 418/7, endanger Spartan control of the Northern Peloponnese.[33] That such fears were justified is shown by an inscription first published in 1987 with the text of a sympolity treaty between Mantinea and Helisson, a small political community on the Western border of the Mainalon massif, quite far away from Mantinea.[34]

The implications of this treaty in terms of political history have so far received surprisingly little attention. However, it sheds new light not only on the relationship between Sparta and Mantinea in the late fifth and early fourth century, but also on the ways and means used by Peloponnesian polities in order to create and protect autonomous zones of action for themselves. Having discussed the date of this treaty in depth elsewhere, I do not intend to repeat my arguments here. Suffice it to say that, after considering the various options, the sympolity treaty has to be dated before 385.[35] What are the implications of such a date for the historical interpretation of this document? In order to find an answer, it is necessary to consider the situation of Mantinea before 418. For the first phase of the Peloponnesian War, some hints in Thucydides point to a close relationship between Mantinea and Helisson. Even though Helisson itself is not mentioned, it is possible to infer from Thucydides (4.134.1; 5.29.1; 5.33.1; 5.47.1; 5.67.2; 5.81.1) that, at the latest during the Archidamian War, the Mantineans had succeeded in building in Southwestern Arcadia a small hegemony of their own, which extended to Maenalia, of which Helisson was part. Thucydides uses for this the terminology of hegemonic symmachy, and based on Thomas Heine Nielsen's comprehensive investigation, we may suppose that Mantinea's hegemony was structured like the larger hegemonic symmachies, such as the Delian and Peloponnesian Leagues.[36] It is perfectly understandable that the Spartans were keen to dissolve such regional hegemony within their

---

[33] On the history of the relationship between Sparta and Mantinea see the summary accounts in Amit 1973:121–182; Nielsen 2002:389–391.

[34] Te Riele 1987 (= SEG 37.340); see also Dubois 1988; IPArk 9.

[35] Funke 2004:431–433.

[36] Nielsen 1996:79–84; Nielsen 2002:367–372; see already Cartledge 1987:257–259.

own sphere of influence. Therefore, when Mantinea too, soon after 418, had to acquiesce in a peace with Sparta, one of the main points of the treaty was that the Mantineans had to "give up their rule over the *poleis*" (Thucydides 5.81.1: τὴν ἀρχὴν ἀφεῖσαν τῶν πόλεων) and thereby to renounce control over extended parts of Arcadia.

We can therefore conclude that from the mid-twenties of the fifth century at the latest, and until 418/7, Helisson, like the majority of the other polities of northern Mainalia, was almost certainly linked to Mantinea by an alliance. After that, such ties were necessarily severed by the treaty between Sparta and Mantinea. Since, however, we have every reason to date the sympoly between Mantinea and Helisson before 385, we can see it as evidence that, at the beginning of the fourth century, Mantinea was again attempting to build up its power, especially against Sparta but also against other neighboring *poleis* such as Tegea, by extending the citizen body. In this connection, one thinks especially of the Corinthian War. The Mantineans probably exploited Sparta's weakness at that point, in order to win back the position of power that had been taken away from them by the thirty-years peace with Sparta. In the sympoly treaty, the reference to "the other *poleis*" (SEG 37.340 line 9: κατάπερ ἐν ταῖς ἄλλαις πόλισι) suggests strongly that at that point other polities, too, possibly former allies of the Mantineans, had concluded a sympoly with them. This reference to further *poleis* and the long distance between Mantinea and Helisson show with full clarity the political significance of such agreements.

The fact that Mantinea was now no longer using treaties of alliance, but rather sympolities, was certainly a clever trick to circumvent the corresponding clauses of the thirty-years peace with Sparta. Of prime importance was the insight that a sympoly ensured a much stronger bond than any sort of alliance. It seems that the Mantineans were operating already at the beginning of the fourth century with an instrument of constitutional law that was going to be applied on a much larger scale and with even more success in the foundation of the Arcadian League in 370. The example of the fusion of Argos and Corinth in 392 shows that other *poleis*, too, were able to resort to sympoly or to similar systems in order to strengthen their autonomous position in the balance of power in the Peloponnese.[37] This emergence of sympoly, attested impressively by the case of Mantinea, can be observed also in other parts of the Greek world, but it seems to be particularly

---

[37] On this fusion, see Robinson's contribution to this volume, and cf. Moggi 1976:242–250 (= Nr. 39); Funke 1980:82n29; Tuplin 1982; Whitby 1984; Moggi 1996:159f.

pronounced in the Peloponnese. Here, the relations and conflicts between polities were characterized in a peculiar way by the interplay between the autonomy of the *polis* and regional—that is, ethnic—cohesion. The tendency towards sympolity across the boundaries of the individual *poleis* may in many ways have been determined by foreign policy, especially insofar as it worked in opposition to Sparta. However, it is also the political consequence of a conspicuous phenomenon: the "ethnicization" of the political world of the Peloponnese at the end of the fifth and beginning of the fourth centuries BCE.

In this contribution, I have tried to focus on some political aspects of this phenomenon as case studies, in order to offer a background of sorts for the examination of the assumed "politics of ethnicity." What I have tried to show on the political level has another side on the level of ideology. The tendency to overstep the narrow borders of the *polis* corresponds to the attempt at founding or recovering the identity of the group beyond the *polis*. Whether we think of the Mantineans, who went to the Mainalon massif not only to reinforce their influence there, but also to recover the bones of Arkas and bring them to Mantinea,[38] or of Lykomedes, who conjured up the autochthony of of the Arcadians against all political pretensions from outside,[39] ethnicity became a political argument.

Bibliography

Amit, M. 1973. *Great and Small Poleis. A Study in the Relations between the Great Powers and the Small Cities in Ancient Greece.* Brussels.

Beck, H. 1997. *Polis und Koinon. Untersuchungen zur Geschichte und Struktur der griechischen Bundesstaaten im 4. Jahrhundert v. Chr.* Historia Einzelschriften 114. Stuttgart.

Beck, H. 2000. "Thebes, the Boiotian League, and the 'Rise of Federalism' in Fourth Century Greece." *Presenza e funzione della città di Tebe nella cultura greca* (ed. P. A. Bernardini) 331–344. Pisa.

Behrwald, R. 2005. *Hellenica von Oxyrhynchos. Herausgegeben, übersetzt und kommentiert.* Darmstadt.

Beister, H. 1970. *Untersuchungen zu der Zeit der thebanischen Hegemonie.* Bonn.

---

[38] Pausanias 8.9.3–4; 8.36.8; on this, see Nielsen 2002:403f.

[39] Xenophon *Hellenica* 7.1.23–24. Herodotus 2.171.3; 8.78,1 and Thucydides 1.2.3 show that Lykomedes could count on older and widespread notions.

11

Beister, H. 1973. "Ein thebanisches Tropaion bereits vor Beginn der Schlacht bei Leuktra. Zur Interpretation von IG VII 2462 und Paus. 4,32,5 f." *Chiron* 3:65–84.

Beister, H. 1989. "Hegemoniales Denken in Theben." *Boiotika. Vorträge zum 5. Internationalen Böotien-Kolloquium* (eds. H. Beister and J. Buckler) 131–153. Münchener Arbeiten zur Alten Geschichte 2. Munich.

Buckler, J. 1980. *The Theban Hegemony, 371-362 B.C.* Harvard Historical Studies 98. Cambridge, MA.

Buckler, J. 2003. *Aegean Greece in the Fourth Century BC.* Leiden.

Cartledge, P. 1987. *Agesilaos and the Crisis of Sparta.* Baltimore.

Curtius, E. 1889. *Griechische Geschichte. III: Bis zum Ende der Selbständigkeit Griechenlands.* Berlin. Sixth Revised Edition.

Dubois, L. 1988. "À propos d' une nouvelle inscription arcadienne." *BCH* 112:279–290.

Dušanić, S. 1970. *The Arcadian League of the Fourth Century.* Belgrade.

Figueira, T. J. 1999. "The Evolution of the Messenian Identity." *Sparta: New Perspectives* (eds. S. Hodkinson and A. Powell) 211–244. London.

Funke, P. 1980. *Homónoia und Arché. Athen und die griechische Staatenwelt vom Ende des Peloponnesischen Krieges bis zum Königsfrieden (404/3 - 387/6 v. Chr.)* Historia Einzelschriften 37. Wiesbaden.

Funke, P. 1998. "Die Bedeutung der griechischen Bundesstaaten in der politischen Theorie und Praxis des 5. und 4. Jh. v. Chr." *Politische Theorie und Praxis im Altertum* (ed. W. Schuller) 59–71. Darmstadt.

Funke, P. 2004. "Sparta und die peloponnesische Staatenwelt zu Beginn des 4. Jahrhunderts und der Dioikismos von Mantineia." *Xenophon and his World* (ed. C. Tuplin) 427–435. Historia Einzelschriften 172. Stuttgart.

Gehrke, H.-J. 1985. *Stasis. Untersuchungen zu den inneren Kriegen in den griechischen Staaten des 5. und 4. Jahrhunderts v. Chr.* Munich.

Grandjean, C. 2003. *Les Mésséniens de 370/369 au 1er siècle de notre ère. Monnayages et histoire.* Athens.

Grote, G. 1888. *History of Greece.* London.

Gschnitzer, F. 1978. *Ein neuer spartanischer Staatsvertrag und die Verfassung des Peloponnesischen Bundes.* Beiträge zur klassischen Philologie 93. Meisenheim.

Hamilton, C. D. 1979. *Sparta's Bitter Victories: Politics and Diplomacy in the Corinthian War.* Ithaca.

Hamilton, C. D. 1991. *Agesilaus and the Failure of Spartan Hegemony.* Ithaca.

Hodkinson, S., and Hodkinson, H. 1981. "Mantineia and the Mantinike: Settlement and Society in a Greek *Polis*." *ABSA* 76:239–296.

Hornblower, S. 2002. *The Greek World 479-323 BC*. London. Third Revised Edition.

Hornblower, S. 1990. "When was Megalopolis Founded?" *ABSA* 85:71–77.

Kiechle, F. 1959. *Messenische Studien. Untersuchungen zur Geschichte der messenischen Kriege und der Auswanderung der Messenier*. Kallmünz.

Lehmann, G. A. 2001. *Ansätze zu einer Theorie des griechischen Bundesstaates bei Aristoteles und Polybios*. Abhandlungen der Akademie der Wissenschaften in Göttingen. Philologisch-Historische Klasse 3.242. Göttingen.

Luraghi, N. 2002. "Becoming Messenian." *JHS* 122:45–69.

Meyer, E. 1978. "Messene/Messenien." *RE* Suppl. 15: 136–289.

Moggi, M. 1976. *I sinecismi interstatali greci*. Pisa.

Moggi, M. 1996. "I sinecismi greci del IV secolo a.C." *Le IVe siècle av. J.-C. Approches historiographiques* (ed. P. Carlier) 259–271. Paris.

Nielsen, T. H. 1996. "A Survey of Dependent *Poleis* in Classical Arkadia." *More Studies in the Ancient Greek Polis* (eds. M. H. Hansen and K. A. Raaflaub) 63–105. Historia Einzelschriften 108. Stuttgart.

Nielsen, T. H. 2002. *Arkadia and its Poleis in the Archaic and Classical Periods*. Göttingen.

Ogden, D. 2004. *Aristomenes of Messene: Legends of Sparta's Nemesis*. Swansea.

Peek, W. 1974. *Ein neuer spartanischer Staatsvertrag*. Abhandlungen der Sächsischen Akademie der Wissenschaften Leipzig. Philologisch-Historische Klasse 65.3. Berlin.

Rhodes, P. J., and Osborne, R., eds. 2003. *Greek Historical Inscriptions 404-323 BC*. Oxford.

te Riele, G. J. M. G. 1987. "Hélisson entre en sympolitie avec Mantinée: une nouvelle inscription d'Arcadie." *BCH* 111:167–190.

Roebuck, C. A. 1941. *A History of Messenia from 369 to 146 B.C.* Chicago.

Shipley, G. 2004. "Messenia." *An Inventory of Archaic and Classical Poleis* (eds. M. H. Hansen and T. H. Nielsen) 547–568. Oxford.

Shrimpton, G. S. 1971. "The Theban Supremacy in Fourth-Century Literature." *Phoenix* 25:310–318.

Sordi, M. 1974. "Propaganda politica e senso religioso nell'azione di Epaminonda." *CISA* 2:45–53.

Tuplin, C. J. 1982. "The Date of the Union of Corinth and Argos." *CQ* 32:75–83.

Tuplin, C. J. 1984. "Pausanias and Plutarch's Epameinondas." *CQ* 78:346–358.

Tuplin, C. J. 1987. "The Leuctra Campaign: Some Outstanding Problems." *Klio* 69:72–107.

Tuplin, C. J. 1993. *The Failings of Empire: A Reading of Xenophon Hellenica 2.3.11-7.5.27.* Historia Einzelschriften 76. Stuttgart.

Whitby, M. 1984. "The Union of Corinth and Argos: A Reconsideration." *Historia* 33:295–308.

Yates, D. C. 2005. "The Archaic Treaties between the Spartans and their Allies." *CQ* 55:65–76.

II

Achaea and the Peloponnese in the Late Fifth-Early Fourth Centuries

Klaus Freitag

T HE PRESENT CONTRIBUTION INVESTIGATES the relationship of Achaea to Sparta in the late fifth and early fourth centuries BCE[1] in order to find out whether ethnicity played a role in that relationship and, if so, in which contexts. For this reason, I will not discuss the ethnogenesis of the Achaeans, especially since C. Morgan's work,[2] some in combination with J. Hall,[3] has provided fundamental observations on the evidence and illuminated many aspects of the mechanisms that caused the ethnic identity of the Achaeans to emerge.[4]

The Achaeans of the Northern Peloponnese probably did not belong to the Peloponnesian League led by Sparta before 417 BCE. Two years earlier, in 419 BCE, the Athenian Alcibiades had marched through the Peloponnese with Athenian and allied troops, and on this occasion the Athenians reached Patrai in Achaea, where Alcibiades decided to connect the acropolis of the city to the harbor by long walls. However, the intervention of Corinth and Sikyon prevented the realization of the project.[5] It is not possible to put such information in a concrete political context from an Achaean perspective. Not only is it unclear how the other Achaean cities reacted to this situation, but we do not even know whether or not Patrai followed an independent course that led

---

[1] Still fundamental for this period is Larsen 1953; Anderson 1954; Koerner 1974; Rizakis 1995.

[2] Especially Morgan 2002. Morgan 1988, 1991, 2000.

[3] Morgan and Hall 1996.

[4] Walbank 2000. See now also Moscati Castelnuovo 2002.

[5] Thucydides 5.52.2.

the citizens to join Alcibiades—whatever this meant in concrete political and diplomatic terms.

At any rate, a little later Thucydides mentions briefly that after the battle of Mantinea the Spartans introduced in Achaea a new order of their liking (Thucydides 5.82.1). We can only speculate on the precise implications of this. In 417 BCE in the cities of the Achaeans, and also at the level of the Achaean League—if such a federal unit already existed at this time—the democratic constitutions, supported by a strong peasantry,[6] were transformed into "moderate" oligarchic regimes. "Moderate" means that access to active and passive voting rights was confined to citizens of hoplite status, and possibly above a certain age, thereby limiting the number of citizens with full rights. However, after the Spartan intervention the number of citizens with full political rights was probably still rather high, especially since the political order in the individual Achaean cities in the following years remained generally unchallenged and relatively stable.[7] Based on Thucydides' laconic comments, it is only a supposition that manipulation of the political structures of the Achaeans by the Spartans was a sort of punishment for their cooperation with the Athenians under Alcibiades.[8]

Whether the Achaeans as a whole or the individual cities became full members of the Peloponnesian League is unclear, as is how long they belonged to the League.[9] It is possible that the Spartans concluded some sort of special alliance with the Achaean League. The citizens of Pellene, close to Sikyon, who belonged to the Achaean *ethnos*, had taken their own political course earlier on, splitting from the other Achaeans and becoming allies of Sparta as an independent and self-conscious political entity.[10] Among the admirals honored with statues in the monument dedicated by Lysander at Delphi to commemorate the battle of Aigospotamoi, Axionikos, the captain from Pellene, is called by Pausanias *Akhaios ek Pellenes*, an Achaean from Pellene,[11] but we cannot be certain that the city at this point belonged to the Achaean federation. However, the epithet "Achaean" makes it clear that the Pellenians considered themselves as belonging to the Achaean *ethnos*.

As Mauro Moggi has recently shown in a fundamental contribution, it is unclear whether a federal state existed as the form of political organization

---

[6] See Robinson 1997:73–78 and especially Gehrke 1985:13–15.
[7] Gehrke 1985:14.
[8] Larsen 1953:802–803.
[9] Koerner 1974:480–483.
[10] Thucydides 2.9.2–3; 5.58.3–4.
[11] Pausanias 10.9.10.

of the Achaeans already in the fifth century BCE.[12] It is entirely possible that the Achaeans completed the last step from loose cooperation based on ethnicity to a federal state with a developed constitution under the leadership of Sparta and as members of the Peloponnesian League. At any rate, it is important to stress that the Spartans did not take any measure, even later, to eliminate a common political organization of the Achaeans, whatever its form. Rather, there are reasons to think that the Spartans recognized the integrity of the Achaean federal state. At any rate, the Achaeans belonged to the Peloponnesian League as a unit and expressed their will, within the limits granted by the structure of the League, with one single voice. It is possible that in the Peloponnesian League the Achaeans had one vote with Pellene having a separate one, as the Lysandrian monument indicates.

From the time of the Peloponnesian War to the year 362 BCE, the situation in Achaea seems relatively stable. The Achaeans reacted occasionally, but were generally rather inactive and favored the conservation of the status quo as far as Peloponnesian politics was concerned. Already in the fifth century they had kept out of major conflicts. They did not join the alliance against Persia,[13] and at the beginning of the Peloponnesian War, according to Thucydides, the whole of the Peloponnese was on Sparta's side except Argos and Achaea, which was connected by *philia* to both sides.[14] Of the Achaeans, only Pellene fought on the Spartans' side from the outset, while the others joined only later.

Before 389 BCE, the Achaeans had granted the federal citizenship to the Kalydonians.[15] This measure is extremely important for two reasons:

1. The political procedure of the Achaeans shows that by this time there was a sort of double citizenship, i.e. the Kalydonians possessed, like the other Achaeans, both citizenship of their own city and citizenship of the federal state.[16] The existence of forms of federal organization along these lines can be seen in inscriptions from the late fifth century. A *Som[ ] ophon Achaios Olenios* shows up in the famous inscription from Sparta listing contributors and contributions to Sparta's war fund (edited by W.T. Loomis with new fragments).[17] This man from Olenos, an Achaean city west of Patras, is indicated with a sequence of personal name, ethnic name, and city ethnic,

---

[12] Moggi 2002. See also Corsten 1999:160–168; Giacometti 2001; Roy 2003.
[13] Freitag 1996b.
[14] Thucydides 5.9.2–3.
[15] Xenophon *Hellenica* 4.6.1.
[16] Beck 1997:55–66.
[17] Loomis 1993:297–308. Smarczyk 1999.

as will become usual in later times. This suggests the existence of a double level of citizenship, tied to Olenos' membership in the Achaean state.[18] Dates proposed for this inscription vary between the Peloponnesian and the Corinthian War. An Attic honorary decree from the year 399 BCE shows a similar situation: the honoree is a certain Aristeas, an Achaean from Aigion (*ton Akhaion ton Aigia*).[19] These documents should be compared to a recently published inscription from Gorgippia, a Milesian colony on the northern shore of the Black Sea. It is a grave inscription dated between 490 and 480 BCE and commemorating one Philoxenos, son of Kelon, who came "from Helike of the Peloponnese" (*Pelaponnaso ex Helikes*). The inscription does not yet refer to Helike as Achaean; rather, in order to specify the location of the distant city of the deceased, it mentions its location in the Peloponnese.[20]

2. While sources that concentrate on Panhellenic or Peloponnesian developments, as already pointed out, show the Achaeans as rather inactive and neutral, they did engage in noteworthy political activities in a specific area: the coastal region of the Gulf of Corinth facing Achaean territory. Expanding their range of action across the gulf, the Achaeans were also crossing their ethnic borders in the strict sense of the word. In the Homeric *Catalogue of Ships* the cities of Pleuron and Kalydon were still Aetolian,[21] but during the archaic and classical ages they had drifted apart from Aetolia and in the fifth century according to Thucydides they were located in a region called "Aeolis."[22] With this extremely ambivalent designation, the inhabitants of the coastal region between Oiniadai and Kalydon were possibly trying to relocate themselves on the map of Greek ethnic identities in a way that facilitated cooperation between their region and (for instance) Achaeans, Boeotians, and Corinthians, and at the same time separated them decidedly from Aetolia in the strict sense. The integration of Kalydon in the Achaean *koinon*, which cannot be precisely dated, is not to be explained only as a consequence of some specific political situation, but rather as the result of close economic and cultural relations, which grew over a long time. The contacts seem to have been especially close between the coastal areas around Kalydon and Patrai. This is shown by several indices: the place-name Olenos is found both in Achaea and on the Aetolian coast facing Achaea;[23]

---

[18] On this see the observations of Rizakis 1995:342.
[19] SEG 40.54. IG II² 13. On this, see Rizakis 1995:348.
[20] Boltunova 1986:59–61. (SEG 36.718.)
[21] Homer *Iliad* 2.635–640.
[22] Bommeljé 1988.
[23] Evidence in Bölte 1937.

according to Thucydides, the people of Zakynthos, at the entrance of the Gulf of Corinth, were descended from the "Achaeans of the Peloponnese"—whoever exactly these Achaeans should be understood to be;[24] and when Achaeans participated in Pericles' expedition against Oiniadai in the mid-fifth century, this probably happened against the background of the pre-existing political project aiming to take control of the Aetolian-Acarnanian coast and create there a sphere of influence.[25] If the Athenians had successfully established a lasting foothold in Oiniadai, they would probably have left the city to the Achaeans, by the same token as they gave nearby Naupaktos to the Messenians. In any case, during the fourth century Pleuron, Kalydon, and for a while also the Western Locrian city of Naupaktos and possibly other places on the Aetolian and Locrian coast such as for instance Phana, belonged to the Achaeans.[26]

In 389 BCE the Achaeans were compelled to put a garrison in Kalydon to defend it against attacks from the Acarnanians. In this time of need, they sent an embassy to Sparta to ask for military support.[27] The military situation had become more critical because the Acarnanians were supported by their allies the Boeotians and Athenians, the latter having also stationed a fleet in the harbor of the nearby Acarnanian city of Oiniadai.[28] The envoys of the Achaeans made it clear to the Spartans that they felt they were being treated unjustly by them. According to Xenophon, they spoke as follows: "We for our part, Spartans, join you in war whenever you order us to and follow you wherever you lead us; but now that we are besieged by the Acarnanians and their allies, the Athenians and Boeotians, you take no thought for us. Now we cannot hold out if the situation remains like this, but either we shall abandon the war in the Peloponnese and all of us cross over and make war against the Acarnanians and their allies, or else we shall make peace on whatever terms we can."[29] According to Xenophon, the Achaeans reinforced their complaint with the implied threat to abandon the Peloponnesian League if in the future they did not receive any effective military help from the Spartans. Therefore the ephors and the assembly decided to march with the Achaeans against the Acarnanians. Two *morai* led by Agesilaos and followed by a corresponding proportion of allied troops crossed the gulf with

---

[24] Thucydides 2.66.1.
[25] Thucydides 1.111.2–3. Larsen 1953:798–802; Freitag 1996a.
[26] Merker 1989. On Phana, see Pausanias 10.18.1–3.
[27] Xenophon *Hellenica* 4.6.1.
[28] Xenophon *Hellenica* 4.6.14.
[29] Xenophon *Hellenica* 4.6.1–2.

the full strength of the Achaeans to invade Acarnania. The Spartan king was able quickly to gain the upper hand and to inflict severe damage on the Acarnanians, but the Achaeans were not at all happy with the course of the expedition.[30] They insisted that Agesilaos should attack certain Acarnanian cities, but in fact he was not able to conquer any of them. As the fall came, Agesilaos retreated from Acarnania. At this point, the Achaeans maintained that Agesilaos had not achieved anything, because he had not taken a single city, neither by spontaneous surrender nor by conquest.[31] Xenophon's report shows that the political and military goals of the Achaeans were not merely defensive: they clearly hoped to gain control of further cities thanks to Agesilaos' intervention. When the following year the Spartan king threatened to invade Acarnania again, the Acarnanians signed a peace with the Achaeans and concluded an alliance with the Spartans.[32]

It is noteworthy that the relationship of Sparta with the Achaean League did not change after the King's Peace, at least to the extent that apparently in Sparta nobody thought that the Achaean League should be dissolved. The relationship seems to have remained intact, although it is only in connection with the catastrophe of Helike that the ancient sources again offer information on the foreign policy of the Achaean League. The destruction of Helike and Bura happened in 373 BCE.[33] A point that has not received much attention in research so far must be emphasized: at the moment of the catastrophe there were ten Spartan ships in the harbor of Helike.[34] The Spartan fleet used that harbor to control the Gulf of Krisa and especially the crossings from Boeotia. Moreover, with their interests in Asia Minor the Spartans played a role in the turn of events that ancient tradition saw as the cause of the catastrophe. In the classical age, Helike had in the sanctuary of Poseidon Helikonios a very important religious center. In current research, the early Achaean League is seen as a sort of amphiktyony around the sanctuary of Poseidon at Helike.[35] Already in the *Iliad* Helike—together with nearby Aigai—is mentioned as an important place in the cult of Poseidon.[36] The events surrounding the catastrophe are known especially thanks to Diodorus and Strabo, both depending on older authors, especially Ephorus and Herakleides

---

[30] Xenophon *Hellenica* 4.6.4.
[31] Xenophon *Hellenica* 4.6.13.
[32] Xenophon *Hellenica* 4.7.1; Xenophon *Agesilaos* 2.20, with Tuplin 1993:74–75.
[33] Lafond 1998.
[34] Aelian *On the characteristics of animals* 11.19.
[35] Tausend 1992:21–25.
[36] Homer *Iliad* 8.203; 13.21.

Pontikos. The story began before 373 BCE in connection with the activities of the Ionians intended to restore the Ionian cultic community. The reason for this, according to Diodorus, was that their common festival had been moved to Ephesos.[37] Following the advice of the Delphic oracle, again according to Diodorus, they were interested in cultic objects from Helike, which had belonged to their forefathers. Strabo diverges from Diodorus on this and says that the Ionians intended to ask for no less than the cult statue of Poseidon, and to fall back on the cultic objects from the sanctuary only if their first request was rejected.[38] According to Diodorus, the embassy first appeared in front of the Achaeans, who accepted their request with an official decree of the League (*dogma*). However, the inhabitants of Helike in this situation remembered an oracle according to which they would be in danger if Ionians sacrificed at the altar of Poseidon, and accordingly rejected their request. They also submitted that the sanctuary was not the common property of the Achaeans, but their own. When the Ionians nevertheless showed up in Helike, the Helikians destroyed their property and captured the *theoroi*. This sacrilege, according to Diodorus, provoked the destruction of the city by Poseidon. Strabo diverges on some details: in his version, the embassy of the Ionians turned with their request directly to Helike, not first to the federal government of the Achaeans. Only when they heard the rejection did they make contact with the federal organs of the Achaeans.[39] After the favorable decision of the League, the envoys went back to Helike only to receive a renewed rejection. Strabo does not mention any direct offence by the Helikians against the embassy. Pausanias, however, goes so far as to say that "Achaeans" expelled Ionian suppliants from the sanctuary and murdered them. The implacable wrath of Zeus Hikesios contributed to the destruction of the city.[40] At any rate, the following year Helike was totally destroyed by a devastating seaquake.

In spite of discordances between the sources, there is no serious reason to doubt the historicity of the Ionian embassy. Under the supervision of Delphi, a close web of political and religious-cultural relations between Ionians, Spartans, Achaeans and Helike had been activated, as L. Prandi has shown in a fundamental study.[41] Further evidence underlines

---

[37] Diodorus 15.49.1.
[38] Strabo 8.7.2.
[39] Strabo 10.7.2.
[40] Pausanias 7.1.1–5.
[41] Prandi 1989.

the ancestral ties between the sanctuary of Poseidon of Helike and the cities of Asia Minor, especially those that belonged to the Ionian League, whose original cult center was on the Mykale Peninsula.[42] According to the most common version, the Achaeans had always been in the Peloponnese, like the Arcadians, but what later became their land, on the coast of the Gulf of Corinth, had originally belonged to the Ionians.[43] The Achaeans had been chased away from their original fatherland and in their turn expelled the Ionians from the Peloponnese. However, they did not terminate the cult at Helike, but rather continued it. In mentioning the twelve cities that formed the Ionian amphiktyony, Herodotus speculates that already when they were in the Peloponnese the Ionians might have been divided into twelve communities.[44] Later authors expand this story. Helike was supposedly the place from which the Ionians fled the Achaeans. Teisamenos, grandson of Agamemnon and son of Orestes, allegedly died fighting against the Ionians and was buried in Helike. Later, following an injunction from the oracle of Delphi, the Spartans brought home the bones of Teisamenos and buried them in Sparta.[45] This story has been the object of controversy, too, because it could simply be a reduplication of the transferral of Orestes' bones from Tegea narrated by Herodotus.[46] The Spartans' ambivalent relationship to the Achaean heritage is visible in other instances, too: when, according to Herodotus, the Spartan king Kleomenes answered the priestess on the Athenian acropolis, who had received him, saying that access to that sanctuary was forbidden to Dorians, with the words "I am an Achaean, no Dorian,"[47] he was exploiting the different levels of identity of the Greeks. In this case, Kleomenes, or rather whoever invented this story, pushed the Dorian identity into the background in favor of a tradition in which the Spartan kings could connect their origin to Perseus or Herakles.[48]

The Achaeans remained on the side of Sparta even after the battle of Leuctra. Polybius and Strabo say that in 371 BCE the Thebans and Spartans submitted their quarrel to arbitration by the Achaeans.[49] According to

---

[42] Moggi 1996; Schilardi 1998.

[43] Smarczyk 2000. See also Helly 1997.

[44] Herodotus 1.145.

[45] Leahy 1955; Malkin 1994:28–30. Thommen 2003:52 speaks of an "Achaian idea ... which relegated the Dorian roots to the background."

[46] Herodotus 1.67–68; Pausanias 3.3.5–7; 8.54.4.

[47] Parker 1998. See also Wickert 1961:11.

[48] On this see the overview by Thommen 2000.

[49] Polybius 2.39.8–10; Strabo 8.7.1.

Polybius, after the Thebans' victory Greece was dominated by uncertainty. In such a situation, both Thebans and Spartans chose to ask the Achaeans, alone among the Greeks, for arbitration in their disputes, not because the Achaeans were particularly powerful, for actually back then they were almost the least powerful of all Greeks, but rather because of their reliability and justice in all respects—a reputation they enjoyed among all Greeks without exception at the time. Certainly Polybius' passage is biased and exaggerated in its insistence on the Achaeans' lack of power, as well as on their high repute and valor, which has often led scholars to consider this passage a late construct by Polybius himself and to reject its historicity, especially since there is no evidence for a decision by the Achaeans. John Buckler writes: "It is simpler and more satisfying to conclude that the purported arbitration never took place except in the patriotic excesses of Achaean tradition."[50]

In the following years, it is unclear how the relationship between Sparta and the Achaeans should be characterized. Xenophon says that the Achaeans remained neutral in 367/6 BCE: they had progressively drifted away from Sparta without joining the Theban alliance.[51] Again Pellene was the first target of Theban attacks and was compelled to pass to the Theban side in 369 BCE, probably together with neighboring Sikyon.[52] Only in 367/6 BCE did the Thebans and their Peloponnesian allies turn their attention explicitly to Achaea, which had remained generally neutral up to that point. Their precise goals and the background to their actions are controversial.[53] At any rate, the Thebans wanted to consolidate their prestige and re-establish their reputation inside the Boeotian-Peloponnesian alliance after the failure of peace negotiations.

At this time, the Achaean cities were still ruled by oligarchies. When Epaminondas invaded Achaea in 367/6 BCE, it is clear that no major military clashes took place, but rather the ruling oligarchies agreed with Epaminondas that they would enter an alliance with Thebes on condition that their regimes remained untouched and nobody was exiled. After guaranteeing these conditions, Epaminondas retreated without further military activities, according to Xenophon.[54] Diodorus however mentions a concrete

---

[50] Buckler 1978, quote from 94.
[51] Xenophon *Hellenica* 7.1.42.
[52] Xenophon *Hellenica* 7.1.18; Diodorus 15.68.2; 15.75.2; Pausanias 9.15.4. On Pellene in this period, see Gehrke 1985:14. See also Roy 1971:589.
[53] Buckler 1980:179–183.
[54] Xenophon *Hellenica* 7.1.42.

military initiative by the Theban: after taking control of Achaea, he "liberated," according to Diodorus,[55] the cities of Dyme, Kalydon, and Naupaktos, expelling from them the Achaean garrisons. It is worth noting that, in spite of the agreement, Epaminondas did intervene with force in the Achaean sphere of influence, in that he made sure that Achaean garrisons were evicted from three strategically important positions. Clearly the Achaeans had, to protect these places, installed garrisons in advance, organized by and according to a decision of their League. The Thebans depicted their intrusion into the internal affairs of the Achaeans in a propagandistic way as a liberation. Besides Dyme, the measure affected Kalydon and West Locrian Naupaktos, which also belonged to the Achaeans at this time. All three were coastal cities, important as such and also for controlling access to the Gulf of Corinth. This decision may have been related to Epaminondas' plan to create a Boeotian fleet, but it is impossible to tell for sure who took control of Kalydon and Naupaktos. Considering that the Aetolians had already shown interest in Naupaktos at the time of Agesilaos' expedition of 389 BCE, it is likely that they took control of them, all the more so since they were now allies of the Thebans.[56]

Nobody was happy with Epaminondas' acts. The Peloponnesian allies, especially the Arcadians, Achaean exiles who hoped to return home, and not least internal opponents of Epaminondas at Thebes made sure that his decisions would be radically overturned. An argument that emerged was that the actions had favored the Spartans.[57] Theban harmosts were sent to Achaea, and they made sure that the ruling elite had to abandon the cities and was replaced by democratic regimes. The exiles, who had mostly retreated to Elis, mustered their forces soon thereafter and were able to bring all the Achaean cities back under their control one after the other, using force where necessary.[58] The democratic interlude in Achaea did not last long. After the old order had been re-established, the Achaeans were again securely on the Spartan side. When Elis changed sides in 365/4 BCE and left the Theban-Peloponnesian alliance, and the conflict against the Arcadians escalated, the Achaeans stood on Elis' side together with the Spartans and helped the Eleians as far as they could.[59]

---

[55] Diodorus 15.75.2. On this, see Merker 1989.
[56] Merker 1989.
[57] Xenophon *Hellenica* 7.1.43.
[58] Xenophon *Hellenica* 7.1.43.
[59] Xenophon *Hellenica* 7.4.17.

In the history of the fifth and fourth centuries BCE the Achaeans usually appear as a unit, settled in a relatively clearly defined territory in the Northern Peloponnese, from Cape Araxos to the Sikyonian border. The list of members of the Achaean League is also relatively constant: Herodotus (1.145), Pseudo-Skylax (34), Polybius (2.41.7–8), Strabo (8.7.4) and Pausanias (7.6.1) show a noteworthy continuity over time. Variations and new appearances can be easily explained case by case, especially in the course of the expansion of the Achaean *koinon* during the third century BCE.[60] Ethnic homogeneity, or more carefully put, a feeling of belonging together, did not, however, automatically mean a sympolity or a federal state in the strict sense. Pellene, which belonged to the *ethnos*, mostly went its own way, developing early on a particularly close relationship to Sparta because of its own interests and outlying geographic position. The main pattern in common political initiatives by the Achaeans from early on was characterized by neutrality in the Peloponnese and since 417 BCE a close connection to Sparta, and furthermore an active interest in the Aetolian-Acarnanian coastal region. When, during the second half of the fifth century, Achaea moved towards a more strict form of federal constitution, it was soon ready and able to integrate cities like Pleuron, Kalydon, and Naupaktos, which strictly did not belong to the Achaean *ethnos*.

The Achaeans bore a name rich in tradition.[61] In the Homeric poems "Achaeans" is a name that indicates on the one hand the inhabitants of a relatively clearly defined territory (Northern Greece; the Northern Peloponnese including Argos; and Crete), on the other, the Greeks who convened against Troy. However, it is totally unclear when the name Achaeans was used for and by the inhabitants of the Northern Peloponnese. Suggestions vary from assuming a tradition going back very early into the post-Mycenaean period to the idea that the usage was consolidated only during the sixth century, possibly under Spartan influence.[62] It should also be noted that during the classical age the name was not used only by the Achaeans of the Peloponnese, but also by those of central Greece, who participated as "Achaeans" in the Delphic Amphiktyony[63] and whose cities harbored cults of gods with the epithet "Panachaean."[64]

---

[60] On this see SEG 15.254, from the year 122 BCE.
[61] Stern 1980:67–70.
[62] Koerner 1974:458–459.
[63] Lefèvre 1998:87–89.
[64] See Reinders 1988:162–164.

Like Catherine Morgan, I also tend to favor a later date for the emergence of an Achaean identity in the Northern Peloponnese, which is attested for the first time in Herodotus.[65] However, this means—again a point demonstrated convincingly by Morgan—that the phenomenon of Achaean colonization in southern Italy has to be interpreted as a complex process that can be understood in general terms only in the light of archaeological evidence and research on ethnicity.[66] The South-Italian "Achaeans" developed their conceptions of their own origin especially in competition with other South Italian Greeks, and these processes soon had repercussions in mainland Greece.

From the point of view of the present volume, the result of this investigation is essentially negative. Ethnic arguments played no perceptible role in the relations between Achaeans and Spartans towards the end of the fifth century and at the beginning of the fourth. Between Spartans and Achaeans, power relations and interests were clear and well defined. Under Spartan leadership the Achaeans had been able not only to stabilize their federal structure, but also to obtain territorial expansion on the northern coast of the Gulf of Corinth. Ideological conflicts centered upon ethnicity between Spartans and Achaeans—assuming that they ever took place with any intensity—had been settled long before the fourth century.

Bibliography

Anderson, J. K. 1954. "A Topographical and Historical Study of Achaia." *ABSA* 44:72–92.

Beck, H. 1997. *Polis und Koinon. Untersuchungen zur Geschichte und Struktur der griechischen Bundesstaaten im 4. Jahrhundert v. Chr.* Stuttgart.

Bleckmann, B. 1993. "Sparta und seine Freunde im Dekeleischen Krieg. Zur Datierung von IG V 1, 1." *ZPE* 96:297–308.

Bölte, F. 1937. "Olenos (4)." *RE* 17.1:2435.

Boltunova, A. I. 1986. "Inscriptions from Georgippia (russ.)." *VDI* 1986:43–61.

Bommeljé, S. 1988. "Aeolis in Aetolia. Thuc. 3.102.5 and the Origins of the Aetolian *Ethnos*." *Historia* 37:297–316.

Brunel, J. 1953. "À propos des transfers de cultes: un sens méconnu du mot ἀφίδρυμα." *RPhil* 27:21–33.

---

[65] See Morgan 2002.

[66] Greco 1998; Osanna 2000; Wilson 2000; Papadopoulos 2002.

Buckler, J. 1978. "The Alleged Achaian Arbitration after Leuktra." *SO* 53:85–96.

Buckler, J. 1980. *The Theban Hegemony 371-362 B.C.* Cambridge MA.

Corsten, T. 1999. *Vom Stamm zum Bund. Gründung und Territoriale Organisation griechischer Bundesstaaten.* Munich.

Freitag, K. 1996a. "Der Acarnanische Bund im 5. Jh. v. Chr." *Akarnanien. Eine Landschaft im antiken Griechenland* (eds. P. Berktold et al.) 75–86. Würzburg.

Freitag, K. 1996b. "Eine vergessene Notiz zur Geschichte Achaias im 5. Jahrhundert v. Chr. bei Herodot (8, 36, 2)." *Historia* 45:123–126.

Gehrke, H.-J. 1985. *Stasis. Untersuchungen zu den inneren Kriegen in den griechischen Staaten des 5. und 4. Jahrhunderts v. Chr.* Munich.

Giacometti, D. 2001. "L'Acaia fra VI e V sec. a.C." *RSA* 31:7–41.

Greco, E. 1998. "Le fondazioni degli Achei in Occidente." *Helike II.* (eds. D. Katsonopoulou et al.) 335–347. Athens.

Greco, E., ed. 2002. *Gli Achei e l'identità etnica degli Achei d'Occidente.* Paestum.

Helly, B. 1997. "Arithmétique et histoire. L'organisation militaire et politique des Ioniens en Achaïe à l'époque archaïque." *Topoi* 7:207–262.

Koerner R. 1974. "Die staatliche Entwicklung in Alt-Achaia." *Klio* 56:457–495.

Lafond, Y. 1998. "Die Katastrophe von 373 v. Chr. und das Verschwinden der Stadt Helike in Achaia." *Naturkatastrophen in der antiken Welt* (eds. E. Olshausen and H. Sonnabend) 118–123. Stuttgart.

Larsen, J. A. O., 1953. "The Early Achaean League." *Studies Presented to David Moore Robinson on his Seventieth Birthday* (ed. G. E. Mylonas and D. Raymond) 2:797–815. St. Louis.

Leahy, D. M. 1955. "The Bones of Tisamenus." *Historia* 4:26–38.

Lefèvre, F. 1998. *L'Amphictionie pyléo-delphique. Histoire et institutions.* Paris.

Loomis, W. T. 1992. *The Spartan War Fund: IG V 1, 1 and a New Fragment.* Stuttgart.

Malkin, I. 1991. "What is an *Aphidruma*?" *ClAnt* 10:77–96.

Malkin, I. 1994. *Myth and Territory in the Spartan Mediterranean.* Cambridge.

Merker, I. L. 1989. "The Achaians in Naupaktos and Kalydon in the Fourth Century." *Hesperia* 58:303–311.

Moggi, M. 1996. "L'excursus di Pausania sulla Ionia." *Pausanias Historien.* 79–116. Geneva.

Moggi, M. 2002. "Sulle origini della Lega Achea." In Greco 2002:133–142.

Morgan, C. 1988. "Corinth, the Corinthian Gulf and Western Greece during the Eighth Century B.C." *ABSA* 83:313–338.

Morgan, C. 1991. "Ethnicity and Early Greek States." *PCPS* 37:131–163.

Morgan, C. 2000. "Politics without the Polis: Cities and the Achaean Ethnos, c. 800–500 BC." *Alternatives to Athens. Varieties of Political Organization and Community in Ancient Greece* (eds. R. Brock and S. Hodkinson) 189–211. Oxford.

Morgan, C. 2002. "Ethnicity: the example of Achaia." In Greco 2002:95–116.

Morgan, C., and Hall, J. 1996. "Achaian Poleis and Achaian Colonisation." *Introduction to an Inventory of Poleis* (ed. M. H. Hansen) 164–232. Copenhagen.

Moscati Castelnuovo, L. 2002. "Dyme achea ed epea." *Identità e prassi storica nel Mediterraneo greco* (ed. L. Moscati Castelnuovo) 159–171. Milan.

Osanna, M. 2000. "Zwischen Dorern, Ionern und Indigenen: Die Achäer und die Anderen im archaischen Großgriechenland." *Gegenwelten: zu den Kulturen Griechenlands und Roms in der Antike* (eg. T. Hölscher). 245–262. Munich.

Papadopoulos, J. K. 2002. "Minting Identity: Coinage, Ideology and the Economics of Colonization in Akhaian Magna Graecia." *CAJ* 12:21–55.

Parker, R. 1998. *Cleomenes on the Acropolis.* Oxford.

Prandi, L. 1989. "La rifondazione del Panionion e la catastrofe di Elice (373 a. C.)" *CISA* 15:43–59.

Reinders, R. H. 1988. *New Halos: A Hellenistic Town in Thessalia, Greece.* Utrecht.

Rizakis, A. D. 1995. *Achaie I. Sources textuelles et histoire regionale.* Athens.

Robinson, E. W. 1997. *The First Democracies: Early Popular Government outside Athens.* Stuttgart.

Roy, J. 1971. "Arcadia and Boeotia in Peloponnesian Affairs, 370–362 B. C." *Historia* 20:569–599.

Roy, J. 2003. "The Achaian League." *The Idea of European Community in History* (eds. K. Buraselis and K. Zoumboulakis) 81–95. Athens.

Schilardi, D. 1998. "Helike and Ionia." *Helike* (ed. D. Katsonopoulou et al.) 283–289. Athens.

Smarczyk, B. 1999. "Einige Bemerkungen zur Datierung der Beiträge zu Spartas Kriegskasse in IG V, 1, 1." *Klio* 81:45–67.

Smarczyk, B. 2000. "Die Ionier Kleinasiens." *Antike Randgesellschaften und Randgruppen im östlichen Mittelmeerraum* (eds. H.-P. Müller and F. Siegert) 46–74. Münster.

Stern, E. M. 1980. "Zeus und die Tempel von Paestum." *MNIR* 42:43–70.

Tausend, K. 1992. *Amphiktyonie und Symmachie. Formen zwischenstaatlicher Beziehungen im archaischen Griechenland.* Stuttgart.

Thommen, L. 2000. "Spartas Umgang mit der Vergangenheit." *Historia* 49:40–53.

Thommen, L. 2003. *Sparta. Verfassungs- und Sozialgeschichte einer griechischen Polis.* Stuttgart.

Tuplin, C. J. 1993. *The Failings of Empire: A Reading of Xenophon Hellenica 2.3.11-7.5.27.* Historia Einzelschriften 76. Stuttgart.

Walbank, F. W. 2000. "Hellenes and Achaians." *Further Studies in the Ancient Greek Polis* (ed. P. Flensted-Jensen) 19–33. Stuttgart.

Wickert, K. 1961. *Der peloponnesische Bund von seiner Entstehung bis zum Ende des archidamischen Krieges.* Dissertation, University of Erlangen-Nürnberg.

Wilson, J.-P. 2000. "Ethnic and State Identities in Greek Settlement in Southern Italy in the Eighth and Seventh Century BC." *The Emergence of State Identities in Italy in the First Millennium BC* (ed. E. Herring and K. Lomas) 31–43. London.

III

Elis

James Roy

Background

IN THE DARK AGE THERE WAS LIMITED SETTLEMENT in northern and central Elis, grouped principally in the Peneios valley and the Alpheios valley.[1] Then between the Dark Age and the archaic period the communities of the Peneios valley must somehow have coalesced to form a political unit. The details of this process are not recoverable from archaeological or literary evidence; but the process certainly included a number of developments that were of crucial importance for the later history of Elis. Firstly, Elis became the principal settlement and presumably the political focus of the community.[2] Secondly, at least by the sixth century and probably earlier the new community expanded its influence over neighbouring areas. Thirdly, in the process of expansion a distinction was established between territory of the Elean state proper and other territories that were subordinated to the Elean state. These developments have to be deduced from our wider knowledge of Elean history rather than demonstrated from surviving evidence: in fact ancient accounts of Elean expansion are dominated by concern with competition between Elis and Pisatis for control of Olympia.

These accounts of warfare between Elis and Pisatis, though varying and even contradictory in detail, have been broadly accepted by many modern scholars (including the present writer). Recently, however, a view originally

---

[1] Eder 2001b.

[2] On the early history of settlement on the site of the town Elis see Eder and Mitsopoulos 1999.

propounded by Niese has been revived and developed with good arguments by several scholars:[3] put simply, the central proposition of these arguments is that the concept of Pisatis arose in the fourth century, and with it a suitably elaborated history for Pisatis (and in due course, anti-Pisatan counter-history). Scholars adopting this view do, however, generally agree that in the classical period Pisatis (as it became) was an integral part of the Elean state proper.[4] This view of a late-emerging Pisatis is very attractive. One minor comment on it is that Elean expansion must have led to some complications in the area near Pisatis since the three minor states of Marganeis, Amphidoloi, and Letrinoi, situated side by side west of Olympia, all became *perioikoi* of Elis; some consideration of which we are entirely unaware must have induced Elis to make these three insignificant communities into subordinate allies rather than including them in the Elean state proper. More importantly it seems that, even if Pisatis had no authentic collective archaic past, some sentiment of regional identity was emerging by the end of the fifth century, since the unnamed group who sought to take over control of Olympia at the end of the Elean-Spartan war (Xenophon *Hellenica* 3.2.31) must have been from the Pisatan area.[5]

The term *perioikoi* is not attested in Elean documents, and is used of communities within the region Elis only by non-Elean writers. It is nonetheless used in this paper as a very convenient shorthand for those communities that were subordinated to the Elean state. There presumably were such *perioikoi* at least from the early sixth century. Some agreement between the Elean state and the communities of Akroreia (which lay east of Elis) to secure the border area between northern Elis and northwestern Arcadia is extremely plausible (if unattested) before major Elean expansion southwards. The eventual extent of Elean expansion is most clearly seen in accounts of the Spartan-Elean war c. 400.[6] North of the Alpheios the perioikic territories were Letrinoi, Amphidolia, and Marganeis (all in an area near

---

[3] Nafissi 2003, Möller 2004, and Giangiulio in this volume.

[4] E.g., Möller 2004:265. Ruggeri (2004:52–53, 196–197 and elsewhere) takes the view that the Pisatans, though controlled by Elis from the later archaic period, did not become Elean citizens until 400 (i.e. the end of the Elean-Spartan war); this view leaves the status of the Pisatans in the fifth century unclear, and would cause difficulties in explaining the peace terms at the end of the war, when Pisatis remained Elean although Elis lost all its subordinate communities.

[5] Unless one regards Xenophon's reference to these counter-claimants as anachronistic, provoked by knowledge of Pisatis' separation from Elis and control of Olympia in the 360s, as suggested by Nafissi in discussion at Münster.

[6] Roy 1997b. On the war generally see Schepens 2004.

Olympia to the west); four communities of Akroreia (northeast of Olympia and east of Elis); and Lasion (east of Akroreia). Everything else was Elean in the narrow sense, including Pisatis around Olympia and the coast at least as far south as Pheia. South of the Alpheios as far as the Neda everything was perioikic between the coast and Arcadian territories.

Geographical Scope of Expansion

No attempt by Elis to expand northwards into Achaea is known. Such expansion would not have been too surprising, since Strabo 8.3.9 reports that some called Dyme an Epeian city, the Epeians being the original inhabitants of Elis.[7] Moreover passage between Elis and Dyme in western Achaea was fairly easy, though protected by fortification at Teichos Dymaion,[8] and ancient reports that the 28th Olympiad (668 BCE) was organised by the Pisatans because the Eleans were occupied with a war against Dyme, though quite probably unhistorical, show awareness of the route.[9] In the Spartan-Elean war of c. 400 Agis led his Spartan and allied troops into Elis from Achaea, and subsequently Achaeans, like others, used the opportunity offered by this same war to pillage Elis (Xenophon *Hellenica* 3.2.23–24, 26). However, though military operations northwards would have encountered no geographical difficulty at least, there is no evidence that in the later archaic or classical periods the Eleans tried to gain control over any Achaean territory.

The frontier between Elis and Arcadia fluctuated.[10] For instance Pherecydes (FGH 3 F 161) described Phrixa as Arcadian, presumably referring to his own day, while Herodotus (4.148) described it as Minyan, and it eventually became Triphylian (Polybius 4.77.9). Also Lepreon sought help from Elis before the Peloponnesian War because it was at war with (unspecified) Arcadians (Thucydides 5.31.2). Despite shifts along this frontier, in the archaic and classical periods it was never possible for the Eleans to penetrate deep into territory claimed by Arcadians.

According to Herodotus (4.148) Elis was making a major effort in his own lifetime to extend its control over Triphylia (to use the name anachronistically). Therefore by the time the Eleans extended their control to the

---

[7] Strabo 8.3.9; on the report see Rizakis 1995:521, cf. 160.

[8] On Teichos Dymaion see Rizakis 1995:449 and 504, and Morgan and Hall 1996:188–189.

[9] Julius Africanus *Ol.* 28, Eusebius *Chronicon* 1.28; cf. Philostratus *de Gymnastica* 7 = C264: see Rizakis 1995:10, 129, and 371.

[10] Roy 2000.

Neda, Messenia south of the Neda was securely held by the Spartans and there was no possibility of further Elean expansion southward. It is in fact quite possible that Sparta helped Elis to establish control over Triphylia as Strabo 8.3.33 says,[11] since there would have been advantages for Sparta in having the territory adjacent to Messenia under the control of an ally.

The Eleans thus pursued a policy of expansion at least from the early sixth century, directed mainly southwards within the limits outlined above. This policy was still being pursued vigorously in the fifth century. The expansion was not achieved solely by military means, for Lepreon voluntarily associated itself with Elis (Thucydides 5.31.2) and Epeion was bought by Elis (Xenophon *Hellenica* 3.2.30–31). Nonetheless the expansion, though complex, was probably pursued mainly by force, as Herodotus 4.148 records the subjugation of the Minyan cities in Triphylia.[12]

In the late fifth century Elis either held as strictly Elean territory or dominated as perioikic territory an area bounded by Achaea in the north, Messenia in the south, and Arcadia in the east. All purely Elean territory lay north of the Alpheios, but, since we do not know the precise limits of the perioikic areas north of the Alpheios, it is impossible to calculate exactly the extent of purely Elean territory. It was, however, certainly very large by Greek standards. Yalouris estimated the total area of Elean and perioikic territory north of the Alpheios at 2120 km², while Swoboda estimated the area of Elean territory as 1160 km² and that of perioikic territory as c. 1500 km², but his calculations included Pisatis among perioikic territory.[13] It seems safe at any rate to assume that purely Elean territory amounted to well over 1000 km².

The Eleans' Image of Themselves

The Eleans developed over time an elaborate mythical past through which they expressed their ethnic identity, as a very recent and full analysis by Gehrke (2003) has shown. The material was clearly being reworked in the classical period, often in a tendentious way. For instance, Ulf (1997) has analysed ancient accounts of the origins of the Olympic Games, and, *inter alia*, his analysis points to the strongly pro-Elean tendency of Ephorus' account. Pro-Elean accounts of how the games had been run were also

---

[11] Roy 2002b:259–260, noting the chronological uncertainties in the reports by Strabo in 8.3.30 and 8.3.33.

[12] On the expansion see Roy 2002b:259–260.

[13] Yalouris 1972:96, Swoboda *RE* 5.2422 on Elis.

produced: Wacker (1998) has recently produced a review of the early victor-lists suggesting that there was strong pro-Elean bias both in the work of the Elean Hippias (which does not appear to have been widely consulted by later chronographers) and in the victor-list of the Elean Aristodemos, possibly the same man as the Elean of the same name who won an Olympic victory in 388 BCE. Other history was also written in a pro-Elean spirit: Bilik (1998–1999) has shown that Ephorus gave a strongly pro-Elean account of the Elean-Spartan war of c. 400.[14]

The most obvious focus for the expression of pro-Elean views was the sanctuary of Zeus at Olympia, once the Eleans took control of it. It would take too long to analyse the wealth of material from Olympia, and only a few items are selected here as illustrations. The Eleans enjoyed a remarkable number of Olympic victories from the fifth century onwards, and as a result there was a very large number of victors' statues dedicated in the sanctuary by Eleans.[15] Other items put in the sanctuary by Elis may have shown more sympathy for the viewpoints of others, but interpretation is difficult. Herrmann (1987:3) sees the sculptural decoration on the temple of Zeus built by the Eleans from the 470s or 460s as appealing to several groups, with the myth of Pelops on the east pediment being local/Olympic, while the Herakles myth on the metopes was of general Dorian interest, and the battle of the centaurs on the west pediment was panhellenic. Kyrieleis (1997), however, sees Pelops on the east pediment as an indication of the political ambitions of Elis, and Heiden (2003) sees an expression of a connection between Thessaly and Elis on the west pediment. Jacquemin (2001a:299–300), accepting accounts of early Elean conflicts, sees in Pausanias' account of the sanctuary at Olympia not so much a panhellenic setting for games in honour of Zeus as a panelean sanctuary uniting the two main elements of the Elean community, the Eleans of the Peneios valley and the Pisatans of the Alpheios. It seems that as the sanctuary developed it offered the visitor a complex set of messages, no doubt read by different Greeks in different ways. Some of the messages were of course not Elean at all: Olympia offered many Greeks a setting in which to project their self-image.[16] Olympia had, however, to be at the same time panhellenic and Elean: the Games were the most obvious expression of panhellenism, but the Eleans could also assert the

---

[14] Bilik's argument that Ephorus' source was Hippias of Elis has however been questioned by Nafissi 2003:29n59.

[15] Crowther 1988; Jacquemin in Casevitz, Pouilloux, and Jacquemin 2002:xii.

[16] See for instance on the western Greeks, Ioakimidou 2000.

Elean nature of the sanctuary. They did so, for instance, on the coins struck after Elis regained control of Olympia, lost during the Elean-Arcadian war of 365–362: on these Elean staters appeared a female figure and the legend 'Olympia,' interpreted—convincingly—by Ritter (2001) as Elis proclaiming its restored control of Olympia after the brief Pisatan regime. And Olympia was of course a functioning sanctuary between the Olympiads, the scene of continuing ritual that was largely Elean.[17]

Olympia had probably served the Eleans as a location for public display before they gained control of the sanctuary. There was certainly settlement at the site of the later town of Elis from the eleventh or tenth century BCE, and public building is identifiable archaeologically from the early sixth century.[18] There was clearly a town of Elis before the reported synoikism of 471, but it is not clear on present evidence that it was used as a location for major public display of images or monuments expressing Elean identity. There is also a striking lack of major religious sanctuaries in and around the Peneios valley, in contrast to the region south of the Alpheios where there were major sanctuaries at Samikon, known from literature, and at the exca-vated site at Kombothekra.[19] Olympia therefore probably served as the main focus of display for the communities of the Peneios valley even before Elis gained control of the sanctuary: the cult centre existed from the eleventh century, and had clearly gained considerable popularity by the seventh century.[20]

Cohesion within the Elean State

There were various communities within Elean territory other than the town of Elis, such as the two ports at Kyllene and Pheia and the site exca-vated at Armatova that was probably Elean Pylos.[21] The need to accom-modate a number of settlements has led some scholars to regard Elis as a federal state. Walter, for instance, has recently made such a suggestion, and van Effenterre and Ruzé write without comment about "la Confédération des Eléens."[22] Siewert (1994:30) cites other scholars who have taken a similar view, but himself argues firmly against the suggestion that the Elean state

---

[17] Jacquemin 2001b.
[18] Eder and Mitsopoulos 1999.
[19] Samikon: Strabo 8.3.13; Kombothekra: Sinn 1978, 1981. See also Taita 2001.
[20] Morgan 1990:57–105, Eder 2001a.
[21] Roy 2002b 254–255. On Armatova: Coleman 1986. Generally on Elean and perioikic settlement see Roy 1999.
[22] Walter 1993:121; van Effenterre and Ruzé 1994–1995 e.g. 1.21.

was a "Stammstaat." Nafissi (2003:48) has recently argued for an "etnico-federale" state in Elis, but the phenomena leading to his conclusion could be explained by the theory of the "dependent state" evolved by the Copenhagen *Polis* Centre.[23] There is in fact no ancient evidence of a federal constitution in the Elean state, and so no reason to suppose that federalism was used as a means of satisfying a range of local interests within Elis.

It is also very difficult to know how far, if at all, the reported synoikism of Elis catered to a range of interests within Elis. In or around 471/0 BCE a synoikism of Elis took place, according to both Diodorus Siculus 11.54.1 and Strabo 8.3.2. The two reports may quite possibly derive directly or indirectly from a common source, in which case by far the most likely such source would be Ephorus. Given this ancient evidence it is difficult to deny that the synoikism occurred, but it is impossible to determine what the synoikism actually involved, despite a good deal of modern speculation that the synoikism was linked to a variety of other developments in Elis.[24] Its significance within the Elean state and in Elis' relations with other communities is wholly obscure.

Pisatan Separatism

The Elean state proper (as opposed to the network of Elis' *perioikoi*), though large and including important communities besides the town of Elis, appears to have held together satisfactorily, until separatist tendencies began in Pisatis.[25] Pisatis was certainly part of purely Elean territory at the time of the Elean-Spartan war c. 400, and there is no clear ancient evidence that it was ever perioikic.[26] There are, however, signs that a Pisatan identity began to appear at the end of the fifth century (unless it can be supposed to have survived from much earlier, even though Pisatis had been Elean for generations). At the end of the Spartan-Elean war of c. 400,[27] when the Spartans were deciding on the terms to be imposed in the peace, an unnamed group put in a claim to administer Olympia in place of the Eleans: the Spartans nonetheless allowed the Eleans to retain control because the others were χωρῖται (i.e. "rustics", Xenophon *Hellenica* 3.2.31). The counter-claimants can hardly be other than Pisatan.

---

[23] Hansen and Nielsen 2004:87–94.

[24] Roy 2002b.

[25] On Pisatis see recently Nafissi 2001 and 2003, Möller 2004; on settlement in Pisatis see Roy 2002a.

[26] Roy 1997b:283–284, 297–298: see Nafissi 2001:311 correcting the interpretation of Pausanias 5.10.2 in Roy 1997b:310n12.

[27] On which, see Schepens 2004.

Later, when in 365 BCE war broke out between Elis and the Arcadian Confederation, and the Arcadians were able to detach Pisatis from Elis, Pisatis became an independent state.[28] There is clear surviving evidence that the Pisatans exercised the functions of a Greek state: a decree; treaties with Arcadia, Akroreia, Messenia, and Sikyon; gold coins minted by Pisa.[29] The Pisatan state is not heard of again after the battle of Mantinea in 362 and presumably rapidly returned to Elis, which had regained control of Olympia before the Olympic Games of 360. Pisatis may in fact have been something of a puppet-state used by the Arcadians: it was often said that the Olympic Games of 364, organised by the Pisatans and regarded as a non-Olympiad by the Eleans (Diodorus 15.78.3), were held by the Pisatans and the Arcadians (Xenophon *Hellenica* 7.4.28–9, Diodorus 15.82.1, Pausanias 6.4.2) or even by the Arcadians alone (Pausanias 6.8.3, 6.22.3, cf. Xenophon *Hellenica* 7.4.35). Given the Arcadian interest in exploiting an independent Pisatis, it is hard to know how far the Pisatans themselves took the initiative in forming their own state, but at the very least the Arcadians must have found Pisatans willing to collaborate with them.

From the late fifth century onwards—setting aside any possible earlier conflicts between Pisatis and Elis—those Pisatans who sought independence from Elis are known to have acted only when an outside power was in a position to help them: Sparta c. 400 and the Arcadians in 365. Nonetheless these repeated episodes in which Pisatans opposed Elis or sought to detach themselves from Elis, suggest that at least some Pisatans had a sense of Pisatan identity and a willingness to act on it. If one accepts that the concept of Pisatis emerged only in the fourth century, then it must be supposed to have given rise to strong sentiments in order to generate the large and persisting body of Pisatan myth-history preserved in later Greek writers.[30]

Thus development of an Elean identity within the territory of Elis proper did not wholly overcome the alternative, rival identity at least occasionally displayed by Pisatans. There is, however, no evidence of such conflict of identity elsewhere in Elis proper. In fact the terms in which Herodotus 8.73.1–3 writes of the peoples of the Peloponnese suggest that in his day Elean identity was well established north of the Alpheios. There were, he says, seven

[28] On the events of 365–362 see Roy 1994:203–204, Nielsen 2002a:118–119, 483–484.
[29] Decree: IvO 36 = DGE 422; treaties: Ringel, Siewert, and Taeuber 1999; coins: Head 1911:426. See Nafissi 2003 and Ruggeri 2004:178–207.
[30] Möller 2004:263–265 shows that in the Pisatan area there were elements of myth-history that could be combined into a Pisatan past.

ethne in the Peloponnese. Two—Arcadian and Kynourian—were autochthonous. One—Achaean—was originally Peloponnesian but had moved within the Peloponnese. The other four had all come to the Peloponnese from elsewhere: Dorian, Aetolian, Dryopian, and Lemnian. Of these, the Eleans alone were Aetolian. Herodotus admittedly offers only a very brief survey of the supposed *ethne*, but he seems nonetheless to treat the area north of the Alpheios as broadly Elean, taking no particular account of either Pisatans or perioikic communities in the area.[31]

Elis and the *Perioikoi*[32]

When the Eleans began to lose some of their subordinate territories from the early Peloponnesian War onwards, their determination to recover and retain anything they had lost seems to have been unwavering. For instance, in the 420s with Spartan support Lepreon was able to free itself from Elean control (Thucydides 5.31.1–5). Then in 418, when Elis was allied to Athens, Argos, and Mantinea, the allied forces first operated against Orchomenos in Arcadia and then debated what to do next. Eventually they decided to proceed against Tegea. The Eleans, however, had urged the allies to help them retake Lepreon, and, when they failed to persuade the others, they went home in anger (Thucydides 5.62.1–2). It is hard to avoid the impression that Thucydides relates this episode in such a way as to bring out the Eleans' blinkered focus on their own interests in Triphylia. Again at a peace conference in 371/0 the Eleans, according to Xenophon *Hellenica* 6.5.2, formulated their claim to communities in Triphylia in very blunt terms: these *poleis*, they said, were theirs.

Thanks to a recently published inscription we know that Elis' relations with the *perioikoi* were, at least by c. 500, structured as an alliance.[33] That was still true in 420, as Thucydides 5.47 shows. The Eleans were naturally the dominant partners. The alliance seems to have been built up through a series of alliances with individual communities. IvO 9 of c. 500 is probably an early example of such an alliance, with the otherwise unknown community of Ewaoioi.[34] Lepreon also formed such an alliance with Elis (Thucydides 5.31.2).

It has been suggested that local communities around Olympia formed an amphictyony to administer the sanctuary. Taita (1999 and 2002) has

---

[31] Herodotus was perfectly capable of recording a complex ethnic interaction in a limited region, as 4.148 on Triphylia shows.

[32] Generally on Elis' relations with its *perioikoi* see Roy 1997b and Ruggeri 2004.

[33] Ebert and Siewert 1997; see also Roy 1997b:292–293.

[34] Roy and Schofield 1999.

provided a very full exposition of both the relevant ancient evidence and modern views for and against the idea of such an amphictyony. She concludes that such an amphictyony did exist, at least until c. 460 BCE, but the evidence for it is slight. The only explicit evidence for such a body is provided by Tzetzes *Chiliades* 12.363–364, and Tzetzes is by no means always a reliable witness. The arguments expressed against the idea of an amphictyony by Gauthier and the reservations of Sordi still have force, and it is difficult to accept the existence of such a body.[35]

Elis does, however, seem to have used its domination of Olympia as a means of exercising control over other states, both perioikic and non-Elean.[36] In the treaty between Elis and the Ewaoioi[37] any penalty for breach of the treaty by either party is to be paid to Olympian Zeus: since Elis dominated the god's sanctuary, it would have a clear advantage in the event of a dispute. When the Anaitoi and Metapioi made a treaty of friendship (IvO 10), any question of a breach of the treaty was to be determined by officials at the sanctuary, thus giving Elis considerable influence over the two, presumably small, communities. In IvO 16, a fragmentary and difficult text concerning Skillous, penalties for wrongful conduct are to be paid to Olympian Zeus, again giving Elis considerable influence. When Lepreon agreed to cede half its territory to the Eleans in order to secure an alliance with Elis, the Eleans allowed the Lepreates to continue to cultivate the land on regular (presumably annual) payment of one talent to Olympian Zeus (Thucydides 5.31.2), which would have allowed religious sanctions for non-payment had not Sparta intervened between Elis and Lepreon. Elis then tried to use an Olympic court as an instrument against Sparta in 420.[38]

Elis may have also used other methods to create links between itself and perioikic communities. We learn that a cult of Artemis was transferred from Elis to Letrinoi (Pausanias 6.22.10), and that, conversely, a cult-statue of Poseidon was transferred from Samikon to Elis (Pausanias 6.25.5–6), but no date is recorded for either of these movements.[39] Pausanias 6.22.10 says that Elis had friendly relations with Letrinoi "from the beginning," but this

---

[35] Gauthier 1972:43–45; Sordi 1984:29–30; Roy 1997b:296 with note 89; Gehrke 2003:18; Nafissi 2003:41n139; Möller 2004:257.

[36] Roy 1997b:296–7.

[37] IvO 9: Roy and Schofield 1999.

[38] Thucydides 5.49.1–50.4: Roy 1998.

[39] Jacquemin in Casevitz, Pouilloux, and Jacquemin 2002:302 suggests that the statue of Poseidon was transferred in the period 245–146 BCE; Ruggeri 2004:107–108 suggests a date after 146.

judgment overlooks the fact that c. 400, when the Spartans invaded Elis, Letrinoi deserted Elis to join the Spartans (Xenophon *Hellenica* 3.2.25). There is certainly evidence that by the second half of the fifth century some Greeks had come to regard perioikic territory as part of an Elean region. As noted above, Herodotus 8.73.1–2 does not distinguish the ethnic identities of the communities in the area north of the Alpheios. More explicitly, Thucydides 5.34.1 describes Lepreon as being on the border between Lakonike and Eleia: he must have considered that all Triphylia north of Lepreon, if not Lepreon itself, belonged to Eleia.[40] Aristophanes *Birds* 149 calls Lepreon itself Elean.[41] This sense that the whole region was Elean did of course ultimately lead to its being unified within the Elean state, but probably not until 146 BCE.[42]

In the late fifth and earlier fourth centuries, however, many of the perioikic communities were by no means ready to accept an Elean identity. From the earlier Peloponnesian War onwards, despite Elis' determination to maintain its domination of its *perioikoi*, they were often able to break away, and in so doing many of them adopted a different ethnic identity. The first such problem for Elis arose over Lepreon, and was exacerbated by Sparta's readiness to support Lepreon against Elis (Thucydides 5.1.5); why Sparta became willing to help undermine Elis' domination of its *perioikoi* is not clear, but the breakdown in friendship between Sparta and Elis had very serious consequences. The bad relations between Elis and Sparta continued to the end of the fifth century, when Sparta undertook a war in order to detach all the *perioikoi* from Elean control.[43] It is notable that once Sparta launched a sustained invasion of Elis in that war, several perioikic communities abandoned Elis and joined the Spartans: Xenophon *Hellenica* 3.2.25 names Lepreon, Makiston, Epitalion, Letrinoi, Amphidoloi, and Marganeis. The terms imposed by Sparta when it won the war are in part difficult to establish,[44] but it is at any rate clear that Sparta insisted that Elis relinquish control of all *perioikoi*. What is interesting for the subject of the present volume is how some of the former *perioikoi* adopted new identities.

The perioikic communities south of the Alpheios were united into a new Triphylian state. Siewert (1987–1988) regarded this new creation as ephemeral

---

[40] Roy 1997b:311n17.

[41] Hornblower 2000:223n6.

[42] Roy 1999.

[43] Among the considerable literature on these events see Roy 1997b:291–292, Roy 1998, and Hornblower 2000. On the war see Schepens 2004.

[44] Roy 1997a, 1997b:299–304; Schepens 2004; Ruggeri 2004:21–28.

and serving the interests of Sparta, but Nielsen (1997) has put forward good arguments for the view that unity in the area was in the interests of the local communities, allowing them to resist Elean attempts to re-establish control over them. Ruggeri (2001–2002 and 2004:73–143) has analysed the political and constitutional history of the Triphylian state, known especially from two inscriptions (both cited in full by Ruggeri).

Akroreia also became a separate state.[45] In Akroreia there were four *poleis*, namely Alion, Eupagion, Opous, and Thraistos.[46] In 394 the Akroreians sent a collective military contingent to support Sparta (Xenophon *Hellenica* 4.2.16), and may therefore have formed a federal state. Certainly the Akroreian communities acted collectively in making a dedication at Olympia jointly with the non-Akroreian Alasyes,[47] but the dedication could equally well have been made while Akroreia was still perioikic or after it was separated from Elis.[48] Siewert 1987–1988 regards the Akroreian state, like the Triphylian, as ephemeral and designed to serve Spartan interests; but it is notable that it was created with some regard for local identities: this is shown by the fact that it did not include Lasion, which lay close to Akroreia to the east and was detached from Elis at the same time as Akroreia. Both Xenophon (*Hellenica* 3.2.30, 4.2.16) and Diodorus (14.17.8) distinguish Lasion from Akroreia, and Lasion remained separate from the new Akroreian state, as is shown by its separate military contingent sent to the Peloponnesian League forces in 394 (Xenophon *Hellenica* 4.2.16).

In fact, c. 400 Lasion was being claimed by Arcadians, according to Xenophon (*Hellenica* 3.2.30). Since there was no Arcadian confederation at the time, and since, if Lasion was claimed by a particular Arcadian city-state like Psophis or Thelpousa, Xenophon would have had no reason not to say so directly, the phrase presumably means that some Arcadians claimed that Lasion shared their Arcadian ethnic identity.[49] Such a claim would fit well with the fact that Lasion became Arcadian a generation later.

Elis made considerable efforts to recover control of its lost perioikic territories, and had some success, particularly north of the Alpheios, though significant areas, including Triphylia and probably also Lasion, were not recovered. Because the evidence is patchy and hard to interpret, it is diffi-

---

[45] Siewert 1987–1988; Ruggeri 2004:144–161.
[46] Diodorus 14.17.8; Xenophon *Hellenica* 7.4.14 writes of *poleis* in Akroreia, but names only Thraustos, i.e. Thraistos, individually.
[47] Siewert 1991 no. 3.
[48] Siewert 1987–1988:8n3.
[49] Roy 2000:138, Nielsen 2002a:98.

cult to be sure exactly how much Elis had recovered by the battle of Leuctra in 371. Tuplin (1993, especially 183–185) offers a cautious and detailed analysis of the question.[50]

After Leuctra the political situation in the Peloponnese changed greatly as Spartan power declined (but did not disappear) and the Arcadian confederation came into being. Both Lasion and Triphylia declared themselves Arcadian, and joined the Arcadian confederation (Xenophon *Hellenica* 7.1.26; Xenophon does not name Lasion in this passage, but it is widely recognised that "the others" must refer to Lasion, because of *Hellenica* 7.4.12). Claims that Lasion was Arcadian had apparently already been raised c. 400, and it is not surprising that Lasion chose to be politically Arcadian in the 360s. For Triphylia to become Arcadian was a greater shift in ethnic identity, but it seems to have been welcomed by the Arcadians, who included Triphylos among the sons of their mythical ancestor Arkas on the Arcadian monument dedicated in these years at Delphi (CEG 2.824).[51] It is not clear whether the Arcadian confederation admitted Triphylia to the confederation as a single member or as several *poleis*.[52] In 365 Elis, or Arcadian exiles backed by Elis, captured Lasion, but it was soon recaptured by the Arcadian confederation (Xenophon *Hellenica* 7.4.12–13, Diodorus 15.77.1). Given the Eleans' evident desire to recover their former perioikic communities (e.g. Xenophon *Hellenica* 7.1.26), it seems clear that in adopting formally an Arcadian identity and joining the Arcadian confederation, Triphylia and Lasion were also protecting themselves against the threat of renewed Elean domination.

In the 360s Elis and Arcadia, originally allies against Sparta in 370, became estranged, and by 365 were at war. The war allowed the Arcadians to detach from Elis both Akroreia[53] and Pisatis.[54] Neither of these territories now became Arcadian, though it was probably at this time that Pisatis was linked to Arcadia by a mythical marriage of Pisos to Olympia, daughter of Arkas.[55] Instead Pisatis and Akroreia became independent states, and an

---

[50] See also Ruggeri 2004:36–42.
[51] Ruggeri 2004:95–96 also draws attention to the hitherto neglected figure Triphyle, mother of Klytios and so ancestor of the Klytiad line of seers at Olympia.
[52] Nielsen 1997:152–155, Ruggeri 2004:140–143.
[53] Xenophon *Hellenica* 7.4.14: the Arcadians did not capture Thraistos on this occasion, and it is unknown whether they took it later. The Eleans had evidently recovered Akroreia, though we do not know when.
[54] Nielsen 2002a:118–119.
[55] Nielsen 2002a:118–119.

alliance of Arcadia, Akroreia, and Pisatis was created.[56] An ancient identity for Pisatis was elaborated (or revived), and the collective identity of the Akroreians recovered the political form that it had had at the beginning of the fourth century. The two new states are not heard of again after the end of the Arcadian-Elean war in 362, and they presumably reverted to Elis, which certainly regained control of Olympia (Xenophon *Hellenica* 7.4.35).

Thus the collective identities of communities within Elis and its perioikic territory were frequently exploited in the period from the end of the Peloponnesian War to the 360s. Triphylia was created. Akroreia's collective identity was given independent political form, twice. Lasion developed an Arcadian identity, probably from the early fourth century and certainly in the 360s. Triphylia too became Arcadian, in a remarkable adaptation of its still fairly new collective identity. The ancient identity of Pisatis, expressed in accounts of the region's early history, was elaborated. No doubt in this catalogue of shifting identities there was a degree of opportunism, but it is hard to believe that all these developments were due simply to cynical political manoeuvring. Triphylia for instance, whose identity evolved in the most remarkable way, could presumably have secured Arcadian support against Elis in the 360s by an alliance rather than by actually becoming Arcadian. The exceptional case of Letrinoi, Amphidoloi, and Marganeis, the three insignificant communities west of Olympia, is illuminating because, though feeble on their own, they were included neither in the new Triphylian nationality after the Elean-Spartan war nor in either the Triphylian nationality or the adjacent Pisatan nationality in the 360s. Underlying sentiment helped both to shape and to limit the identities that emerged among the Elean *perioikoi* in the fourth century, and these three small communities were neither Triphylian nor Pisatan, just as Lasion was not Akroreian. Adopting a common identity, so far as sentiment allowed, became a common method of seeking to secure a community's freedom from the threat of Elean control.

It is notable that in every single case the shift in identity was away from Elis. Despite some signs that an extended Elean identity, extending as far south as the Neda, was beginning to emerge by the later sixth century, Elis was evidently unable to offer any counter-attraction to the prospect of freedom from Elean domination. When faced with a choice between being attached to Elis and being attached to Elis' neighbour Arcadia, those *perioikoi* who had the choice chose either alliance with Arcadia or actual Arcadian identity. Evidently Elis' traditional distinction between the Elean state

---

[56] Ringel, Siewert, and Taeuber 1999; Ruggeri 2004:184–188.

proper and its *perioikoi*[57] was too strong to be overcome when Elis needed to find a way to hold on to its subordinate allies.

From the Peloponnesian War to the 360s, Elean foreign policy, when not dominated by the Peloponnesian League, was heavily influenced by the desire to find allies who would help Elis retain or recover its *perioikoi*. Of course other considerations also influenced external policy, not least internal conflicts in Elis itself that would take too long to explore here.[58] In general, however, Elis suffered greatly from a failure to find an answer to the potent appeal that the prospect of a separate identity made to many of its *perioikoi*.

Bibliography

Bilik, R. 1998–1999. "Hippias von Elis als Quelle von Diodors Bericht über den elisch-spartanischen Krieg?" *AncSoc* 29:21–47.

Bultrighini, U. 1990. *Pausania e le tradizioni democratiche (Argo e Elide)*. Padua.

Casevitz, M., Pouilloux, J., and Jacquemin, A., eds. 1999. *Pausanias: Description de la Grèce. Livre V: L'Elide (I)*. Paris.

Casevitz, M., Pouilloux, J., and Jacquemin, A., eds. 2002. *Pausanias: Description de la Grèce. Livre VI: L'Elide (II)*. Paris.

Coleman, J. E. 1986. *Excavations at Pylos in Elis*. Hesperia Supplement 21. Princeton.

Crowther, N. B. 1988. "Elis and the Games." *AC* 57:301–310.

Ebert, J., and Siewert, P. 1997. "Eine archaische Bronzeurkunde aus Olympia mit Vorschriften für Ringkämpfer und Kampfrichter." *Agonismata. Kleine philologische Schriften zur Literatur, Geschichte und Kultur der Antike* (ed. J. Ebert) 200-236. Stuttgart.

Eder, B. 2001a. "Continuity of Bronze Age Cult at Olympia? The Evidence of the Late Bronze Age and Early Iron Age Pottery." *Potnia. Deities and Religion in the Aegean Bronze Age* (eds. R. Laffineur and R. Hägg) 201–209. Liège.

Eder, B. 2001b. "Die Anfänge von Elis und Olympia: zur Siedlungsgeschichte der Landschaft Elis am Übergang von der Spätbronze- zur Früheisenzeit." *Forschungen in der Peloponnes* (ed. V. Mitsopoulos-Leon) 234–243. Athens.

---

[57] Ruggeri 2004:35–36 and 46–53 (and elsewhere) redevelops the argument that Elis granted citizenship to its *perioikoi* in (or shortly before) 368 and withdrew it by 364. Having argued (Roy 1997b:297–298) that no such grant was made, I hope to support that view with fresh arguments at a forthcoming conference.

[58] See Gehrke 1985, Bultrighini 1990.

Eder, B. and Mitsopoulos, V. 1999. "Zur Geschichte der Stadt Elis vor dem Synoikismos von 371 v. Chr." *ÖJ* 68 Beiblatt:1–40.

Gauthier, P. 1972. *Symbola. Les étrangers et la justice dans les cités grecques.* Nancy.

Gehrke, H.-J. 1985. *Stasis. Untersuchungen zu den inneren Kriegen in den griechischen Staaten des 5. und 4. Jahrhunderts v. Chr.* Munich.

Gehrke, H.-J. 2003. "Sull'etnicità elea." *Geographia Antiqua* 12:5–22.

Hansen, M. H., and Nielsen, T. H., eds. 2004. *An Inventory of Archaic and Classical Poleis.* Oxford.

Head, B.V. 1911. *Historia numorum.* Oxford. Second Edition.

Heiden, J. 2003. "Thessalische Lapithen in Elis. Zur Deutung des Westgiebels von Olympia." *AA* 1. Halbband:183–190.

Herrmann, H.-V. 1987. "Einführung." *Die Olympia-Skulpturen* (ed. H.-V. Herrmann) 1–28. Darmstadt.

Hornblower, S. 2000. "Thucydides, Xenophon, and Lichas: were the Spartans Excluded from the Olympic Games from 420 to 400 B.C.?" *Phoenix* 54:212–223.

Ioakimidou, C. 2000. "Auch wir sind Griechen! Statuenreihen westgriechischer Kolonisten in Delphi und Olympia." *Nikephoros* 13:63–94.

Jacquemin, A. 2001a. "Pausanias, le sanctuaire d'Olympie, et les archéologues." In Knoepfler and Piérart 2001:283–300.

Jacquemin, A. 2001b. "Pausanias, témoin de la religion grecque dans le sanctuaire d'Olympie." *Olympie.* (ed. A. Pasquier) 181–213. Paris.

Knoepfler, D., and Piérart, M. eds. 2001. *Editer, traduire, commenter Pausanias en l'an 2000.* Geneva.

Kyrieleis, H. 1997. "Zeus and Pelops in the East Pediment of the Temple of Zeus at Olympia." *The Interpretation of Architectural Sculpture in Greece and Rome* (ed. D. Buitron-Oliver) 13–28. Hanover.

Maddoli, G., and Saladino, V. 1995. *Pausania: Guida della Grecia. Libro V: L'Elide e Olimpia.* Milan.

Maddoli, G., Nafissi, M., and Saladino, V. 1999. *Pausania: Guida della Grecia. Libro VI: L'Elide e Olimpia.* Milan.

Möller, A. 2004. "Elis, Olympia und das Jahr 580 v. Chr. Zur Frage der Eroberung der Pisatis." *Griechische Archaik. Interne Entwicklungen—externe Impulse* (eds. R. Rollinger and C. Ulf) 249–270. Berlin.

Morgan, C. 1990. *Athletes and Oracles. The Transformation of Olympia and Delphi in the Eighth Century B.C.* Cambridge.

Morgan, C., and Hall, J. M. 1996. "Achaian *poleis* and Achaian colonisation." *Introduction to an Inventory of Poleis* (ed. M. H. Hansen) 164–232. Acts of the Copenhagen Polis Centre 3. Copenhagen.

Nafissi, M. 2001. "La prospettiva di Pausania sulla storia dell'Elide: la questione pisate." In Knoepfler and Piérart 2001:301–321.

Nafissi, M. 2003. "Elei e Pisati. Geografia, storia e istituzioni politiche della regione di Olimpia." *Geographia Antiqua* 12:23–55.

Nielsen, T. H. 1997. "Triphylia: An Experiment in Ethnic Construction and Political Organisation." *Yet More Studies in the Ancient Greek Polis* (ed. T. H. Nielsen) 129–162. Papers from the Copenhagen Polis Centre 4. Stuttgart.

Nielsen, T. H. 2002a. *Arkadia and its Poleis in the Archaic and Classical Periods.* Göttingen.

Nielsen, T. H., ed. 2002b. *Even More Studies in the Ancient Greek Polis.* Papers from the Copenhagen Polis Centre 6. Stuttgart.

Ringel, E., Siewert, P., and Taeuber, H. 1999. "Die Symmachien Pisas mit den Arkadern, Akroreia, Messenien, und Sikyon. Ein neues Fragment der 'Arkadischen Bündnisstele' von 365 v. Chr." *Bericht über die Ausgrabungen in Olympia* (ed. A. Mallwitz and K. Herrmann) 11:413–420. Berlin.

Ritter, S. 2001. "Münzbilder im Kontext: Zeus und Olympia auf Elischen Stateren des 4. Jahrhunderts v. Chr." *Konstruktionen von Wirklichkeit: Bilder im Griechenland des 5. und 4. Jahrhunderts v. Chr* (eds. R. von den Hoff and S. Schmidt) 89–105. Stuttgart.

Rizakis, A. D. 1995. *Achaïe I. Sources textuelles et histoire régionale.* Meletemata 20. Athens.

Roy, J. 1994. "Thebes in the 360s BCE." *CAH²* 6:187–208. Cambridge.

Roy, J. 1997a. "Spartan Aims in the Spartan-Elean War of c. 400. Further Thoughts." *Electronic Antiquity* 3. http://scholar.lib.vt.edu/ejournals/ElAnt/V3N6/roy.html.

Roy, J. 1997b. "The *Perioikoi* of Elis." *The Polis as an Urban Centre and as a Political Community* (ed. M. H. Hansen) 282–320. Acts of the Copenhagen Polis Centre 4. Copenhagen.

Roy, J. 1998. "Thucydides 5.49.1–50.4: The Quarrel between Elis and Sparta in 420 B.C., and Elis' Exploitation of Olympia." *Klio* 80:360–368.

Roy, J. 1999. «Les cités d'Élide.» *Le Péloponnèse. Archéologie et histoire* (ed. J. Renard) 151–176. Rennes.

Roy, J. 2000. "The Frontier between Arkadia and Elis in Classical Antiquity." *Polis and Politics* (eds. P. Flensted-Jensen, T. H. Nielsen, and L. Rubinstein) 133–156. Copenhagen.

Roy, J. 2002a. "The Pattern of settlement in Pisatis." In Nielsen 2002b:229–247.

Roy, J. 2002b. "The Synoikism of Elis." In Nielsen 2002b:249–264.

Roy, J. and Schofield, D. 1999. "IvO 9: A New Approach." *Horos* 13:155–165.

Ruggeri, C. 2001–2002. "L'état fédéral de la Triphylie: remarques sur l'histoire politique et constitutionelle." Πρακτικὰ τοῦ ϛ' Διέθνους Συνεδρίου Πελοποννησιακῶν σπουδῶν. 2:165–176. Peloponnesiaka Supplement 24. Athens.

Ruggeri, C. 2004. *Gli stati intorno a Olimpia. Storia e costituzione dell'Elide e degli stati formati dai perieci elei (400-362 a.C.).* Historia Einzelschriften 170. Stuttgart.

Schepens, G. 2004. "La guerra di Sparta contro Elide." *Ricerche di antichità e tradizione classica* (ed. E. Lanzilotta) 1–89. Tivoli.

Siewert, P. 1987–1988. "Triphylien und Akroreia. Spartanische 'Regionalstaaten' in der westlichen Peloponnes." Πρακτικὰ τοῦ γ' Διέθνους Συνεδρίου Πελοποννησιακῶν σπουδῶν. 2:7–12. Peloponnesiaka Supplement 13. Athens.

Siewert, P. 1991. "Staatliche Weihungen von Kesseln und anderen Bronzegeräten in Olympia." *MDAI(A)* 106:81–84.

Siewert, P. 1994. "Eine archäische Rechtsaufzeichnung aus der antiken Stadt Elis." *Symposion 1993: Vorträge zur griechischen und hellenistischen Rechtsgeschichte* (ed. G. Thür) 17–34. Akten der Gesellschaft für Griechische und Hellenistische Rechtsgeschichte 10. Vienna.

Sinn, U. 1978. "Das Heiligtum der Artemis Limnatis bei Kombothekra. Elische Lekythen." *MDAI(A)* 93:45–82 with Tafeln 21–26.

Sinn, U. 1981. "Das Heiligtum der Artemis Limnatis bei Kombothekra II: Der Kult." *MDAI(A)* 96:25–71 with Tafeln 7–16 and Beilage 4.

Sordi, M. 1984. "Le implicazioni olimpiche della guerra d'Elide." *Problemi di storia e cultura spartana* (ed. E. Lanzilotta) 145–159. Università di Macerata Pubblicazioni della Facoltà di Lettere e Filosofia 20. Rome.

Taita, J. 1999. "Un'Anfizionia ad Olimpia? Un bilancio sulla questione nell'interpretazione storiografica moderna." *Quaderni di Acme* 39:149–186.

Taita, J. 2000. "Gli Aitoloi di Olimpia. L'identità etnica delle comunità di vicinato del santuario olimpico." *Tyche* 15:147–188.

Taita, J. 2001. "Confini naturali e topografia sacra: i santuari di Kombothékras, Samikon e Olimpia." *OTerr* 7:107–142.

Taita, J. 2002. "Rapporti fra il santuario di Olimpia e lo stato di Elide."
Quaderni di Acme 54:131–161.

Tuplin, C. J. 1993. *The Failings of Empire: A Reading of Xenophon Hellenica 2.3.11–7.5.27.* Historia Einzelschriften 76. Stuttgart.

Ulf, C. 1997. "Die Mythen um Olympia—politischer Gehalt und politische Intention." *Nikephoros* 10:9–51.

van Effenterre, H. and Ruzé, F., eds. 1994–1995. *Nomima: Recueil d'Inscriptions Politiques et Juridiques de l'Archaïsme Grec.* 2 volumes. Rome.

Wacker, C. 1998. "The Record of the Olympic Victory List." *Nikephoros* 11:39–50.

Walter, U. 1993. *An der Polis teilhaben. Bürgerstaat und Zugehörigkeit im archaischen Griechenland.* Historia Einzelschriften 82. Stuttgart.

Yalouris, N. 1972. "The City-State of Elis." *Ekistics* 33.195:95–96 (February 1972).

IV

Triphylia from Elis to Arcadia

Claudia Ruggeri

ΡΙΦΥΛΙΑ AND ITS INHABITANTS, the Τριφύλιοι, provide an important example of the creation of a new ethnic identity that can be dated to a precise historical context and investigated at the very moment of its emergence. Even more interestingly, some thirty years after its emergence this ethnic identity was transformed in order to make the Triphylians members of the Arcadian *ethnos*.

I.1. Triphylia: The New Ethnic Identity Created around 400 BCE

The name *Triphulia* and the ethnic *Triphulioi* were created after the end of the war between Sparta and Elis, probably to be dated around 400 BCE.[1] Among other conditions, the Eleans were compelled by the peace treaty to give autonomy to the cities of the *perioikoi*.[2] The *perioikoi* were the communities that inhabited the area located between the rivers Alpheios and Neda, the area which from the beginning of the fourth century came to be called Triphylia, and, north of the Alpheios, the Letrinians, the Amphidolians, the Marganians, the Akroreians, and Lasion. As will be shown below (I.3), the name *Triphulia* and the ethnic identity of the *Triphulioi* did not exist before. Only at the beginning of the fourth century, after becoming independent from Elis thanks to the Spartan intervention, did the cities south of the Alpheios take a common name and create a shared ethnic identity as part of

---

[1] Scholars disagree on the exact date of the war; see most recently Schepens 2004:73–85; Ruggeri 2004a:16n1–2. I would like to take the opportunity to thank Peter Funke and Nino Luraghi for inviting me to the conference in Münster and for the friendly and fruitful discussion of certain points in my paper.

[2] Xenophon *Hellenica* 3.2.30–31; Diodorus Siculus 23.34.1; Pausanias 3.8.5. Siewert 1987:276; Roy 1999:155; Nielsen 2002:239; Ruggeri 2004a:64–65.

a complex process whose result was the establishment of political and military unity in the form of a federal state.

The evidence on the Triphylian state at the beginning of the fourth century is composed of two inscriptions of the Triphylians, to be dated within the first thirty years of the century, that record the grant of Triphylian citizenship to some individuals. Besides providing information on some Triphylian magistracies, these documents show that Triphylia was a federal state (see I.5).[3] The ethnic *Triphulios* as part of a personal name is attested in an Athenian funerary inscription of the second half of the fourth century, i.e. for somebody who was probably born in the first half of the century.[4] Finally, the Triphylians had an eponymous hero, Triphylos, who was probably created at the time of the emergence of the Triphylian federal state; the tradition on Triphylos that we know from an Arcadian dedication in Delphi and from Polybios cannot be dated earlier than 369 BCE, that is, to the year when Triphylia was annexed to the Arcadian federal state, since it calls Triphylos a son of Arkas.[5]

I.2: The Role of the Spartans

Because the liberation of the *perioikoi* from the hegemony of the Eleans around 400 was brought about by their military intervention, an obvious question to ask is whether the Spartans also had an important role in forming the states of the Elean *perioikoi*, in particular that of Triphylia, which is the object of our present enquiry. The origin of the Spartans' effort in defense of the autonomy of the Elean *perioikoi*, which had already started with their intervention in support of Lepreon against Elis in the third quarter of the fifth century,[6] was in fact their hostility towards the Eleans, which became even more open when the Eleans allied themselves with Athens, Argos and Mantinea in 420 BCE.[7] The aim was to force the Eleans under their own hegemony and to weaken their military power by

---

[3] SEG 35.389; 40.392; Siewert 1987:275–277. For a complete bibliography of the inscriptions: Ruggeri 2004a:73n160–161.

[4] IG II² 10461.

[5] FdD 3.1.3; CEG 824. The group of statues and the inscription are also described by Pausanias 10.9.5. The descent of Triphylos from Arkas is attested also by Polybius 4.77.8. Nielsen 2002:249–250; Ruggeri 2004a:94–96.

[6] Thucydides 5.31.1–5. Formally, the war of the Spartans against the Eleans was provoked by the question of the *perioikoi*: Xenophon *Hellenica* 3.2.23; Diodorus Siculus 23.17.5–6; Pausanias 3.8.3. The issue of the *perioikoi* was used as a pretext but the motive for the war was control over Olympia: Sordi 1984a:21, 24; Sordi 1984b:149, 152.

[7] Thucydides 5.47.9.

breaking the system of alliances with the *perioikoi*, which the Eleans had created. At the time of the peace around 400, by undoing the *summachiai*[8] of the Eleans, the Spartans deprived them of the military tributes and received the *perioikoi*, now autonomous, and the Eleans themselves into the Peloponnesian League.[9] It is also very likely that the Spartans favored the formation of the new independent states of the *perioikoi*, and there is occasional evidence of Spartan intrusion in questions of internal competence of the Triphylian state. Such is the case, for example, with the settlement of Xenophon in Skillous, only four kilometres from Olympia. One of the goals of this measure, though probably not the sole one, must have been for the Spartans to have an informant in the *polis* which, until 371/0, was one of the cities that formed the federal state of Triphylia.[10] Another piece of evidence regarding the important role played by the Spartans in the formation process of the state of Triphylia could be the Spartan element in the genealogy of the eponymous hero of the Triphylians, Triphylos, who in the Arcadian dedication of 369 at Delphi is the son of Arkas, but on the maternal side descends from Amyklas, king of Sparta.[11]

---

[8] *On the* summachiai of the Eleans with the *perioikoi* see I.3 and n19 below.

[9] Xenophon *Hellenica* 4.2.16. Siewert 1987–1988:8–10. Sparta's hegemonic policy was the cause of the war against Elis: Schepens 2004:85–89; Nafissi 2003:26–27. Falkner has emphasized among the objectives of Sparta control of the two ports of Elis, Kyllene and Phea: Falkner 1996:17–25; Falkner 1999:385–394; Roy 1997a:299–304; Roy 1997b.

[10] The settlement of Xenophon in Skillous is to be dated between 390 and 386 BCE and the sources agree in attributing responsibility to the Spartans: Xenophon *Anabasis* 5.3.7; Diogenes Laertius 2.52; Pausanias 5.6.5. On the subject Ruggeri 2004a:119–132; Ruggeri 2004b; Sordi 2005:15–20, who believes that Xenophon founded an actual colony at Skillous.

[11] In the dedication to the Arcadians at Delphi, (see n5 and below, II.1) Triphylos appears as one of the sons of Arkas. However, in his description of the monument Pausanias (10.9.5) highlights the important detail that, unlike the other sons of Arkas who appear in the dedication, Triphylos was not a son of Erato, but of Laodamia, daughter of Amyklas, king of Sparta. This reference to Amyklas certainly has a precise meaning, which, however, is not entirely clear (Ruggeri 2004a:95n253). According to Nilsson 1951:80, through Amyklas, the Triphylians wanted to record the importance of the Spartan intervention in obtaining autonomy from Elis at the end of the fifth century. Ioakimidou 1997:329 hypothesizes instead that the reference to Amyklas reveals the intention of the Arcadians to emphasize that, if in the past the Spartans had exercised control over Triphylia, it now belonged to them. It seems to me unlikely that the Arcadians, in a dedication for victory over the Spartans, could have an interest in recording the role of Sparta in the formation of Triphylia. Instead, Triphylos' mother could be a remnant of a genealogical tradition from before 369, one created, that is, at the beginning of the fourth century by the Triphylians and the Spartans at the time of the birth of the federal state of Triphylia and of the creation of the eponymous hero Triphylos himself. At this time, one could easily envision Triphylos being said to be descended from Amyklas king of Sparta, with Arkas not yet present in the genealogy. Thirty or so years later, at the time when the Triphylians abandoned the

I.3: The *Poleis* of the Area between the Rivers Alpheus and Neda before 400 BCE

Until the beginning of the fourth century, the communities which inhabited the area between the rivers Alpheus and Neda were separated from each other: Nielsen[12] has already demonstrated that in the fifth century they did not possess a concept of common ethnic identity and were not united politically. Some literary and epigraphical sources on these communities from the fifth century, attest to them being *poleis* in the political sense of the word: first of all, Lepreon, which had sent 200 hoplites for the war against the Persians and which was commemorated by the ethnic name of its citizens, Λεπρεᾶται, in the Greek dedications at Delphi and Olympia for the victory at Plataea,[13] was already at the time a *polis*. In the second half of the fifth century, before the outbreak of the Peloponnesian War but at a date which cannot be established with any more certainty, the Lepreans concluded a treaty of alliance with the Eleans; up to that moment, they were an autonomous *polis*, not yet under the hegemony of the Eleans.[14] In a dedication at Olympia dated between 450 and 425, Skillous too is defined as a *polis*.[15] Herodotus, in the passage where he refers to the foundation by the Minyans of the cities of Lepreon, Makiston, Phrixa, Pyrgos, Epion, and Noudion, uses the word *poleis*.[16] Xenophon too, both when referring to events in the fifth century, and to others in the fourth, calls the communities of Triphylia *poleis*. Furthermore, Xenophon uses the ethnic names of Lepreon, Epitalion, and Makiston, this last also as part of a personal name, Σιλανὸς Μακίστιος, one of the participants in Cyrus' expedition against Artaxerxes, and, referring to the inhabitants of Skillous, uses the term *politai*.[17]

There are many indications that suggest that in the fifth century, the *poleis* of the area south of the Alpheus were under the control of the Eleans. First, an inscription in Olympia dated to the last quarter of the sixth century, which twice mentions τοὶ Ϝαλεῖοι καὶ ἁ συμαχία, has been interpreted by

---

alliance with Sparta to enter into the federal state of the Arcadians, the tradition of the descent of Triphylos from the Spartans was still too fresh to be erased and replaced with a new one, and this is why, even though it might have been slightly uncomfortable for the Arcadians, it was inserted into the new Arcadian genealogical tradition.

[12] Nielsen 2002:233–247.

[13] Herodotus 9.28.4; ML 27; Pausanias 5.23.1–3.

[14] Thucydides 5.31.2.

[15] IvO 16; van Effenterre and Ruzé 1994–1995:1n56.

[16] Herodotus 4.148.4.

[17] Xenophon *Hellenica* 3.2.23; 30; 6.5.2; 7.1.26; *Anabasis* 5.3.9–10; 7.4.16.

Siewert as evidence that the *perioikoi* of the Eleans were formally *summachoi* of Elis, obviously in an alliance dominated by the latter.[18] The submission of Lepreon to the Eleans was also accomplished in this way. For, according to Thucydides (5.31.2–4), the treaty of military alliance, which has been mentioned above, was concluded between the Lepreans and the Eleans in the second half of the fifth century, before the beginning of the Peloponnesian War, when the former called the latter to help them in a war against the Arcadians, agreeing to give in exchange half of their territory. At the end of the war, the Eleans had taken possession of these lands and had imposed on the Lepreans a tribute of a talent to be paid every year to Zeus of Olympia in exchange for allowing them to continue inhabiting and cultivating the lands. As has already been mentioned, the inscription which cites τοὶ Ϝαλεῖοι καὶ ἁ συμαχία has to be dated to the end of the sixth century, but we do not know which *perioikoi* around this date were *summachoi* of the Eleans. However, according to Thucydides, Lepreon had become a *summachos* around the third quarter of the fifth century, was then detached from Elis by the Spartans, but came back under the hegemony of the Eleans around the end of the fifth century.[19] The comment made by Herodotus (4.148.4) according to whom the cities of Lepreon, Makiston, Phrixa, Pyrgos, Epion, Noudion had been devastated by the Eleans "in his own time" (ἐπ' ἐμέο) is not very clear and must be interpreted as evidence either for the conflict which led to the submission of these cities or of a conflict between the Eleans and the cities of the *perioikoi*, which had already, all or in part, become their allies. It is, however, certain that the Eleans considered the cities of the *perioikoi* as their own, or, to use Xenophon's expression, as "booty" (*Hellenica* 3.2.23: ἐπιληίδας): for, according to Xenophon, it was with these words that the Eleans had tried to defend their rights over the cities of the *perioikoi* against the Spartans, who, on the other hand, thought the cities should be left autonomous. Two other pieces of evidence from the fifth century confirm that not only did the Eleans consider the communities of the *perioikoi* their own, but that this had been acknowledged as the state of affairs by the other Greeks. The first is a passage from Aristophanes' *Birds* of 414, which considers Lepreon an Elean

---

[18] Siewert 1994:256–264; Ebert and Siewert 1997. Siewert's interpretation is generally accepted: Roy 1997a:292–293; Roy 1999:155; Roy 2002:252; Nielsen 2002:242–244; Ruggeri 2004a:18; 68; Nafissi 2003:25. The *summachia* of the Eleans with the unidentified Ewaioi (IvO 9), about whom we do not know if they were *perioikoi* of the Eleans or not, is to be dated around 500. On the inscription: Roy and Schofield 1999:155–165.

[19] Falkner 1999:389–393; Ruggeri 2004a:120–121.

city;[20] the second is another passage from Thucydides which attests to the area south of the Alpheus up to Lepreum being called Ἠλεῖα in the second half of the fifth century.[21]

To sum up, the communities of the area south of the Alpheus, many if not all of which were *poleis* in a political sense at least in the fifth century, did not, up until the end of the war of the Spartans against the Eleans in 400, share a common ethnic identity and were not united amongst themselves; they had in common only the fact that they were all ruled by the Eleans, who most likely acquired their power over the *perioikoi* in different stages, first taking the Alpheus valley, and then moving south in order to control Lepreon around the beginning of the second half of the fifth century.

Some of the communities of the area, we do not exactly know how many and which, took part in the amphiktiony of the sanctuary of Poseidon at Samikon on the central coast of Triphylia. Our sources do not allow us to place the existence of this amphiktiony within a precise time-frame, but several clues point back to a time before the creation of the federal state of the Triphylians at the beginning of the fourth century, a time in which the *poleis* were independent, instead of being politically united, which means the fifth century or even earlier.[22] Strabo's passage signaling the existence of the amphiktiony contains the following information (8.3.13): καὶ τὸ Σαμικὸν μετὰ ταῦτα, ὅπου τὸ μάλιστα τιμώμενον τοῦ Σαμίου Ποσειδῶνος ἱερόν· ἔστι δ' ἄλσος ἀγριελαιῶν πλέων· ἐπεμελοῦντο δ' αὐτοῦ Μακίστιοι· οὗτοι δὲ καὶ τὴν ἐκεχειρίαν ἐπήγγελλον, ἣν καλοῦσι Σάμιον· συντελοῦσι δ' εἰς τὸ ἱερὸν πάντες Τριφύλιοι. "Then there is Samikon, where the sanctuary of Poseidon Samios, which is the object of very great devotion, lies. It is in a sacred grove full of wild olive trees; the Makistians used to take care of it: they would announce the sacred truce they called Samian. All the Triphylians contribute to the maintenance expenses of the sanctuary." It should firstly be noted that in the era of Strabo and his source the term *Triphulioi* did not possess a political connotation apart from referring to the inhabitants of Triphylia, which had become a mere geographical name. Strabo's passage on the sanctuary of Poseidon, which probably derives from Artemidorus, though we do not know who the ultimate source was, describes not only the center of a

---

[20] Aristophanes *Birds* 149: τὸν Ἠλεῖον Λέπρεον.

[21] Thucydides 5.34.1. Nielsen 2002:233.

[22] On the amphiktiony of the sanctuary of Poseidon, see Tausend 1992:19–21, who also believes it to be very ancient, although for reasons different from the ones mentioned here.

cult worshipped by the inhabitants of the region, but also the participation of the cities of Triphylia in the upkeep of the sanctuary via the payment of a tribute. Taking care of the sanctuary was up to the city of Makistos, which was not far from Samikon, but inside Triphylia, near the modern village of Skillountia (Mazi) which, during the celebration of the god's festival, would announce the sacred truce. The sanctuary of Poseidon was thus the center of an amphiktiony of the Triphylians, as expressed by the verb συντελοῦσι. As I have attempted to show elsewhere,[23] the existence of this amphiktiony, run by the Makistians, who must have occupied one of the most important cities of the area, certainly predated the decline of Makistos, which occurred during the course of the third century BCE. For, around the third decade of the third century, Makistos did not exist any more, and had long since disappeared by the time of Artemidorus and Strabo.[24] The reference to *ekecheiria*—that is a sacred truce proclaimed within the precincts of a regional cult, rather than an international one like the one near Olympia, to allow for the Triphylians to participate in the feast of Poseidon—suggests the independence of the *poleis* of the region, and the possibility of the existence of armed conflicts between the cities of the amphiktiony.[25] The organization of an amphiktiony to take care of the cult and the organization of common festivals, bears witness to the existence of contact and some kind of cohesion between the inhabitants of the region that adhered to it, but does not suggest either a shared ethnic identity or a common military policy. On the other hand, the very fact that the communities around the sanctuary of Poseidon at Samikon decided to unite in an amphiktiony shows an attempt to organize themselves and give themselves some common rules, using the amphiktiony as a unifying element in the absence of a stronger one.

I.4: The Name Triphylia

In the process of the creation of a common ethnic identity, the first thing the communities south of the Alpheus had to do was to give themselves a name and the one chosen was *Triphulioi*: "those of the three tribes," or "those formed from the three tribes." The very etymology of the name points to the artificial nature of what had been created, since it was necessary to go back to three different tribes for a common ethnicity. So even the name confirms what we inferred from the sources: that there was no ethnic unity in the

---

[23] Ruggeri 2001–2002:173–175; Ruggeri 2004a:96–102.
[24] Nielsen 1997:134n35; Roy 1999:157; Ruggeri 2004a:100.
[25] I thank Peter Siewert for discussion of the significance of *ekecheiria*.

area before the beginning of the fourth century. What these three tribes were was not clear to the ancients, as Strabo, who knows different traditions on the origin of the name, testifies, and it is not clear to us either. In addition, it should be noted that an ethnic identity is composed of common elements that can be real or fictitious: so we cannot know how serious the reference to the three tribes actually is; we only know that the Triphylians presented themselves in this way. Even Strabo was not certain which three tribes formed Triphylia (8.3.3): Τριφύλιοι δ' ἐκλήθησαν ἀπὸ τοῦ συμβεβηκότος, ἀπὸ τοῦ τρία φῦλα συνεληλυθέναι, τό τε τῶν ἀπ' ἀρχῆς Ἐπειῶν καὶ τὸ τῶν ἐποικησάντων ὕστερον Μινυῶν καὶ τὸ τῶν ὕστατα ἐπικρατησάντων Ἠλείων· οἱ δ' ἀντὶ τῶν Μινυῶν Ἀρκάδας φασίν, ἀμφισβητήσαντας τῆς χώρας πολλάκις ... The three tribes would thus have been the Epeians, the Minyans, and the Eleans or instead of the Minyans, the Arcadians. It is clear that Strabo has gathered different and contradictory versions. The reference to the Eleans has no value, firstly because the Ϝαλεῖοι, the "inhabitants of the valley," i.e. of the so-called *koilê* Elis, the valley of the Peneus, did not reside in Triphylia, and secondly because it is extremely improbable that the Triphylians, at the time of independence from the Eleans, against whom they rebelled by going over to the Spartans during the war at the end of the fifth century, would have wanted to include the Eleans in their origins or affirm that one of the tribes that made them up were the Eleans.

With the passing of the centuries, the traditions on the origin of the name have grown, and Stephanus of Byzantium knew different interpretations of the name which were no longer tied exclusively to three tribes: Τριφυλία, ἡ Ἧλις. λέγονται καὶ Τρίφυλοι παρὰ τὸ οἰκισθῆναι ἀπὸ τριῶν φυλῶν ἢ ἀπὸ τριῶν πυλῶν ἢ ἀπὸ Τριφύλης τῆς Κλυτίου μητρός.

We find an important tradition on the peoples south of the Alpheus in Herodotus, who obviously was not yet aware of the formation of the state of Triphylia nor of the name. Speaking of the Minyans, descendants of the mythical Argonauts, Herodotus (4.148.4) tells how after having chased the Paroreatans and the Kaucones from their land, they divided it into six parts and founded the cities of Lepreon, Makistos, Phrixai, Pyrgos, Epion, and Noudion. It is possible that these are the three tribes from which the Triphylians wanted to trace their origins at the beginning of the fourth century, because besides Herodotus many other traditions from Homer to Strabo record these populations in the area.[26] It is also clear that the tradi-

---

[26] The presence of the Minyans in the region finds confirmation in the name of the river Minyeios (Homer *Iliad* 11.722), identified in the sources of Strabo (8.3.19; 8.3.28) and

tion of the Minyans in the foundation of the six cities is a myth of origins already circulating in the fifth century,[27] a myth that brought together the six cities mentioned by Herodotus, but not all those that in the fourth century made up Triphylia, because at least Skillous, Epitalion, Hypana, and Typaneai are missing. It is impossible to know whether Herodotus omits these cities because they were not considered Minyans or for other reasons.

These different traditions, going back to different periods, seem to suggest a general picture along the following lines. Until the end of the fifth century, the autonomous *poleis* south of the Alpheus shared neither any sense of common ethnic identity nor any form of political unity, and presumably possessed various myths of origins, amongst which was the one referring to the foundation of six cities by the Minyans. With the formation at the beginning of the fourth century of the federal state of Triphylia, a new mythical tradition specific to the Triphylians and valid for all the cities of the area was created. It is possible to respond to the doubts expressed many years ago by Bölte, who could not believe that the term Triphylia had come into being only in the fourth century, by looking at the issue from this perspective. He believed that the term had to be much older because it made reference to tribes that did not exist any more in historical times.[28] This, however, is exactly what we would expect when studying the emergence of a new concept of ethnic identity which, at its inception at the beginning of the fourth century, was based not on factual reality but on mythical tradi-

---

Pausanias (5.6.2–3) as the Anigros which flowed by Samikon. The Minyans were a Boeotian population gathered around Orchomenos and tied to the south of Thessaly; in the valley of the Alpheus as in Triphylia, toponyms and mythical characters are attested which correspond to others known in the area of Boeotia and Thessaly. This information must be interpreted as the memory of the migrations of populations in the Peloponnese coming from these regions. Eder 1998:186–187; Ruggeri 2004a:84–86.

[27] Nielsen 2002:234.

[28] Bölte 1939:186: "Greek scholars combined [*scil.* the information they had]; they did not have access to a real tradition any more. This would be hard to understand if Niese (Niese 1910:13) were right to maintain that the name originated at the beginning of the fourth century, an expression that hides the process in the deepest darkness. Another observation brings to the same conclusion. In historical times there were no more tribes in this area, but autonomous communities. Therefore a name that presupposes the existence of three tribes must be very old" (*Die griechischen Gelehrten haben also kombiniert; eine wirkliche Überlieferung war ihnen nicht mehr erreichbar. Das wäre schwer verständlich, wenn Niese (Niese 1910:13) recht hätte mit der Ansicht, der Name habe sich gebildet im Anfang des 4. Jhdts., ein Ausdruck, der den Vorgang in tiefstes Dunkel hüllt. Es lässt sich aber zeigen, daß der Name älter sein muss. Zu demselben Ergebnis führt eine andere Überlegung. In der historischen Zeit gibt es in dieser Gegend keine Stämme mehr, sondern nur autonome Gemeinden. Deshalb muss ein Name, der die Existenz von drei Stämmen voraussetzt, sehr alt sein*).

tions projected into the past, like that of the arrival in the region of the Minyans, descendants of the Argonauts, or that of the Kaukones who lived there before their arrival.

I.5: The Federal State of Triphylia

The creation of the ethnic concept of the Triphylians at the beginning of the fourth century was part of the complex process of the formation of the federal state of the Triphylians. The federal state is attested by two inscriptions, one of which was found near the modern Skillountia (Mazi), where the remains of ancient Makistos are located, while the other, of uncertain origin, consists of two decrees granting Triphylian citizenship to people mentioned in the respective documents and, in one of the decrees, to their descendants.[29] The contents of these documents give us some information about the organization of the state of Triphylia: the decrees were issued by the council, or more probably by the federal assembly of the Triphylians; as regards magistracies, the federal college of the *damiurgoi* is mentioned.[30] One of the documents bears witness to the position of the κατάκοος, a federal officer who probably acted as a secretary or witness.[31] One of the grants of citizenship regards in particular the *polis* of Makistos: in fact, the Triphylians decided that the people inscribed on the tablet would be Makistians, that is citizens of Makistos, residents there with all the rights of citizens including the right to hold the magistracies of the city. In granting citizenship, the Triphylians specify the *polis* in which the beneficiaries of the decree must live: these receive both Triphylian citizenship and that of the *polis* of Makistos. In this document we thus have evidence of the existence of the double citizenship (the federal one, and that of the individual *poleis* of the federation) which is a fundamental characteristic of Greek federal states. In the other inscription, the new citizens receive along with their citizenship the ἀτέλεια πάντων; here we have information about the existence of τέλη, that is, federal taxes,[32] given that this decree, much shorter than the other one, concerns itself only with the federal level and does not

---

[29] See n3.

[30] Nielsen 2002:253; Ruggeri 2004a:133–138.

[31] Siewert 1987:277 believes that a *katakoos* carried out the duties of a secretary analogous to a *grammateus*, with the difference that the name *katakoos* descends from an epoch preceding the use of writing as one of the functionary's duties. See also Ruggeri 2004a:139–140: the interpretations offered are those of "listener," "witness," or public investigator subsequently called to recount and testify.

[32] Nielsen 2002:254; Ruggeri 2004a:139–140.

specify that the new citizens will become members of any particular *polis*. Finally, Xenophon's passage (*Hellenica* 4.2.16) on the Greek forces in the battle of Nemea (394) shows that the Triphylians, as allies of the Spartans, had sent a contingent of hoplites to join the army of the Peloponnesian League: if the cities of Triphylia had organized and sent a common contingent they surely also possessed a federal army.

From the study of dialectal characteristics present in the inscription found at Skillountia, and from those present in other documents found in the area of Triphylia dated between the fifth and the beginning of the fourth century, it seems that we can establish, despite the scarcity of the documents, that the dialect spoken in the region, which is Elean, shows local variants. While in the northern part of Triphylia the dialect possesses all the characteristics typical of Elean, the psilosis, the rhotacism at the end of the word and the accusative plural in –οις instead of –ους, in an inscription from Kombothékra in the center of Triphylia and in one from Lepreon in the south of the region, aspiration is certainly present.[33] In the context of the study of the formation of the concept of ethnic identity and of the federal state of the Triphylians this confirms that speaking the same language, which can naturally be an element favorable to the formation of an ethnic identity common to a community, is not necessarily a determining factor, and that linguistic diversity does not present an obstacle to the processes of unification once they have been set in motion.[34] In addition, slight dialectal differences in Triphylia should not come as a surprise once we have considered the artificiality of the process through which ethnic unity had been created by the Triphylians, who defined themselves as those "formed by the three tribes." Furthermore, as the differences between dialects spoken in the north and center-south of Triphylia did not hamper the process of forming a common ethnic identity, so the fact that the Triphylians did not speak Arcadian did not hinder their entry into the Arcadian federation and their acceptance of the Arcadian ethnic identity.[35]

II.1: The Triphylians become Arcadians

The Triphylians remained allies of the Spartans until after the battle of Leuctra in the summer of 371/0; Xenophon recounts that Lepreon was still on the side of the Spartans during their expedition against Mantinea

---

[33] Siewert 1987:275–276; Ruggeri 2000:117–121; Ruggeri 2004a:87–93.
[34] Nielsen 2002:51.
[35] Nielsen 2002:23–24, 51.

(*Hellenica* 6.5.11). The reason why Xenophon mentions only the 'Lepreans' in this passage instead of writing 'Triphylians'—we would expect that the whole federation would take part in the expedition with a common contingent—is not entirely clear. We do know that the Eleans took advantage of the Spartans' defeat at Leuctra to re-capture some of the communities of the *perioikoi*, such as Skillous and maybe some other cities in the north of Triphylia, and this might have provoked the lack of coordination between the members of the federation. As for the attempt to re-capture the *perioikoi*, we know that the Eleans delivered a military attack after Leuctra and that certainly at the time of the peace negotiations in Athens in 371/0 they still had not re-captured Triphylia, which on that occasion they claimed as their own in front of the other Greeks.[36] Right afterwards, however, the Eleans took Skillous, as we learn from some ancient sources on the life of Xenophon, who at the time lived in the *polis* where he had been installed by the Spartans. Now Xenophon had to leave, seeking refuge first in Lepreon, until that city ceased to be on the side of the Spartans, and then at Corinth.[37] We do not know of any other conquests of the Eleans in Triphylia, but it is possible that other cities in the north of the region had been re-captured.[38] At any rate, the Eleans carried out other conquests north of the Alpheus, re-capturing the Amphidolians, the Letrinians, the Marganeans, and the cities of Akroreia.[39]

---

[36] Xenophon *Hellenica* 6.5.2: Ἠλεῖοι δὲ ἀντέλεγον ὡς οὐ δέοι αὐτονόμους ποιεῖν οὔτε Μαργανέας οὔτε Σκιλλουντίους οὔτε Τριφυλίους· σφετέρας γὰρ εἶναι ταύτας τὰς πόλεις. This passage is much debated by the moderns because Xenophon separates Skillous from the rest of Triphylia, of which in fact it was a part, and because the Eleans, in their claims on the *perioikoi*, fail to record, together with the Marganeans, the inhabitants of Skillous, and the Triphylians, four other communities: the Letrinians, the Amphidolians, the Akroreians, and Lasion. On possible solutions, see Tuplin 1993:183–184; Roy 1997a:284–285n20; Ruggeri 2004a:37–38.

[37] Diogenes Laertius 2.53; Pausanias 5.6.6. Roy 1999:155–156; Ruggeri 2004a:38–41.

[38] The position of Epitalion, not far from Skillous and situated at the crossing point of the Alpheus, on the borders of Elis and the territory of the Letrini, very probably recaptured by the Eleans, was a critical one. Ruggeri 2004a:41.

[39] The re-capture of these communities on the part of the Eleans is confirmed by the increase in Elean territorial tribes, as attested by Pausanias for the Olympics of 368 and followed by a reduction of their number already in force at the Olympics of 364 (5.9.5–6): in 368 the Elean tribes had been taken from ten to twelve and this change should certainly be related to the military conquests of the Eleans that occurred between the end of 371/70 and 370/69, just as the reduction of the tribes from twelve to eight before 364 should be related to the Elean defeats in the war against the Arcadians in 365/4 with the ensuing loss of three cities in Akroreia and Pisatis. Gschnitzer 1958:13n16; Bultrighini 1990:160–162; Ruggeri 2004a:35–45. Cf. Roy 1997a:297–298.

Instead, the sources make it clear that by 369 Triphylia had already become Arcadian, and this transition must have occurred after the Spartan expedition against Mantinea—in which, as I have mentioned, the Lepreans took part—and so at the time of the Theban expedition to the Peloponnese in 370/69. The Arcadians, allies of the Thebans, of the Eleans, and of the Argives, dedicated a monument at Delphi to celebrate their victory over the Spartans during the invasion of Laconia. The monument was a group of nine bronze statues accompanied by an epigram: the statues represented the mythical genealogy of the Arcadians and portrayed Apollon, Kallistos, Nike, Arkas, and the sons of Arkas: Apheidas, Elatos, Azan, Triphylos, and Erasos.[40] Since the sons of Arkas stand for the ethnic tribes of the Arcadians, the Triphylians are implicitly counted as one of those tribes: it is clear that in connection with the entry of Trihpylia in the federal state of the Arcadians, the hero Triphylos had been inserted into the genealogy of the Arcadians, with the Triphylians becoming for all intents and purposes Arcadian.[41] There is also an interesting passage on the Triphylians' change of ethnic identity in Xenophon: when the Eleans asked the Arcadians to return the cities that had been taken away from them in the past by the Spartans "they noticed that their requests were being ignored and that, instead, the Arcadians had a high regard for the Triphylians and those who had detached themselves from Elis, because they declared themselves to be Arcadians" (*Hellenica* 7.1.26: τοὺς δὲ Τριφυλίους καὶ τοὺς ἄλλους τοὺς ἀπὸ σφῶν ἀποστάντας περὶ παντὸς ποιουμένους, ὅτι Ἀρκάδες ἔφασαν εἶναι). The "others," who like the Triphylians had entered into the federation of the Arcadians, were the Lasians.[42] The assumption of Arcadian ethnic identity on the part of the Triphylians gives us information on aspects pertinent to the concept of ethnic membership: firstly, as noted by Nielsen, the Arcadian federal state was "ethnically exclusive,"[43] which means that no-one who did not share the same ethnic identity could become a member of the federation. Furthermore, this process shows how the Arcadian ethnic identity functioned as an umbrella for distinct local identities. The Triphylians had their own ethnic

---

[40] See n5. Other proofs of the entry of Triphylia into the Arcadian federation are the sending of a citizen of Lepreon in 367 as official ambassador of the Arcadians to the court of the king of Persia in Susa (Xenophon *Hellenica* 7.1.33; Pausanias 6.3.9) and an inscription of the Arcadian federation from which we learn that the Lepreans were sending magistrates to the federal council (IG V 2.1).

[41] Roy 1999:155; Roy 2000:144–146; Nielsen 2002:263–264; Ruggeri 2004a:42–44.

[42] Xenophon *Hellenica* 7.4.12. Roy 2000:138, 143–144.

[43] Nielsen 2002:23–24.

identity which was absorbed by the Arcadian *ethnos*. The Triphylians' own identity, as we have seen, subsumed those of the other communities that constituted it. In this series of "multiple identities," the Triphylians' example resembles those of the other sub-groups of the Arcadian *ethnos* such as the Mainalians or the Parrhasians, which also comprised different communities, some of which were *poleis* in a political sense.[44]

In conclusion, it is possible to speculate on the motives which probably determined Triphylia's entry into the newly-formed Arcadian federation, which had for some time been disputing with the Eleans over the cities near the border. The Triphylians clearly acted out of political opportunity. Sparta was in a moment of deep crisis and accordingly could not guarantee help to the *perioikoi* against the expansionistic designs of the Eleans, who had immediately taken advantage of the favorable situation to attack some of the cities that Sparta had taken away from them in 400 at the end of the war. For this reason in 370/69 the cities of Triphylia did not hesitate to abandon their allies the Spartans to go over to the side of those who until then had been their enemies, but could still offer more effective help against the Eleans.[45] Perhaps most significant is the example of Lepreon, which at the beginning of the second half of the fifth century was still in conflict with the Arcadians, and was on the side of Sparta against the Arcadians in the expedition against Mantinea just after Leuctra, but which, a year later, had already become Arcadian.

Bibliography

Bölte, F. 1939. "Triphylia." In *RE* 7 A 1:186–201.

Bultrighini, U. 1990. *Pausania e le tradizioni democratiche. Argo ed Elide.* Padua.

Ebert, J., and Siewert, P. 1997. "Eine archaische Bronzeurkunde aus Olympia mit Vorschriften für Ringkämpfer und Kampfrichter." *Agonismata. Kleine philologische Schriften zur Literatur, Geschichte und Kultur der Antike* (ed. J. Ebert) 200–236. Stuttgart.

Eder, B. 1998. *Argolis, Lakonien, Messenien. Vom Ende der mykenischen Palastzeit bis zur Einwanderung der Dorier.* Vienna.

van Effenterre, H. and Ruzé, F. , eds. 1994–1995. *Nomima. Recueil d'inscriptions politiques et juridiques de l'archaïsme grec.* 2 volumes. Rome.

---

[44] Nielsen 2002:115–116, 266–269.
[45] Siewert 1987–1988:12; Nielsen 2002:261–262.

Falkner, C. 1996. "Sparta and the Elean War, ca 401/400 B.C.: Revenge or Imperialism?" *Phoenix* 50:17–25.

Falkner, C. 1999. "Sparta and Lepreon in the Archidamian War. (Thuc. 5.31.2–5)." *Historia* 48:385–394.

Gschnitzer, F. 1958. *Abhängige Orte im griechischen Altertum.* Munich.

Ioakimidou, Ch. 1997. *Die Statuenreihen griechischer Poleis und Bünde aus spätarchaischer und klassischer Zeit.* Munich.

Nafissi, M. 2003. "Elei e Pisati. Geografia, storia e istituzioni politiche della regione di Olimpia." *Geographia Antiqua* 12:23–55.

Nielsen, T. H. 1997. "Triphylia: An Experiment in Ethnic Construction and Political Organisation." *Yet More Studies in the Ancient Greek Polis* (ed. T. H. Nielsen) 129–162. Historia Einzelschriften 117. Stuttgart.

Nielsen, T. H. 2002. *Arkadia and its Poleis in the Archaic and Classical Periods.* Göttingen.

Niese, B. 1910. "Drei Kapitel eleischer Geschichte." *Genethliakon* 3–47. Berlin

Nilsson, M. P. 1951. *Cults, Myths, Oracles and Politics in Ancient Greece.* Lund.

Roy, J. 1997a. "The *Perioikoi* of Elis." *The Polis as an Urban Centre and as a Political Community* (ed. M. H. Hansen) 282–320. Acts of the Copenhagen Polis Centre 4. Copenhagen.

Roy, J. 1997b. "Spartan Aims in the Spartan-Elean War of c. 400. Further Thoughts." *Electronic Antiquity* 3. http://scholar.lib.vt.edu/ejournals/ ElAnt/V3N6/roy.html.

Roy, J. 1999. "Les cités d'Élide." *Le Péloponnèse* (ed. J. Renard) 151–176. Rennes.

Roy, J. 2000. "The Frontier between Arkadia and Elis in Classical Antiquity." *Polis and Politics* (eds. P. Flensted-Jensen, T. H. Nielsen, and L. Rubinstein) 133–156. Copenhagen.

Roy, J. 2002. "The Synoikism of Elis." *Even More Studies in the Ancient Greek Polis* (ed. T. H. Nielsen) 249–264. Stuttgart.

Roy, J., and Schofield, D. 1999. "IvO 9: A New Approach." *Horos* 13:155–165.

Ruggeri, C. 2000. "Note sulle divergenze nel dialetto e nella forma delle lettere tra le iscrizioni del centro-sud della Trifilia e quelle dell'Elide." *ZPE* 133:117–121.

Ruggeri, C. 2001-2002. "L'état fédéral de la Triphylie. Remarques sur l'histoire politique et constitutionnelle." Πρακτικὰ τοῦ ϛ' Διέθνους Συνεδρίου Πελοποννησιακῶν σπουδῶν. 2:165–176. Peloponnesiaka Supplement 24. Athens.

Ruggeri, C. 2004a *Gli stati intorno a Olimpia. Storia e costituzione dell'Elide e degli stati formati dai perieci elei (400-362 a.C.).* Stuttgart.

Ruggeri, C. 2004b. "Senofonte a Scillunte." *Athenaeum* 92:451–466.

Schepens, G. 2004. "La guerra di Sparta contro Elide." *Ricerche di antichità e tradizione classica* (ed. E. Lanzillotta) 1–89. Tivoli.

Siewert, P. 1987. "Die neue Bürgerrechtsverleihung der Triphylier aus Mázi bei Olympia." *Tyche* 2:275–277.

Siewert, P. 1987–1988. "Triphylien und Akroreia. Spartanische 'Regionalstaaten' in der westlichen Peloponnes." *Πρακτικά τοῦ γ' Διέθνους Συνεδρίου Πελοποννησιακῶν σπουδῶν.* 2:7–12. Peloponnesiaka Supplement 13. Athens.

Siewert, P. 1994. "Symmachien in neuen Inschriften von Olympia. Zu den sogenannten Periöken der Eleer." *Federazioni e federalismo nell'Europa antica* (ed. L. Aigner-Foresti, et al) 257–264. Milan.

Sordi, M. 1984a. "Il santuario di Olimpia e la guerra d'Elide." *CISA* 10:20–30.

Sordi, M. 1984b. "Le implicazioni olimpiche della guerra d'Elide." *Problemi di storia e cultura spartana* (ed. E. Lanzillotta) 145–159. Università di Macerata Pubblicazioni della Facoltà di Lettere e Filosofia 20. Rome.

Sordi, M. 2005. "Note senofontee." *Aevum* 79:17–22.

Tausend, K. 1992. *Amphiktyonie und Symmachie. Formen zwischenstaatlicher Beziehungen im archaischen Griechenland.* Stuttgart.

Tuplin, C. J. 1993. *The Failings of Empire: A Reading of Xenophon Hellenica 2.3.11–7.5.27.* Historia Einzelschriften 76. Stuttgart.

V

The Emergence of Pisatis

Maurizio Giangiulio

Emergence, or Re-emergence?

A T THE END OF THE NINETEENTH CENTURY probably no ancient historian would have doubted that the Pisatans had been the inhabitants of the Alpheios' valley, which in the first decades of the sixth century BCE the Eleans subdued and stripped of control of the Olympic Games. Many would have shared the opinion expressed by Georg Busolt that Pisatis and Triphylia were to the Eleans what Messenia was for the Spartans.[1] Moreover, it was taken for granted that the Pisatans' group identity did not get lost, but re-emerged in the fourth century and that key elements of the historical tradition about the Pisatans were available—at least in part—to late writers such as Strabo and Pausanias.[2] Apparently, both the Pisatan-Elean relationship of the fourth century and the late literary record could not be understood except in the light of a receding past. Everything was to be explained by admitting that before the sixth century the Pisatans had been an autonomous ethnic group.

It comes as no surprise, then, that the conception advanced in 1910 by Benedictus Niese did not find acceptance. Niese boldly tried to challenge the consensus root and branch, arguing that in the archaic age an autonomous Pisatan polity did not exist beside Elis, and that the ancient accounts of the struggles between the Pisatans and the Eleans are to be taken as late invention.[3] Niese's view was subversive enough to be marked out by Beloch as

---

[1] Busolt 1878:171–172.
[2] See, for instance, Viedebantt 1930.
[3] Niese 1910:esp. 27.

"mistaken" and by Wilamowitz as "inconceivable";[4] hardly ever mentioned since, it has always been dismissed. Until recently, neither Strabo's and Pausanias' accounts of the struggles, nor the overall picture of the Pisatan-Elean relationship as drawn by the nineteenth-century scholars have been called into question—the most notable exceptions being H. T. Wade-Gery and A. Andrewes.[5] Significantly, Ernst Meyer's discussion of the evidence, which remains the most comprehensive and perceptive,[6] maintains that "Pisa's past political autonomy cannot be doubted and that the tradition about Pisa's ancient rights to the Olympic Games is so reliable that nobody in ancient times could reject it completely."[7]

It is only in very recent times that the role played by the Pisatans in the history of Elis and the overall character of their ethnicity have been seen in a new light. Pisatan studies are now on the move.[8] Niese's argument is now taken into account and has already stimulated new research; for instance, based on a better understanding of Pausanias' account of Elean archaic history, we can now rule out the notion that it presupposes a genuine historical tradition going back to the archaic age.[9] As for Pisatan ethnicity, it has been persuasively argued that the Pisatans can hardly have developed a group identity before the fourth century BCE,[10] and were never able to exhibit an ethnic consciousness.

The time has come to interpret the literary record in the context of the events of the late classical age, rather than to see it in the light of a receding historical background. It is widely held, now, that our information about archaic Greek history—as J. K. Davies remarked—"is the production of a continually changing tradition which is at least semi-oral, owes a great deal more to poetic utterance and mythic modes of thought than to anything else, and is generated more by the changing needs of a continually shifting present than by a scholarly urge to reconstruct a static but receding past."[11] From this point of view, to focus on the fourth-century dynamics which took place in the Alpheios valley can shed light not only on obscure

---

[4] Beloch, 1912:38n1; Wilamowitz-Moellendorff 1922:481.
[5] Wade-Gery 1925:544f; Andrewes 1956:62–63.
[6] Meyer 1950.
[7] Meyer 1950:1749.57–61.
[8] See Nafissi 2001; Nielsen 2002:118–119; Roy 2002; Gehrke 2003; Nafissi 2003; Möller 2004; Ruggeri 2004.
[9] For a thorough discussion of Pausanias' account see now Nafissi 2001.
[10] See Gehrke 2003; Möller 2004.
[11] Davies 1994:200.

historical events, but also on the needs of a changing present which shaped both Pisatan identity and the image of the past intentionally projected by the Eleans and the Pisatans.

In a sense, Busolt was right. Pisatis can really be seen as some sort of Messenia. But the reason is not that in both of them an ethnic group brought into subjection could finally gain its independence, rather that in both cases—*si parva licet* ...—it is the fourth-century historical context that triggered crucial changes as far as collective identity and perceptions of the past are concerned.[12]

Pisa and the Pisatans in the Fourth Century BCE: the Independent State

In 365 war broke out between Elis and the Arcadians.[13] The Eleans, who claimed Lasion, now incorporated in the Arcadian Confederacy, had already cut themselves off from the Boeotian-Peloponnesian alliance, and concluded alliances with Sparta and the Achaeans.[14] On the other side, the Boeotian-Arcadian alliance concluded in 370 was apparently still in place,[15] and the Arcadians had the support of Athens, Thebes, Argos, Sikyon, the Messenians and the Pisatans.[16] In the late summer of 364 the Eleans attacked the Pisatans and the Arcadians, who had gained control of the Olympian sanctuary, but were repelled after a violent struggle in the sacred precinct itself. The Pisatans, who maintained that they were the first to have had control of the sanctuary, celebrated the Olympic Games.[17] They had evidently begun to play a new role, as both their foreign policy and their claims to the Olympic Games show. It is in this context that the political community of the Pisatans came to take shape; or to put it more precisely, that Pisa was constituted as an independent state,[18] as the epigraphic evidence seems to show beyond any doubt.

---

[12] On Messenian identity see Luraghi 2001 and Luraghi 2002.

[13] On the war see Roy 1971 (esp. 593 on the chronological problems), and Roy 1994:203–204.

[14] Xenophon *Hellenica* 7.4.17.

[15] Roy 1971:595–596.

[16] See Xenophon *Hellenica* 7.1.44–45; 7.4.4–6, 17, 19–20, 27–29; for Messenia and Sikyon see also the inscription at n19 below; for the Pisatans see Diodorus 15.78.2.

[17] See Xenophon *Hellenica* 7.4.28–32 and Diodorus 15.78.2–3 (the discrepancies can be traced back to Diodorus' source); on Pisatan presidency of the Games see also Pausanias 6.4.2 and 6.22.3.

[18] Niese 1910:16; Meyer 1950:1754; Roy 1971:594; Nielsen 2002:118; Ruggeri 2004:178–181, and the references cited there (n566). As for the date of Pisatan independence, 365 at the very latest is more probable than 364.

More than one inscription makes clear that the Pisatans concluded international treaties. A decree of the Arcadian Confederacy, which ratifies a bilateral alliance between Pisa and Akroreia on one side, and the Arcadians on the other confirms that Pisa was backing the Arcadian Confederacy.[19] And another inscribed decree, which is to be taken as Pisatan, shows that Pisa was also allied to Sikyon and Messenia.[20] Moreover, the Pisatans created *proxenoi* and *thearodokoi*,[21] and despatched *thearoi*; remarkably, one of these *proxenoi* is a Sikyonian politician hostile to Sparta who had an important role in Sikyonian policy-making.[22] Clearly, a coherent foreign policy of the Pisatan state was at work.

As for the Pisatan state itself, the decrees and the treaties show that it now had formal mechanisms by which it made decisions; and civil magistracies were in place (three *hellanodikai*) which had the same name as the Elean ones, but differed from them in number and prerogatives.[23] Importantly, the Pisatan state now possessed an apparently well-defined political shape: as the treaties show, the Pisatans had a democratic *politeia*.[24] It cannot go unnoticed in this context that the Pisatan state minted a coinage which can be taken as evidence for civic self-expression: the gold and silver coins we know display on the obverse the head of Zeus Olympios, and on the reverse the legend ΠΙΣΑ.[25]

The newly established identity of the Pisatan community played a role at the international level. More specifically, what needs to be better under-

---

[19] The text of the fragmentary decree (SEG 22.339; 29.405) is now to be read in the version of Ringel, Siewert and Taeuber 1999:414–417 (where another fragment is published which had been briefly noted by Mallwitz 1981:99–101; cf. SEG 32.411); see also SEG 49.466A and Ruggeri 2004:159–161.

[20] SEG 22.339; 32.411; SEG 49.466B; see now Ringel, Siewert and Taeuber 1999:417–420; Ruggeri 2004:185–186.

[21] IvO 36; Syll.3 171 (cf. Rhodes and Lewis 1997:95 number 36), on which see esp. Perlman 2000:64–65, 175 and Ruggeri 2004:187n603, 188.

[22] The Pisatan *proxenos* should be identified with the Sikyonian *stratêgos* appointed in 368/7 (Xenophon *Hellenica* 7.1.44–46 and Diodorus 15.70.3); cf. Perlman 2000:64–65.

[23] For a thorough discussion of the Elean *hellanodikai*, see Ruggeri 2004:46–53.

[24] Both in the alliance between Pisa and the Arcadians (n19 above, lines 8–9) and of Pisa with Sikyon (n19 above, line 10) occur the words *damos* and *politeia* with reference to the political regime and the constitutional order of the *polis* (apparently Pisa). Ringel, Siewert and Taeuber 1999:417 take the word *politeia* as meaning "oligarchic constitution": for a good argument against this view, see Ruggeri 2004:160–161, 201–202.

[25] Babelon 1901–1914:3.764–68 no. 1180–1182; Seltman 1921:3, 56–58 no. 173–174; Kraay 1976:106 figure 333; Ruggeri 2004:182n582; for a perceptive treatment of iconography see Ritter 2001.

stood, as Nielsen remarked quite recently,[26] is the reason why the Pisatans did not join the Arcadian Confederacy,[27] as the Triphylians did,[28] and contented themselves with concluding an alliance with it. In other words, why did the Arcadians not suggest the Pisatans should become Arcadians, when they had incorporated the Triphylians into the confederacy and made the Triphylian eponym Triphylos one of the sons of Arkas?[29] As we shall see later on, there is no need to assume that Pisatan identity was older and more "natural" than Triphylian identity, so that the Pisatans could not really be claimed as Arcadians. It may be suggested that the true reason is that Pisatan identity was especially attached to Olympia, and that the Olympian traditions could not be appropriated by the Arcadians any more than the sanctuary itself. So the Arcadian Confederacy gained control of the sanctuary by closely linking to itself the puppet state of the Pisatans and their newly constructed traditions that focused on Olympia. It is usually claimed that the Arcadians could not make the Pisatans into Arcadians and that this is precisely the reason why they kept the Pisatans outside the confederacy: they could be seen as no more than allies, or, as the mythical genealogies had it, as people descended from the husband of Arkas' daughter.[30] But one has the impression that in those years the Arcadians had to solve the crucial problem of showing adequate grounds for celebrating the Olympic Games together with the Pisatans. On one side, the Pisatan puppet state which was claiming the sanctuary was to be related to the Arcadians, but could not be identified with them; on the other, the Olympian sanctuary itself was to be credited with an Arcadian identity: and this is the reason why Olympia, the personification of the sanctuary, came to be known as Arkas' daughter.[31]

Before proceeding further, it may be useful to question some common assumptions about the Pisatan state. It is widely held that it embraced Pisatis,[32] that is to say the area which stretched from the Alpheios River to

---

[26] Nielsen 2002:119.

[27] As Niese 1910:27 and Meyer 1950:1753 maintained.

[28] Xenophon *Hellenica* 7.1.126; see Nielsen 2002:255n126, 263; Ruggeri 2004:42, 140–143.

[29] See CEG 824; cf. Pausanias 10.9.5. See Ruggeri's contribution in the present volume.

[30] On Pisos as husband of Arkas' daughter (Olympia) see Oros in *Etymologicum Magnum* 623, 16–17. In his *Ethnika,* Oros (fifth century CE) could still gather reliable mythographical details, drawing on learned late-Hellenistic sources; on Oros see Reitzenstein 1897:322f and Alpers 1981:87–101.

[31] On Olympia as personification of the sanctuary see Ritter 2001:92n10.

[32] See, for instance, Roy 1971:584 ("Pisatis, including Olympia, became an independent state"); Roy 2000:144; Ruggeri 2004:197.

Mt. Pholoë and from Amphidolia and Marganeis to the Erymanthos River.[33] Moreover, the list of the "eight Pisatan *poleis*" known to Apollodorus of Athens in the second century BCE (Strabo 8.3.31) is taken to go back to the time of Pisatan independence.[34] Yet, it is to be pointed out that there are no strong reasons at all to think that it was Pisatis as a whole that became an independent polity; in other words, we cannot exclude the possibility that when Pisa was constituted as a polis its territory was limited to a small area surrounding Olympia. The name Pisa itself gives an interesting clue. The coins with the legend ΠΙΣΑ and the head of Zeus Olympios may suggest that we are dealing with the name of the area of the Olympian sanctuary, which in the fifth century could alternate with Olympia, as its occurrences in Pindar and Herodotus show.[35] At the time of Pisatan independence, when the Pisatans took charge of the Olympic Games, the name could aptly express the claims of the Pisatans to the sanctuary. Therefore, it seems most likely both that Pisa's territory was limited to a fairly restricted area not extending far from the Olympian sanctuary, and that not all the local communities which ancient geographers and grammarians took as Pisatan belonged to the Pisatan state. But there is more to it than that, because it is actually far from clear that at the time of Pisatan independence a full fledged notion of Pisatis as a sub-regional unit was already in place. I would surmise that the notion of Pisatis itself is of learned origin and that it goes back to the Hellenistic age, perhaps to Demetrius of Skepsis.[36] It probably was a conception that permitted the systematic arrangement of the information collected by grammarians and geographers about the small communities in the area around Olympia.

Now, if an archaic polis called Pisa did not exist, as is generally acknowledged,[37] the collective ethnic "Pisatans" could not go back to a receding past, and it is not to be taken as having undergone a process of "politicisation"; rather, it would have been created in later times, in the context of the formation of both a Pisatan identity and a Pisatan community.

It becomes apparent, at this point, that the problem of the group identity of the Pisatans needs to be reconsidered. It can in fact be shown that

---

[33] On the geography of Pisatis see Meyer 1950:1736–1744, esp. 1743–1744; Roy 2002; Ruggeri 2004:188–197.

[34] Maddoli, Nafissi and Saladino 1999:364–65, 369; Nafissi 2001:307n16; Ruggeri 2004:197.

[35] Siewert 1991.

[36] See fr. 5 Gaede in Athenaeus 8.346bc; for a thorough discussion of the conceptions of ancient Pisatis advanced by Hellenistic geographers, see Meyer 1950:1739–1743.

[37] Meyer 1950:1746, 21–25.

such identity was constructed in the fourth century, but to take it to be merely a side effect of the formation of the Pisatan state would be simplistic. It seems more complex processes were involved.

Pisatan Identity in the Making

As for Pisatan identity, one cannot help but be struck by its attachment to Olympia. Pisatan coinage displays both the name 'Pisa' and the image of Zeus Olympios, and it was in this way that the newly constituted political community claimed a very close link to Olympia. It comes as no surprise, then, that when the Elean-Arcadian war came to an end, in 362, and the Eleans took charge of the sanctuary again, they too asserted their claims to Olympia: the coins they struck exhibited the image of Zeus and the personification of Olympia which the Pisatans, in turn, had appropriated by making her the wife of their mythical ancestor Pisos.[38] But there is more evidence about the Pisatan and Elean claims to Olympia. When the Pisatans celebrated the Olympic Games they maintained that they were the first to have had control of the sanctuary, and in order to assert this claim they resorted to a set of mythical arguments (τισι μυθικαῖς καὶ παλαιαῖς ἀποδείξεσι χρώμενοι).[39] This piece of information goes back at least to Ephorus,[40] and can be compared with a reference in Apollodorus of Athens to ancient stories (*palaia*) about the first establishment of the Olympic Games which gave expression to the Elean and Pisatan rival claims.[41] As Jacoby remarked,[42] Apollodorus was acquainted with the same information as Ephorus, which should be taken to go back to a fourth-century debate. As for the Pisatan *palaiai apodeixeis*, we can only guess at their content, but it is worth noticing that a well-informed source reports that the first founder of the Olympic Games had been Pisos, the eponymous hero of Pisa.[43] It goes without saying that in this way the

---

[38] On the Elean issues featuring Olympia, see Seltman 1921:58 no. 175 and Ritter 2001:91n8.

[39] Diodorus 15.78.2.

[40] As is well known, eighteenth-century *Quellenforschung* established that Diodorus' Greek and Persian narratives of books 11–15 depend on Ephorus; for a brief review of the arguments see Stylianou 1998:49–50.

[41] See FGH 416 T 5 in Strabo 8.3.30.

[42] FGH IIIb Kommentar zu nr. 297–607 [Text], 234.29–39; [Noten], 149n34.

[43] Phlegon of Tralles FGH 257 F 1; cf. *Scholia* on Plato *Republic* 465d, p. 230 Greene. As for Phlegon's information, it is important to remark that besides reflecting the fourth-century Elean and Pisatan diverging traditions on the prehistory of Olympia it bears the traces of other, more "conciliatory" traditions which are apparently influenced by the historical situation of the years following the peace concluded in 363/2: see Nafissi 2001:321 and n57; Möller 2004:251f.

eponymous hero is made responsible for the origins of Olympia, and, even more importantly, it is the Pisatans who founded the Games well before the arrival of Oxylos and the Eleans. Pisos, who embodies the collective Pisatan "personality," is "the first," and it is precisely the circulation of such stories about Pisos that explains why the Pisatans claimed to have been the first to have control of the sanctuary. So, we can safely assume that stories about the role played by Pisos in the prehistory of the Olympic Games were an integral part of the *palaiai apodeixeis* which the Pisatans circulated.

According to Apollodorus the Pisatans maintained that when the Trojan War broke out they were *hieroi tou theou*.[44] In other words, the Olympian holy truce would have been first instituted by the Pisatans. But the Eleans too claimed to be a people sacred to Zeus since the time when they took possession of the land, as Ephorus reports.[45] One should assume, then, that these claims had been an integral part of the fourth-century debate about the prehistory of Olympia, and that the mythological arguments presented by the Pisatans were meant also to support their claims to the establishment of the Olympian truce. In this way the Pisatans not only placed special emphasis on their association with Olympia, but claimed for themselves as well an extraordinary religious quality.

Now, as for the origin of the Pisatan *muthikai* and *palaiai apodeixeis*, their specific reference to Olympia makes clear that the Pisatan presidency of the Olympic Games in 364 needed a convincing set of charter-myths. This is confirmed by the genealogy of the Pisatan founder of the Games. For Pisos' genealogy is shaped by, or fitted to, the needs of the present, namely the foreign relations of the Pisatan state in the fourth century. In fact, Pisos is provided with a wife called Olympia, who is known in mythology as the daughter of the Arcadian eponym Arkas.[46] We are evidently dealing with a genealogical manipulation to be put in the framework provided by the alliance between Pisa and the Arcadian Confederacy. The genealogy establishes

---

[44] See Apollodorus of Athens FGH 416 T 5, lines 21–22.

[45] See FGH 70 F 115 p. 72, lines 9–12 in Strabo 8.3.33; cf. Polybius 4.73.9–74.1; Diodorus 8.1; 14.17.11. We should not take for granted that Diodorus 14.17.11 ultimately derives from Hippias of Elis (for this view see FGH IIIb [Noten], 144; Bilik 1998–1999:27–28, 35–37); more probably he depends on the Oxyrhinchus Historian (Schepens 2004:46–55). Be that as it may, the holy truce (*ekekheiria*) should be seen as an Elean invention going back to the Classical age, and possibly to the times of the Spartan-Elean war at the beginning of the fourth century: see FGH 4A 3.1026 F 8a (J. Bollansée), Rigsby 1996:41–44, Bilik 1998–1999:27–28, 35–37.

[46] See n30 above.

a close link between the Pisatans and the Arcadians, without obliterating the Pisatans' identity by making them Arcadians.

There remains an important point which deserves our attention. Certain hints actually suggest that the invention of a Pisatan tradition may be seen to have extended to Pisatan prehistory as a whole, rather than being limited only to the origins of the Olympic Games. This process involved, in particular, stories about Pisos, Salmoneus and Oinomaos: these deserve a closer look because they can be traced back—at least in part—to the archaic age.

As for Pisos, it is important to recall that he had been represented on the so called "Kypselos' chest" in Hera's temple at Olympia,[47] a Corinthian votive gift going back to the first decades of the sixth century, as is now widely agreed.[48] On the chest Pisos featured as one of the heroes participating in the funeral games for Pelias. Now, the Argonautic myth played a role in archaic Corinth,[49] and the funeral games for Pelias are a common subject in archaic art. But how are we to explain the fact that Pisos, in particular, is one of the competitors? I would surmise that Pisos was displayed on the chest because he was important at Olympia, and that the same holds true for Pelops, Hippodamia and Oinomaos.[50] There is no reason to deny that Pisos was already the eponymous hero of Pisa/Olympia.

If this is so, Pisos' involvement in the funeral games for Pelias could have been meant to emphasize the Aeolian connection that was an integral part of the local identities of the communities of the Alpheios' valley. Aeolus' son Salmoneus, in fact, was the eponymous hero of the Pisatan Salmone near the river Enipeus,[51] not far from Olympia, and in the fourth century he was known as a king of Pisatis.[52] Now, Pelias was the son of Salmoneus' daughter Tyro, and the myth of her rape by Zeus on the river Enipeus either had been

---

[47] See Pausanias 5.17.5–19 for the description of the monument, and 17.9 for Pisos. On Kypselos' chest see, most recently, Splitter 2000 (esp. 26–27 on Pisos).

[48] Splitter 2000:50–51.

[49] For the references to the bibliography see Splitter 2000:27n103.

[50] For Onomaus, Pelops and Hippodamia on Kypselos' chest see Pausanias 5.17.7; on their association with Olympia, see nn57, 62 below.

[51] Diodorus 4.68.1; Strabo 8.3.32 C 356; Apollodorus *Bibliotheke* I 89; Stephanus of Byzantium, v. Σαλμώνη; see also West, 1985:65n76. On Salmoneus see J. Ilberg, ML 4 (1909–15), s. v. and E. Simon, LIMC 7.1, 653–655. On Salmone see Panayotopoulos 1991; Mandl and Ruggeri 2000, and esp. Roy 2002:237.

[52] See Ephorus FGH 70 F 115 p. 71.l.27, which makes Salmoneus the king of Epeians and Pisatans who was responsible for Aitolus' flight from Elis to Aetolia; this implies the Elean origin of Aitolus and is to be seen, then, as an integral part of a local Elean tradition on which Ephorus drew (see Gehrke 2003).

originally located in the area of Olympia, as West maintains,[53] or, if it was originally a Thessalian myth, it must have aroused great interest among the people of the Enipeus' and Alpheios' valleys. Pisos' genealogy itself reflects this Aeolian connection: Pisos is said to have been the son of Aeolus' son Perieres,[54] or of Perieres' son Aphareus.[55] This could fit the alliance between the Pisatan state and Messene in the 360s, but it does not necessarily follow from this that we are dealing with a fourth-century invention, as Astrid Möller maintains.[56] I would not discount the possibility that this genealogical detail goes back to the archaic age. If it is so, we are faced with an attempt to establish a link between Pisos and the Aeolids.

We should also take into account the possibility that in the fourth century the Pisatans appropriated and manipulated older mythological narratives centered on Oinomaos. On the one hand both Oinomaos himself and the myth of Hippodamia's suitors are to be seen as strongly attached to Olympia;[57] on the other hand Oinomaos' Pisatan identity is an integral part, as Pindar shows, of his mythical personality.[58] One is tempted to take Oinomaos as embodying the idea that Olympia and Pisa were almost the same thing, and it is worth remembering that Pisatan coinage implies the same idea: it is not by chance, then, that the evidence indicates many efforts made by the Eleans to discriminate between Olympia and Pisa. As for the attachment of the Pisatans to Oinomaos, it is useful to draw attention to the role played both by Oinomaos as founder of the Pisatan Harpina—and as son of Harpina herself[59]—and Hippodamia's myth in shaping the Pisatan landscape: the tomb of the suitors was located near Harpina,[60] the grave of the mares of one of the suitors was near the River Parthenias,[61] and the river itself took its name from one of these mares.[62] Moreover, Pisa itself came to be seen as Oinomaos' *polis*.[63] Given these premises, it would be surprising if Oinomaos' mythical personality had not been intrinsic to the newly

---

[53] West 1985:142–143.

[54] Pausanias 5.17.9; 6.22.2.

[55] *Scholia* on Theocritus 4.29–30b (cf. Pausanias 4.2.2).

[56] Möller 2004:259.

[57] See Howie 1991; Kyrieleis 1997. On Oinomaos at Olympia, see Pausanias 5.14.7; 20.6–7.

[58] Pindar *Olympian* 1.70; cf. Strabo 8.3.31 C 356; Diodorus 4.73.1; Pausanias 5.1.6; 5.20.6.

[59] Pausanias 6.21.8; Dyspontion too was founded by Oinomaos' son Dysponteus (Pausanias 6.22.4; but he is a son of Pelops in Stephanus of Byzantium 245.12–246.2).

[60] Pausanias 6.21.9.

[61] Pausanias 6.21.7.

[62] Pausanias 6.21.7.

[63] Diodorus 4.73.1.

constructed collective identity of the fourth-century Pisatans. One probably should explain in the same way those traditions about Pelops which show—though Pelops was crucially important for the Eleans and for the control of Olympia[64]—that he had close links with many communities of the Alpheios' valley. It is perfectly possible, then, that this is the reason why the Pisatans claimed Pelops' remains.[65]

As far as we can see, in all these cases we are dealing with narratives which in the archaic age had been employed by the local communities of the Alpheios' valley in the construction of a culturally significant past. We should assume, then, that when the Pisatans gained independence, they recovered those narratives and used them to articulate the newly constructed Pisatan identity.

We must now consider whether the sense of identity developed by the Pisatans in the fourth century is to be taken as an ethnic consciousness. We can take for granted that "ethnic identity is socially constructed and subjectively perceived,"[66] and that, consequently, it is almost impossible to determine as an objective category. But it is crucially important both to focus on what distinguishes the ethnic group from other social groups and to trace the features on which the perception of cultural uniqueness of a given group is based. From this point of view, not all of the features by which we can identify ethnic groups are to be taken as being crucial to the present discussion. Some of them, in fact, are important in other associative groups too, and so are not exclusive to the ethnic group, while not all of them are liable to be subjectively constructed as "criteria" of ethnicity. As is well known, Anthony Smith isolated six identifying marks of an ethnic group: the existence of a collective name, a myth of common descent, a shared history, a distinctive shared culture, an association with a specific territory, and a sense of solidarity.[67] Now, in the light of the above remarks, it would seem preferable to see the common myth of descent, the connection with a specific territory,

---

[64] On the Olympic ritual for Pelops (Pindar *Olympian* 1.90–93; Pausanias 5.13.1) see Slater 1989 and Krummen 1990:158–168; for his role as founder of Olympia and of the Olympic Games see Pindar *Olympian* 1.24, 94f; Pausanias 5.8.2; Phlegon FGH 257 F 1, 6; cf. Lee 2001:48–51.

[65] On Pelops' remains in Pisa see Pausanias 5.13.4 (cf. 6.21.1: Pelops had ruled over the Pisatans). For Pelops' association with other communities see Pausanias 6.22.1 (his remains in Harpina); Lycophron 53–54; Pausanias 6.22.6 (one of the sons of Pelops as founder of Letrinoi).

[66] Hall 1997:19.

[67] See Smith 1986:22–31, discussed, most recently, by Hall 1997:25 and Nielsen 2002:48–50.

and the emphasis on a shared history as ranking paramount among the features that identify an ethnic group.

To turn now to the Pisatans, the first point to be made is that the genealogical details about Pisos we are dealing with do not appear to reflect, except to a limited extent, the recognition of a putative shared ancestry. It is reasonable to doubt that the Pisatans possessed a real myth of descent. As for the connection to a territory, one should notice that no emphasis is given to the region where the Pisatans as a group reside, to the homeland of the ethnic group. And if we keep in mind that places are crucial for cultural memory, it becomes most relevant that there is no Pisatan homeland featuring as *lieu de mémoire*, as Pierre Nora would have it.[68] It comes as no surprise, then, that we have no evidence for the name Pisatis being used as the name of a region in the fourth century. Apparently, the notion of a region called Pisatis emerged only later. It was Olympia, instead, that had a mythical and symbolic quality for the Pisatans, but even Olympia was not seen as a proper sacred centre of a homeland. It is not so much that Olympia was the centre of the Pisatan world, as that Olympia and Pisa were seen by the Pisatans as two sides of one and the same coin. One could say, in this connection, that Pisatan identity mainly consisted in claiming Olympia as Pisatan.

All in all, one has the impression that Pisatan ethnic identity remained underdeveloped and feeble. This impression becomes stronger when we ask ourselves to what extent the Pisatans possessed a shared history. We have seen that the Pisatans claimed to have founded the Olympic Games, that Oinomaos probably was of paramount importance for their identity, and that some Pisatan communities traced their origins back to him. On the other hand, there is no trace of a Pisatan genealogical history, nor, for instance, of any attempt to claim Nestor and his kingdom as Pisatan. It remains to be investigated whether Pisatan traditions about the history of the Olympic Games had existed. But before looking in detail at this problem, it deserves to be emphasised that the picture we have been drawing so far does not easily fit in with the hypothesis that in the fourth century the Pisatan independent state was built upon a Pisatan identity rooted in a receding past and a well established ethnic consciousness. In other words it is doubtful—to say the least—that it was the identity of a group calling itself "the Pisatans"

---

[68] Nora 1984–1992. As is well known, the crucial relevance of space for group memory has been pointed out by Maurice Halbwachs (Halbwachs 1941; Halbwachs 1950:130–167) and is now seen as one of the most important features of cultural memory (Assmann 1992:1.3.3).

that became politicised and set in motion the development which led to the formation of a new political unit. We should rather admit that it is the newly constituted Pisatan polity that played a decisive role in shaping a Pisatan group identity.

We have seen that Pisatan identity is a fourth-century cultural construct. Now, it is crucial to determine when it took shape. The role played by the formation of an independent Pisatan polity in 364 is apparent, but there are hints that a Pisatan identity started gradually to emerge earlier, in the first decades of the century.

We should take into account, then, what happened at the beginning of the century. When the Spartan-Elean war broke out,[69] the Alpheios valley, both to the north and to the south of the river, was thrown into turmoil, and many communities which had the status of subordinate allies of the Eleans, seceded from them.[70] At the end of the war with the Spartans the Eleans had to leave independent all those communities and, in addition, the Triphylian towns, Phrixa, Epitalion, Letrinoi, the Amphidolians, the Marganians, the Akroreians, and the town of Lasion.[71] So it was that Elis was deprived of her mini-empire, as Paul Cartledge put it.[72]

Although Olympia and the area surrounding it had been directly involved in the war, no community situated in close proximity to the sanctuary raised any claim to independence. Apparently, a subordinate Pisatan community acting as such did not exist, but the war set in motion an important development. According to Xenophon (*Hellenica* 2.2.31) the idea that the presidency of the Olympic Games belonged to the Eleans by right was questioned, and Sparta considered stripping the Eleans of the presidency, maintaining that the sanctuary did not belong to them in ancient times. This comes as no surprise, since in 420 BCE the Eleans had excluded the Spartans from Olympia.[73] But there is more to it than that. Xenophon says that some

---

[69] Xenophon *Hellenica* 3.2.21–31; Diodorus 14.17.4–12; 34.1–2; Pausanias 3.8.3–5; see Sordi 1984a; 1984b; Unz 1986; Bultrighini 1990:232f; Tuplin 1993:183f; 201–205 (esp. on chronological problems), and, most recently, Schepens 2004.

[70] Xenophon *Hellenica* 3.2.25

[71] Xenophon *Hellenica* 3.2.30 (for a good discussion of the textual problems see Nafissi 2003:26n31).

[72] Cartledge 1987:353.

[73] Thucydides 5.49–50, on which see esp. Roy 1998 and Hornblower 2000, who plausibly argues that the Spartans were not excluded for the two decades after 420, and that they were re-admitted shortly before the Olympic year 416. Be that as it may, "it is entirely plausible that the Spartans should have long resented even a short-term ban which had been lifted many years previously" (Hornblower 2000:223n27).

people were raising a claim to the presidency against the Eleans, but the Spartans did not trust these rival claimants because they were rustic and would not be competent to preside over the sanctuary.[74] These rival claimants must be the Pisatans, or, more probably, the inhabitants of one or more of the local communities in the district of Olympia: what happened in 364, when the independent state of Pisa and the Arcadians organized the Games, helps explain the meaning of Xenophon's reference to the "rival claimants." As James Roy remarked,[75] the pejorative term (*khoritai*) should not be pressed as evidence of any particular structure in politics or settlement, but the fact that in the area surrounding Olympia no community joined the revolt probably suggests that Sparta's view of the rival claimants, and their lack of group consciousness or of any sense of political solidarity, are to be seen as two sides of one and the same coin.

Niese maintained that this passage of Xenophon, which is now widely held to be reliable,[76] could not have been written before 364 and that it has to be taken as a late insertion.[77] Indeed, we should allow that Xenophon's treatment of the Spartan-Elean war was written after 362,[78] and that this is the reason why some inaccuracies are easily traceable.[79] As for the passage about the rival claimants, it is reasonable to assume that it has been written with hindsight, but I see no strong reason to assume that Xenophon back-dated the origins of the quarrel over Olympia in the light of the historical events of the sixties. Therefore, the Spartan-Elean war can be regarded as a fitting historical context for the origins of the quarrel. The claims to the Olympian sanctuary had evidently been triggered by the Spartan intervention and by the liberation of many subordinate allies of the Eleans. It is probable that, given a situation of such unrest, the communities of what became Pisatis began to feel different from the Eleans. So, the crisis of the Elean mini-empire was making way for new identities and new political organizations. It was in those years, it seems, that the idea of questioning the Elean right to control Olympia was emerging for the first time. Moreover, one gets

---

[74] Xenophon *Hellenica* 3.2.31: οἱ δὲ Λακεδαιμόνιοι τοῦ μέντοι προεστάναι τοῦ Διὸς τοῦ Ὀλυμπίου ἱεροῦ, καίπερ οὐκ ἀρχαίου Ἠλείοις ὄντος, οὐκ ἀπήλασαν αὐτούς [scil. τοὺς Ἠλείους], νομίζοντες τοὺς ἀντιποιουμένους χωρίτας εἶναι καὶ οὐχ ἱκανοὺς προεστάναι.

[75] Roy 2002:240.

[76] Sordi 1984a:157f; Bultrighini 1990:239, 243; Roy 1997:283 and n13; Roy 2002:240; Ruggeri 2004:26, 190; Möller 2004:261.

[77] Niese 1910:11n5, 44.

[78] Tuplin 1993:29f; Dillery 1995:12f

[79] Nafissi 2003:31.

the impression that the Elean right to control Olympia was the burning issue of the first decades of the century. Hippias' *Olumpionikôn anagraphê*, probably published at the beginning of the fourth century, strongly affirmed it and projected it back into the past,[80] and we should also assume that pamphlets and *logoi* like Gorgias' *Olumpikos* and *Encomium of the Eleans* discussed it.[81] Thus, the claims to Olympia raised against the Eleans are to be seen as an integral part of a wider cultural and political context, in which a discussion began to take place that contributed to the formation of a Pisatan group consciousness.

Constructing the Past

As is well known, until recently scholarship used to take for granted that an historical Pisatan tradition dating back at least to the seventh century existed, which the Eleans felt themselves compelled to manipulate. Of course, Elean traditions did exist which presupposed both the Elean presidency of the Olympic Games and the Elean rule over the Pisatans and the neighbouring communities. Probably they were not unlike the tradition reported by Pausanias 6.22.2–4, and should be seen as fiercely hostile to the Pisatans.

It may be useful to compare the other traditions on Elis' struggle against Pisa for control of Olympia. For both Apollodorus and the ancient chronographic tradition Pisatan control of Olympia was long-lasting.[82] However, once again the Elean rights to Olympia and to Pisatis are taken for granted: the Eleans feature as the founders of the Games, and Pisatan control of the sanctuary is seen as bound to come to an end. As is well known, these traditions bulk large in modern discussions. For it is widely believed that, although we are presented with an Elean reinterpretation of Olympia's history, reconstruction of the original events is not impossible. The Pisatans would have controlled the sanctuary from time immemorial, then, in the early sixth century, the Eleans would have conquered Pisatis and taken in charge the Olympics; but, in order to provide justification for their conquest,

---

[80] FGH IIIb Kommentar zu Nr. 297–607 [Text], 222.15–18; [Noten], 144–145n10.

[81] FGH IIIb Kommentar zu Nr. 297–607 [Text], 222.18–20; [Noten], 145n11.

[82] See Apollodorus of Athens FGH 416 T 5. 28–31 ("After the twenty-sixth Olympiad, when they had got back their home-land, the Pisatans themselves went to celebrating the Games... But in later times Pisatis again fell into the power of the Eleans, and thus again the direction of the Games fell to them") and (Africanus) Eusebius *Chronicle* I 194f Schoene [92 Karst] = FGH 416 T 5ab (the Pisatans had charge of the Olympic Games from the thirtieth to the fifty-second Olympiad [572 BCE]).

they would have represented themselves as the founders of the Games who had been unlawfully stripped of control of Olympia by the Pisatans.

Now, this view of the traditions we have been discussing so far is based on two assumptions that turn out to be very questionable. The first is that there existed an unchanging Pisatan tradition dating back at least to the seventh century, which the Eleans felt themselves compelled to manipulate. The second is that the Eleans could not deal with the genuine memories which recorded Pisatan control of Olympia before the Elean conquest simply by omitting them. So the Elean tradition could not help but reinterpret the historical situation and the tradition, obviously a Pisatan one, which recorded it.

As for the first assumption, one should admit that, given the Elean conquest of Pisatis in the early sixth century and its incorporation into the Elean state, two centuries later nothing would have prevented the Eleans from disposing of the early Pisatan history of Olympia. As for the existence of genuine Pisatan memories, besides noticing that there are no traces of them whatsoever, one should note that if we envisage them as a local tradition dating back to the archaic age and transmitted by word of mouth, then we must presuppose a "social surface" for that tradition and, as a consequence, an archaic Pisatan community playing an historical role as such. But this view of Elean-Pisatan relations and of the overall character of the alleged Pisatan tradition does not fit the evidence well. For instance, both the early-fifth century grant of Chaladrian citizenship to Deukalion,[83] where Pisa features as a place-name, and the mentions of Pisa in Pindar and Herodotus,[84] do not imply a Pisatan community. If previously an independent Pisatan community had existed, it surely would have left more substantial traces in the historical record.

If this line of argument is right, then we should assume that the temporary Pisatan control of Olympia featuring in these traditions, which take for granted both the Eleans' right to the sanctuary and the original Elean rule over Pisatis, turns out to be a concession made to the fourth-century Pisatan claims. In other words, it seems probable that we are dealing with an intentional construction of the past whereby the Eleans intended to facilitate the incorporation of the Pisatan polity into the Elean state. From this

---

[83] IvO 11 = van Effenterre and Ruzé 1994, number 21 (500–475 BCE: Jeffery 19902:220 no. 8); for a good discussion of the problems involved, see, most recently, Nafissi 2003:43–44.

[84] Cf. Herodotus 2.7.1–2 and Pindar *Olympian* 1.18, 2.3, 3.9, 6.5, 8.9, 10.43, 13.29, 14.23; *Nemean* 10.32; *Parthenia* 2.49 Snell-Maehler.

point of view, it may be useful to pay attention to a whole series of traditions about the mythical and historical past of Olympia which, instead of taking the Pisatans and the Eleans as two conflicting communities, speak of their relationship in conciliatory terms. We should refer at least to the account of the foundation of the Olympic Games by the Spartan Lycurgus, the Elean Iphitos and the Pisatan Cleosthenes[85] and to the story of the Sixteen Women, who settled by arbitration the feud between Eleans and Pisatans.[86] The story of Chamynos, the loyal Pisatan, and of the role played by him in the origins of the sanctuary of Demeter Chamyne is also pertinent,[87] but may be of later origin. We are dealing with narratives which, as Massimo Nafissi remarked,[88] fit well the historical context of the years following the end of Pisatan independence in 362, when we see Olympia under Elean control and the Eleans backing the Spartans. But one should remember that *homonoia* ("like-minded identification") was a burning issue in those times,[89] and that the Eleans were left with the problem of the Pisatans. They had to be integrated into the Elean political organization, but their newly acquired identity could not be obliterated. Thus, we can suppose that effort was being put in by the Eleans to restructure the past according to the needs of the present. The traditions at issue clearly reflect this effort.

Thus far I have argued on one hand that neither a Pisatan community, nor a Pisatan tradition played a role in the archaic history of Elis; and on the other, that a whole complex of Elean traditions has to be seen within the framework provided by the needs of a rapidly shifting fourth-century horizon. We are left with the problem of how to understand the archaic historical context. There is no space here to discuss the early history of Olympia and of the Alpheios' valley, both to the north and to the south of the river, but I would surmise that, if the Elean aristocracies of the Peneios' valley had controlled the Alpheios' valley from time immemorial, the Elean narratives about the archaic struggles for the presidency of the Olympic Games between Eleans and Pisatans could hardly have been concocted, even

---

[85] Aristotle fr. 533 Rose in Plutarch *Lycurgus* 1.2; Phlegon FGH 257 F 1; Pausanias 5.20.1; see Nafissi 2001:309–310, Nafissi 2003:33.

[86] Pausanias 5.16.5.

[87] Pausanias 6.21.1.

[88] Nafissi 2001:318–321, Nafissi 2003:33–34, 37.

[89] Cf. the inscription (IvO 260: Ϝαλείων περὶ ὁμονοίαρ) on the base of a huge statue of Zeus dedicated by the Eleans at Olympia (Pausanias 5.24.4), and the reference to *homonoia* in Phlegon's account of the origins of the Olympic Games (FGH 257 F 1; *Scholia* on Plato *Republic* 465d, p. 230 Greene); for a discussion of the historical situation and the ideological issues involved see Nafissi 2001:321 and n57, Ruggeri 2004:198–200.

at the time of the independent Pisatan state. This is the reason why I am prepared to assume that there is a kernel of truth in such narratives. Perhaps they presuppose dim memories of conflicts between communities of the lower Alpheios' valley which attached their identity to Olympia, Oinomaos and Salmoneus on one side, and the aristocracies of the Peneios' valley on the other. As for the Pisatan "tyrants" Pantaleon, Damophon and Pyrrhus, it is impossible to know who they really were. Pantaleon and his son Pyrrhus could be seen as kings,[90] while Pyrrhus' brother Damophon is labelled as tyrant.[91] Perhaps they cannot be taken as "true" tyrants,[92] but are to be seen as local dynasts who tried to establish a special relationship between the communities of the lower Alpheios' valley and the Olympian sanctuary. Be that as it may, we cannot in any case take at face value the Elean tradition about the sixth century conquest of Pisatis. The Elean conquest and the archaic Pisatan state are better removed from the historical context.

The case of the Pisatans shows how even in Classical times an ethnic identity and a political community could be created, exist for a while, and then fade away. We are inclined to think that collective identities tend to go back to a receding past, and that, though processes may be at work whereby they become enfeebled for a time, they are bound to re-emerge. Yet this does not hold true for the Greeks. For them, both political organization and corporate identity depended on how communities understood and expressed themselves. Both had to meet the needs of a shifting present, and could be easily modified.

From this point of view, one should not say that the Greeks were in the grip of the past.

Bibliography

Alpers, K. 1981. *Das attizistische Lexicon des Oros. Untersuchung und kritische Ausgabe der Fragmente*. Berlin.

Andrewes, A. 1956. *The Greek Tyrants*. London.

Assmann, J. 1992. *Das kulturelle Gedächtnis. Schrift, Erinnerung und politische Identität in frühen Hochkulturen*. Munich.

Babelon, E. 1901–1914. *Traité des monnaies grecques et romaines*. Paris.

---

[90] Pausanias 6.22.2,4, and Heraclides Lembus *Excerpta Politiarum* 21.1–3 Dilts (Pantaleon).
[91] Pausanias 5.16.5.
[92] As now De Libero 1996:220–222 sees them.

Beloch, K. J. 1912. *Griechische Geschichte I. Die Zeit vor den Perserkriegen 1.* Strasburg.

Bilik, R. 1998–1999. "Hippias von Elis als Quelle von Diodors Bericht über den elisch-spartanischen Krieg?" *AncSoc* 29:21–47.

Bultrighini, U. 1990. *Pausania e le tradizioni democratiche: Argo ed Elide.* Padova.

Busolt, G. 1878. *Die Lakedaimonier und ihre Bundesgenossen.* Leipzig.

Cartledge, P. 1987. *Agesilaos and the Crisis of Sparta.* London.

Davies, J. K. 1994. "The Tradition about the First Sacred War." *Greek Historiography* (ed. S. Hornblower) 193–212. Oxford.

Dillery, J. 1995. *Xenophon and the History of His Times.* London.

van Effenterre, H., and Ruzé, F., eds. 1994. *Nomima. Recueil d'inscriptions politiques et juridiques de l'archaïsme grec. I.* Rome.

Gehrke, H.-J. 2003. "Sull'etnicità elea." *Geographia Antiqua* 12:5–22.

Halbwachs, M. 1941. *La Topographie légendaire des Evangiles en Terre Sainte. Étude de mémoire collective.* Paris.

Halbwachs, M. 1950. *La Mémoire collective.* Paris.

Hall, J. M. 1997. *Ethnic Identity in Greek Antiquity.* Cambridge.

Hornblower, S. 2000. "Thucydides, Xenophon, and Lichas: Were the Spartans Excluded from the Olympic Games from 420 to 400 B.C.?" *Phoenix* 54:212–225.

Howie, G. 1991. "Pindar's Account of Pelops' Contest with Oenomaus." *Nikephoros* 4:55–120.

Jeffery, L. H. 1990. *The Local Scripts of Archaic Greece: A Study of the Origin of the Greek Alphabet and its development from the Eighth to the Fifth Centuries B.C.* Oxford. Revised Edition.

Kraay, C. M. 1976. *Archaic and Classical Greek Coins.* Berkeley.

Krummen, E. 1990. *Pyrsos Hymnon. Festliche Gegenwart und mythisch-rituelle Tradition als Voraussetzung einer Pindarinterpretation (Isthmie 4, Pythie 5, Olympie 1 und 3).* Berlin.

Kyrieleis, H. 1997. "Zeus and Pelops in the East Pediment of the Temple of Zeus at Olympia." *The Interpretation of Architectural Sculpture in Greece and Rome* (ed. D. Buitron-Oliver) 13–27. Washington, DC.

Lee, H. M. 2001. *The Program and Schedule of the Ancient Olympic Games.* Hildesheim.

De Libero, L. 1996. *Die archaische Tyrannis.* Stuttgart.

Luraghi, N. 2001. "Der Erdbebenaufstand und die Entstehung der messenischen Identität." *Gab es das Griechische Wunder? Griechenland zwischen dem Ende des 6. und der Mitte des 5. Jahrhunderts v. Chr.* (eds. D. Papenfuß and V. M. Strocka) 279–303. Mainz.

Luraghi, N. 2002. "Becoming Messenian." *JHS* 122:45–69.

Maddoli, G., Nafissi, M., and Saladino, V. eds. 1999. *Pausania. Guida della Grecia. VI. L'Elide e Olimpia*. Milan.

Mallwitz, A. 1981. "Neue Forschungen in Olympia (Theater und Hestiaheiligtum in der Altis)." *Gymnasium* 88:97–122.

Mandl, G. C., and Ruggeri C. 2000. "Eine pisatische Siedlung bei Neráïda/Pérsaina im Hinterland von Olympia." *OTerr* 6:45–54.

Meyer, E. 1950. "Pisa, Pisatis." *RE* 20.2:1732–1755.

Möller, A. 2004. "Elis, Olympia und das Jahr 580 v. Chr. Zur Frage der Eroberung der Pisatis." *Griechische Archaik. Interne Enwicklungen—Externe Impulse* (eds. R. Rollinger and C. Ulf) 249–270. Berlin.

Nafissi, M. 2001. "La prospettiva di Pausania sulla storia dell'Elide. La questione pisate." *Éditer, traduire, commenter Pausanias en l'an 2000* (eds. D. Knoepfler and M. Piérart) 301–321. Geneva.

Nafissi, M. 2003. "Elei e Pisati. Geografia, storia e istituzioni politiche della regione di Olimpia." *Geographia Antiqua* 12:23–55.

Nielsen, T. H. 2002. *Arkadia and its Poleis in the Archaic and Classical Periods*. Göttingen.

Niese, B. 1910. "Drei Kapitel eleischer Geschichte." *Genethliakon* 1–47. Berlin.

Nora, P. ed. 1984–1992. *Les Lieux de mémoire I-III*. Paris.

Panayotopoulos, G. 1991. "Questions sur la topographie éléenne. Les sites d'Héracleia et de Salmoné." *Achaia und Elis in der Antike* (ed. A. D. Rizakis) 275–282. Athens.

Perlman, P. J. 2000. *City and Sanctuary in Ancient Greece. The Theorodokia in the Peloponnese*. Göttingen.

Reitzenstein, R. 1897. *Geschichte der griechischen Etymologika. Ein Beitrag zur Geschichte der Philologie in Alexandria und Byzanz*. Leipzig.

Rhodes, P. J. and Lewis, D. M. 1997. *The Decrees of the Greek States*. Oxford.

Rigsby, K. J. 1996. *Asylia. Territorial Inviolability in the Hellenistic World*, Berkeley.

Ringel, E., Siewert, P., Taeuber, H. 1999. "Die Symmachien Pisas mit den Arkadern, Akroreia, Messenien und Sikyon. Ein neues Fragment der 'arkadischen Bündnisstele' von 365 v. Chr." *Bericht über die Ausgrabungen in Olympia* (ed. A. Mallwitz and K. Herrmann) 11:413–420. Berlin.

Ritter, S. 2001. "Münzbilder im Kontext: Zeus und Olympia auf elischen Stateren des 4. Jahrhunderts v. Chr." *Konstruktionen von Wirklichkeit. Bilder im Griechenland des 5. und 4. Jahrhunderts v. Chr.* (eds. R. von den Hoff and S. Schmidt) 89–105. Stuttgart.

Roy, J. 1971. "Arkadia and Boeotia in Peloponnesian Affairs, 370-362 B.C." *Historia* 20:569–599.

Roy, J. 1994. "Thebes in the 360s BC." *CAH2* 6:187–208. Cambridge.

Roy, J. 1997. "The Perioikoi of Elis." *The Polis as an Urban Centre and as a Political Community.* (ed. M. H. Hansen) 282–320. Copenhagen.

Roy, J. 1998. "Thucydides 5.49.1–50.4: The Quarrel between Elis and Sparta in 420 B.C., and Elis' Exploitation of Olympia." *Klio* 80:360–368.

Roy, J. 2000. "The Frontier between Arkadia and Elis in Classical Antiquity." *Polis and Politics* (eds. P. Flensted-Jensen, T. H. Nielsen, and L. Rubinstein) 133–156. Copenhagen.

Roy, J. 2002. "The Patterns of Settlement in Pisatis. The 'Eight *Poleis*'." *Even More Studies in the Ancient Greek Polis* (ed. T. H. Nielsen) 229–247. Stuttgart.

Ruggeri, C. 2004. *Gli stati intorno a Olimpia. Storia e costituzione dell'Elide e degli stati formati dai perieci elei (400-362 a.C.).* Stuttgart.

Schepens, G. 2004. "La Guerra di Sparta contro Elide." *Ricerche di antichità e tradizione classica* (ed. E. Lanzillotta) 1–89. Tivoli.

Seltman, C. T. 1921. *The Temple Coins of Olympia.* Cambridge.

Siewert, P. 1991. "Die frühe Verwendung und Bedeutung des Ortsnamens <Olympia>." *MDAI(A)* 106, 65–69.

Slater, W. J. 1989. "Pelops at Olympia." *GRBS* 30:485-501.

Smith, A. D. 1986. *The Ethnic Origins of Nations.* Oxford.

Sordi, M. 1984a. "Le implicazioni olimpiche della guerra d'Elide." *Problemi di storia e cultura spartana* (ed. E. Lanzillotta) 143–59. Rome.

Sordi M. 1984b. "Il santuario di Olimpia e la guerra d'Elide." *CISA* 10:20–30. Milan.

Splitter, R. 2000. *Die "Kypseloslade" in Olympia. Form, Funktion und Bildschmuck: eine archäologische Rekonstruktion.* Mainz.

Stylianou, P. J. 1998. *A Historical Commentary on Diodorus Siculus. Book 15.* Oxford.

Tuplin, C. J. 1993. *The Failings of Empire: A Reading of Xenophon Hellenica 2.3.11-7.5.27.* Historia Einzelschriften 76. Stuttgart.

Unz, R. K. 1986. "The Chronology of the Elean War." *GRBS* 27:29–42.

Viedebantt, O. 1930. "Forschungen zur altpeloponnesischen Geschichte. 2. Elis und Pisatis." *Philologus* 85:23–41.

Wade-Gery, H. T. 1925. "The Growth of the Dorian States." CAH 3:527–570, 762–764.

West, M. L. 1985. *The Hesiodic Catalogue of Women: Its Nature, Structure, and Origins.* Oxford.

von Wilamowitz-Moellendorff, U. 1922. *Pindaros.* Berlin.

VI

Arcadia

Ethnicity and Politics in the Fifth and Fourth Centuries BCE[*]

Maria Pretzler

THE EMERGENCE OF ARCADIAN IDENTITY, and its culmination in the foundation of an Arcadian state in 370 BCE, was a crucial factor in the disintegration of the Peloponnesian League. With very few exceptions Arcadia becomes visible in the ancient literary sources only in the late archaic period, at a time when most of the region, if not all, was already part of Sparta's growing Peloponnesian League.[1] A united Arcadia as we see it in the 360s BCE is, in fact, one extreme in a wide range of decisions and actions adopted by Arcadian cities in relation to a common regional identity that we can observe in the archaic and classical periods. The sources often document a very fragmented political landscape in which Arcadian cities did not hesitate to abandon pan-Arcadian concerns in favor of co-operation with an outside ally. Yet in 370 BCE Arcadia seemed ready for political unification at very short notice.

In this paper I trace the emergence of a common Arcadian identity in an environment that, on the surface, does not seem conducive to such a development. I start with an investigation of the nature of Arcadian identity in 370 BCE, especially focusing on the arguments that were deployed

---

[*] I am grateful to Thomas Heine Nielsen for his advice and suggestions for this paper which, as his support in all matters Arcadian, have been invaluable. Thanks are also due to the organizers and participants of the Münster conference, in particular Nino Luraghi and Jim Roy. Last but not least, I would like to thank the anonymous referee for many helpful comments.

[1] Ste Croix 1972:97 assumes that by 540 almost the whole Peloponnese was allied to Sparta. This excludes Argos and probably all of the Achaean cities, most of which joined the league during the Peloponnesian War, or just before.

to convince all Arcadian cities to abandon particularism for a while and to support a common Arcadian cause. This is followed by a study of pan-Arcadian ideas and actions before 370 BCE, as developed and expressed in the region, and especially in relations between Arcadians and outsiders. Sparta has a special role to play in this story: concerted Arcadian action recorded in our sources usually takes place in opposition to the region's ambitious southern neighbor, or in the context of the activities of Sparta's Peloponnesian League.

Arcadian Rhetoric and the Foundation of the Arcadian State

The Spartan defeat at Leuctra in 371 BCE triggered developments in Arcadia that, although in themselves short-lived, had lasting consequences for Sparta and, ultimately, for the whole Peloponnese.[2] The initiative probably lay with Mantinea, broken up into villages in 385 BCE by a Sparta at the height of her powers after the King's Peace.[3] The Mantineans lost no time in undertaking a synoecism and in rebuilding their walls. Many Arcadian cities gave them their support,[4] a sign of pan-Arcadian feelings which are especially remarkable in the light of Mantinea's small-scale imperialist tendencies in the fifth century.[5] Tegea, Mantinea's neighbor and only rival in Arcadia, underwent a *stasis* in which the pan-Arcadian democrats gained the upper hand over a sizeable pro-Spartan party.[6] With both major cities on board the Arcadians proceeded to found a federal state, and although some cities, such as Orchomenos and Heraia, were reluctant to join,[7] support seems to have been widespread.

This development is remarkable because an apparently fragmented area managed to create a sophisticated territorial state in such a short time. In Arcadia no single hegemonic city could on its own impose a federal agenda, as Thebes did in Boeotia, and there is no evidence for a long standing tradition of tribal cohesion as in Aetolia: tribal states existed within Arcadia, but, as we shall see, before 370 BCE there had probably never been an organization that included the whole region. The new Arcadian state was, it seems, inspired by anti-Spartan sentiments, but this was not a sufficient criterion to allow membership: prospective members of "doubtful Arcadian-ness,"

[2] Nielsen 2002:475–477, Roy 1974, Larsen 1968:180–195.
[3] Xenophon *Hellenica* 5.2.1–8; on Mantinea as initiator: Larsen 1968:183, Dušanić 1970:285.
[4] Xenophon *Hellenica* 6.5.5; Elis also contributed to Mantinea's new wall.
[5] Nielsen 2002:367–372.
[6] Xenophon *Hellenica* 6.5.6, Diodorus 15.59.1–4.
[7] Xenophon *Hellenica* 6.5.11.

such as the Triphylians, needed to be "Arcadianized" by a manipulation of Arcadian myth-history.[8] This suggests that the Arcadian federal state was indeed defined by, and founded upon, Arcadian identity.

Xenophon provides an example of explicitly Arcadian sentiment in a speech given in 369 BCE by Lycomedes of Mantinea, one of the "founding fathers" of a unified Arcadia.[9] The speech documents enormous Arcadian confidence based on two main factors: firstly, Arcadian autochthony and the claim that the Arcadians are the only true Peloponnesians, and secondly, that the Arcadians were the most numerous people and the strongest and bravest warriors, which made them indispensable for both Sparta's and Thebes' success.

Xenophon's Lycomedes, it seems, has a well-defined concept of what it means to be Arcadian, and in this speech he uses this sense of Arcadian identity as a political argument, advocating a policy of independent action. This passage in Xenophon's *Hellenica* represents the only fairly contemporary summary of how the ethnic identity card may have been played in the context of political debate in Arcadia. Xenophon must have known Arcadia well, and he had certainly made acquaintance with Arcadians among Cyrus' Ten Thousand.[10] His bias against most of Sparta's enemies, however, makes it necessary to assess this passage very carefully. Would Arcadians have recognized this image of themselves? Would they have approved? Would outsiders have recognized these arguments as typically Arcadian? Let us look at Lycomedes' claims in turn.

It was common knowledge among the Greeks that the Arcadians were autochthonous inhabitants of the Peloponnese. Fragments of Hesiod's work suggest that Arcadian genealogy was an issue from the earliest days of Greek literature, and Hecataeus, still in the archaic period and well outside Arcadia, also dealt with the subject. All versions of this genealogy suggest that Arcadians were seen as different from their neighbors: they are descended from Pelasgos, which makes them autochthonous, just as Xenophon's Lycomedes claims.[11] Arcadians are the only Peloponnesians still to live in their original homeland, since according to Greek tradition

---

[8] CEG 824 (*FdD* III 3, Pausanias 10.9.5–8), Polybius 4.77.8, Pausanias 5.5.3–6; Nielsen 2002:248–252.

[9] Xenophon *Hellenica* 7.1.23-24. Lykomedes: Xenophon *Hellenica* 7.1.39, 7.4.2, Diodorus 1.562.2, 15.67.2.

[10] Roy 1972b.

[11] Hesiod fr. 162 W, fr. 163 W, fr. 23a 32 W. Hecataeus *FGH* 1 F 6, F 9, F 29a, F 29b; Pherecydes *FGH* 3 F 5, F 82a, F 135a, F 156–161, Asios in Pausanias 8.1.4; cf. Pausanias 8.1.4-4.4.

the Achaeans, also autochthonous Peloponnesians, left the Argolid for the formerly Ionian region of Achaea when the Dorians invaded.[12]

Arcadian identity is first and foremost dependent on this common ancestry. In fact, most Arcadian cities were fairly mechanically linked to the Arcadian genealogy by an eponymous founder who was seen as a son of Lycaon, son of Pelasgos. One list of Lycaon's sons, possibly based on a fifth-century original,[13] is preserved in Apollodorus' work, another was compiled by Pausanias, probably from contemporary oral tradition: he specifically looked for remains of the small communities which were wholly or partly deserted after their inclusion in the synoecism of the Arcadian League's new capital, Megalopolis, and the genealogy presented in his *Periegesis* conveniently includes those he was able to locate.[14]

The development of local mythical history suggests that, as Arcadian identity developed, the (mythical) history of the region was adapted as well, a process that should be expected in the context of an emerging and perhaps expanding ethnic identity.[15] Such changes are also reflected in the changing accounts of the origins of Triphylia which apparently "became" Arcadian in the space of a few decades in the early fourth century,[16] just in time to be included in the new federal state. When the Arcadians set up their monument in Delphi, probably in 369 BCE, their eponymous hero, Arkas, had "acquired" an additional son, Triphylos, and as if to stress the point, a son of Triphylos, Erasos, was included, too.[17] This monument is a crucial piece of evidence because it represents an authentic record of the self-representation of the Arcadian League in the 360s BCE, and the significant remains of the original base together with Pausanias' detailed description provide an excellent record. The league set up a series of statues representing the most important figures in the Arcadian genealogy,[18] including Arkas with his sons and his mother Kallisto, and the inscription specifically stresses Arcadian autochthony. The context of the monument is also poignant, because it was placed at the entrance of the sanctuary, a location dominated by Argive and

---

[12] Herodotus 8.73, cf. 2.171, Thucydides 1.2.3.

[13] Apollodorus 3.8–9; fifth-century source: Nielsen 2002:235–236 with n. 36; Callmer 1943:45–46, van der Valk 1958:142, Hejnic 1961:55.

[14] Pausanias 8.3.1–5, cf. 8.27.1–8; Roy 1968.

[15] Nielsen 2002:92–97, see *Iliad* 2.605–8.

[16] Nielsen 2002:230–265, Herodotus 4.148. See Ruggeri, this volume.

[17] CEG 824 (*FdD* III 3), Pausanias 10.9.5–8. See also Polybius 4.77.8–10.

[18] Pausanias 10.9.5-6 refers to the monument as Tegean, but the main inscription (CEG 824 lines 1–2) identifies it as a dedication of the Arcadians.

Spartan dedications. This emphasized the powerful message of a new, strong and self-confident Arcadia as an aspiring Peloponnesian power, presented in one of the most public spaces in the Greek world, and it seems perfectly compatible with the image presented by Xenophon's Lycomedes.

Arcadian identity did not just come with a long genealogy; there were also some traits which were seen as typical for the region and its people. Most of these are, in fact, alluded to in the *Iliad*'s *Catalogue of Ships*, a text that, although notoriously difficult to date, almost certainly predates all other preserved literary information about Arcadians except probably Hesiod.[19] The passage, with its references to the mountainous landscape, to flocks pastured in Arcadia (specifically in Orchomenos), and to inhabitants who are excellent fighters but not acquainted with the sea, remained a crucial reference point for the Arcadian image well into the Roman imperial period. To these typical Arcadian traits one might add piety, poverty and, perhaps connected to the idea of the extreme age of the Arcadian people, a certain reputation for a primitive lifestyle.[20] The Arcadian dialect was also distinct from other dialects used in the Peloponnese, and just as inscriptions record specific features of local variety we have to assume that it must have been possible to tell the difference between the spoken language of an Arcadian and that of his Dorian, Elean or Achaean neighbors.[21] It is, however, not clear whether the ancient Greeks ever acknowledged the existence of a specific Arcadian regional dialect in the same way as they thought of Attic or Boeotian.[22] The Triphylians are an interesting test case: the dialect recorded in their inscriptions is Elean (in some places with slight variations).[23] Nevertheless the Arcadians were willing to accept them into their tribe: what made the Triphylians Arcadian was not their dialect but their putative ancestry.

Lycomedes' speech singles out Arcadian prowess in warfare, the Arcadian quality most relevant for a claim to political power. The idea that Arcadians had always allowed others to use their services instead of going to war on their own behalf seems to have been proverbial by the second half of the fifth century: about 425 BCE Hermippos included mercenaries from Arcadia in a list of stereotypical products of different regions.[24] The comic

---

[19] *Iliad* 2.603–614.
[20] Nielsen 2002:74–83, Pretzler 2005:526–527.
[21] For a detailed discussion of the Arcadian dialect see Dubois 1986.
[22] See Nielsen 2002:50–52, 75–76, with Hall 1995, Hall 1997:170–181.
[23] Striano 1991, Ruggeri 2000.
[24] Hermippos fr.63 (Köck), in Athenaios 1.27F.

poet Plato uses the expression Ἀρκάδας μιμεῖσθαι, which describes someone fighting for others while suffering only defeat at home.[25] This reference is ambiguous: it might point to the Arcadians as long-standing allies of Sparta, or it could refer to mercenary service. The latter is likely to be the interpretation that would have come to most Greeks' minds, because Arcadians had a reputation for serving as mercenaries in the Greek world and beyond. From Herodotus' Arcadians who, after Thermopylae, are trying to sell their military services to the Persians,[26] to the several thousand among Cyrus' Ten Thousand,[27] the region was famous for exporting good soldiers, but also troops that might support any cause as long as payment was adequate. This reputation was certainly based on fact: for example, Roy calculates that the Arcadians with Cyrus represented at least eight percent of the adult male population of Arcadia at a time when yet others were employed elsewhere, for example in Sicily.[28]

Lycomedes' (or rather Xenophon's) reference to Arcadians whose efforts in war bring about others' success sounds suspiciously similar, and it certainly plays on the same stereotypes. The audience's knowledge of Arcadian warriors' prowess in mercenary service would help to emphasize the point the speaker is trying to make, although in this context the reference is primarily to Arcadians fighting as (unpaid!) allies of the large powers in Greece, namely Sparta and recently also Thebes. The old Arcadian stereotype is skillfully adapted to fit a bid for an Arcadian state that acts independently of any of the large powers, and Lycomedes goes so far as to hint at the possibility that Arcadia could become a major player in its own right. We know from Athenian sources how markers of local identity were used in public speeches, particularly to underline patriotic statements.[29] Xenophon probably drew on such traditions when he composed Lycomedes' speech, and he produced a credible translation of recognized Arcadian stereotypes into rhetorical arguments. Xenophon's version of Arcadian patriotic sentiment in a political context is likely to have appeared plausible to Greeks in general, and it was probably familiar enough to Arcadians, too.

---

[25] Borgeaud 1988:21–22, 197–198n109; Plato Comicus (active at least 428–389 BCE) fr. 99 (Köck); see also Xenophon *Hellenica* 3.5.12 (set in 395 BCE); Nielsen 2002:81–82.

[26] Herodotus 8.26.2.

[27] Roy 1967:308–309 calculates that there were 4000 at least. Cf. Parke 1933:14–16, Demand 1990:48–49.

[28] Roy 1999:346–348, see also Fields 2001.

[29] Loraux 2006, esp.132–171, 263–304.

The Development of Arcadian Identity

The Arcadian view is, in fact, difficult to determine because most references to Arcadia reflect what outsiders thought about Arcadians: the region's image was relatively clearly defined some time before we see Arcadians themselves declare their Arcadian identity. In the context of this paper it is particularly important to understand how they reconciled their loyalty to a city or local tribal community with their regional identity. In order to understand the pan-Arcadian sentiments that helped to drive political unification after the battle of Leuctra it is necessary to investigate evidence for a regional identity before the league was founded. As far as possible this enquiry must be based on original classical sources, because in spite of its quick demise the Arcadian league is likely to have had a lasting impact on pan-Arcadian symbols and rhetoric, not least by creating Megalopolis, a city that still retained many monuments of pan-Arcadian significance in the Roman period, and that was itself a lasting memorial of regional unification.[30]

Nielsen collects all instances of the regional ethnic in inscriptions and texts, and he does detect a distinct pattern: Arcadians often, but by no means always, chose to call themselves Ἀρκάς, and it was also possible to combine the regional label with a city ethnic: "an Arcadian from Tegea."[31] It does not seem surprising that the regional ethnic (as used by Arcadians themselves) is usually found outside the region itself, but even then the label "Arkas" was by no means universally adopted. Epigraphic references to Arcadians outside Arcadia show a good deal of variation. The fourth century lists of *naopoioi* at Delphi include Arcadians who chose to be known by their city ethnics, alongside others who preferred the regional label Ἀρκάς, without any apparent correlation with the state of the Arcadian League at the time or with the size or prominence of the city in question.[32] Roy's observations of Xenophon's usage in the *Anabasis* offer a more detailed insight into such personal preferences. Xenophon usually labels personal acquaintances from Arcadia with their city ethnic, while he uses the more general ethnic "Arcadian" when he does not know an individual well. This would suggest that in close interactions with other Greeks these Arcadians preferred to

---

[30] Pausanias 8.30.1-8.32.5, Nilsson 1972:18–22, Jost 1973:264–256, Jost 1985:220–235. Note Pausanias 8.53.9, a "common hearth of the Arcadians" in Tegea, which should probably also be seen in the context of the Arcadian League of the 360s BCE and the sentiments, symbols, and rhetoric it created.

[31] Nielsen 2002:54–66.

[32] Nielsen 2002:63–64 with n96, appendix II.

stress their local identity, but as first identification in conversation with an outsider they might choose the regional ethnic before indicating their *polis* or tribal community.[33]

Given that a large part of classical Arcadia consisted of well-established *poleis*, it is perhaps quite surprising how easily some Arcadians did adopt the regional ethnic in place of a city ethnic. Like most Greeks, Arcadians had more than one identity to choose from, and they would have made use of whichever label seemed to be most advantageous or prestigious in a particular context. The relatively common use of the Arcadian ethnic suggests that it was particularly well recognized abroad and therefore a useful category to be associated with. In an "international" context Arcadian identity was apparently attractive, or at least preferable to the exclusive use of less-recognizable city ethnics. The generally positive image that Arcadians enjoyed in the Greek tradition, from their most impressively ancient pedigree to the fearsome warrior image, may well have added to the wide appeal of Arcadian-ness. We should also consider that the Arcadian ethnic may have been acceptable alongside city identities exactly because during most of its history Arcadia was not a political unit. This meant that regional and local identities could co-exist without much friction, unlike, for example, in Boeotia where regional identity became a threat to local identities because it served Thebes as a means of coercing its neighbors into the Boeotian League.[34]

The most striking epigraphical evidence for a common Arcadian identity can be found in the late fourth-century victory lists set up at the sanctuary on Mount Lykaion.[35] They present various outsiders with their city ethnics, but Arcadians are all listed as Ἀρκάς. Not only is the use of the regional ethnic unique for inscriptions found in Arcadia, the complete omission of city-ethnics for all Arcadians is not paralleled anywhere else, even outside the region. This has to be seen as a deliberate and particularly strong pan-Arcadian gesture, and although the inscriptions date to a period after the demise of the federal state, they show that Mount Lykaion was seen as a location particularly appropriate for extravagant Arcadian gestures. The importance of this pan-Arcadian sanctuary can, in fact, be traced back into an earlier period: Xenophon reports that Cyrus consented to interrupt his

---

[33] Roy 1972b.

[34] Examples for Boeotian rhetoric as a threat: Thucydides 2.2.1–4, 3.61.1, 3.64 (cf. 3.55–56), 7.57.5; Xenophon *Hellenica* 5.1.32–33, 6.3.19.

[35] IG V 2.549, 550. Nielsen 2002:61–63 & appendix I.

march to allow his Arcadian mercenaries to celebrate the Lykaia festival.[36] Not only are the Arcadians the only mercenaries among the Ten Thousand to be singled out in this manner, it is also remarkable that men hailing from many different cities regarded a common regional festival as so important that they managed to convince their non-Arcadian Greek commanders and their Persian employer to grant them the opportunity to celebrate it.

It seems clear, then, that by the early fourth century BCE Arcadian identity was well established, regarded as an appropriate substitute for local identities in some circumstances and developed sufficiently to be useful as a political tool. Such a politicized sense of identity must have emerged over time as individuals, cities or regional organizations turned individual political agendas into Arcadian causes. We need to ask, therefore, under what circumstances pan-Arcadian rhetoric may have become an attractive political tool.

The most striking example for apparently common Arcadian activity is a large but enigmatic series of coins which started some time before the mid-fifth century and continued for some decades, possibly as the largest coinage in the Peloponnese.[37] These coins bear the image of Zeus Lykaios and an unidentified goddess; there is also a legend APKAΔIKON, usually in abbreviated form. As Nielsen shows conclusively, it is very unlikely that there ever was an Arcadian state, or any kind of fully fledged pan-Arcadian organization before the foundation of the federal state in the fourth century.[38] Nielsen stresses the connection of the *Arkadikon* coinage with the sanctuary on Mount Lykaion; as already mentioned, this was a particularly important place for a common regional identity.[39] There is no evidence that the Lykaion was under firm control of one *polis* before its inclusion in the territory of Megalopolis. Communities in the area lived in villages and small towns and were organized in tribes. The initiative could have come from an organization of states around the sanctuary, a putative Arcadian amphiktyony, as Nielsen suggests, although such an organization is not attested in

---

[36] Xenophon *Anabasis* 1.2.10, Roy 1972b:134–135, Ma 2004, esp. 338–343, cf. Parker 2004:139–140. See also Bergese 1995:111–112: a dedication to Zeus Lykaios found in Sicily; connected with the many mercenaries who were hired in Sicily?

[37] Williams 1965, Kraay 1976:98.

[38] Nielsen 2002:120–157, Nielsen 1996. One suggestion was that a league was created by Cleomenes I: see especially Wallace 1954, but evidence for events (most prominently Herodotus 9.33, 9.35) in fifth-century Arcadia contradict the idea of a long-lasting comprehensive league. See Roy 1972a; cf. Andrewes 1952.

[39] Nielsen 2002:145–152, Nielsen 1996:56–61, Head 1911:444–445, 447–448 ("festival coinage").

the sources.[40] It seems more likely that the *Arkadikon* coinage represents the attempt by one or more individual powers to harness Arcadian symbols and sentiments for their own ends.

Fifth-century history provides us with a number of examples where regional rhetoric may have been seen as useful in initiating or consolidating the co-operation between different states or political groups in the region, even if none of these efforts seems to have achieved a coalition that included all of Arcadia. Such developments would also have made a significant contribution to a clearer definition of Arcadian identity and the symbols that could best represent it. We cannot rule out that some cities or individuals had pan-Arcadian aspirations as early as the archaic period; both Tegea and Mantinea may have been influential, and it seems that Kleitor also managed to assert power over neighboring communities.[41] There is, however, not enough evidence to evaluate these developments in any detail and to determine whether any bid for regional power before the Persian Wars went hand in hand with pan-Arcadian aspirations.[42]

The earliest attested example shows us an outsider attempting to find a common Arcadian symbol to rally his followers in the region. Herodotus reports that Cleomenes I was planning to unite the Arcadians to strengthen his position against political opponents in Sparta, and he expected his new allies to swear an oath of allegiance by the Styx River in northern Arcadia.[43] These plans probably never came to fruition because Cleomenes was recalled to Sparta before he had formed his Arcadian coalition. The Styx is not usually presented as a place of Arcadian identification, and if we are dealing with a glimpse of a genuinely native tradition, it was soon abandoned, perhaps when the Lykaion became the main focus of regional identity. However, the Styx does seem an unlikely choice for such a role, not only because of its extremely remote location, but also because of its ominous connections with the underworld. It is possible that this episode represents an idea imposed by an outsider (Cleomenes? Herodotus or his source?) not in response to some Arcadian tradition, but rather as a nod to the river's famous role in the Homeric epics where it serves the gods as a guarantor of their most holy

---

[40] See Nielsen 2002:150–152.

[41] Tegea: note the successful defence against Spartan aggression; the attack on Tegea is connected to Spartan designs on all of Arcadia (Herodotus 1.66); Mantinea: Pausanias 5.26.6 with Richter 1939:194–201; Kleitor: inscription mentioning spoils "from many cities," Pausanias 5.23.7 with Richter 1939:199–201.

[42] Nielsen 2002:185–188, Roy 1972a:336, 339–340; cf. Roy 1972c.

[43] Herodotus 6.74–75.

oaths.[44] In any case, this episode shows that using an Arcadian agenda for political ends was feasible in the early fifth century BCE, or at least that a few decades later, around the middle of the century, Herodotus could present this story as a plausible interpretation of the king's actions.[45]

Among the Arcadians themselves the two largest cities, Tegea and Mantinea, were particularly keen to exploit regional politics for their own ends. Tegea's anti-Spartan stance after the Persian wars apparently led to an alliance with Argos, and Tegea probably became the leader of an alliance, referred to by Herodotus as "all Arcadians except Mantinea," which was active between 479 and 465 BCE and was defeated by the Spartans in the battle of Dipaia.[46] In 423 BCE, when Tegea opposed its neighbor Mantinea with the help of the Spartans, it still had some allies of its own, presumably also Arcadians.[47] Fifth-century Tegea engaged in some hefty pan-Arcadian and anti-Spartan rhetoric with the aim of showing itself as the traditional leader of the region. Herodotus, who probably visited the city around the mid-fifth century, records a number of examples.[48] In the temple of Athena Alea, a sanctuary of more than merely local importance, he saw the chains of Spartans who had allegedly been taken prisoner in a conflict before the foundation of the Peloponnesian League. This represents a monumentalization of the ancient conflict between Tegea and Sparta which is scarcely thinkable in a city as faithful to Sparta as the Tegeans had been at Plataea. It does, however, suit a state at the head of an anti-Spartan coalition. The historical conflict is conveniently shown as Sparta's first step towards a conquest of all of Arcadia which was at least considerably delayed by Tegean resistance.[49] The mythical history of Tegea also supplied a crucial part of the royal genealogy of Arcadia. One of the Arcadian-Tegean kings, Echemos, was credited with defeating Hyllos, the son of Heracles, with the result that the Heraclidae (in effect the Dorian ancestors of the Spartans) stayed out of the Peloponnese for another three generations. Herodotus' Tegeans use this essentially anti-Dorian story as an argument to remind the Spartans of their right to a privileged position in the phalanx at Plataea.[50] Pausanias' description of Tegea stresses this anti-Spartan role of Tegea even more, but

---

[44] *Iliad* 2.755, 14.247, 15.37; *Odyssey* 2.185.
[45] Roy 2001:266, Nielsen 2002:84–85.
[46] Herodotus 9.35, Nielsen 2002:142–145, 366–367; see also Andrewes 1952.
[47] Thucydides 4.134.
[48] Herodotus 1.66–68, 9.26–28.
[49] Herodotus 1.66.
[50] Herodotus 9.26.

it is impossible to determine how much of the tradition and monuments mentioned date back to the time before 370 BCE.[51] Herodotus' evidence alone is, however, sufficient to demonstrate that at least in the fifth century Tegea made a conscious effort to present itself as a long-standing champion of the Arcadian cause, particularly against Sparta.

By the latter half of the fifth century Mantinea was just as eager to show pan-Arcadian tendencies as its southern neighbor. Its coinage shows acorns and bears alongside the traditional Mantinean emblem, the trident. Both are very Arcadian motifs, the bear because Arkas' mother Kallisto was turned into a bear, and acorns are connected with the image of the earliest origins of the Arcadians: before the invention of agriculture they were said to have lived on acorns, a fact which made βαλανηφάγοι ("acorn eaters") an appropriate epithet for Arcadians in a Delphic oracle quoted by Herodotus.[52] Thucydides reports that by 423 BCE Mantinea had gained control over a fairly large part of Arcadia which included Parrhasia (part of the area later incorporated in the territory of Megalopolis) and probably also parts of central Arcadia.[53] Like Tegea, Mantinea therefore had reason to resort to Arcadian, as opposed to purely Mantinean, themes. The period of Mantinean expansionism also offers the most likely background for an initiative to transfer the bones of Arkas to Mantinea, a bold move which suggests a serious claim to pan-Arcadian leadership.[54] Mantinean policies in this period also had a strong anti-Spartan flavor, especially after 420 BCE, when the Arcadian city joined an alliance with Athens, Argos and Elis, and in 418 BCE Sparta had to take military action to put a halt to their activities. It is therefore likely that, just as with Tegea earlier in the century, Mantinea's pan-Arcadian rhetoric was closely connected with a struggle against Sparta. In this context it is also interesting to observe that even in the euphoric days after the battle of Leuctra some Arcadians were apparently skeptical about a pan-Arcadian movement. Orchomenos in particular had to be coerced into the new league: a city that could probably look back on a long struggle against its neighbor Mantinea's expansionist tendencies had good reasons to remember

---

[51] Pausanias 8.45.3, 47.2, 47.4, 48.4–5, 53.10, 54.4. Pretzler 1999:109–111, 114–118. See also Pretzler 2007:152–153.

[52] Herodotus 1.66, cf. Pausanias 8.1.6.

[53] Nielsen 2002:367–372, Thucydides 4.134.1–2, 5.28.3–5.29.2, 5.33.1–3, 5.4.7, 5.67.2, 5.81.1.

[54] Pausanias 8.9.3, 8.36.8, for the date see Hejnic 1961:29, Jost 1985:128, Bergese 1995:25, Nielsen 2002:403–404, esp. n460.

that causes presented as Arcadian might not be equally beneficial to all Arcadians.[55]

The two great cities of Arcadia were probably not alone in playing the Arcadian card when it seemed politically opportune. Pan-Arcadian claims may have been used in different contexts, and by different parties. For example, Xenophon reports that "the Arcadians" were claiming Lasion (in east Elis) as Arcadian, probably in 397 BCE.[56] He does not explain who these Arcadians are. All of them? Part of Arcadia? A neighboring Arcadian city such as Psophis or Thelpusa? Xenophon may be projecting the circumstances of his own time (post-370 BCE) into the past, but he suggests that someone was using a pan-Arcadian agenda well before the political unification of the region. There is also an intriguing example of coins from Methydrion and Orchomenos with a number of designs depicting the myth of Kallisto and the birth of Arkas. Nielsen suggests that this coinage might be connected to Orchomenos' own efforts to assert influence over cities in its vicinity, namely the creation of a *sunteleia* which probably included Methydrion.[57] We have to assume that by the fourth century, the "Arcadian argument" was not just used by the big players, and it is possible that under some circumstances, Arcadians may have used pan-Arcadian rhetoric to support a common cause, independent of the interests of one of the cities that had long used regional identity to serve their own ends.

Such ostensibly (if not geographically comprehensive) pan-Arcadian activities were probably the driving force behind the creation of the *Arkadikon* coinage. If we follow Kraay in dating the beginning of the series just before the mid-fifth century, the best candidate for initiating this coinage is Tegea's alliance, which fought Sparta at Dipaia. Cleomenes' activities in Arcadia predate the earliest coins, while Mantinea's rise in the second half of the fifth century comes too late.[58] This would also explain why Tegea, a large and relatively prosperous city, apparently did not mint coins of its own for most of the fifth century.[59] As long as Tegea was the leader

---

[55] Xenophon *Hellenica* 6.5.10–11, Diodorus 15.59.4. Cf. Thucydides 5.61–62 (418 BCE); see also Roy 1971:571–572.

[56] Xenophon *Hellenica* 3.2.30.

[57] Head 1911.451, Nielsen 2002:355–357. Cf. Head 1911.452, a fourth-century coin of Pheneos showing Hermes with the infant Arkas; in some specimens the child is even identified by a legend.

[58] Dates: Kraay 1976:98.

[59] Nielsen 1996:56; Head 1911.454: start of Tegean coins in c. 420 BCE. Possible archaic coinage: Nielsen 2002:594.

of a substantial Arcadian alliance it would have had the clout to determine the use of Arcadian symbols and to initiate a regional coinage which may then have continued well beyond the period of Tegea's greatest influence. In the variable political climate of fifth-century Arcadia no single substantial Arcadian organization is likely to have survived as long as the *Arkadikon* coinage, but pan-Arcadian rhetoric and symbols clearly proved useful in different situations. Under such circumstances the minting of *Arkadikon* coins may well have been interrupted, or perhaps there were even several cities which struck coins of this type at different times: both scenarios would account for the distinct die sequences identified by Williams.[60] The focus on Zeus Lykaios would suggest a commitment to a pan-Arcadian rhetoric which could be seen as more inclusive than any symbol closely connected to Tegea itself, particularly the city's major goddess, Athena Alea. The control over (or access to) the Lykaion sanctuary might have played a role in Tegea's conflict with Mantinea in the area of Oresthasion and Ladokeion, not far from Mount Lykaion.[61]

Particular modes of ethnic argumentation adopted by the Arcadians owed much to forms of political discourse practiced in other parts of Greece. In fact, the defining features of Arcadian identity may be the result of an ongoing dialectic process that took place while other identities, especially those connected to the Dorians, simultaneously emerged in the archaic Peloponnese. Arcadian pride in autochthonous origins seems a perfect answer to Sparta's Dorian rhetoric which centered on the "return" or migration of the Heraclidae to the Peloponnese.[62] It is possible that this was already an issue in the sixth century when the Spartans tried to stake a claim to pre-Dorian heritage by transferring the bones of Orestes and his son Teisamenos to Sparta.[63] This particular mode of exploiting mythical history was then in turn adopted by the Mantineans when they transferred the bones of Arkas from Mainalos to their own city.[64]

Such forms of "ethnic discourse," developed in the context of interstate politics, would invite Arcadians to think in regional categories, and it seems that ultimately, this made political unification a conceivable option, even if

[60] Williams 1965.
[61] Thucydides 4.134, 5.29.1, Nielsen 2002:372–373.
[62] Hall 1997:34–66, cf. Thucydides 1.2.3, Herodotus 8.73.
[63] Transfer of bones by Sparta: Herodotus 1.67–68, cf. Pausanias 8.54.4, 3.11.10 (Orestes), Pausanias 7.1.8 (Teisamenos); de Ste Croix 1972:96, Leahy 1955, Dowden 1992:91, Welwei 2004.
[64] Pausanias 8.9.3, cf. 8.36.8.

it remained practically impossible as long as Sparta was in control. When the opportunity finally came, the Arcadians were ready to act together as a group, at least for a few years.

The Influence of Sparta

Sparta was the outside factor which had the most significant influence on the development of Arcadian identity, and it is therefore to Sparta that we now turn. Sparta's aggression and her alliance with all Arcadian cities and communities within the Peloponnesian League were instrumental in shaping the crucial preconditions for the unification of Arcadia which proved so destructive for the whole alliance in the crisis after Leuctra.

In the ancient sources Arcadian opposition to Spartan aggression and control is the most conspicuous aspect of this relationship. Many texts written after 370 BCE are probably influenced by hindsight and by Arcadian anti-Spartan sentiments that outlasted the Peloponnesian League by centuries, not least because Sparta continued to pose a threat to her immediate neighbors.[65] In spite of this continuing friction the relationship between Sparta and individual Arcadian allies could be very good,[66] and it should not be forgotten that most of the time Arcadian cities enjoyed considerable freedom to pursue their own policies; even wars between Sparta's allies were not an unusual occurrence.[67]

Opposition to Sparta was nevertheless a crucial factor in the formation of Arcadian identity. In general, group identities depend on the existence of the "other" which is perceived as being outside the group, and different from it. Conflict with such an opponent will usually increase group cohesion.[68] Sparta seems to have been very aggressive in the archaic period, with a focus on its neighbors beyond Messenia certainly in the seventh century, and possibly as early as the eighth.[69] At the same time at least the evidence from the sanctuary of Athena Alea at Tegea suggests that from the protogeometric period onward there was also close cultural interaction with Laconia.[70] The Arcadians had ample opportunity to get to know their

---

[65] Pretzler 1999:114–119.
[66] E.g. Tegea in 479, and again from c. 365 to 370; Nielsen 2002:142–145.
[67] Wars among league members: e.g. Thucydides 1.103.4, 4.134, 5.29.1, 5.33, Xenophon *Hellenica* 5.4.36. de Ste Croix 1972:120–122. See also Roy 1972b:339–340, Roy 2001:265.
[68] Smith 1986:37–38.
[69] Osborne 1996:184–185.
[70] Voyatzis 1999:143–145.

southern neighbor and to observe contrasts that could help them define their own ethnic identity.

After the battle of Leuctra pan-Arcadian activities constituted a deliberate move away from Spartan influence. Anti-Spartan rhetoric was rife in much of Greece by this point, because Sparta's heavy-handed policy after the King's Peace gave ample reason for discontent. The Mantineans, who played a leading role in the move towards Arcadian unity, had a particularly good cause to bear grudges against the state that had forced them to abandon their urban center, and to settle in separate villages.[71] By the time Tegea was embroiled in *stasis* it was clear that the unification of Arcadia depended on a struggle of democrats against pro-Spartan oligarchs.[72] Since, as we have seen, much of the pan-Arcadian rhetoric that developed in the fifth century was closely connected with opposition to Sparta, it was probably easy to adapt already existing ideas and symbols to the new circumstances. The foundation of Megalopolis in particular was an Arcadian federal project which combined a regional agenda with overt anti-Spartan measures. The new city was created by the synoecism of a large part of southern and southwestern Arcadia, which up to this point was organized by tribes and small towns or villages. This region had been strategically important for the Spartans, because it offered access from Laconia to Messenia, and that route was now blocked by a major new fortified settlement.[73] Moreover, the conspicuous construction of a new "Great City," emphasized by its programmatic name, symbolizes the power of the new Arcadian League, but it also responds to a long tradition of tensions created by Sparta's opposition to urbanization projects, be it the construction of city walls or the foundation of urban centers by synoecism, which found its most extreme expression in the *dioikismos* of Mantinea in 385 BCE.[74]

The Spartans were not necessarily the only outsiders who contributed to the definition of Arcadian-ness: the prime choice of the "significant other" for ethnic identification may vary in different areas and periods.

---

[71] Xenophon *Hellenica* 5.2.1–8, 6.5.5–6.5.11.

[72] Xenophon *Hellenica* 6.5.6–9. Roy 1971:569–571.

[73] Pausanias 8.27.1–8, Diodorus 15.72.4. Note that there is a dispute about the date (371/0 BCE or 368/7 BCE). If the later date is chosen the foundation of Messene (369 BCE) may have been a further incentive or inspiration, although direct Theban involvement is ruled out by most commentators. Nielsen 2002:414–442, Hornblower 1990 esp. 75–77, Demand 1990:111–118, Moggi 1976:293–325, Braunert and Petersen 1972, Larsen 1968:185–186, Niese 1899.

[74] Demand 1990:59–72, see also Braunert and Petersen 1972.

Argos may have been seen as a serious threat in the archaic period, and one would expect that anti-Elean rhetoric became an especially useful aspect of Arcadian identification at a time when the Triphylians tried to distance themselves from Elis by "becoming" Arcadian. As it turned out in the 360s BCE, however, sentiments against Elis or Thebes, which became crucial issues for the Arcadian confederation, were not enough to keep the region together. After Epaminondas' Peloponnesian campaign that established Messenia as an independent state, Sparta was no longer equally perceived as a threat by all Arcadians. Soon it became clear that there was no other factor that could replace Sparta as common unifying enemy and therefore guarantor for strong pan-Arcadian sentiments. The result was that individual cities' concerns, class-consciousness, and even a common Peloponnesian sentiment (for Sparta, against Thebes) could overrule specifically Arcadian interests.[75] Even in her defeat as hegemon of the Peloponnese Sparta proved that she was the crucial factor for Arcadian identification, whose absence ultimately meant failure for the pan-Arcadian project. In fact, anti-Spartan sentiment was such an integral part of Arcadian identity that it can still be seen in Polybius' attitudes, and, even later, in Pausanias' record of Arcadian traditions.[76]

There is yet another way in which Sparta contributed to the consolidation of Arcadian ethnicity, namely by making the Arcadian cities and tribal communities part of the Peloponnesian League. It is generally thought that warfare is a significant factor in the emergence of ethnic communities, but it is more difficult to assess the effect of warfare within the context of a large alliance. If I may offer a bold comparison to illustrate my point, the impact of the Roman system of alliances on the peoples and states of Italy shows this effect particularly clearly. By giving an originally disparate group of communities, tribes and states a means of forging contacts and by fostering interaction within the peninsula the Romans not only created an unprecedented military machine, they also contributed to the formation of a new Italian identity which enabled their allies to unite against their masters in the Social War.[77] Many factors that contributed to this development in Italy, such as the status of Italians and Romans in provinces overseas and the role of Latin as a means of communication and identification in a multilingual environment, have no parallels on the Peloponnese. The states and ethnic

---

[75] Xenophon *Hellenica* 7.4.33–7.5.3.
[76] Pretzler 1999.
[77] Keaveney 1987:3–39.

groups within Sparta's league were culturally and politically less hetero-geneous to begin with, but as in Italy, decades of membership in a highly active military alliance were bound to promote communication between member states and increase the allies' experience with war and politics on a scale that a small *polis* could hardly have allowed them to gain. The activi-ties of the Peloponnesian league, particularly in the Peloponnesian War, also contributed to the prosperity of Arcadian cities because on one hand the region was never a major theatre of the war, while on the other hand Sparta's allies were probably entitled to a share of the booty acquired in successful campaigns.[78]

At first glance the Spartans were apparently not interested in the large regional and ethnic groups to which their allies belonged; in fact, it has been claimed that they deliberately followed a policy of "divide and rule." The league was organized by member states, namely cities and small tribal communities: Sparta made treaties with individual states,[79] troops were usually recruited by community, not by region, and the phalanx was apparently not composed along ethnic lines.[80] However, in practice regional or ethnic links between allies would have played an important role, espe-cially on campaign. Contingents supplied by small member states could be so small that on their own they could hardly make up an effective section of the phalanx, especially when Sparta did not need the full strength of its allied army and commanded its members just to send a proportion of their full force. Such small contingents would have been dependent on close co-operation and personal acquaintance with men from other cities just to ensure the cohesion necessary to keep the phalanx together.[81] In the fifth century league campaigns became almost an annual event, and it is likely that fighting and campaigning with other Peloponnesians fostered cohesion among Sparta's allies.

How, then, would this contribute to Arcadian identity specifically? The region contained a particularly large number of very small states which would need to be organized in manageable units, and smaller *ethne* within Arcadia, especially Parrhasians, Mainalians, Eutresians, and Kynourians, may have been treated as units, although they did also contain *poleis* which

---

[78] Callmer 1943:98–99.

[79] Tausend 1992:174, de Ste Croix 1972:106–116, Kagan 1969:13–30, Kahrstedt 1922:81–82.

[80] E.g. Plataea: Herodotus 9.28.3–31.5, cf. 9.26.1–2; cf. Plutarch *Moralia* 193B; Pritchett 1974:190, 194–199, Hanson 1999:205–208.

[81] Hanson 1989:117–123; allied armies could find it difficult to achieve cohesion within the phalanx: Pritchett 1974:190–193, 206.

may have had individual treaties with Sparta.[82] Ancient authors sometimes group together all Arcadians—or at least those from the smaller cities—when they speak of the contingents making up Peloponnesian forces, and this might reflect actual practice within the league.[83] There is also some evidence that at times, when they seemed useful for organizational purposes, major regional units were also acknowledged by the Spartans. For example, according to Thucydides the league levied ships by region in 412 BCE, and Diodorus suggests a regional organization of league troops in the early 370s BCE.[84]

The league gave the Arcadians experience in warfare beyond the means of individual cities, which may explain the efficiency of federal Arcadian troops (the *Eparitai*) especially mentioned by Xenophon; the new state's commanders and individual soldiers could already draw on the experience in large scale warfare.[85] A similar effect also seems to be apparent in Xenophon's *Anabasis*: by 400 BCE the Arcadians among the Ten Thousand showed a group cohesion that seems surprising in a particular section of a mixed army of mercenaries. Although they came from various cities, and were probably originally recruited through different commanders, they fought together in an organized contingent (called τὸ Ἀρκαδικὸν), and they made their own decisions by casting votes in an assembly.[86] This organized group knows how to argue its Arcadian case, using superior numbers and military prowess as an argument, just as Lycomedes of Mantinea does in the speech discussed at the beginning of this paper,[87] and as Arcadians may quite possibly also have done when they were on campaign with the Peloponnesian League. They were also willing to work together with other Peloponnesians, for example Eleans or Achaeans, while at the same time displaying a certain hostility towards Spartans, and, more explicitly, against

---

[82] The Mainalians sent troops to fight with the Spartans in 418 BCE, Thucydides 5.67.1. On individual cities within these tribes see Roy 1972d 48–49; e.g. Thucydides 5.33.2 (*poleis* in Parrhasia), Xenophon *Hellenica* 6.5.12 (Eutaia in Mainalia); see also Pausanias 8.3.1–4, 8.27.3–14, 8.28.1.

[83] E.g. Herodotus 7.202, 8.72; Thucydides 5.60.3 5.57; Nielsen 2002:153.

[84] Thucydides 8.3.2, Diodorus 15.31.2.

[85] Xenophon *Hellenica* 7.4.19–27; cf. Diodorus 15.62.1–2, 15.67.2. Note that the number and exact nature of the Arcadian federal troops is disputed. Parke 1933:92–93, Pritchett 1974:223, Thompson 1983:154–158.

[86] Xenophon *Anabasis* 4.8.18–19, 6.4.10–11; Roy 1967:296–309. See also Roy 2004, esp. 272–276, Hornblower 2004.

[87] Xenophon *Anabasis* 6.2.9–11, cf. Xenophon *Hellenica* 7.1.23.

non-Peloponnesians.[88] As we have already seen, these Arcadians also knew how to express and celebrate their common regional identity within a multinational group of other Greeks and non-Greeks.[89] It seems likely that this particularly Arcadian, and to an extent Peloponnesian (Elean, Achaean), behavior was influenced by a long experience of service within the large, mixed armies of the Peloponnesian League.

Membership in the Peloponnesian League also meant participation in league assemblies where members could discuss and influence the common course of action. Although the league was nominally a set of alliances between Sparta and individual cities, fellow members did work together, and cities could seek support among members for particular causes, as shown by Corinth's canvassing just before the outbreak of the Peloponnesian War.[90] Among the members of the league, the Arcadians with their many communities constituted the biggest ethnic block. This does not mean that they automatically decided and voted along ethnic lines, but the negotiation of supraregional policies in this context may also have contributed to a recognition of common interests, especially among the smaller cities. Could an "Arcadian" claim to Lasion have been made in this context?[91] The Peloponnesian League was quite possibly the first arena for Arcadian arguments in a wider, "international" political context.

The Spartans were certainly aware and often wary of ethnic groups within their league. They were willing to back an ethnic state in Triphylia where it could serve their own ends, but they were clearly aware of the danger that such an ethnic movement could pose for themselves and their league. In Arcadia traditional rivalries between cities offered good opportunities to control the rise of a comprehensive anti-Spartan pan-Arcadian movement. Some cities were evidently more worried about their nearest neighbors than about Sparta, for example Orchomenos and Tegea who were often willing to back whoever was fighting their common neighbor Mantinea. In the fifth century both Tegea and Mantinea managed to assemble sizeable anti-Spartan coalitions but neither succeeded in uniting the whole region.[92] In 418 BCE the Tegeans were apparently on the verge of civil war in favor of the pan-Arcadian, anti-Spartan cause. Sparta recognized the imminent

---

[88] Xenophon *Anabasis* 6.1.30, 6.2.9–10.

[89] Xenophon *Anabasis* 1.2.10 (Lykaia), cf. 6.1.11 (Arcadian dances).

[90] Thucydides 1.119–120.

[91] Xenophon *Hellenica* 3.2.30.

[92] Herodotus 9.35, Thucydides 4.1.134; Nielsen 2002:367–374.

danger of a united Arcadia and acted immediately and with full force.[93] In the following period, before the battle of Leuctra, Mantinea continued to be the main proponent of Arcadian and anti-Spartan sentiments, while Sparta relied on a number of loyal cities, presumably ruled by elites whose security depended on the hegemon, to prevent regional co-operation from getting out of hand. Once the King's Peace gave Sparta a free hand, she disbanded Mantinea into villages which were obliged to send separate army contingents on league campaigns. This drastic action may have been intended as a clear Spartan message against the pressure for larger regional units in general, and pan-Arcadian aspirations in particular. As the developments after the Spartan defeat at Leuctra showed, however, the time for regional/ethnic politics had definitely come.

Conclusions

The Arcadian bid for independence from Sparta in 370 BCE spelled the end of Sparta's role as a major power in Greece. Within about a year the Arcadians transformed their region of heterogeneous communities into a sophisticated federal state. There is no doubt that this movement was founded upon an appeal to a well-defined sense of Arcadian identity.

In spite of the very fragmentary sources we can trace the development of Arcadian identity back into the archaic period when communities in a region recognized as a distinct entity by outsiders started to develop a common sense of self. This regional identity existed alongside a set of numerous local community identities. For most of the late archaic and classical periods before 370 BCE these communities were members of the Peloponnesian League which was, in fact, the only political organization that united them all, albeit within a much larger framework that also included many other states. In the fifth century Tegea and Mantinea created regional leagues within this framework, and it is likely that both used Arcadian rhetoric to gain support. Neither managed to unite all of Arcadia, but they quickly came into conflict with Sparta.

After its conflicts with leagues of Arcadians and other ethnic-regional groupings within its alliance in the fifth century, Sparta was wary of such activities and tried to control anti-Spartan—and therefore presumably also regional—sentiments, which probably only strengthened the sense of a common Arcadian identity. These were ideal circumstances for the develop-

---

[93] Thucydides 5.64.1–2.

ment of an explicitly anti-Spartan pan-Arcadian rhetoric which was crucial for unification after the battle of Leuctra. It took the removal of Spartan control, the very factor that had been so instrumental in the development of Arcadian identity, to create a functioning political movement that encompassed the whole region. In the absence of that cohesive factor, namely Sparta as an enemy all Arcadians could agree on, that unity was very short-lived indeed.

Bibliography

Andrewes, A. 1952. "Sparta and Arcadia in the Early Fifth Century." *Phoenix* 6:1–5.

Bergese, L. B. 1995. *Tra ethne e poleis. Pagine di storia arcade.* Pisa.

Borgeaud, P. 1988. *The Cult of Pan in Ancient Greece.* Chicago. Translated by K. Atlass and J. M. Redfield.

Braunert, H. and Petersen, T. 1972. "Megalopolis: Anspruch und Wirklichkeit." *Chiron* 2:57–90.

Callmer, C. 1943. *Studien zur Geschichte Arkadiens bis zur Gründung des arkadischen Bundes.* Lund.

Demand, N. H. 1990. *Urban Relocation in Archaic and Classical Greece: Flight and Consolidation.* Bristol.

Dowden, K. 1992. *The Uses of Greek Mythology.* London.

Dubois, L. 1986. *Recherches sur le Dialecte Arcadien.* Louvain-La-Neuve.

Dušanić, S. 1970. *Arkadski Savez IV Veka.* Belgrade.

Fields, N. 2001. "Et Ex Arcadia Ego." *AHB* 15.3:102–130.

Hall, J. M. 1995. "The Role of Language in Greek Enthicities." *PCPhS* 41:83–100.

Hall, J. M. 1997. *Ethnic Identity in Greek Antiquity.* Cambridge.

Hanson, V. D. 1989. *The Western Way of War.* New York.

Hanson, V. D. 1999. "Hoplite Obliteration: The Case of the Town of Thespiai." *Ancient Warfare. Archaeological Perspectives* (eds. J. Carman and A. Harding) 203–477. Gloucestershire.

Head, B. V. 1911. *Historia Numorum.* Oxford. Second Edition.

Hejnic, J. 1961. *Pausanias the Perieget and the Archaic History of Arcadia,* Rozpravy Československé Akademie věd Řada společenských věd, Roč. 71. sešit 17. Prague.

Hornblower, S. 1990. "When was Megalopolis Founded?" *ABSA* 85:71–77.

Hornblower, S. 2004. "'This was Decided' (*edoxe tauta*): The Army as *polis* in Xenophon's *Anabasis*." In Lane Fox 2004:243–263.

Jost, M. 1973. "Pausanias en Mégalopolitide." *REA* 75:241–267.

Jost, M. 1985. *Sanctuaires et cultes d'Arcadie.* Etudes Péloponnésiennes 9. Paris.

Kagan, D. 1969. *The Outbreak of the Peloponnesian War.* London.

Kahrstedt, U. 1922. *Griechisches Staatsrecht I.* Göttingen.

Keaveney, A. 1987. *Rome and the Unification of Italy.* London.

Kraay, C. M. 1976. *Archaic and Classical Greek Coins.* London.

Lane Fox, R. ed. 2004. *The Long March: Xenophon and the Ten Thousand.* New Haven.

Larsen, J. A. O. 1968. *Greek Federal States.* Oxford.

Leahy, D. M. 1955. "The Bones of Tisamenus." *Historia* 4:26–38.

Loraux, N. 2006. *The Invention of Athens: The Funeral Oration in the Classical City.* Second edition, New York.

Ma, J. 2004. "You Can't Go Home Again. Displacement and Identity in Xenophon's *Anabasis.*" In Lane Fox 2004:330–345.

Moggi, M. 1976. *I sinecismi interstatali greci. Vol. I: Dalle origini al 338 a. C.* Pisa.

Nielsen, T. H. 1996. "Was there an Arkadian Confederacy in the Fifth Century?" *More Studies in the Ancient Greek Polis* (eds. M. H. Hansen and K. Raaflaub) 39–62. Stuttgart.

Nielsen, T. H. 2002. *Arkadia and its Poleis in the Archaic and Classical Periods.* Göttingen.

Nielsen, T. H., and Roy, J. eds. 1999. *Defining Ancient Arkadia.* Copenhagen.

Niese, B. 1899. "Beiträge zur Geschichte des Arkadischen Bundes: 2. Wann ward Megalopolis gegründet?" *Hermes* 34:527–542.

Nilsson, M. P. 1972. *Cults, Myths, Oracles, and Politics in Ancient Greece.* Lund.

Osborne, R. G. 1996. *Greece in the Making 1200–479 BCE.* London.

Parke, H. W. 1933. *Greek Mercenary Soldiers: From the Earliest Times to the Battle of Ipsos.* Oxford.

Parker, R. 2004. "One man's Piety: The Religious Dimension of the *Anabasis.*" In Lane Fox 2004:131–153.

Pretzler, M. 1999. "Myth and History at Tegea: Local Tradition and Community Identity." In Nielsen and Roy 1999:89–129.

Pretzler, M. 2005. "Polybius to Pausanias: Arkadian Identity in the Roman Empire." *Ancient Arkadia* (ed. E. Østby) 521–531. Athens.

Pretzler, M. 2007. *Pausanias: Travel Writing in Ancient Greece.* London.

Pritchett, W. K. 1974. *The Greek State at War II.* Berkeley.

Richter, G. M. A. 1939. "Greek Bronzes Recently Acquired by the Metropolitan Museum of Art." *AJA* 43:189–201.

Roy, J. 1967. "The Mercenaries of Cyrus." *Historia* 16:287–323.

Roy, J. 1968. "The Sons of Lykaon in Pausanias' Arcadian King-List." *ABSA* 63:287–292.

Roy, J. 1971. "Arcadia and Boeotia in Peloponnesian Affairs." *Historia* 20:569–599.

Roy, J. 1972a. "An Arcadian League in the Earlier Fifth Century BCE?" *Phoenix* 26:334–341.

Roy, J. 1972b. "Arcadian Nationality as seen in Xenophon's *Anabasis.*" *Mnemosyne* 25:129–136.

Roy, J. 1972c. "Orchomenus and Clitor." *CQ* 22: 78–80.

Roy, J. 1972d. "Tribalism in Southwestern Arkadia in the Classical Period." *Acta Antiqua Academiae Scientiarum Hungaricae* 20:43–51.

Roy, J. 1974. "Postscript on the Arcadian League." *Historia* 23:505–507.

Roy, J. 1999. "The Economies of Arkadia." In Nielsen and Roy 1999:320–381.

Roy, J. 2001. "Arcadia—How Far From the Greek Miracle?" *Gab es das Griechische Wunder? Griechenland zwischen dem Ende des 6. und der Mitte des 5. Jahrhunderts v. Chr.* (eds. D. Papenfuß and M. Strocka) 263–275. Mainz.

Roy, J. 2004. "The Ambitions of a Mercenary." In Lane Fox 2004:264–288.

Ruggeri, C. 2000. "Note sulle divergenze tra le iscrizioni della Trifilia e dell'Elide." *ZPE* 133:117–121.

Smith, A. D. 1986. *The Ethnic Origins of Nations.* Oxford.

de Ste Croix, G. E. M. 1972. *The Origins of the Peloponnesian War.* London.

Striano, A. 1991. "Remarques sur le prétendu sous-dialecte de la Triphylie." *Achaia und Elis in der Antike* (ed. A. D. Rizakis) 139–143. Athens.

Tausend, K. 1992. *Amphiktyonie und Symmachie. Formen zwischenstaatlicher Beziehungen im archaischen Griechenland.* Stuttgart.

Thompson, W. E. 1983. "Arkadian Factionalism in the 360's." *Historia* 32:149–172.

van der Valk, M. 1958. "On Apollodori *Bibliotheca.*" *REG* 71:100–168.

Voyatzis, M. E. 1999. "The Role of Temple Building in Consolidating Arkadian Communities." In Nielsen and Roy 1999:130–168.

Wallace, W. P. 1954. "Kleomenes, Marathon, the Helots, and Arkadia." *JHS* 74:32–35.

Welwei, K.-W. 2004. "Orestes at Sparta: the Political Significance of the Grave of the Hero." *Spartan Society* (ed. T. Figueira) 219–230. Swansea.

Williams, R. T. 1965. *The Confederate Coinage of the Arcadians in the Fifth Century BCE.* New York.

VII

Messenian Ethnicity and the Free Messenians
Nino Luraghi[*]

THE BIRTH OF AN INDEPENDENT POLITY in Messenia, in what used to be the western part of the Spartan state, represents the most conspicuous change that the ethnic revival of the early fourth century brought to the political map of the Peloponnese. Although both its extension and its internal structure varied in the following centuries in ways that are difficult to appreciate precisely,[1] the new Messenian polity surpassed in magnitude and long-term resilience all the new ethnic and political entities that emerged in those years. Observing the symbolic expressions of the new polity and the ways in which it positioned itself on the cultural map of Greece and found its place in the shared past of the Greeks, we gain insights into the dynamic mixture of tradition and innovation that always accompanies ethnogenesis. Furthermore, the controversial history of the Messenians between the sixties of the fifth century and the age of Epaminondas offers a unique opportunity to observe the interaction of ethnicity and international politics in classical Greece.

1. Messenians in the Fifth Century

After the disappearance of their predecessors sometime during the archaic period, the fifth century saw the return of the Messenians to the political landscape of Greece. To be sure, they did not appear at first in the area they were most closely associated with, the area we are used to calling Messenia.

[*] The present contribution forms a part of a wider project, which has meanwhile appeared in book form (Luraghi 2008). The author wishes to thanks the participants to the Münster conference and the anonymous referee for their helpful comments.
[1] After Roebuck 1941, see now Grandjean 2003, with groundbreaking work on the numismatic evidence.

The first polity that called itself "the Messenians" arose in Sicily, on the site of the ancient Chalcidian colony of Zancle, which was re-founded in 488 or thereabouts by the tyrant of Rhegion Anaxilaos and called Messene. The name of the new colony was apparently part of a broader cultural policy implemented by the tyrant, who considered himself of Messenian descent, to promote the Messenian element in his own city and cut Rhegion loose from its Chalcidian heritage.[2] The new Messenian identity that emerged on the Straits of Messina shows elements that would remain characteristic of the Messenian identity for centuries to come.[3] In other ways, though, this first manifestation of the Messenian identity was different from what came after. Most strikingly, all early documents emanating from this new polity, including its coins and dedications of war booty at Olympia, call its citizens *Messênioi*, using the Ionic form of the ethnic instead of the Doric form *Messanioi*. This probably means that Dorianism had not yet been recognized as a necessary component of the Messenian identity, as it later would.[4]

After the earthquake that shattered the southern Peloponnese in the sixties of the fifth century, a new group calling itself "the Messenians" emerged, and this time it was in Messenia. This group was formed by Helots and *perioikoi* who seceded from Sparta. Ultimately their revolt failed and the rebels, after resisting for many years entrenched on Mount Ithome, had to surrender to the Spartans, but they did so from a relatively strong position, and were able at least to gain the right to leave the Peloponnese. The Athenians settled them in Naupaktos in Ozolian Locris, where the Messenians remained for more than half a century, until after the end of the Peloponnesian War.[5] During the *pentekontaetia*, the Messenians of Naupaktos seem to have been involved in various campaigns in Northwestern Greece,[6]

---

[2] Rhegion was supposedly a joint Chalcidian-Messenian colony; see Luraghi 1994:193–215 with further references.

[3] Most conspicuously, the adoption of modified forms of Spartan cults and myths; see e.g. Luraghi 1997 on the cult of Artemis.

[4] As suggested by Hall 2003:154n62. Note however that the dedications of weapons by the Methanioi strongly suggest that the idea that the Messenians were actually Dorians originated in Messenia itself, in connection with the fifth-century revolt at the latest; see Luraghi 2001a:288–289. For the use of the ethnic in the Ionic form by the Messenians of Sicily, see the dedications of weapons in Olympia SEG 24.313, 314 (victory over the Mylaioi, soon after the foundation, Luraghi 1994:213), 304, 305 (victory over the Locrians, before 477 BCE, Luraghi 1994:216) and Mikythos' dedications, IvO 267–269 (after 467 BCE, Luraghi 1994:226). On coins, the shift from the Ionic to the Doric form seems to occur around 450 BCE, Caccamo Caltabiano 1993:67–69.

[5] On the revolt following the earthquake, see Luraghi 2001a.

[6] See Freitag 1996:78–82; Jacquemin and Laroche 1982:198–199.

but their most prominent deeds were performed during the Peloponnesian War. Besides participating in Demosthenes' campaign in Aetolia in 426,[7] the Messenians played a decisive part in forcing the surrender of the Spartiates blockaded on the island of Sphacteria during the Pylos campaign.[8] For more than a decade, from the Spartan surrender on Sphacteria in the summer of 425 until 408, with an interval of two years,[9] Pylos was garrisoned by Messenians from Naupaktos, later joined by Helots and possibly *perioikoi* who had deserted from both Messenia and Laconia. Meanwhile, Messenians from Naupaktos participated in the Sicilian expedition, summoned by Demosthenes in 413 (Thucydides 7.31.2) and, under Conon's guidance, in the repression of the pro-Spartan faction in Corcyra in 410 (Diodorus 13.48).

Clearly, after they left the Peloponnese under the truce that ended the revolt, the Messenians acted as a political community—a *polis* on the move. Their situation was highly peculiar. We cannot tell under precisely what conditions they held Naupaktos, but it is clear that they did not consider it their real residence. A recently published inscription from Naupaktos records some sort of agreement between Messenians and Naupaktians, who appear to be acting as two independent political communities, living side by side.[10] This confirms what could be inferred, although with less certainty, from the dedicatory inscription of the Nike of Paionios (see below), which called the dedicators "Messenians and Naupaktians." The Messenians did not see themselves as colonists, founding a new city, witness the fact that they did not change their own name or the name of the place where they settled. Neither were they prepared simply to dissolve into the local, pre-existing political community: far from becoming Naupaktians or renaming their new place of residence "Messene," the Messenians conceived of them-selves as a polity in exile, temporarily displaced, obviously in hopes of being able eventually to return to their real fatherland in the Peloponnese. The way in which historians occasionally designate them, *hoi Messênioi hoi en Naupaktôi*, captures this peculiar situation very clearly.[11]

---

[7] Thucydides 3.94–98; see also 3.105–113. Note that, according to Thucydides, it was the Messenians who urged Demosthenes to undertake the campaign and offered advice. Collaboration between Demosthenes and the Messenians of Naupaktos would continue in the Pylos campaign.

[8] Thucydides 4.36.

[9] From the late summer of 421 to the winter of 419; see Thucydides 5.35.6–7 and 5.56.2–3.

[10] Matthaiou and Matrokostas 2000–2003.

[11] Thucydides 2.9.4, Diodorus 12.60.1.

Beside their seeing themselves as a *polis* in exile, there was another aspect that made the Messenians untypical: they were in a sense an open-ended polity. All the Helots and *perioikoi* who succeeded in joining them became themselves Messenian, regardless of where exactly in *Lakonikê* they came from. When the Athenians agreed to withdraw the Messenian garrison from Pylos in 421, Thucydides (5.35.7) describes those who were evacuated as Messenians, Helots and others who had deserted from the *Lakonikê*, and adds that they were settled on the island of Cephallenia. By 401, all these people were recognized as Messenians.[12]

The new Messenians already show signs of a condition that will affect Messenians for centuries to come, a chronic need to make up for their previous absence from the stage of Greek history. To their inherent weakness in terms of Panhellenic clout the Messenians reacted with what has been aptly called "a virtual *Blitzkrieg* of self-assertion,"[13] appropriately conducted in the Panhellenic sanctuaries. Their victory in a campaign in northwestern Greece was commemorated at Delphi by an extraordinarily conspicuous offer, a triangular pillar of marble, seven meters and a half tall, decorated by two rows of bronze shields and probably topped by a bronze tripod supported by a marble statue.[14] Then, probably immediately after the Peace of Nicias, their most memorable monument was erected, the statue of Nike by the sculptor Paionios of Mende, again on a tall triangular pillar, right in front of the temple of Zeus at Olympia. This time, the defeated enemies, not explicitly mentioned in the dedicatory inscription, certainly included the Spartans, and the most conspicuous deed celebrated by this monument was the Messenians' participation in the campaign of Pylos.[15]

---

[12] Cf. Diodorus 14.34.2. Notice that Thucydides gives signs of not being inclined to take too seriously the Messenian identity of this motley crew, witness his use of the expression "those who are now called the Messenians" (7.57.8). He was not alone in his moderately pro-Spartan take on the Messenian question: as we know from the Attic *stêlai*, Alcibiades' uncle Axiochus, one of the Hermocopids, had named one of his slaves *Messênios*, and since it is quite unlikely that the man was really a Messenian, his name must have been a sarcastic statement about the true nature of "those who are now called the Messenians" (see Rosivach 1999:129n3).

[13] Figueira 1999:215.

[14] Jacquemin and Laroche 1982:192–199, who suggest a date before the thirty-years peace. The dedicatory inscription is SEG 32.550.

[15] For the dedicatory inscription, see Meiggs-Lewis 74. The best study of the monument is still Hölscher 1974, especially helpful on the political implications of the dedication and the Spartans' reaction to it, which confirms that they perceived the monument as a challenge.

It is the Messenians' never-forgotten aspiration to win back their father-land, and not only their consistent loyalty to Athens, that explains why, after the end of the Peloponnesian War, after the successful conclusion of their campaign against Elis, the Spartans decided to evict the Messenians from Naupaktos and from a fortress they occupied on the island of Cephallenia. In 401, according to Diodorus (14.34.2–5), faced by the Spartan onslaught, the Messenians left Naupaktos and Cephallenia with their weapons. Some of them moved to Sicily, to fight as mercenaries for Dionysius the First, but the majority, some three thousand according to Diodorus, went to Cyrene, where they helped the Cyrenaean aristocracy to return to the city from which they had been recently exiled.[16] A few years later, Dionysius settled six hundred Messenian mercenaries in Messana, which he was founding anew after the city had been laid waste by the Carthaginians in 397. Then, however, afraid of annoying his allies the Spartans, the Syracusan tyrant decided to relocate the Messenians to another place, still in Messana's territory. There they founded the city of Tyndaris, a fortress in an important strategic position, defending the approach to Messana along the northern coast of Sicily (Diodorus 14.78.4–6).[17] But the Messenian diaspora must have spread even wider than this. As we happen to know from the *Hellenica of Oxyrhynchus* (15.3), the personal guard of the exiled Athenian admiral Conon was formed by Messenians, too.[18]

The Messenian experience in the second half of the fifth century had shown that Messenian ethnicity could pose a serious threat to Sparta, as underlined both by the expulsion of the Messenians in 401 and, earlier, by the Spartans' insistence in 421 on having among the conditions of the peace the removal of the Messenians from Pylos, even if the Athenians kept a garrison there. It is not clear to what extent the Athenians themselves real-

---

[16] As usual with numbers provided by Greek historians, it is difficult to decide what to do with Diodorus' data. At any rate, Diodorus seems to refer to men of fighting age, and the impression that the largest contingent of the Messenian diaspora was the one that took the route to North Africa is supported by Pausanias (4.26.2), who however says that they went to Euhesperides not Cyrene.

[17] It should not go unnoticed that the name of the new city implies a claim to the Tyndarids, traditionally seen as Spartan (a similar claim in Pausanias 3.26.3 and 4.31.9); this is confirmed by the iconography of the first coins of the new city, which show Helen and the Dioscuri. See Consolo Langher 1965. We have here one example of the construction of a Messenian identity that was based on disputing traditional elements of the Spartan heritage; for more, see below.

[18] The anonymous referee suggests the likely possibility that these Messenians were Messenian-Naupaktian marines from the Ionian War who had stayed loyal to Conon after Aigospotamoi.

ized what kind of weapon against the Spartans the Messenians represented, and to what extent they were willing to make full use of it;[19] certainly, the lesson was not lost on the Argives, who in 419 urged the Athenians to bring back the Messenians to Pylos, alleging that the Spartans had violated the conditions of the peace (Thucydides 5.56.2). The Argives had been enemies of the Spartans for centuries, and they may have had a better appreciation of Peloponnesian politics and of the strengths and weaknesses of the Spartans.[20]

From the revolt to the final expulsion of the Messenians from Naupaktos and Cephallenia, the Spartans' attitude to them changed in an important way. The conditions under which the rebels had left Ithome show that the Spartans back then were unwilling to treat them as anything but fugitive slaves.[21] However, the fact that they did not try to enslave the Messenians in 401 implies some redefinition of their views on the identity of these people. One could certainly see here one more expression of the realism for which the Spartans were famous: a community that had lived free for some five decades, with an uninterrupted record of mostly victorious fighting, could not easily be reduced to slavery again without the danger of provoking a massive revolt. However, this change of attitude, dictated by sheer political realism as it may have been, should not be seen as trivial. Some of the Messenians whom the Spartans were evicting from Naupaktos and Cephallenia had been Helots only a few years earlier.

2. Free Messene and Its Liberators

After the foundation of Tyndaris in 396, the sources are completely silent as to the whereabouts of the Messenians for more than two decades. Then, as if from nowhere, came the liberation of Messenia by the allied army led by Epaminondas into the southern Peloponnese in the fall of 370/69. After invading and ravaging Laconia, the army, formed by the Boeotians and their central Greek allies, and by Arcadians, Eleans, and Argives, marched into Messenia. There, Epaminondas founded an independent Messenian state, whose pivotal point was a large fortified settlement at the foot of Mount Ithome.[22] The choice of the site made sense in a number of ways. Mount

---

[19] Lewis 1977:28.

[20] Further indications of the Argives' awareness that Messenia could be turned into Sparta's Achilles' heel are discussed below.

[21] Thucydides 1.103.1 and Figueira 1999:234–235.

[22] For a detailed reconstruction of the campaign, with references to sources and bibliography, see Buckler 1980:70–90.

Ithome has a central position in Messenia, overlooking both the Stenyklaros plain to the north and the lower Pamisos valley to the south. It was within easy reach of Arcadia by way of the Derveni pass, and accordingly, it could be defended in case of a Spartan counterattack, which was definitely to be expected. Moreover, the site had important symbolic overtones. Even though the legends of the Messenian resistance in the archaic period that we find in Pausanias probably originated later, Mount Ithome was associated with the revolt against Sparta in the fifth century. If there was a monument of Messenian resistance, that was Mount Ithome.

The creation of a free polity in Messenia was a striking development, and one wonders who conceived this rather bold plan. Objectively speaking, the final result of the campaign of 370/69, with Sparta still alive but crippled, suited the interests of the Thebans better than those of the other allies. Epaminondas' personal initiative is stressed in the sources (e.g. Diodorus 15.66.1) and should probably be seen behind a decision that was going to have important consequences both for the initial survival of Messene and for the history of Messenia for centuries to come, the decision to fortify Ithome. Still standing today for long stretches, the imposing fortification wall was the most impressive component of the city for an ancient visitor. Built in stone up to the top, nine kilometers long, it was a true masterpiece of military architecture, exploiting the nature of the terrain to the best effect. Pausanias (4.27.7) explicitly connects the construction of the wall with the liberation of Messenia, insisting that it was built in an extraordinarily short time, and recent studies have shown that in terms of architectural technique a date soon after the liberation of Messenia is likely. Comparison with other fortifications points to the involvement of Theban military architects in the enterprise.[23] This massive work betrays a realistic attitude towards the new polity's chances of survival if faced with a Spartan onslaught and without external help. Epaminondas must have thought that the Messenians simply had to be in a condition to resist long enough for a rescue army to reach them. The permanence of a strong garrison in the city once Epaminondas left (Diodorus 15.67.1) confirms this point. However, both on a symbolic and on a material level, the imposing walls of Ithome defined in a new way the status of this settlement vis-à-vis the rest of Messenia and the Greek world at large.

---

[23] By far the most detailed investigation of the fortifications of Messene is provided by Müth-Herda 2005:42–139. I would like to thank Silke Müth-Herda for providing me with a copy of her dissertation.

Beyond this, it is unclear to what extent Theban initiative left its mark on the new polity. Some sources call Epaminondas its founder, but they may be taken as speaking in a rather loose and unspecific sense. Much later, Ithome—by that time calling itself Messene—seems indeed to have worshipped Epaminondas as founder,[24] but there is no evidence that might suggest considering either Ithome or the whole Messenian polity as a colony of Thebes: none of the ties that normally existed between colonies and mother cities, such as common cults and names of tribes and other civic subdivisions, are documented in their case. This is not surprising, after all. As the Messenians saw it, the birth of their free state was in reality a restoration of something that was supposed to have existed in the past, not a foundation in the strict sense of the word, and the Thebans clearly concurred: the ancestral rights of the Messenians were the foundation of the legitimacy of the new polity, which correspondingly had to depict itself as the revival of something that had already existed in the past.

Beside the Thebans, Argives and Arcadians both appear to have played an important role in the rebirth of Messene. Pausanias (4.26.7) highlights the intervention of the Argive general Epiteles, chosen to lead an army from Argos to found Messene anew. Epiteles was pointed by a dream towards the place on Mount Ithome where, at the time of the final Spartan conquest of Messenia, the Messenian hero Aristomenes had buried a bronze hydria that contained the texts of the mysteries of the Great Goddesses of Andania. Much in this story shows signs of later elaboration. However, some support for Pausanias' depiction of the Argives' participation may come from the fact that one of the tribes of the new Messenian polity carried the name of the Argive Heraclid Daiphontes, like an Argive *phatra* also did (see below). Moreover, a number of clues seem to suggest that the Argives had been keenly aware for quite a while of the fact that rule over Messenia was the cornerstone of Spartan supremacy. The tradition about the division of the Peloponnese among the Heraclids, which implicitly questioned this situa-

---

[24] Pausanias mentions two statues of Epaminondas in Messene, one in the stoa of the Asklepieion, built approximately in the first half of second century BCE (see Chlepa 2001:79–80), the other in the *hierothusion* (Pausanias 4.31.10 and 32.1 respectively; see Themelis 2000:45). Especially the position of the former, among the main gods of Messene, suggests that the Theban general was regarded in some sense as the founder of the city. However, *pace* Leschhorn 1984:164–166, there is no evidence for a cult for Epaminondas in Messene. The facility with which the sentence "By my counsels ... holy Messene receives at last her children" from the epigram that accompanied Epaminondas' statue in Thebes (Pausanias 9.15.6) is paraphrased by Pausanias as "Epaminondas was the founder (*oikistês*) of Messene" (Pausanias 9.15.5; cf. also 14.5) is a warning.

tion, seems to have originated in Argos, possibly in the first decades of the fifth century,[25] and according to Thucydides (5.69.1) before the battle of Mantinea in 418 the Argive commanders fired up their troops by reminding them that they were fighting to reestablish *isomoiria*, that is, equality in the division of the Peloponnese—surely a reference to Sparta's domination over Cresphontes' lot, i.e. Messenia. Finally, as mentioned above, the Argives seem to have seen the point of having Messenians in Pylos better than the Athenians themselves had. But this is as close as we can get to definite proof that the liberation of Messenia was really an Argive idea.

In the first years after the liberation, the Arcadians were very active in campaigns that resulted in a significant expansion of the original territory of the free Messenians. They unsuccessfully attacked Asine, probably in the summer of 369/8 (Xenophon *Hellenica* 7.1.25), then conquered Kyparissia and Koryphasion, on the western coast of Messenia, in 365 (Diodorus 15.77.4), adding them to the Messenian territory. Much as the Arcadians were instrumental in the survival of the new polity, however, they had not spent the last two centuries waiting for the right moment to cut down the Spartan supremacy, as the Argives had. On the whole, it is probably correct to connect the Arcadians' role in the consolidation of Messene with the trend towards a more independent and self-conscious foreign policy on their part, a trend that Xenophon suggests was gaining strength during the sixties.[26]

3. The New Messenians: The Party Line(s)

Given that the legitimacy of the new polity depended on its being the restoration of an entity that had existed before, defining the identity of the new Messenians was crucial, and controversy on this point is to be expected. If the evidence we have is anything to go by, the parties involved in fact held radically divergent views of the identity of the citizens of the new polity.[27] For the Spartans, whose take on the issue can be reconstructed based on Isocrates' *Archidamos*, these people were their former slaves, unduly manumitted by the Thebans, and not the "true Messenians."[28] We are in no position to tell how accurately Isocrates reflects real Spartan views, our only guarantee being that those views were certainly known to Isocrates' audi-

---

[25] Luraghi 2001b.

[26] Pretzler, this volume.

[27] Dipersia 1974:54–61 collects the basic evidence; see also Grandjean 2003:54–57. For the Spartan and Theban views, see Asheri 1983:36–39 and Luraghi 2002:63.

[28] Isocrates *Archidamos* 28; as Dipersia 1974:58 subtly notes, this speaks to shared perceptions of slavery, trying to win for the Spartans the sympathy of the other Greeks.

ence.[29] One wonders who, in Isocrates' view, would have qualified as "the true Messenians." The Theban line, as reflected in statements attributed to Epaminondas by late sources and most explicitly in the epigram that accompanied his statue, again according to later sources, was that Messene had been liberated and repopulated by bringing back the Messenians from exile. This same view is found in sources that can for other reasons be expected to be more sensitive to the Theban line.[30]

One point needs emphasizing, because it has not always received the attention it deserves: according to the Theban version of the liberation of Messenia, there were no Messenians left in the region itself at the time of Epaminondas' campaign, which should imply that all descendants of the ancient Messenians had left the country after the revolt in the fifth century at the latest. This is made explicit in Pausanias, but is clearly presupposed by Diodorus and Plutarch as well. None of them speaks of liberation of Messenians living in Messenia, and for that matter, no ancient source does. Paradoxically, on this point the Thebans agreed with the Spartans, in that both denied, directly or by implication, that descendants of the once free Messenians lived in the region at the time of Epaminondas' expedition.

The rest of Greece seems to have taken these conflicting views of the identity of the new Messenians for the expressions of propaganda they were. The clearest evidence of this is provided by the Athenian orator Lycurgus. In his speech against Leocrates, delivered in 330 BCE, he mentioned Troy and Messene as two examples of cities that had been deserted by their inhabitants at some point in the past and never recovered. According to Lycurgus, five hundred years after its destruction Messene had been repopulated by people assembled randomly (*Against Leocrates* 62). Certainly Lycurgus did not intend to question the legitimacy of the free Messenian state, but he took for granted that the citizens of this state were not the descendants of the Messenians of the past, and he expected his audience to concur. Even Diodorus (15.66.1), an author who is clearly dependent on sources on the

---

[29] Jehne 1994:11n21 with further references. The fact that similar views are voiced by the Spartans in Xenophon, *Hellenica* 7.4.9 speaks moderately in favor of taking Isocrates' *Archidamos* as a reasonably reliable representation of Spartan views.

[30] The epigram is quoted in full only by Pausanias 9.15.6, but seems to have been quite well-known; Cicero, *Tusculan disputations* 5.17.49 quotes the first verse. The *grande rentrée* of the Messenians appears in Diodorus 15.66.6, in Plutarch's *Pelopidas* 24.5 and *Life of Agesilaos* 34.1, and, with fuller detail, in Pausanias 4.26.5, who specifies that Epaminondas summoned the Messenians from Italy, Sicily, and Euhesperides, where they had fled when the Spartans, after defeating Athens, had expelled them from Naupaktos.

whole not hostile to the Thebans, describes the foundation saying that Epaminondas, after summoning all the Messenians he could find, opened up citizen rights in the new city to whoever wished to partake of them.

4. The New Messenians: Facts on the Ground

It should be clear that both the Spartan and the Theban version of the identity of the Messenians were meant to underpin either side's take on the Messenian issue in the struggles that followed the liberation.[31] Although there may be some truth to each of them, neither can be taken as a reliable guide to what was happening on the ground. This leaves us in a difficult position, where the best we can do is to discuss the probability of different scenarios and different approaches.

In the first place, it will be helpful to look at the topography of the new Messenian state, since after all, when Messenia was liberated, it may have been less densely populated than other parts of the Peloponnese, but it was certainly not uninhabited. The city that was growing out of a pre-existing perioikic settlement by Mount Ithome was only a component of the new polity.[32] First of all, the Plain of Stenyklaros and the Soulima Valley, in all likelihood Spartiate land tilled and inhabited by Helots, certainly became part of free Messene, and probably, judging by later history, formed the territory of the new city of Ithome. Moreover, other perioikic settlements became part of Messene, although in some cases it is difficult to tell exactly when. According to Pausanias (4.26.5), Epaminondas had been told by a dream to give back to the Messenians "their fatherland and their *poleis*," and later Pausanias indeed refers briefly to the reconstruction of the "other *poleis*" as taking place parallel to the foundation of Ithome, which he anachronistically

---

[31] The return of Messene under Spartan control was the clause that pushed the Thebans to refuse the peace that Philiskos of Abydos was trying to broker in 368 (Xenophon *Hellenica* 7.1.27); the freedom of Messene was one of the requests of Pelopidas at Susa and one of the conditions of the peace the Thebans unsuccessfully tried to have the Greeks agree upon in 367 (Xenophon *Hellenica* 7.1.36, 7.1.39; Diodorus 15.81.3). See Jehne 1994:79–90, Grandjean 2003:65–67.

[32] Roebuck 1941:37n54 first realized that the new city itself was called Ithome, while Messene was the name of the new Messenian polity, which probably included more towns, former perioikic settlements, connected to Ithome in some sort of federation. Recently, Grandjean 2003:93–98 has argued against Roebuck; note however that the ethnic "Ithomaeans" is by far the most likely supplement for SEG 43.135 line 9, adding one more source to Roebuck's dossier. See also Plutarch *Pelopidas* 24.9, not considered by Grandjean, and compare the use of "Messene" as name of the region in fifth-century authors such as Pherecydes (fr. 117 Fowler = FGH 3 F 117), Hellanicus (fr. 124a and 125 Fowler = FGH 4 F 124 and 323a F 23), Euripides fr. 1083, and Aristophanes *Lysistrata* 1141

calls Messene (4.27.7). Only in the case of Korone, Kyparissia and Koryphasion is ancient evidence available. As noted above, the latter two were compelled to become part of Messene by the Arcadians in 365/4. Korone, according to Pausanias (4.34.5), was formerly called Aipeia and was founded anew when the Thebans brought the Messenians back to the Peloponnese. Its founder was the Boeotian Epimelides of Koroneia. The Arcadian onslaught on Asine, probably in the summer of 369/8, confirms that the western coast of the Messenian gulf north of Asine was not Lacedaemonian any more at that time. If Korone was really founded anew, however formally, it might parallel Ithome, which also rose on the site of a former perioikic town, one that had been the cradle of the revolt in the fifth century but seems nevertheless to have been in continuing existence in the second half of the century.[33]

More problematic is the fate of the important perioikic settlements east of the Pamisos, Thouria, Pharai and Kalamai. In the late first century BCE Kalamai apparently worshipped an Arcadian hero, which may point to some role played by the Arcadians in its joining Messene; if this were the case, 369 or the years immediately thereafter would be the most likely context.[34] In the case of Thouria, which had taken part in the revolt after the earthquake, definite evidence shows that it had become Messenian again by 322, but strong arguments suggest making it a part of free Messenia from the outset, especially its fortification wall, built in isodomic ashlar masonry in the early fourth century, using the same technique that was used also at Ithome.[35] On balance, the most likely assumption seems to be that at least Thouria and Pharai, and probably also Kalamai, were part of the new Messenian state from the beginning: even if they did not join it of their own free will—which

---

[33] Note that Pausanias' insistence on the fact that the city at the foot of Mount Ithome had no predecessors in the centuries before could betray the attempt to disguise the continuity between new Messenians and old *perioikoi*, and would match the representation of the new polity as formed totally by old Messenians returning from exile, which was the official Theban line.

[34] IG V 1.1370, lines 24–25. On Hippothoos see Pausanias 8.5.4; 10.3 (sacrilege and death) and especially 45.7 (Hippothoos depicted in the Calydonian hunt on the pediment of the mid-fourth century temple of Athena Alea, the most prominent monument of Tegea); there was a tribe Hippothoontis in Tegea, IG V 2.39 and 40, Pausanias 8.53.6. It should be noted however that a Spartan Hippothoos appears in the list of the sons of Hippokoon killed by Heracles given by Apollodorus (3.10.5).

[35] On the fortification walls of Thouria, see Hope Simpson 1966:123–124, whose chronology is to be revised in light of Müth-Herda 2005. For the likelihood that Thouria joined Messene in 369, see also Shipley 2004:566. Traces of offerings connected with one of the Bronze Age chamber tombs at Thouria, whose start coincides with the liberation of Messenia, would point in the same direction; see Chatzi-Spiliopoulou 2001.

is not at all unlikely considering Thouria's track record—the Thebans and their allies can scarcely have left these settlements alone, so close to Ithome and with no natural obstacles in between.

Of course, even if we could determine with certitude the territorial extension of free Messene, we would still not know exactly who formed its citizen body, for after all an exchange of population on a large scale cannot be ruled out *a priori*. However, a general look at the inhabitants of *Lakonikê* in the years before Epaminondas' expedition suggests that quite a few of them may not have needed a lot of persuasion to become citizens of the new polity. Unrest among the Helots is normally assumed, and with good reason, although the picture of universal revolt as soon as the Theban army invaded Laconia, found in some ancient sources (Xenophon *Hellenica* 7.2.2; *Life of Agesilaos* 2.24), is certainly exaggerated. After all, with Epaminondas just across the Eurotas as many as 6,000 Helots were ready to fight for Sparta in return for the promise to be liberated if they fought well (Xenophon *Hellenica* 6.5.29).[36] Among the *perioikoi*, not normally suspected of having a seditious disposition by modern scholars, discontent with the Spartiates must have been fairly widespread. According to Xenophon (*Hellenica* 6.5.25), an embassy of *perioikoi* had approached Epaminondas as he still hesitated to march into the Spartan territory, offering themselves as hostages and assuring the Theban that, if he only dared to march further, all the *perio-ikoi* would revolt against the Spartiates—already now, they said, they hardly responded when summoned to arms. At least some *perioikoi* really joined the invading army and participated in Epaminondas' campaign (*Hellenica* 6.5.32). Incidentally, these Laconian *perioikoi* must have formed part of the citizen-body of the new city, since they could hardly expect that the Spartans would leave them in peace as soon as the Theban army had left Laconia. On the other hand, perioikic settlements south of Sparta were laid waste by Epaminondas, and the harbor of Gytheion resisted the Theban onslaught (Xenophon *Hellenica* 6.5.32). In other words, it seems that the rifts in the Spartan state which became conspicuous on the occasion of Epaminondas' invasion were not clear-cut and did not simply run between Helots on the

---

[36] Although the measure was exceptional, the practice was not new. Between 425 and 369, the Spartans seem to have had recourse rather frequently to the recruitment of large contingents of Helots with the promise of freedom (after the campaign for which they had been recruited?), especially for expeditions abroad; these were the Neodamodeis, on whom see Ducat 1990:160–161. Cozzoli 1978:223–224 is probably right to suggest a connection between this phenomenon and Sparta's willingness to allow Dionysius the First to recruit large contingents of mercenaries among the Lacedaemonians (Diodorus 14.44.2; 58.1).

one side and Spartiates and *perioikoi* on the other, nor just between Laconia and Messenia.

In light of this, it is reasonable to assume that Helots and *perioikoi*, especially but not only from Messenia itself, contributed to the population of Messene, in proportions that we cannot quite determine, both with respect to one another and to any other component of the citizen body. An influx of inhabitants from outside the region is also likely. There may not have been too many Messenians of the diaspora among them: Tyndaris prospered after its foundation and there is no evidence that its population moved away in high numbers.[37] However, even if we do not assume an open invitation to join the new polity, as Diodorus seems to suggest, a suitably ecumenical approach could probably find "old Messenians" quite close to home: one of the earliest sources on the Second Messenian War, a passage from Callisthenes quoted by Polybius (4.33.5 = FGH 124 F 23), speaks of Messenian exiles finding refuge in Arcadia at that time, and it would not be surprising if their "descendants" were among the new Messenians.

In conclusion, we should not be too far from the truth in assuming the population of free Messene to have been comprised of former inhabitants of the region, free and unfree, refugees from Laconia, and settlers from abroad. A close look at their cults confirms the general accuracy of this conclusion and helps to some extent in defining the proportions.

5. Messenian Identity in the Fourth Century

The most revealing evidence on how the new Messenians articulated their identity comes from the names of their tribes. As a number of inscriptions from Ithome/Messene shows, the citizen body was divided into five tribes, called Hyllis, Kleolaia, Aristomachis, Kresphontis and Daiphontis.[38] The presence of two of these tribes at Thouria and possibly of one of them at Korone suggests that they applied to all the free Messenians, as one would expect anyway given the usual association between tribes and ethnic identity.[39] The names of the Messenian tribes are transparent. Hyllos was the son of Heracles, Kleolaios Hyllos' son and the father of Aristomachos, who was in his turn Kresphontes' father. Daiphontes was a Heraclid from Argos, who

---

[37] In favor of the presence of Messenians of the diaspora, see now Grandjean 2003:57.

[38] Jones 1987:146–148.

[39] On the tribes at Thouria, see IG V 1.1386, and Jones 1987:148–149. The tribe Kleolaia seems to be mentioned in an inscription from Petalidi, ancient Korone, which has been made known recently, SEG 48. 514 J; the second line should read]λεολαιας δευ[, as I could verify during a visit to the Benaki Museum in Kalamata in March 2005.

had married Temenos' daughter Hyrnetho. The choice of these heroes as eponymous for the tribes is remarkable. In the Greek world, the names of subdivisions of the citizen body were typically related to ethnic identity, although not in a systematic way: Dorians normally had the three ancestral tribes of the Pamphyloi, Hylleis, and Dymanes, and often a fourth one, and Argadeis, Aigikoreis, Geleontes, and Hopletes recurred in many Ionian cities, though rarely all together.[40] Considering that the Messenian revolt in the fifth century and the myth of the Dorian invasion had established the Messenians as members of the Dorian *ethnos*, we might have expected the new Messenians to adopt the names of the Dorian tribes, or at least some of them. Actually, this happened only in the case of the tribe Hyllis. The remaining names delineate a subtle and creative strategy of ethnic self-definition. Exploiting the ambivalence between Heraclids and Dorians in the traditions on the division of the Peloponnese, the Messenians were able to connect themselves to a supposed ancestral Heraclid heritage, which constituted the main mythic charter providing legitimacy to the new Messenian state,[41] while at the same time diverting attention from the Dorian identity they shared with the Spartans—a component of their ethnicity they could not altogether erase, since it had been emphasized by fifth-century Messenians.

However, the new tribal names went much further in placing the new political community on the mythic-historical map of Greece in a very precise way. Heraclid myths were particularly important at Argos. Daiphontes, eponymous of one of the Messenian tribes, was a very prominent character in Argive myth-history: he was Temenos' son-in-law and successor, *de facto* or only *in pectore* depending on the version of the myth. He was also the eponymous of a *phatra* at Argos, while another Argive *phatra* was named after Kleolaios.[42] Moreover, the Heraclid heritage formed a strong bond between the Messenians and their new protectors the Thebans: Heracles was a quintessentially Boeotian and more specifically Theban hero. His cult seems to have played a part in the initiation of the warriors of the Sacred Band, the elite Theban unit that had crushed the Spartan hoplites at Leuctra; right before the battle, allegedly the weapons dedicated in the temple of Heracles

---

[40] On Dorian and Ionian tribes, see Roussel 1976:193–263.

[41] Luraghi 2001b.

[42] On Daiphontes' genealogy, see Pausanias 2.19.1. Harder 1991:126–128 discusses various versions of his role in the succession to Temenos. On the *phatrai* of the Daiphontees and Kleodaidai at Argos see Piérart 1985:282–284. On the Argive *phatrai*, subdivisions of the tribes, see also Jones 1987:113.

at Thebes had disappeared, signifying that the hero himself was preparing to join the fight.[43] It is important to note that in exactly the same years the Argives themselves were emphasizing their Heraclid heritage to create a mythic connection with Thebes: the "hemicycle of the kings," a series of ten bronze statues dedicated at Delphi in the aftermath of the alliance between Thebes and Argos and the liberation of Messenia, depicted Heracles and his Argive ancestors all the way back to Danaos.[44] This parallel strengthens the idea that the Heraclid names of the Messenian tribes were meant to establish a connection with the mythic heritage of Thebes. The assemblage of eponymous heroes of the tribes showcased the ancestral claim of the Messenians to their fatherland, while at the same time emphasizing their mythic connections to Argos and Thebes. This peculiar mix of tradition and innovation, or rather this innovation disguised as the most ancestral of traits, defines fourth-century Messenian ethnicity in an important way.

The extremely consistent and slightly artificial picture offered by the Messenian tribes becomes more concrete and problematic once we compare it with the deities worshipped in post-liberation Messenia. In Greek culture, cults were associated with ethnicity at least as closely as tribal names were.[45] Messenian cults offer evidence for how the Messenians constructed their identity, and also how their identity may have been perceived by other Greeks.

Among the cults documented in Mavromati-Messene itself, only a few can be traced back to the age of the liberation. This is probably the case with the cult of Zeus Ithomatas, practiced in a sacred enclosure on the top of the mountain.[46] Archaeological evidence from there is scarce, but the very first coins struck by the Messenians show an image of Zeus Ithomatas, in an old-fashioned style that was probably meant to suggest some traditional pedigree for the new polity.[47] Material evidence going back to the fourth century is not abundant in the urban area, either, since the sanctuary of Asclepius

---

[43] The "miracle" is reported by Xenophon *Hellenica* 6.4.7; cf. Callisthenes FGH 124 F 22a, Diodorus 15.53.4, the latter crediting Epaminondas with engineering it. Note that the Herakles' Theban connections were made explicit at Messene in the assemblage of statues in the western *stoa* of the Hellenistic Asklepieion, where Herakles and the personification of the city of Thebes flanked Epaminondas; see Themelis 2000:43.

[44] See Pausanias 10.10.5 and, on the form and political meaning of the monument, Salviat 1965.

[45] On the pervasive connection between cults and ethnicity in Greek culture see Parker 1998:16–21.

[46] See Zunino 1997:103–107.

[47] Grandjean 2003:59–65.

was completely rebuilt at a later date, covering up to a large extent the traces of earlier phases. The cult in the archaic sanctuary omega-omega continues undisturbed from the archaic period to the late fourth or early third century, when the shrine was totally rebuilt, apparently after being destroyed by a fire. Some of the rather scanty evidence on the early architectural phases of the sanctuary may refer to new buildings erected at the time of the liberation of Messenia.[48] The cult of the Dioscuri is explicitly attested by a votive inscription on a bronze shield dating slightly before the destruction (SEG 45.302). It is not completely certain how far back this cult goes, but the iconography of the dedications would be consistent with their presence from early on. In other words, the cult of the Dioscuri may conceivably have been introduced in this sanctuary at the time of the liberation of Messenia, but it is at least as likely that it simply continued from the period before. The same can be said with more confidence of the kourotrophic deity whose cult is suggested by the iconography of archaic terracottas from the omega-omega sanctuary.[49] In the soundings south of the later temple of Asclepius traces of buildings and an altar have been found that can be connected with Epaminondas' foundation, but even here it is impossible to say with certainty, on the basis of the votives of classical date, which deity or deities were worshipped in this shrine. Asclepius is extremely likely to have been among them, given his importance in the later history of the sanctuary and the fact that anatomic ex-votos have been found among the materials associated with these early buildings.[50] Traces of cult go back to the archaic age, and it is ultimately only the fact that the cult of Asclepius was apparently expanding precisely in the late fifth and early fourth century that suggests that it may have been introduced here at the time of the liberation of Messenia. Also to be dated in the fourth century, probably close to 369, is a small prostyle temple dedicated to Artemis Orthia.[51]

Asclepius was still a new god in the early fourth century. Even though his early temple may not have been as uniquely prominent among the sanctuaries of the new city as the later Doric temple would be, it is fair to say that the location of his cult speaks in favor of its importance from the beginning. One of the traditions about Asclepius' birth connected it with Messenia, espe-

---

[48] See Themelis 1998:157–161
[49] Papaefthymiou 2001–2002.
[50] Themelis 2000:22–23.
[51] Themelis 1994:101–106.

cially with the eastern coast of the Messenian gulf,[52] and this could explain to some extent why he became part of the pantheon of the new city. Besides the popularity of the cult in the early fourth century, its relative novelty, and the traditions on the Messenian origin of the god, there may be one further reason for its introduction into the pantheon of the free Messenians. The center from which the cult of Asclepius spread was Epidauros, a long-standing object of Argive covetousness and therefore a staunch ally of Sparta, one of the very few that did not desert the Spartans after Leuctra.[53] One version of the myth of the Heraclids in the Argolid attributed the conquest of Epidauros to Daiphontes. By Pausanias' time at the latest, the Epidaurians had appropriated Daiphontes and his wife Hyrnetho, daughter of Temenos, but the quarrel between Argives and Epidaurians as to which city had Hyrnetho's tomb (Pausanias 2. 28.3–7) suggests that Daiphontes, too, was a likely object of dispute, in which case one can see the two sides interpreting in diverging ways Daiphontes' role at Epidaurus: founder for the Epidaurians, conqueror for the Argives. It would be tempting to see in the Messenian cult of Asclepius also the reflection of an attempt by the Argives to hijack the main god of their enemies the Epidaurians. However, given the fragmentary nature of the evidence, this hypothesis has to remain somewhat tentative.

Apart from the strongly Messenian Zeus Ithomatas and the probable newcomer Asclepius, the other cults documented at Ithome in the early fourth century have a striking point in common: an obvious connection with a Spartan heritage. This is hardly surprising in the case of the cults in the sanctuary omega-omega, which simply continued from the time before the liberation. Even in this case, the iconography of the terracotta plaques shows from the fifth century to the fourth no appreciable change that might suggest changes in the deities worshipped in the sanctuary.[54] If one of them was Artemis in her function of kourotrophic goddess, one may speculate about a connection with the little temple *in antis* dedicated to Artemis Orthia. Be that as it may, Artemis Orthia had herself, if possible, an even stronger Spartan flavor than the Dioscuri, worshipped in the sanctuary.[55]

---

[52] Luraghi 2006:180–181.

[53] On the conflictual relations between Epidauros and Argos, see now Piérart 2004:27–30.

[54] On the iconography of the plaques, admittedly not very specific, see Themelis 1998.

[55] The same combination of cults with strong Spartan associations (Apollo Karneios), local cults (the river-god Pamisos), and possible newcomers (the Great Gods at Andania) is found in Messenian territory. See the evidence collected in Zunino 1997 and for the possible Boeotian origin of the Great Gods, see Guarducci 1934:84.

Of course, there can be no serious doubt as to the fact that the new Messenians put in place discursive strategies to explain the embarrassing presence of prominently Spartan cults in their pantheon, and both in the case of Artemis Orthia and in that of the Dioscuri we seem to catch a glimpse of those strategies.[56] However, aetiology and myth offered a much more malleable surface than actual cult did, which is why the cults of the new Messenians present such an intriguing picture. De-Laconizing the landscape must have been one of the highest cultural priorities in free Messenia, and yet, rather than give up the Spartan gods and try to replace them, the new community by and large preferred to cling to them, reinterpreting the origin of their cults when it was necessary or possible. The assemblage of deities worshipped in the earliest times of free Messenia makes sense only if we admit that the new Messenians had a strong reason to regard those cults as theirs. This situation was the result of the combination of two interrelated factors. The first is the fact that Spartan traits were part of the Messenian identity from its first manifestation, in Rhegion and Sicilian Messene in the early fifth century. The second must be a very strong Lacedaemonian component in the population of the new Messenian polity. The fact that the written sources, ideologically biased as they are, tend to ignore such a component should not surprise or worry us too much.

6. Messenian Ethnogenesis

In the end, one has the impression that in some key aspects the emergence of the new Messenians in the fourth century resembled fifth-century Messenian ethnogenesis. To be sure, massive external intervention in the form of Epaminondas' campaign and later of ongoing military activity by the Arcadians in southwestern Messenia constitutes an important difference, and the likely influx of population from outside the region was a new factor, too. Beside this, though, the foundation of Messenian identity was still the same: opposition to Sparta. As Thomas Figueira (1999:224) put it, "instead of reflecting genealogy, feeling 'Messenian' or identifying oneself as 'Messenian' appears to be inversely correlated with the degree of compliance with the Spartan government and with the Spartiates as a social class." Figueira refers to the fifth century, but his formulation seems to hold true to a significant extent for the citizens of free Messene, as well.

---

[56] Luraghi 2002:65.

The idea that, in spite of a myth of foundation based on an exile and return story, the roots of the new Messenian ethnogenesis of the fourth century lay partly in Messenia itself may receive some support from a very important and characteristically Messenian class of evidence, later materials deposited in Bronze Age tombs.[57] The interpretation of this corpus of evidence is anything but straightforward. In very general terms, since there can be little doubt that Bronze Age tombs were recognized as such, the cult practiced in them was in all likelihood addressed to previous inhabitants of the region. It may be less than crucial from our perspective to decide whether such previous inhabitants were seen as heroes or as ancestors by the worshippers.[58] In either case, they were clearly perceived as a powerful presence that had to be appeased, and one that had a particularly close connection to the territory. Cult created a special relationship between the worshippers and these powers. For an understanding of the meaning of this relationship, the perceptions of the past in whose framework it was embedded are of decisive importance. We cannot be absolutely certain that, prior to the liberation of Messenia, these ancestral dead were not seen as part of a purely Laconian view of the past of the region, but by the mid-fifth century the idea that the region west of the Taygetos was a later addition to the original Spartan lot was widespread enough to suggest that most probably the Bronze Age tombs were seen as pre-Spartan and by implication as Messenian. The absence of comparable evidence of cult at Bronze Age tombs from Laconia somewhat reinforces this conclusion.

In spite of the circumstantial arguments that can be brought to its support, this conclusion is and cannot but be hypothetical. The fact that on the whole the evidence for cult at Bronze Age tombs is much more abundant for the period after 369, and that in some cases the cult seems to start right at the time of the liberation, speak in favor of this hypothesis.[59] The alternative, that the cults may have expressed the attempt of some groups to claim superior status for themselves by hijacking the Bronze Age dead as their own ancestors, cannot be ruled out completely, but the nature of the cultic activities involved, mostly of a rather modest level and apparently discontinuous, does not offer strong support to it. On the whole, it seems more likely that we

---

[57] The best survey of the evidence is Boehringer 2001:243–325; add now Chatzi-Spiliopoulou 2001.

[58] See the discussion in Antonaccio 1995:245–268. At any rate, the terracotta plaques strongly suggest heroic cult, especially considering the parallels from Laconia; see Boehringer 2001:291.

[59] Alcock 1991.

are dealing with a claim of autochthony, or, in other words, that worshipping local heroes or ancestors in post-liberation Messenia equaled an expression of Messenian ethnicity. But then, it seems reasonable to assume a similar explanation from the beginning for those cults that start before the liberation and continue into free Messenia.

If this conclusion is acceptable, then the chronological distribution of the evidence has striking implications from our point of view. The relative lateness of the evidence from the Pylos region could be connected to the fact that this region had to be won militarily by the Arcadians before it became part of the new Messenian polity. In the area of Nichoria, not far from Korone, the respective timeline of interest for Mycenaean graves and liberation from Sparta is completely different, in what could be a revealing way. Offerings in the graves start around 425, suggesting that Messenian ethnicity may already have been brewing here for some forty to fifty years until finally the area became overtly Messenian. Where the stimuli came from may be indicated by the scanty evidence from the hills overlooking the Pylos bay and from the highlands that connect that area and the northwestern corner of the gulf of Messenia, and the chronological coincidence between possible statements of Messenian identity in the form of worship of autochthonous heroes or ancestors and the presence of Messenians of Naupaktos at Pylos may not be accidental.[60]

This reading of the evidence, hypothetical as it is, could add in an important way to the reconstruction of Messenian ethnogenesis in the fourth century. It would confirm that this phenomenon had an important local dimension. Although the liberation did come abruptly and by external intervention, the Messenian identity was smoldering in Messenia itself. Affirmations of Messenian identity may well have been an early expression of a disaffection analogous to the one that came to the fore among the *perioikoi* of Laconia at the time of Epaminondas' invasion in 369. Even more than in the case of the revolt after the earthquake, it is impossible to tell for sure if the carriers of the Messenian identity in late fifth-century Messenia were Helots or *perioikoi*. The latter are likely to be archaeologically more visible. In the case of Nichoria, the cult in the *tholos* F is but one manifestation of renewed human presence on the plateau, and is apparently accompanied by a substantial building whose foundations made of large limestone blocks

---

[60] Figueira 1999:240n56.

have been tentatively identified by the excavators as belonging to a temple.[61] This might suggest connecting the area with the perioikic town that became Korone. However, it would probably be wrong, especially at this date, to take an either-or approach to this question. In all likelihood, both Helots and *perioikoi* were involved in the claim of Messenian identity expressed by tomb worship.

7. Conclusion

To conclude, the birth of a free Messenian polity was made possible by an extraordinary convergence of favorable conditions. It could not have happened without the Theban victory at Leuctra and subsequent invasion of Laconia. Arcadian and Argive involvement was clearly very important, and a peculiar ethnic dynamic in the Peloponnese must have made it easier for the new ethnic entity to be accepted as such. However, the preexistence of Messenian ethnicity and the fact that it had meanwhile gained some acceptance throughout the Greek world were necessary preconditions for the success of the new polity carved out of the Lacedaemonian state. Massive external influence on the shape of Messenian ethnicity should not completely divert our attention from the very important fact that cultic activity at Bronze Age tombs may point to the articulation of claims of Messenian identity from the last decades of the fifth century in parts of the region that would become free Messene in 369. If that is correct, upon gaining their freedom thanks to the Theban victory, these Messenians probably sacrificed their own constructions of their past to the Messenian master narrative that was to survive in the written sources, without any contrasting voice but the—equally self-interested, equally implausible— Spartan image of the city of slaves.

---

[61] See Coulson and Wilkie 1983:337 and plan 7-2. The building is much more substantial than those whose traces have been located in the pre-third-century strata of the omega-omega complex and in the courtyard of the Asklepieion at Mavromati/Messene. The pottery associated with the building appears to be contemporary with the pottery found in the *tholos*.

Bibliography

Alcock, S. E. 1991. "Tomb Cult and the Post-Classical *Polis*." *AJA* 95:447–467.

Antonaccio, C. M. 1995. *An Archaeology of Ancestors: Tomb Cult and Hero Cult in Early Greece*. Lanham.

Asheri, D. 1983. "La diaspora e il ritorno dei Messeni." *Tria corda. Scritti in onore di Arnaldo Momigliano* (ed. E. Gabba) 27–42. Como.

Boehringer, D. 2001. *Heroenkulte in Griechenland von der geometrischen bis zur klassischen Zeit. Attika, Argolis, Messenien*. Berlin.

Buckler, J. 1980. *The Theban Hegemony, 371-362 B.C.* Cambridge MA.

Caccamo Caltabiano, M. 1993. *La monetazione di Messana. Con le emissioni di Rhegion dell'età della tirannide*. Berlin.

Chatzi-Spiliopoulou, G. 2001. "Ὁ 6ος θαλαμοτὸς τάφος τῶν Ἑλληνικῶν Ἀνθείας στὴ Μεσσηνία." *Forschungen in der Peloponnes* (ed. V. Mitsopoulos-Leon) 285–298. Österreichisches Archäologisches Institut Sonderschriften 38. Athens 2001.

Chlepa, E.-A. 2001. *Μεσσήνη. Τὸ Ἀρτεμίσιο καὶ οἱ οἶκοι τῆς δυτικῆς πτέρυγας τοῦ Ἀσκληπιείου*. Athens.

Consolo Langher, S. 1965. "Documentazione numismatica e storia di Tyndaris nel sec. IV a. C." *Helikon* 5:63–96.

Coulson, W. D. E., and Wilkie, N. 1983. "Archaic to Roman Times: The Site and Environs." *Excavations at Nichoria in Southwest Greece*. 3:332–350. Minneapolis.

Cozzoli, U. 1978. "Sparta e l'affrancamento degli Iloti nel V e nel IV secolo." *MGR* 6:213–232

Dipersia, G. 1974. "La nuova popolazione di Messene al tempo di Epaminonda." *Propaganda e persuasione occulta nell'antichità* (ed. M. Sordi) 54–61. Milano.

Ducat, J. 1990. *Les Hilotes*. Athens.

Figueira, T. J. 1999. "The Evolution of the Messenian Identity." *Sparta: New Perspectives* (ed. S. Hodkinson and A. Powell) 211–244. London.

Freitag, K. 1996. "Der Akarnanische Bund im 5. Jh. v. Chr." *Akarnanien. Eine Landschaft im antiken Griechenland* (eds. P. Berktold, J. Schmid and C. Wacker) 75–86. Würzburg.

Grandjean, C. 2003. *Les Messéniens de 370/369 au 1er siècle de notre ère. Monnayages et histoire*. Athens.

Guarducci, M. 1934. "I culti di Andania." *SMSR* 10:174–204.

Hall, J. M. 2003. "The Dorianization of the Messenians." *Helots and their Masters in Laconia and Messenia* (eds. N. Luraghi and S. E. Alcock) 142–168. Cambridge, MA.

Harder, A. 1991. "Euripides' Temenos and Temenidai." *Fragmenta Dramatica* (ed. H. Hofmann and A. Harder) 117–135. Göttingen.

Hölscher, T. 1974. "Die Nike der Messenier und Naupaktier in Olympia." *JDAI* 89:70–111.

Hope Simpson, R. 1966. "The Seven Cities offered by Agamemnon to Achilles." *ABSA* 61:113–131.

Jacquemin, A., and Laroche, D. 1982. "Notes sur trois piliers delphiques." *BCH* 106:191–218.

Jehne, M. 1994. *Koine Eirene. Untersuchungen zu den Befriedungs- und Stabilisierungsbemühungen in der griechischen Poliswelt des 4. Jahrhunderts v. Chr.* Stuttgart.

Jones, N. F. 1987. *Public Organization in Ancient Greece: A Documentary Study.* Philadelphia.

Leschhorn. W. 1984. *Gründer der Stadt. Studien zu einem politisch-religiösen Phänomen der griechischen Geschichte.* Stuttgart.

Lewis, D. M. 1977. *Sparta and Persia.* Leiden.

Luraghi, N. 1994. *Tirannidi arcaiche in Sicilia e Magna Grecia, da Panezio di Leontini alla caduta dei Dinomenidi.* Florence.

Luraghi, N. 1997. "Il mito di Oreste nel Regno dello Stretto." *Mito e storia in Magna Grecia* 333–346. Naples.

Luraghi, N. 2001a. "Der Erdbebenaufstand und die Entstehung der messenischen Identität." *Gab es das griechische Wunder? Griechenland zwischen dem Ende des 6. und der Mitte des 5. Jahrhunderts v. Chr.* (ed. D. Papenfuß and V. M. Strocka) 279–301. Mainz.

Luraghi, N. 2001b. "Die Dreiteilung der Peloponnes. Wandlungen eines Gründungsmythos." *Geschichtsbilder und Gründungsmythen* (ed. H.-J. Gehrke) 37–63. Würzburg.

Luraghi, N. 2002. "Becoming Messenian." *JHS* 122:45–69.

Luraghi, N. 2006. "Messenische Kulte und messenische Identität in hellenistischer Zeit." *Kult—Politik—Ethnos* (eds. K. Freitag, P. Funke and M. Haake) 169–196. Stuttgart.

Luraghi, N. 2008. *The Ancient Messenians: Constructions of Ethnicity and Memory.* Cambridge.

Matthaiou, A. and Mastrokostas, E. 2000–2003. "Συνθήκη Μεσσηνίων καὶ Ναυπακτίων." *Horos* 14–16:433–454.

Müth-Herda, S. 2005. *Messene. Topographie und Stadtplan in spätklassischer und hellenistischer Zeit.* Dissertation, Berlin.

Papaefthymiou, V. 2001–2002. "Σύμπλεγμα τριῶν καθιστῶν εἰδωλίων ἀπὸ τὸ ἱερὸ τῆς Δήμητρος καὶ τῶν Διοσκούρων τῆς ἀρχαῖας Μεσσήνης." *Πρακτικὰ τοῦ ϛ´ διεθνοῦς συνεδρίου Πελοποννησιακῶν σπουδῶν (Τρίπολις, 24-29 Σεπτεμβρίου 2000).* 2:129–146. Peloponnesiaka Supplement 24. Athens.

Parker, R. 1998. *Cleomenes on the Acropolis.* Oxford.

Piérart, M. 1985. "Le Tradizioni epiche e il loro rapporto con la questione dorica. Argo e l'Argolide." *Le origini dei Greci. Dori e mondo egeo* (ed. D. Musti) 277–292. Bari.

Piérart, M. 2004. "Deux voisins. Argos et Épidaure. (Mythes, Société, Histoire)." *La città di Argo: Mito, storia, tradizioni poetiche* (ed. P. Angeli Bernardini) 19–34. Rome.

Roebuck, C. A. 1941. *A History of Messenia from 369 to 146 B.C.* Chicago.

Rosivach, V. J. 1999. "Enslaving Barbaroi and the Athenian Ideology of Slavery." *Historia* 48:129–157.

Roussel, D. 1976. *Tribu et cité. Études sur les groupes sociaux dans les cités grecques aux époques archaïque et classique.* Paris.

Salviat, F. 1965. "L'offrande argienne de l'«hémicycle des rois» à Delphes et l'Héraclès béotien." *BCH* 89:307–314.

Shipley, G. 2004. "Messenia." *An Inventory of Archaic and Classical Poleis* (eds. M. H. Hansen and T. H. Nielsen) 547–568. Oxford.

Themelis, P. G. 1994. "Artemis Ortheia at Messene: The Epigraphical and Archaeological Evidence." *Ancient Greek Cult Practice from the Epigraphical Evidence* (ed. R. Hägg) 101–122. Stockholm.

Themelis, P. G. 1998. "The sanctuary of Demeter and the Dioscouri at Messene." *Ancient Greek Cult Practice from the Archaeological Evidence* (ed. R. Hägg) 157–186. Stockholm.

Themelis, P. G. 2000. *Ἥρωες καὶ ἡρῷα στὴ Μεσσήνη.* Athens.

Zunino, M. L. 1997. *Hiera messeniaka. La storia religiosa della Messenia dall'Età Micenea all'Età Ellenistica.* Udine.

VIII

Ethnicity and Democracy in the Peloponnese, 401–362 BCE

Eric Robinson

I N 370 BCE CIVIL STRIFE BROKE OUT in Tegea between a conservative
party favoring Tegea's traditional laws (*patrious nomous*) and a popular,
nationalistic party in favor of all Arcadians coming together *en tô koinô*
to make common decisions. The populists won, but only after they armed
the *dêmos* and gained the aid of Mantineans who arrived in force at Tegea to
help them (Xenophon *Hellenica* 6.5.5–9). The Mantineans had just reunified
and (apparently) redemocratized their city in the teeth of Spartan opposition (Xenophon *Hellenica* 6.5.3–5), and together Mantinea and Tegea provided
the motivating force for the foundation of a new, federal Arcadian state that
would be governed according to democratic principles. Both Xenophon and
Diodorus highlight the role of Lycomedes (a Tegean according to Diodorus
15.59, probably in error; he is a Mantinean in Xenophon *Hellenica* 7.1.23 and
Diodorus 15.62) [1] who persuaded the Arcadians to govern themselves collectively (*es mian sunteleian*), appointing federal officials and convening "The
10,000" (*hoi murioi*) as the main decision-making body for the league. [2] Not all
Arcadian cities joined the league at once: Heraia and Orchomenos initially
resisted and fought alongside the Spartans. [3] Within a very few years,
however, all seem to have joined. A federal proxeny decree dated to the
mid-360s lists participating officials from the major cities of Arcadia, and

---

[1] Stylianou 1998:416.
[2] Xenophon *Hellenica* 7.4.2–3; Diodorus 15.59. On the apparently democratic nature of the
league, see Roy 2000. On the terms "league" vs. "confederacy" (which I use interchangeably
here) and its foundation in Arcadia at this time, see Nielsen 2002:474–477.
[3] Xenophon 6.5.11, 22.

other sources fill in the gaps for most other Arcadian communities.[4] During the decade of the 360s the Arcadian confederacy acted as one of the most powerful political and military forces in the Peloponnese, working actively to protect its cities' territories and oppose the Spartans. In doing so it often promoted democracies or democratic factions, as, for example, in Sicyon and Achaea in 366 and Elis c. 365.[5]

So the rise of the Arcadian league provides a dramatic example of how democratic politics and a national ethnic sense could work together, in this case resulting in the forging of a powerful new political entity in the midst of the Peloponnese. The question this paper will address is the extent to which these two forces—ethnic identity and democratic politics—combined in an effective way to create political change in the fourth-century Peloponnese. Was the Arcadian case an exception, or did it lay out a paradigm for how democracy and ethnicity tended to interact?

Ethnicity, of course, is a complicated term, one that can refer to a variety of real or imagined communities. For the purposes of this study I will construe it broadly, including under the general rubric of "ethnicity" examples of the self-identification of a people with regional kinship groups. In most cases, such as the Arcadians, Achaeans, Triphylians, and Messenians, this interpretation will raise few eyebrows. Things get more complicated in other cases, however, such as the Eleans. Clearly, "the Eleans" could refer to a purely political community, that of the *polis* Elis. However, "Eleans" also referred to the inhabitants of a rather large territory including numerous towns, inhabitants whom Herodotus considered to be ethnically distinct among the peoples of the Peloponnese (8.73). It would not be too great a stretch, then, to think about "the Eleans" in ethnic as well as political terms.[6]

Democracy makes for a more straightforward category, though it is not without its complications in our era. For example, scholars have on occasion sought to downplay the influence of *dêmokratia* in this period. G. E. M. de St. Croix sees it as a failing force which "barely held its own" in the fourth century, as a prelude to its coming destruction in Hellenistic and Roman times.[7] S. Perlman denies that the popular factions struggling against local oligarchic opponents in the era of the Corinthian War had anything

---

[4] IG V 2.1 (=Rhodes and Osborne 2003: nr. 32); Nielsen 2002:477–478.
[5] Xenophon *Hellenica* 7.1.42–46; 7.4.15–17. Nielsen 2002:485–90.
[6] See Roy, this volume, for a discussion of inter-community relations within Elis.
[7] De Ste Croix 1981:295–300 for the fourth century (quotation at 295), 300–317 for the later eras.

to do with democracy, but rather simply pursued an anti-Spartan agenda.[8] But these contentions are hard to square with the general picture of new democratization, re-democratization, continuing democracies, and struggles for democracy attested for the period.[9] It is true, of course, that immediately after the fall of the Athenian empire many popular governments were replaced by oligarchies at Sparta's behest, especially in cities formerly under Athenian rule.[10] But in the decades that followed, Sparta's predominance was rattled and its preference for oligarchic government frequently flouted, not only among major rivals such as Argos, Athens, and Thebes, but also in smaller states closer to home. In this well-established context of vibrant democracy and populist agitation it would be foolhardy to dismiss *dêmokratia* as a political force or assume that when our sources indicate that a faction sought to promote it one must supply further "actual" motives.

Nevertheless, Perlman's emphasis on the importance of Sparta for inspiring policies for and against it in cities of the Peloponnese points to a very real phenomenon. As the most dominant Greek power in the early fourth century, Sparta's influence was vast and sometimes engendered strong opposition. It was indeed a major factor driving political events in the Peloponnese, and thus its role must be carefully considered in studying the relationship between ethnic identity and populist politics in those events. One must be on guard, however, for Xenophon's biases here. It is not just that this key historian favored the Spartan cause, which leads him on occasion to treat unfairly opposing forces (e.g. the Corinthians at *Hellenica* 4.4.1–8, on which see below); but even more, his general perspective is so Spartan-centered that one might easily mistake the *Hellenica*'s narrative focus on Spartan interests and consequences with a reality that was surely more open-ended.

In surveying fourth-century Peloponnesian events for the confluence of ethnic and democratic movements, one quickly discovers that, aside from the case of the Arcadians, the two rarely complemented each

---

[8] Perlman 1964.

[9] The list of Greek cities and regions that our sources suggest continued, attained or struggled to attain *dêmokratia* at some point in the fourth century includes: Achaea, Arcadia, Argos, Corcyra, Corinth, Kos, Kyme, Cyrene, Elis, Ephesos, Eretria, Erythrai, Helisson, Heraia, Heracleia Pontica, Hestiaia/Oreos, Iasos, Olbia, Lokroi, Mantinea, Megara, Miletos, Mytilene, Paros, Phigaleia, Phleious, Rhodes, Syracuse, Thebes. Many more possibilities could be added based on suggestive but inconclusive epigraphic evidence. See Hansen and Nielen 2004; in greater detail, my forthcoming book *Democracy Beyond Athens: Popular Government in the Greek Classical Age.*

[10] See e.g. Xenophon *Hellenica* 3.4.2–7, 3.5.13; Plutarch *Lysander* 13.3–4.

other. Ethnicity might often become tied up with desires for autonomy and freedom in the sense of freeing one's lands from foreign domination, but such ought not necessarily to be equated with *dēmokratia*. Consider the case of the Messenians and the new ethnic state they formed after the defeat of the Spartans at Leuctra. As Luraghi has shown in his contribution to this volume, hatred of others works well as a device to help to forge an ethnic identity,[11] and here the new Messenian citizens, whatever their actual origin and composition (exiles from abroad, helots and/or *perioikoi* from Messenia, helots and/or *perioikoi* from Laconia) used their well-established hostility toward the Spartans to unify the new community as they advanced their project of ethnogenesis, supposing that the new state founded by Epaminondas of Thebes was reviving a old Messenian nation. Xenophon in the *Hellenica* famously omits even to mention the founding of Messenia; our other sources dwell on the reclaiming of ancestral lands and the glorious revival of an old city.[12] But none indicate any specifically democratic or oligarchic political motivations among the Messenians, nor do they give a hint of the constitutional order of the new state. One might guess that, given the constitutional proclivities of Thebes, Argos, and the Arcadians, all of which helped make the newly independent Messenian state possible, a *dēmokratia* resulted. We know at least that Messenia had an *ekklêsia* in which sumbouleutic debate took place.[13] But such factors make for a frail argument, and in fact we have no direct evidence for an incoming Messenian democracy, and some suggestions in later sources that a more conservative government held power.[14] Unlike many other struggles against an overbearing, oligarch-promoting Sparta in this era, references to a populist ideology among the Messenians, before or after the creation of their state, are notably missing.

---

[11] Also a major point in Pretzler's contribution to this volume concerning the formation of the Arcadian state.

[12] Diodorus 15.66; Plutarch *Pelopidas* 24; Pausanias 4.26–27; cf. Isocrates *Archidamus* 22–28.

[13] Aristotle *Rhetoric* 1418b5–11.

[14] Stylianou 1998:436 guesses *dēmokratia* resulted; Meyer 1978:150–151 argues on the basis of later texts that the constitution was oligarchic/timocratic. Shipley 2004:563 challenges Meyer's conclusion, citing various inscriptions from the late fourth century and afterwards which use the word *damos* or otherwise suggest the possibility of democratic institutions, but the effort is not decisive. Grandjean 2003:72 notes the use of *damos* in the inscriptions, but considers the early constitution to be an unknown. Roebuck's older political history of Messenia for the most part ignores the issue, only briefly positing timocracy, though his argument for Arcadian influence in the federal structure of the newly founded government might suggest more populist procedures (Roebuck 1941:109–117).

Similarly, in Elis competing appeals to ethnicity <u>could</u> have had a democratic dimension, but if so our sources are curiously silent about it. As Roy's contribution in this volume makes clear, Elis consistently sought to retain control over territories it long considered to be part of Elis even as some of these communities—in particular the Pisatans and the Triphylians—sought to establish their own separate ethnic identities.[15] Roy suggests that the Eleans may have found themselves especially vulnerable to this kind of ethnic defection because of the longstanding distinctions made between the Eleans proper and *perioikoi* within their state. The two key moments of separation are the aftermath of the Spartan war with Elis c. 400, in which Elis was forced to release from their control a number of towns including Triphylian ones, and the conflict between Arcadia and Elis of the mid-360s, during which the Pisatans were able to establish their own state in association with the Arcadians. As it happens, constitutional conflict could have played a part in both these cases, but, if so, they led to contrasting results.

During the war with Sparta c. 400, Elis encountered internal factional strife. Certain wealthy men, hoping to turn the city over to the Spartans, began a massacre, and made a point of trying to kill Thrasydaios, the popular leader (*prostatês tou dêmou*). The wrong man was slain, however, and when the *dêmos* learned that Thrasydaios still lived, they rallied around him and he led them into a victorious battle against the killers.[16] The next year Thrasydaios opened negotiations with the Spartans: after the Eleans made a number of concessions—including freeing the Triphylians and others, though keeping control over Olympia despite the claims of the Pisatans—the Spartans came to terms with Elis and the two sides agreed to peace and renewed alliance. Importantly, no change in the government of Elis is reported. This fact, plus the earlier triumph of the *dêmos* and their leader Thrasydaios, strongly implies that democracy continued at Elis all through this period.[17] What of the new Triphylian state—did it embrace oligarchy or democracy? The testimony is unclear. Literary sources say nothing, while

---

[15] See also on these two the contributions in this volume by Giangiulio and Ruggeri.

[16] Xenophon *Hellenica* 3.2.21–31; see also Diodorus 14.17.4–12, 14.34.1; Pausanias 3.8.4, 5.4.8, 7.10.2. Gehrke 1985:53–54; Roy 1997.

[17] Compare Xenophon's use of similar terms describing internal politics in Mantinea, a democracy at the time, at *Hellenica* 5.2.3–7. On Thrasydaios as a supporter of Athenian democrats in 404/3, see Plutarch *Moralia* 835F. Roy 1997 does not doubt this, considering that "democracy was solidly rooted among Elean citizens." He further theorizes that Sparta may have hoped to lessen the democracy's influence by taking control of Elis' ports and navy. See also Roy 2004:497.

the relatively new inscriptions upon which reconstructions of Triphylian state structure have been based do not indicate constitutional type.[18] Their concern for matters of citizenship, office holding, and taxation could apply just as well to oligarchies or democracies. The only hint we might glean is that the collective bodies invoked at the start of both documents are not the *dêmos* or the *boulê-and-dêmos* or a popular assembly like the *aliaia* at Argos—typical inscriptional formulae used by democratic states—but simply *Triphulioi*. If this signals an absence of democracy,[19] then the drive for ethnic independence from (democratic) Elis likely ended in oligarchy, a result that would certainly have suited the Spartans who created this opportunity for a new state in the first place.[20]

Things worked out differently in the mid-360s, when Elis triggered a war with the Arcadians after trying to retake some of its formerly dependent communities. Again internal conflict erupted in Elis, and, despite attempts from the democratic Arcadians to aid the populist faction, this time Elean oligarchs came out on top. In the course of the war the Pisatans were able to free themselves and, in conjunction with the Arcadians, briefly take control of Olympia and sponsor the games of 364.[21] What little information we have of the Pisatans' independent undertakings (a few treaties and coins) tells us nothing constitutional. We might presume that Pisatis, which began to trace an Arcadian heritage and seems to have acted as a puppet-state of the democratic Arcadians (even if it probably did not join their federal league),[22] came to be democratically governed itself. So potentially in this case a move for ethnic independence could have gone hand in hand with democratiza-

---

[18] Nielsen 1997:144–151; Ruggeri 2004:133–140.

[19] One cannot be certain about this basis for doubting democracy, as there were no set rules for oligarchic or democratic formulae among the varying practices in decrees from state to state. See Rhodes 1997 for the convenient arrangement of many different examples. Nevertheless, one might go so far as to say that oligarchies in states such as Delphi often invoked the *polis* as a whole in the opening of their decrees, where democracies like the Athenian highlighted the role of the *dêmos* in their formulae.

[20] The motivation for the formation of a separate Triphylian state is usually alleged to be either Spartan desires for greater friendly military resources or the natural wishes of the Triphylians to be able to fend off Elean attempts at reabsorbing the freed cities. See the discussion in Nielsen 1997:151–5.

[21] On joint Pisatan/Arcadian control of these Olympics, Xenophon *Hellenica* 7.4.28–9; Diodorus 15.78, 15.82.1; Pausanias 6.4.2; though other passages refer only to Arcadian sponsorship.

[22] See Nielsen 2002:118–119; Roy 2004:501, and in this volume. The eponymous founder Pisos is said to have married Olympia, the daughter of Arkas (*Etymologicum Magnum* 623.16–17; see Nielsen 2002:118). Giangiulio in this volume stresses the strongly Olympian and Arcadian aspects of the Pisatan identity created in this period.

tion. But in no ancient source is the connection actually made. Furthermore, given the Pisatans' longstanding dissatisfaction with Elean control whether Elis was democratically or oligarchically governed, and the opposite constitutional alignments in Triphylia's move to independence, it would be dubious to argue for any kind of general democratic pattern in the ethnic struggles of Elis' subject communities.

Corinth in the late 390s provides another interesting case that mixes issues of ethnic and *polis* identity with constitutional struggles. In c. 392 traditionally oligarchic Corinth underwent a violent political crisis that resulted in democracy and, ultimately, isopolity and union with Argos, lasting until 386. Xenophon provides the fullest account, a few paragraphs in the course of his narrative of the Corinthian War, at *Hellenica* 4.4.1–8. According to him, "the most and best" of the Corinthians were tiring of the war against Sparta, but were prevented from making peace by a combination of Corinth's allies in the war (Argives, Athenians, Boeotians) with those Corinthians who had received Persian bribes (see 3.5.1) and those who had been most responsible for bringing on the war. Fearing that the would-be peacemakers might turn the city over to the Spartans, the others concocted and executed a murderous plan, killing many of them in the agora and driving others of the "best men" (*beltistoi*) into retreat and potential exile. Upon invitation, some of those driven away returned to city, only to find it governed (as Xenophon conveys from their perspective at 4.4.6) "tyrannically" with metics holding greater influence than themselves and, even worse, with Corinthians having to share citizenship with Argos. Whether we are to understand these metics to have been Argive newcomers or previously disenfranchised Corinthians or something else is unclear.[23] Some of these *beltistoi* found the situation intolerable and determined to rescue their fatherland, to return Corinth to itself and make it free (*peiromenous de tên patrida . . . Korinthon poiêsai kai eleutheran apodeixai*); they would also bring back its *eunomia*. They thus attempted to betray Corinth to the Spartans.

The dramatic language Xenophon uses here invokes the ideal of *polis* freedom and autonomy, but in the service of traditional oligarchy rather than democracy. He writes tendentiously, of course, favoring the faction of the *beltistoi* over their scheming, murdering opponents; he apparently seeks to justify as good and noble the exiles' decision to help Sparta against their own city. One wonders how far the anti-war party had gone before the plot to kill or drive them off hatched.

---

[23] Griffith 1950:247; Whitby 1984:296n3.

Xenophon never actually states that democracy replaced oligarchy at Corinth after the *stasis*, or that political ideology had anything to do with the struggle, but that is the clear implication given the author's juxtaposition of *beltistoi* favoring *eunomia* on the one side and, on the other, revolutionaries who govern like tyrants, exalt metics, and seek to merge the *politeia* with that of (democratic) Argos.[24] Diodorus offers a much briefer picture of events, but his text—if it has been properly emended—shows that an explicit desire for democracy had motivated the revolutionaries from the start (14.86.1).[25] So also implies the Oxyrhynchus historian, who at 2.2-3 (7.2-3 in McKechnie and Kern) describes Corinthians who wished to bring political change to their city (μεταστῆσαι τὰ πρά[γμ]ατα ζητοῦντες) and were hostile to Sparta, much like the Athenians and Boeotians who hated Sparta because of the Spartan practice of supporting opposing political factions within their cities. Political ideology, therefore, seems to have played a major role in the upheaval at Corinth.[26]

Both Xenophon and Diodorus make clear that at some point after the initial revolution, probably two years later in 390, Argos took firmer control of Corinth, marching in a large army and effectively uniting the two polities. This union lasted until the terms of the King's Peace were enforced in 386, at which point the Argives departed, the exiles returned, and Corinth was restored (*autê eph' heautês hê ton Korinthion polis egeneto*), ending its union to

---

[24] His use of the words *oi pleistoi kai oi beltistoi* at 4.4.1 to describe those sick of the war with Sparta cannot be taken to indicate that the majority of Corinthians opposed the populist revolution to come: the *pleistoi* is dropped when it comes to describing who was targeted in the violence or forced to withdraw. Indeed, this expression should probably be taken as a hendiadys born of Xenophon's bias—"the most and the best men" really means "most of the best men."

[25] This emendation—altering the nonsensical Ἐν δὲ τῇ Κορίνθῳ τινὲς τῶν ἐπιθυμία κρατούντων συστραφέντες κτλ. in the text to the more reasonable Ἐν δὲ τῇ Κορίνθῳ τινὲς τῶν ἐπιθυμούντων δημοκρατίας συστραφέντες—has been challenged by Ruzé 1997:307-309. While she does not doubt that internal politics are involved in this episode, she sees no reason to bring in the word *dêmokratia* here and considers Salmon's alternative emendation (Ἐν δὲ τῇ Κορίνθῳ τινὲς τῶν κρατούντων ἐπὶ θυσίᾳ συστραφέντες) to be a better solution (Salmon 1984:355-357). Her objection is reasonable, and though it seems to me that the content of the Xenophon and *Hellenica Oxyrhynchia* passages are in fact suggestive of democratic motivation, it is perhaps a bit adventurous to insert the word here. Other emendations seem possible as well: for example, Ἐν δὲ τῇ Κορίνθῳ τινὲς τῶν κράτους ἐπιθυμούντων συστραφέντες κτλ.

[26] *Contra* Perlman 1964. Perlman sees fear of Sparta as the only motivator for the Corinthian alliance with Argos. Cf. Ruzé 1997:288.

democratic Argos.[27] Clearly, the appeal to *polis* identity that Xenophon attributes to the exiles worked in the service of oligarchy rather than democracy. What of ethnic identity? No historical source mentions it as a factor employed for or against the merging of Corinth into Argos. Yet there was certainly room for a pro-unification argument based on common ethnicity. Both populations were Dorian, of course. But Homer's *Iliad* implies an older and even stronger relationship, describing Corinth as a part of the Argolid: the *Catalogue of Ships* lists Corinth together with Mycenae and other area communities as under Agamemnon's leadership (2.569–580);[28] and, more tellingly, at 6.152–159 Corinth (under the older name Ephyra) is described as being in a nook of Argos (μυχῷ Ἄργεος) and its Sisyphid dynasty subservient to Argive rulers. Pausanias picks up on these Homeric statements—he says at 2.1.1 that Corinthian territory formed a part of Argive land, and he makes explicit reference to the Homeric picture of a Corinth subservient to Argos in the era of the Trojan War (2.4.2)—but he also elaborates a great deal more about its founding dynasty, suggesting that traditions existed for telling an alternative tale of a more independent early Corinth.[29] It is possible to speculate that where Pausanias talks of a dependent city within Argive territory he is relating a version of events promoted by Argos in the early fourth century to help justify the absorption of Corinth, with the alternative line being attributable to contemporary attempts to oppose such a view.

Achaea provides a final example. While the constitutional status of this ethnic region is not well understood for much of its history, it is for one episode in our era.[30] In 366 the Thebans under Epaminondas, aided by the Argives and others, invaded Achaea with the goal of converting the cities there into allies. Initial successes led to negotiations with the aristocratic leaders (*beltistoi*) of the Achaean cities, leaders who promised support for the Thebans. Epaminondas in return did not make changes in the (apparently oligarchic) *polis* constitutions, and prevented the exiling of the elites, after which he departed. But complaints soon arose from populist opponents of the Achaean aristocrats and from the (democratic) Arcadian allies, prompting the Theban assembly to reverse Epaminondas' policy: they sent harmosts into the Achaean cities who, with the help of local popular groups,

---

[27] Quotation from Xenophon *Hellenica* 5.1.34. See also Xenophon *Hellenica* 4.8.34, 5.1.36; Diodorus 14.91–92.

[28] Picked up on by Strabo 8.6.18–19.

[29] 2.1–2.4.4. See Will 1955:237–258 for a discussion of the legends about earliest Corinth.

[30] See for a discussion Freitag, this volume.

drove out the aristocrats and set up *dêmokratiai*. This situation did not last, however, as the aristocratic exiles banded together and launched a military campaign to retake the Achaean cities. The exiles, being numerous, succeeded in their efforts, one by one capturing the cities and bringing about the elites' restoration, after which Achaea pursued a strongly pro-Spartan foreign policy.[31]

What role, if any, did ethnic identity play in these events? Xenophon, our main source, says nothing about it. But we know that a strong Achaean consciousness of common ethnicity went back at least as far as the fifth century and probably farther, and that by the early fourth an Achaean federal league existed, suggesting that this consciousness had been politicized.[32] The aristocrats who negotiated with Epaminondas during his expedition likely were federal representatives,[33] and Diodorus 15.75.2 talks of "Achaean" garrisons that Epaminondas expelled from the cities of Dyme, Kalydon, and Naupaktos. Given the large number (*ouk oligous*) of supporters the aristocrats were able to muster for their campaign of restoration and the evident speed and ease with which they retook the democratic cities (Xenophon *Hellenica* 7.1.43), one can reasonably suppose that the aristocrats benefited from an appeal to collective Achaean opposition to foreign oppressors, represented by the newly arrived Theban governors in the cities. Democratic collaborators (who we know had a hand in driving out the oligarchs) will have been vilified as betrayers of their own people. Some sort of appeal of this kind must have been necessary, for the victories of democrats in the cities over the league oligarchy were popular in themselves. Indeed, Diodorus uses the word *eleutherôsis* to describe the effect on the cities of Theban removal of Achaean garrisons at 15.75.2. This does not surprise for the non-Achaean cities of Kalydon and Naupaktos, which might naturally see the end of Achaean control as liberation;[34] but it is striking that Dyme, an Achaean city itself, could be described in this way. The garrison might possibly have been there to protect the city from outsiders (the Eleans?), but in combination with the use of *eleutherôsis* and the existence of anti-oligarchic movements in Achaea, it seems more likely to have been there to secure

---

[31] Xenophon *Hellenica* 7.1.41–3; Diodorus 15.75.2; FGH 70 F 84. Buckler 1980:185–93.

[32] Morgan and Hall 2004:472–478; Stylianou 1998:380 (*ad* Diodorus 15.49.2).

[33] Buckler 1980:189.

[34] The garrison in Kalydon was initially aimed against the Acharnanians in 389 (Xenophon *Hellenica* 4.6.1); this may have changed over time. But see Freitag, this volume, on the close relationship between Achaeans and Kalydonians and on the league garrisons in 367/6.

Achaean oligarchic control.[35] In the Achaea of 366, therefore, the democratic aspirations of many—suddenly realized with Theban help—must have been countered in some way if we are to explain the swift success enjoyed by the Achaean elites against domestic foes joined with Theban garrisons; appeals based on ethnic unity against non-Achaean oppressors would have made a logical choice.

So what can we make of these episodes altogether? The most obvious conclusion is that the superficially plausible association of democratic ideals with ethnic autonomy is in fact very poorly attested in this period. That it did so in the case of Arcadia in 369 is beyond question; but one is hard pressed to find other explicit examples, despite the healthy number of Peloponnesian states in ethnic and constitutional turmoil in the fourth century. The defection of the Pisatans from Elis c. 364 may provide another occasion, though there (unlike with Arcadia) our sources give no hint of partisan political aims at any step in the process, and a democratic result is not certain. Other episodes are either indeterminate (Messenia) or actually show the reverse, as politicized appeals to ethnic identity probably worked against movements for democratic change or a democratic status quo (Elis/ Triphylia, Achaea). The case of Corinth's revolutionary union with Argos is somewhat ambivalent: appeals to *polis* identity and pride worked for the oligarchs, while legendary ethnic commonalities could have been exploited by democrats (though it is unclear they were).

It is best, then, to consider the increasingly politicized ethnicities of the region in this period as another variable in rather than a predictor of constitutional alignments or outcomes. Just as struggles between elite and populist factions made up part of the political terrain on which states and leaders had to operate, so did ethnic identities. However, where adherence or hostility to the Spartan (and later Theban) local colossus might move in predictable directions when it comes to matters of democracy and oligarchy, it did not in terms of ethnicity. Much more important for the latter is the presence or absence of outside intervention. Interventions allowed the easy galvanizing of ethnic or nationalist sentiment, sparking a desire to defend the homeland or to take advantage of an opportunity to establish a sepa-rate ethnic homeland. In such cases, unlike with democracy and oligarchy, the familiar actors did not have assigned roles: oligarchic Sparta might in one circumstance be the facilitator of ethnic division and its opponent

---

[35] Stylianou 1998:481 (*ad* Diodorus 15.75.2). The presumption of a preexisting oligarchic government stems primarily from Xenophon *Hellenica* 7.1.42, with Thucydides 5.82.1.

in another.[36] The same went for the democratic Argives and Arcadians. In effect, ethnicity represented another realm open for political manipulation, and those most skillful at reading or taking advantage of geopolitical circumstances might succeed in changing the direction of politics in their home communities, or indeed the very definition of the community.

The events in Arcadia of 370, consequently, should be seen as a remarkable convergence of otherwise unpredictable elements. Strongly democratic sentiment had long existed among some Arcadians (most clearly the Mantineans), but the wounding of the Spartan behemoth after Leuctra and the rise of populist sentiment in Tegea gave it new life. Taking advantage of hostility to the (now weakened) Spartans for past interventions—including the harsh *dioikismos* enforced against Mantinea in 385—popular leaders at Tegea and Mantinea were able to combine their causes under the vision of a new national Arcadian state. Sparta's predictably hostile, intrusive response, defeated by the combined forces of the Arcadians and numerous allies, helped cement the new Arcadian league. Democracy, politicized ethnicity, and antipathy to the local hegemon proved to be a potent mixture, but one exploited less often than one might expect.

Bibliography

Buckler, J. 1980. *The Theban Hegemony, 371-362 B.C.* Harvard Historical Studies 98. Cambridge, MA.

Gehrke, H.-J. 1985. *Stasis. Untersuchungen zu den inneren Kriegen in den griechischen Staaten des 5. und 4. Jahrhunderts v. Chr.* Munich.

Grandjean, C. 2003. *Les Messéniens de 370/369 au 1er siècle de notre ère. Monnayages et histoire.* Athens.

Griffith, G. T. 1950. "The Union of Corinth and Argos (392–386 B. C.)." *Historia* 1:236–256.

---

[36] It is possible to see the beginnings of a pattern with Sparta, however. While it clearly supported an ethnic movement in the case of the Triphylian separation from Elis c. 400, this move backfired later when the Triphylians joined with the Arcadians. Meanwhile, in the cases of Messenia and Arcadia Sparta adamantly opposed new ethnic conglomerations, and it also did its best to thwart Argos' union with Corinth, which could have had an ethnic dimension. It did back the oligarchic Achaean confederacy against the Thebans, of course, but this was an old ethnic association, and, according to Freitag in this volume, ethnic issues did not determine relations between Spartans and Achaeans. (Thanks to Nino Luraghi for this suggestion.)

Hansen, M. H., and Nielsen, T. H. 2004. *An Inventory of Archaic and Classical Poleis.* Oxford.

Meyer, E. 1978. "Messene/Messenien." *RE* Suppl. 15: 136-289.

Morgan, C., and Hall, J. M. 2004. "Achaia." In Hansen and Nielsen 2004:472–488.

Nielsen, T. H. 1997. "Triphylia: An Experiment in Ethnic Construction and Political Organisation." *Yet More Studies in the Ancient Greek Polis* (ed. T. H. Nielsen) 129–162. Papers from the Copenhagen Polis Centre 4. Stuttgart.

Nielsen, T. H. 2002. *Arkadia and its Poleis in the Archaic and Classical Periods.* Göttingen.

Perlman, S. 1964. "The Causes and Outbreak of the Corinthian War." *CQ* 14:64–81.

Rhodes, P. J. 1997. *The Decrees of the Greek States.* Oxford.

Rhodes, P. J., and Osborne, R., eds. 2003. *Greek Historical Inscriptions 404-323 BC.* Oxford.

Roebuck, C. 1941. *A History of Messenia from 369 to 146 B.C.* Chicago.

Roy, J. 1997. "Spartan Aims in the Spartan-Elean War of c. 400: Further Thoughts." *Electronic Antiquity* 3. http://scholar.lib.vt.edu/ejournals/ElAnt/V3N6/roy.html.

Roy, J. 2000. "Problems of Democracy in the Arcadian Confederacy 370-362." *Alternatives to Athens* (eds. R. Brock and S. Hodkinson) 308–326. Oxford.

Roy, J. 2004. "Elis." In Hansen and Nielsen 2004:489–504.

Ruggeri, C. 2004. *Gli stati intorno a Olimpia. Storia e costituzione dell'Elide e degli stati formati dai perieci elei (400-362 a.C.).* Historia Einzelschriften 170. Stuttgart.

Ruzé, F. 1997. *Délibération et pouvoir dans la cité grecque de Nestor à Socrate.* Paris.

Salmon, J. B. 1984. *Wealthy Corinth.* Oxford.

Shipley, G. 2004. "Messene." In Hansen and Nielsen 2004:547–568.

de Ste Croix G. E. M. 1981. *The Class Struggle in the Ancient Greek World.* London.

Stylianou, P. J. 1998. *A Historical Commentary on Diodorus Siculus, Book 15.* Oxford.

Whitby, M. 1984. "The Union of Corinth and Argos: a Re-consideration." *Historia* 33:295–308.

Will, E. 1955. *Korinthiaka.* Paris.

IX

The Archaeology of *Ethnê* and Ethnicity in the Fourth-Century Peloponnese

Catherine Morgan

I
T IS NOWADAYS HARDLY CONTROVERSIAL to view *poleis* and *ethnê* not as distinct forms of state, but as tiers of identity with which communities identified with varying enthusiasm and motivation at different times.[*] States were palimpsests of social action, and behaviour enacted over different social and/or physical ranges—across a territory, focused on a specific settlement, or on some other form of association (as, for example, the cult community linked to a specific sanctuary)—left traces in different aspects of the material record.[1] By the late fifth century, a variety of material and textual evidence indicates that certain forms of political decision-making were coming to be lodged in the supra-*polis* register — a register usually described in terms of ethnic identity.[2] This chapter focuses on what happened next; on the development of the ethnic register of political discourse in the Peloponnese through the fourth century, and the way in which this can be traced in terms of material behaviour. This is not to imply that the shifts in behaviour outlined below can be explained primarily in terms of group identity. As will be shown, much flowed from changing local or regional economic and political circumstances; in focusing on the ethnic, we are rather addressing the manner of communication and accommodation of new realities or aspirations.

---

[*] I am grateful to Peter Funke and Nino Luraghi for their invitation to present this paper, and for patient encouragement thereafter. The present version has benefitted greatly from discussion with Jim Roy, Maria Pretzler and Simon Hornblower: I particularly thank John Davies for a detailed critique.

[1] Morgan 2003:1–16 *et passim*.
[2] Morgan 2003:esp. ch. 2.

Bridging the gap between our understanding of the late Archaic—early Classical balance between *polis* and ethnic registers and what we understand of the Hellenistic period is a problem which has yet to be fully addressed. We have more or less succeeded in deconstructing long-held beliefs about the primeval "tribal" roots of the great Hellenistic federal states.[3] But this simply reshapes the problem of characterising and explaining the steps involved in the formation of integrated political superstructures during the third century, and of the role of ethnic identity in this process—in Hans Beck's words, "the perception of .... a federal grammar between *polis* and *ethnos*."[4]

As I have argued in discussing the Early Iron Age and the Archaic period, most of the perceived limitations on using the archaeological record to trace the process of ethnic discourse, and its outcomes in terms of *ethnê*, are a matter of research design rather than being inherent in the available data.[5] This is equally true when investigating the "politics of ethnicity" in the fourth century. This chapter offers an overview of those aspects of material behaviour which played an active role in expressing and shaping ethnic identity on the political level in different regions of the Peloponnese. Admittedly, fourth-century evidence is at present somewhat less than that of preceding and succeeding centuries. Nonetheless, it both foreshadows third-century practices and continues fifth-century developments under new circumstances, and is therefore of considerable interest.

The Nature of the Evidence

By contrast with earlier periods, much of our evidence is now monumental in scale. It includes the patterns of development of major settlements and the construction of particular types of public building in different areas, as well as sculpture and other visual imagery. This shift in scale is not a matter of chance. In comparison with the late Archaic period, fifth-century changes in material behaviour altered the way in which the expression of personal identity must be approached in most areas of the Peloponnese. The votive records of sanctuaries are a notable case. Setting aside monumental dedications, to which we will return, a culture of personal or collective self-expression featuring the consumption of costly resources underwent a major transformation during the fifth century in favour of generic statements in

---

[3] See e.g. Funke 1993 and Morgan 2003:6–7 for a review of past scholarship.
[4] Beck 2003 (quotation at 78); for a review of past scholarship, see Beck 1997:20–29.
[5] Morgan 2003:211–212.

cheaper materials (terracotta figurines, for example).[6] The votive record of city and panhellenic sanctuaries therefore no longer provides good evidence with which to reconstruct personal statements of identity (at least until the late third–second century, when magistracies and euergetism began to be celebrated). But partly as a result, monumental collective offerings gained greater prominence.

There are, of course, exceptions of considerable importance to the present discussion. As Nino Luraghi's chapter shows, Messenian identity in the newly independent state post-369 was built not only from (reconfigured) perceptions of Helot and probably also perioikic identity, but also via a steady stream of material statements which date back to the fifth-century inception of this particular episode of Messenian insurgency.[7] The creation of the material "hinterland" necessary for a shared "past" drew widely on the established vocabulary of collective expression. The results ranged from the joint dedication with the Naupaktians of the Nike of Paionios at Olympia (plus a second statue at Delphi of which only the base survives),[8] to offerings (mostly of fine pottery) at Mycenaean tombs at key locations within the territory to which the Messenians aspired.[9]

Monumental Dedications

A number of contributors to this volume consider in various ways the dedication of monumental or other collective offerings, and their use to create both an immediate impression and *lieux de memoire* which could help to shape longer term perceptions of the dedicating group. Where direct evidence survives, it is clear that the dedication of monuments depicting aspects of the collective myth-history of *ethnê* (complementing those of individual *poleis*) was a notable feature of the fourth-third centuries, and found echoes in the great epic regional histories composed at this time (Rhianos of Bene's *Achaika, Eliaka,* and *Messeniaka,* for example).[10] Of course the ethnic

---

[6] Snodgrass 1989–1990; see also Siewert 1996.

[7] See also Luraghi 2001, 2002 and 2003 (with full accounts of earlier studies). Alcock 2002: ch. 4.

[8] Hölscher 1974; Jacquemin and Laroche 1982:192–204 (the restoration of Naupaktioi in the dedicatory inscription at Delphi is conjectural).

[9] Luraghi, this volume; Alcock 1998; Alcock 1999. On the subsequent history of heroization in the new state, see Themelis 2003: esp. 24–29.

[10] Pearson 1962 remains a useful account of the use of Rhianos' *Messeniaka* in later accounts of the First Messenian War (although on his wider agenda and its opponents, see also Alcock 1999). Delphi: Jacquemin 1999:38–79, 85–86, 184–202. Ioakimidou 1995 offers the most recent review of the evidence but, where dependent on literary testimonia, tends to

labels themselves are not new, and it might reasonably be argued that after Leuctra, when there was no longer any reason to suppress or repress their political use, the evidence merely indicates a new confidence in presenting an established, "unchanging" identity. Yet it is worth considering the extent to which this was in itself a point of rhetoric which served to strengthen a form of identity which was becoming an increasingly powerful complement to more local, *polis* ties.

Perhaps the most prominent case, also considered by Maria Pretzler in this volume, is the group of ethnic monuments set alongside city dedications at Delphi. Discussion should begin with these city dedications, as they provide the context in which the ethnic monuments must be read. The spectacular series of Argive dedications which began in 456 with the Monument of the Epigonoi, culminated around 369 with the Hemicycle of the Kings. This celebrated Argos' alliance with Thebes, and was thus a powerful symbol for the newly "liberated" Peloponnesians.[11] Over the next century or so, the area around the Hemicycle came to be filled with dedications. Immediately after its creation, however, when the area was still relatively empty, the placing close by of a small number of Peloponnesian monuments (including that of Lysander himself) must have created a very strong impression. Particular among these is the group celebrating the so-called autochthonous peoples of Arcadia dedicated by the Arcadian *laos* in ca. 369 (and plausibly linked with the confederacy of 370), which was signed by one of its sculptors as Samolas Arkas.[12] A number of Arcadian cities (Gortys, Kaphyai, Tegea, Mantinea, and Thisoa) had made civic dedications at Delphi during the fifth century, and Orchomenos did so too during the fourth. But this collective monument represents a deliberate departure.[13] To it might be added Pausanias' reference (10.18.2–3) to the Achaean dedication of a statue of Athena which must either date early in the fourth century or to 189 CE, and the series of five monuments dedicated by the *koinon* of the Aetolians from the early third.[14] It would be premature to claim any major departure from the fifth-century predominance of city dedications, not least given the small numbers of extant bases and the doubts surrounding the date of some

---

propose dates close to the event commemorated, which may be unreliable. Borbein 1973 remains a valuable review of the genres of statuary current in the fourth century, and of key developments within them.

[11] Jacquemin 1999:55–56; Ioakimidou 1997:87–92, 241–255.

[12] Jacquemin 1999:257–259; for the Arcadian dedication, see 187, cat. 066.

[13] Jacquemin 1999:62–63; Ioakimidou 1997:119–124, 322–341.

[14] Jacquemin 1999:62–64, 254–256.

of the offerings mentioned by Pausanias. Nonetheless, one should not under-estimate the likely impact not merely of these monuments individually, but of the ensemble they formed.

Coinage

Coinage is a second area where, already during the fifth century, mate-rial statements had come to reflect the political salience of ethnic iden-tity. Not least thanks to Thomas Martin's wide-ranging discussions of the practical function and political value of Greek coinage,[15] from the perspec-tive of a historian and with due acknowledgement of the many controver-sies and uncertainties involved, it is easy to see in broad terms how early coin issues could function as indicators of the political register (regional-ethnic or city) in which certain political and/or economic problems were perceived to be most conveniently addressed. This general formulation must surely be preferred to any implication of formal league authorities. When one considers the range of functions for which a verifiable form of revenue might have been needed — the acquisition of raw materials, military pay, taxes, fines and contributions to name but a few — it is clearly important to see what solutions (or claims to solutions) were advanced and in what way. Hence the considerable scholarly debate surrounding the fifth-cen-tury Arkadikon coinage, which began to be struck later than the first city issues (the obols and triobols or hemidrachms of Heraia ca. 510–470, and perhaps also Mantinea),[16] and most probably continued alongside a growing number of them (including those of Psophis, Pallantion, Pheneos, Alea, Kleitor, Thaliades, and Mantinea).[17] It is precisely this overlap and the inter-action between city, sub-regional ethnic (in the case of the Parrhasians) and regional ethnic issues which have given rise to such a range of (notably religious and military) explanations for the Arkadikon issues.[18] The fact that city issues came from northern and western *poleis*, close to contested borders, and in the east from a city such as Mantinea, which was actively engaged in trade with its eastern neighbours, allows us to postulate distinc-tive needs met by different forms of issue.[19] Indeed, some fifty years ago Charles Seltman noted that the denominations of the Arkadikon coinage

---

[15] Martin 1985:196–218; Martin 1995.

[16] Head 1911:447–449; Kraay 1976:96. Heraia: Williams 1970.

[17] Head 1911:444–456. Nielsen 2002:135–136.

[18] To take only very recent literature, compare, for example, Psoma 1999 with Nielsen 2002:121–152 (the latter with a full review of previous scholarship).

[19] Morgan 2003:82–85.

corresponded to gaps in the Olympic issues of neighbouring Elis.[20] Yet the separate die-sequences attested in the Arkadikon coinage have generally been accepted as evidence that issues were struck in local mints (and here I emphasize merely the principle, rather than the specific locations proposed, which remain matters of disagreement).[21] If so, it would be an over-simplification to see the ethnic and city registers as merely functionally distinct (let alone incompatible, an old argument now rightly rejected).[22] Whatever the immediate economic purpose of the Arkadikon coinage, it also made a wider regional claim with which those who struck and/or used it identified themselves.

Every aspect of this general fifth-century picture continued into the fourth. Most coin issues still represented the interests of individual *poleis*. After the Arcadian capture of Olympia in 365, for example, Pisa struck coinage with iconography which reflects its ancient role in Olympic history.[23] Megalopolis is the case with the widest implications by virtue of the circumstances of its creation. It is perhaps not surprising to find that when the city minted in the 360s, it was the Arkadikon coinage which served as the available model of a widely used, shared issue (quite apart from the historical claims and allusions which it embodied).[24] As ever, the Messenians are the exception: little as we know of the internal organisation of the new state, it surely contained *poleis*, yet the first coin issues carried the ethnic legend.[25] The form chosen, *Messanioi*, may, as Hall suggests, imply a city ethnic derived from the toponym Messene,[26] but in practice the situation was the reverse. The ethnic was already well established in use and it is perhaps hard to see what else the inhabitants of the region would have called themselves: how to name the new town was a less obviously straightforward matter, however. Despite the likely existence of other *poleis* within the territory of post-independence Messenia,[27] *Messanioi* patently had wider significance, and the suggestion that it represents an ideal of community conceived in exile is wholly plausible. "The Messenians" minted silver staters, triobols and obols, plus a bronze issue too. The head of Demeter on the obverse surely reflects

[20] Seltman 1955:97.
[21] Williams 1965:8–15; for critique, see most recently Nielsen 2002:136–140.
[22] Kraay 1976:95–98, with previous bibliography.
[23] Head 1911:426; Ruggeri 2004:181–183; Nielsen 2002:118–119; Giangiulio, this volume.
[24] Nielsen 2002:140–141.
[25] Grandjean 2003:99–101.
[26] Hall 2003:146–155.
[27] Shipley 2004:547–568.

an important cult in a very fertile region (and conceivably, even at this stage, the role of the eponymous heroine Messene as founder),[28] whereas Zeus on the reverse of the stater and triobol must *inter alia* allude to Mt. Ithome.[29]

In concentrating on city issues, one should not ignore larger scale ethnic—if not federal—claims made via coinage. Staters were issued by the Arcadian League soon after 370,[30] and in Achaea, silver coinage (staters and related drachms and hemidrachms) of ca. 370–360 with the legend ΑΧΑΙΩΝ have rightly been seen as evidence for shared interests and collective pride after Leuctra.[31] The Arcadian issue probably reveals most about the aspirations of the cities who struck it, as against those, like Pheneos or Stymphalos, who preferred to strike on much the same model but with their own city legends.[32] Arguably, it is not until after the refoundation of the Achaean League in 280 that we find numismatic evidence for any significant shift in economic and political integration in any wider local or pan-Peloponnesian context (a major and controversial topic in its own right, and beyond the scope of the present discussion). That it took so long for any widespread intensification of coin issues or hierarchy of circulation to emerge begs both political and economic questions, especially when one considers the potential needs for verifiable forms of payment across the Peloponnese through the fifth and fourth centuries, for example for military supply.[33] While there are echoes here of the explanation of military pay offered for the Arkadikon coinage, the implication that commodity supply mechanisms continued to function without straining pre-existing fifth-century economic structures to breaking point is rather important.

The Built Environment: Background and Context

As emphasized, however, the main changes to be observed are in the built environment—in settlement hierarchies, the timing and nature of building programmes, as well as in the popularity and distribution of individual building types. Inevitably, the nature of the evidence makes the chronological focus of this discussion less precise than that of other chapters in this volume. Yet while one might expect some time lag between the creation of

---

[28] Deshours 1993: esp.53–60.

[29] Grandjean 2003:21–48, 59–65; Head 1911:426

[30] Gerin 1986.

[31] Warren 2007:109; see previously, Head 1911:431; Kraay 1976:101. For the wider context supporting this interpretation, see Morgan and Hall 1996:194–196.

[32] Head 1911:452, 454; Schultz 1992; Tausend 1999:66 (M. Pretzler).

[33] The Arcadian picture is thoroughly reviewed by Roy 1999.

institutions and the provision of built facilities and monuments to house and/or express them, the significance of this should not be overestimated. The ability and will to mobilise the human and material resources necessary to build must have rested on perceptions of what was desirable and/or practical, drawn from wider experience of political and social realities.[34] Monumental construction is not merely symbolic in its own right, but illustrates the ability of the patron group to exploit complex social and economic networks. Again, this is of itself nothing new, but the intensity of building activity must have created an unusually rich range of opportunities for craftsmen and contractors willing and able to move freely from project to project across political boundaries, and thus for patrons to display their ability to command.[35] Whether this in turn created competition to assemble a good team with the right materials at the best prices is a matter of speculation. Alison Burford argued that the Epidauros building contracts indicate reliance on personal contacts established via *proxenia* and *theôrodokia* to draw in craftsmen and raw materials from other states at the best possible prices.[36] But if one accepts this argument (and it is not clear that one should), it must be understood within a well-established context of craft mobility. In the same way, while there is quite widespread evidence that *proxenoi* and other such persons took opportunities for personal advertisement via prominent public buildings in the cities in which they served—Antiochos of Lepreon's dedication of the *proedria* seats in the theatre at Megalopolis, for example, soon after the foundation of the city[37]—there is no hard evidence to link this to a specific role in the construction.

Overall, therefore, there may be relatively few direct material counterparts for the ethnic claims attested in our historical sources in the narrow time frame of the first half of the fourth century. But in the longer term, changes in residential and economic development, which themselves imply shifts in underlying perceptions and power relations, had the power to shape the ways in which people interacted and described each other—the experienced landscape which reflected and formed claims of identity.[38] The

---

[34] Coulton 1977:17–20.

[35] Davies 2001:221–223 with primary reference to Delphi: Feyel 2006: part II.

[36] Burford 1969: esp. 35–39.

[37] Fiechter 1931:21–22.

[38] Morgan and Coulton 1997:103–118; Fletcher 1995: chs. 1, 2. Most such work is based in post-industrial environments (classic works include Lynch 1960: chs.1, 3; Saarinen 1976: chs. 4, 5): much remains to be done on the creation of the idea of a built environment in pre-Roman times (see Morgan 2003: ch. 2).

built expression of political ideas, either in the ethnic register or (as will be further argued) in *poleis* previously subservient (*de facto* if not *de iure*) to the great powers of the fifth century, shaped perceptions of the socio-political landscape either as claims to a new reality or, in time, as *lieux de memoire*. It is important to see the fourth century in such terms, as a period of transition, rather than retrospectively, from the perspective of the Hellenistic world of ethnic leagues.

Before turning to the settlement record, however, we should pause to consider the wider context of these changes, since the Peloponnese cannot be understood in isolation. Certain relationships were close to constants. The Corinthian Gulf was always a critical outlet for the mountain economies of the central Peloponnese and central Greece (Phocis, Locris, Aetolia and Boeotia).[39] Arcadian communities practised a diverse range of upland subsistence strategies, with (broadly) a greater emphasis on the traditional triad further east, and on herding further west, and noting the particular demands of high altitudes in the central and northern areas.[40] The need to exchange commodities across eco-zones (with, at the very least, short-distance internal transhumance) must have contributed to complex perceptions of territory and social group boundaries.[41] On a broader level, the strength of Arcadia's links with the outside world, achieved via Achaea in particular, served to open up the regional economy and avoid the cycles of boom or bust characteristic of closed mountain systems through history.[42] In turn, the impact on the development of coastal, "bridge," zones can be traced in a number of ways. An illustration which shows these processes to be well established long before the fourth century is the nature of Achaean script, which combines traits from areas all around the Gulf, and is on present evidence first attested on Ithaca around 700 BCE. It is hardly controversial to suggest that the local character of certain scripts was to a significant extent a deliberate creation: other contributors to this volume demonstrate that it was still a powerful tool into the fourth century in regions such as Messenia or Elis/Pisa. This particular example, however, shows with unusual clarity the vitality of connections focused on the Gulf zone.[43]

---

[39] Freitag 2000: esp. 1–29; Morgan 2003:213–222, although discussion is based on earlier evidence.

[40] Roy 1999.

[41] For a summary of the arguments, see Morgan 2003:168–171.

[42] Bintliff 1997:30–32.

[43] Luraghi forthcoming. Achaean script: Jeffery 1990:221–224, 248–251.

From the fifth century onwards, shifts in the nature and scale of activity along and around the Corinthian Gulf exposed the north coast, and thence the central Peloponnese, to a range of new opportunities and models of political and economic action. Indeed, it is worth considering the extent to which the apparent centrifugal dynamic of the fourth century was something new, or whether fifth-century centripetalism, centered on Sparta and to a lesser extent Argos, was more transitory than might be inferred from the pre-occupations of Thucydides and Xenophon.[44] I suggest that the fourth century saw a partial return to old orientations, but with changes resulting from opportunities created for the Achaean cities in particular by a number of interrelated factors. First, prolonged warfare (the need for harbours and shipping of supplies, for example); secondly, the influence of settlement expansion throughout northwest Greece and the Ionian islands; thirdly, the effect of the removal after 371 of the Spartan military levies recently systematized by Agesilaos (Diod.15.31.1–2) in freeing resources for investment elsewhere.

Changes in what was to become greater Aetolia (including the coastal territories then in other hands) were perhaps the most obvious and most directly experienced by Peloponnesians. This is due both to physical proximity and, at least initially, to Achaean political interests along the northern coast of the Gulf. Kalydon was formally incorporated into an Achaean League (of whatever form) shortly before 389 (Xenophon *Hellenica* 4.6.1) and held into the 360s, and after the demise of Athenian control and a period of independence, Naupaktos was Achaean until 338.[45] The old view that urban development occurred here only in the later fourth-third centuries, after centuries of backwardness, is plainly wrong. At Chalkis, which was incorporated into Aetolia on its removal from Achaea in 366, recent Helleno-Danish fieldwork has revealed evidence of an extensive Archaic precursor to the Classical-early Hellenistic city.[46] And at Naupaktos, the impact of the

---

[44] Accepting that Xenophon's remark (*Hellenica* 7.2.1) "if a state which is small has accomplished many deeds, it is even more fitting to set them forth" was indeed born out by a comparatively large number of references to otherwise ill-recorded *poleis* (Sikyon, for example: Lolos 1998:46–47). Davies 1997 advances the different, but compatible, argument that the pre-371 Spartan alliances in the Peloponnese, and the post-371 alliances aimed at containing Sparta within Laconia, initially led by Arcadia, were effectively mirror images of each other.

[45] Grainger 1999:30–32.

[46] Dietz et al. 1998 and 1999; Dietz et al 2004:175–188 (the conclusion that the Archaic city may have been larger than the Hellenistic, which rests on the establishment of a late Classical cemetery over an Archaic habitation area [Eiring 2004] is intriguing, but requires more investigation).

Athenian garrison and the presence of Messenian exiles is clearly shown in the physical expansion of the *phrourion* and the creation and expansion of town cemeteries through the second half of the fifth century.[47] Yet the later Classical expansion was real, and even though excavation at inland sites has been more limited, the picture here too is clear.[48] The Aetolians were certainly beginning to act more in concert by the 370s, and the Athenian protest to the Aetolian *koinon* made in 367/6 offers good evidence for the existence of a league by this date, even if we do not know its exact constitution.[49] Yet despite their warlike reputation, the Aetolians were no real threat on their own (they required Macedonian aid to take Naupaktos). I merely note that such a physical and political transformation, at that point unparalleled in the Peloponnese, was new, close at hand, and something to which Achaea at least, as the principal coastal state, had to respond.

Changes in the scale and nature of settlement in the Ionian islands may have been of even greater long-term significance in that they reflect a major shift of power to the west. On Kephallenia, so important to Athens through the second half of the fifth century (and host to Messenian exiles at Krane),[50] new, planned cities were laid out from the first half of the fourth century onwards, and there was a general increase in fortified settlements.[51] On Leukas, the main town cemeteries expanded markedly from the mid-fifth century and especially through the fourth (at the end of which the city was walled).[52] The late fifth–fourth century also saw the development of one of the most characteristic forms of rural settlement, the tower residences which combined agricultural and security (defence and observation) functions too. The intensity of exploitation implied by these facilities finds echoes elsewhere in the region.[53] In the case of Ithaca, the island's limited resources and location as a stepping stone between Kephallenia and Leukas

---

[47] Bommeljé et al. 1987:99. For the findings of recent excavations by the 6th EPKA, Patras, see Kolia and Saranti 2004; Saranti 2006.

[48] For gazeteers, see Bommeljé et al. 1987: ch. 6; Freitag, Funke and Moustakis 2004:379–390. Building: Funke 1987 and 1997.

[49] Rhodes and Osborne 2003, 35. On the league: Scholten 2000:13–16; Beck 1997:43–54; Corsten 1999:133–159; Freitag, Funke and Moustakis 2004:379; *contra* Grainger 1999:29–53, who nonetheless infers a form of precursor *koinon* based on the shrine of Apollo at Thermon.

[50] Thucydides 2.7, 2.30–33, 2.80 (Hornblower 1991:290, 362). Randsborg 2002:2.29–31.

[51] Randsborg 2002: vol. I, catalogue group 3.

[52] Andreou 1998 for a summary of evidence from rescue excavations of several decades. Fiedler 1996.

[53] Morris 2001; Morris and Papadopolous 2005 for a wider review of arguments for tower function.

made it a peculiarly sensitive indicator of changes in local economic integration and orientation. Here the fourth century saw the start of major expansion at the two principal settlements, Aetos and Stavros, from a quite small Archaic and early Classical base. The findings of the Stavros Valley Project show intense late Classical and Hellenistic exploitation of the *khôra* of Stavros, and at Aetos, both the pre-war excavations of the British School at Athens, and more recent work by the University of Washington at St Louis point to a major expansion in settlement.[54] Here too, a series of fortifications were established in the late fourth–early third century, including those on the acropoleis of Aetos and (somewhat later) Roussano (east of Stavros), and a tower residence at Ag. Athanasios.[55] The chain of fortified vantage points, running in an arc from Leukas through Ithaca to Kephallenia seems to have been in place by the early third century at the latest. The Leukas canal, navigable again perhaps from the mid-third century onwards (if we can trust Pseudo-Skylax 34), brought Corcyra into this ambit also. For the Peloponnese, the outcome was intensified traffic along the Gulf and a clear power shift westwards: this is most clearly seen in the expansion of Patras and Dyme discussed below.

These complex interconnections provide the wider context for more localised changes in Peloponnesian settlement. Crucially for the Peloponnese, with its complex balance of upland, lowland, and maritime ecologies, these connections were both immediately locally sensitive and had the capacity to explain why certain routes and locations became more or less salient over time. A good illustration is the birth and death of the Azanian *ethnos*.[56] The location of the Azanian cities, neighbouring the *merê* of the Achaean mesogeia (Pharees and Tritaees) and located in fertile upland valleys on the few passes between the central Peloponnese and the coast,

---

[54] The Stavros Valley Project is co-directed by the author (for the British School at Athens) and Dr Andreas Soteriou (35th EPKA, Argostoli). These observations rest on re-examination of (mostly) unpublished data from the pre-war work of the British School at Athens (S. Benton, W. Heurtley) and renewed fieldwork (excavation and survey) conducted in 2002 and 2003, publication of which is in preparation. Aetos: observations based on notes of Benton's (largely unpublished) finds by the late John Cook, and Symeonoglou 1984; Symeonoglou 1985:205–215; Symeonoglou 1986:236–238. See Steinhart and Wirbelauer 2002: ch. 4 for earlier antiquarian finds, which confirm the growing wealth of both centers through the second half of the fourth and third centuries.

[55] Partsch 1890:54–63 remains the most complete account; see also Randsborg 2002:1.109–110; Steinhart and Wirbelauer 2002:110–111, 114–115 for Haller von Hallerstein's drawings of these monuments. Ag. Athanasios: Kontorli-Papadopoulou 2001:320–326; the British School excavations of 1930 and 1937 in the tower area will be published by the author.

[56] Pikoulas 1981–1982; Nielsen and Roy 1998; Morgan 1999:416–424.

makes it easy to understand how, in certain periods (the eighth to sixth centuries for example), they could acquire distinctive material traits, behavioural traditions, and ethnic identity, yet at others be pulled more or less directly into political associations to north and south.[57]

Ethnically, most Azanian cities came to identify themselves as Arcadian, but the chronology of their monumental development shows, to a varying extent, similarity with coastal Achaea. Lousoi is an interesting such case. An Azanian city which identified itself as ethnically Arcadian after the demise of the Azanian *ethnos* (at least by the late fourth or early third century),[58] the chronology of its monumental development is closer to that of coastal Achaea, although details of architectural style show a more even balance of connections to north and south. The late fourth-century Ostbau is the earliest building in a series which included the Temple of Artemis Hemera of ca. 300 (strongly influenced in its architecture by the somewhat earlier Classical temples at Bassai and Tegea), Naiskos D, and then the Hellenistic bouleuterion and fountain house—and such settlement evidence as we have dates at the earliest to the third century.[59] But Lousoi should not be seen as typical either in date or in the development of specific building forms (the chronology of which will be discussed presently). The Pheneos survey, for example, has revealed evidence of towers that were surely more than just military in purpose from the end of the fifth to the mid-third century.[60] Further west, evidence seems closer to the Arcadian pattern outlined below: the theatre at Leontion dates to the second half of the fourth century, and at Kleitor there may perhaps be a fourth-century predecessor to the Hellenistic theatre later used for Achaean League assemblies.[61] Geography, and especially the direction and role of routes of communication, make such a mixed picture readily comprehensible.

From a wider Peloponnesian perspective, we should note the potential for comparative analysis of site hierarchy. It would, for example, be helpful to evaluate features such as settlement size and layout, and important progress in this direction has certainly been made (as discussed below) largely on the basis of surface data.[62] Inevitably, though, conclusions have

---

[57] Petropoulos 1985.

[58] Nielsen and Roy 1998:11, 16, 23–26.

[59] Mitsopoulos-Leon 2001b offers a convenient summary with references; on the temple, see Ladstätter 2001.

[60] Tausend 1999:306–330.

[61] Leontion: Rossetto and Sartorio 1994:251; Kleitor: Petritaki 2001.

[62] Bintliff 1997; Morgan and Coulton 1997:87–88, 91–99, 126–128. The remarks of Osborne

tended to be rather broad-brush, and a lengthy new study would be required if we were to attempt use surface data to draw more detailed comparison of regional development across the Peloponnese while taking full account of the variability both of the data and the methodologies via which they were generated.[63] This would be a worthwhile exercise which would likely add considerably to the account given here, but it is beyond the scope of this short chapter. For present purposes, there are a few cases where real change in the extent and built form of a settlement can be identified. One such is Stymphalos, where geophysical exploration has revealed a newly established, orthogonally planned city, with a theatre and a new temple of Athena. The excavator, Hector Williams, relates this change to synoikism, comparing Stymphalos to Mantinea as a possibly similar conception.[64] But more evidence of this kind is needed before models of ranking can be applied to data on site size and layout over any significant area. At present, monumental construction offers greater scope for documenting a degree of settlement ranking, as well as for varying perceptions of the wider significance of different building forms missing in earlier centuries.

Regional Comparisons

In his recent discussions of the relationship between demography and wider political power, John Bintliff has identified cycles of "urban take off," which were always combined with expansion in rural settlement.[65] In the fifth century the main area of this "take off" corresponded with the political peak of the old *polis* lowlands (i.e. the northwest Peloponnese), in the fourth it reflects the rise of the central and southern Peloponnese, and in the third century we find the rise of Achaea, central and north-western Greece. Bintliff's argument drew on data from a range of surface survey projects, but it echoes what can be observed in monumental investment and raises questions of site hierarchy which merit continuing research.

2004:168–170 are apposite: it is insufficient to focus on the top end of the size scale given the range and pervasiveness of assumptions about the classification and interpretation of site size at each point on the scale. This is not to dismiss the exercise—merely to note the extent and nature of issues involved.

[63] Analogous to Alcock 1993: esp. chs. 2, 3, 4 or, for the Bronze Age, Wright 2004. Alcock and Cherry 2004 contains a wealth of discussion of the problems of intra- and inter-regional comparison, of integrating excavation and survey data, and of establishing standards for comparison of survey projects of different vintage and methodology (see especially papers by Attema and van Leusen; Cunningham and Driessen).

[64] Williams 1983a and 1983b.

[65] Bintliff 1997; Bintliff 1999.

Limitations of preservation and research must be acknowledged (although some building forms—theatres for example—tend to remain more visible than others).[66] The following review is preliminary and uncertainties of detail remain: nonetheless, the results offer a useful point of departure for argument.

We will consider Bintliff's geographical groupings in turn, beginning with Arcadia, where an emergent ranking of *poleis* finds echoes in the epigraphical record (the early fourth-century subjection of Helisson to Mantinea, for example).[67] Significance may be attached to the location of the few cities to erect public buildings in the fourth (or very late fifth) century—and here perhaps the most interesting forms of structure are bouleuteria (for their obvious political implications) and, given their likely multiple uses, theatres.[68] The three major eastern *poleis*, Tegea, Mantinea and Orchomenos, feature strongly, along with Megalopolis.[69] Indeed, Megalopolis, with its large and architecturally innovative theatre, federal Thersilion and (if Pausanias 8.30.9 is correct) city bouleuterion too, offers a snapshot of a perceived ideal of monumental development in the mid-fourth century.[70] The correlation of this physical development with an emerging double (eastern and western) political

---

[66] Frederiksen 2002:67–69.

[67] Rhodes and Osborne 2003: no.14 (SEG 37.340.3–7); Nielsen 2002:345–379, on Helisson and Mantinea see 34, 116–117, 294–295, 359–363 and Funke in this volume.

[68] For a general review of the significance of particular forms of public architecture, see Hansen and Fischer-Hansen 1994; Morgan and Coulton 1997:103–116. Bouleuteria: Gneisz 1990: part A, ch. 1; Hansen and Fischer Hansen 1994:37–44; Theatres: Frederiksen 2002:80–88.

[69] Fourth-century Peloponnesian theatres as listed by Rossetto and Sartorio 1994, in approximate chronological order (and with Arcadian sites underlined): cats. 262 (Megalopolis, post 370), 313 (Mantinea II, fourth-century, after 370), 213 (Phleious, mid fourth-century), 270 (Tegea I late fourth-century), 251 (Leontion late fourth-century), 268 (Orchomenos, late fourth-century with third-century choregic monuments), 153 (Corinth, first cavea under Roman theatre, late fourth-century), 207 (Elis, cavea end fourth-century), 225 (Isthmia II, end fourth-century), 229 (Orchomenos Kalpaki fourth-century with third-century proedria thrones), 255 (Keryneia Mamousia, pre-end fourth-century?), 235 (Kastro Platanias Helleniko, fourth-century cavea). The existence of a theatre at Phigaleia by 375/4 is attested by Diod. 15.40.2. Bouleuteria, as listed by Hansen and Fischer-Hansen 1994: Mantinea (date disputed: Gneisz 1990: cat. 37 dates the first phase to the fourth century), Megalopolis *Thersilion* (ca. 370: Gneisz 1990: cat. 38), Megalopolis (city bouleuterion, date?; for a contrary interpretation, see Gneisz 1990, cat. 39), Olympia (rebuilding?; Gneisz 1990: cat. 47 dates construction phase 3 to 374 or later), Sikyon (late fourth-century); Orchomenos had already built in the fifth century (see also Gneisz 1990: cat. 50). Gneisz 1990 adds to this list Lousoi (cat. 36, fourth/third-century).

[70] For recent research on the theatre, see Karapanagiotou 2001; Karapanagiotou-Oikonomopoulou 2006. On the Agora area: Kreilinger 2006.

focus on "great" *poleis* within Arcadia is important,[71] and is further nuanced by the sites chosen in the fourth century for temple (re-)construction.

Compared with the extent and scale of temple building in Arcadia during the Archaic period, the fourth century saw relatively few locations (re-)developed.[72] But what was undertaken was done on a lavish scale and designed to send out carefully conceived messages to a wide audience. This contrast is not unique to Arcadia: the nature of fourth-century religious building programmes throughout the Peloponnese differed in many respects from that of the previous, sixth-century peak, as will be further discussed. Here, however, the changes correlate with wider patterns of architectural investment. Lavish as they were, temples do not always seem to have been the highest priority for local investment. At Tegea, the fire of 395 which destroyed the Archaic temple necessitated the first rebuilding since the late seventh century. The proposed date of ca. 345–335 for the extant architectural remains leaves a gap of almost 50 years between the fire and the rebuilding.[73] Indeed, Geoffrey Waywell has suggested that if the Ada, Zeus, and Idrieus relief dedicated at this time was a document relief, it may be a thank-offering for a donation of money from the satraps of Mylasa.[74] He further suggests that the subject of the relief sculpture of the altar, the birth and life of Zeus (Pausanias 8.47.4), fits a Carian interest, although the version chosen, with Zeus attended by nymphs, surely also alludes to Mt Lykaion. Certainly, Ionianising sculptural and architectural traits are particularly prominent and the overall effect more elaborate than the slightly later (late fourth- or early third-century) temple of Artemis Mesopolitis in the new upper city of neighbouring Orchomenos.[75]

Scholarly interest has focused on the innovative interior design and rare sculptural decoration of the Tegea temple, and in general, the level of attention paid in the fourth century to such design, and to the role of sculpture in particular, is notable. Sculpture had the power to add symbolic value to an already rich structure. Hence the addition of a frieze to the relatively recently constructed Athenaion in the Triphylian city of Makistos (near modern Skillountia/Mazi) on the Elean border.[76] The subjects of the

---

[71] See also Frederiksen 2002:89–90.

[72] Voyatzis 1999:153–159.

[73] Norman 1984:191–194.

[74] Waywell 1993.

[75] Blum and Plassart 1914; Østby 1990–1991:327–337.

[76] Ruggeri 2004:102–107 reviews the question of the identification of Skillountia with ancient Makistos, and summarizes archaeological findings from the acropolis and cemeteries.

east and west pediments, a gigantomachy and amazonomachy respectively, are both given a distinctive local twist. The gigantomachy, for example, includes elements of the myth of Lykaion, one of whose sons was Mististeus, *oikist* of Makistos.[77] This temple was built in ca. 500, one of a group erected by Triphylian cities (along with those at Prasidaki, Babes, Lepreon, and Kombothekra).[78] It is unclear whether it was erected by Triphylians before the loss of Makistos to the Eleans (at some point before 480) or by the Eleans thereafter, although Nakasis presents a cogent argument for the former, noting that the Eleans used booty from the Triphylians for the Temple of Zeus at Olympia.[79] The temple was maintained through the fifth century, but its sculpture was added after 399 in celebration of the re-liberation of the Triphylian cities between 400 and 367.

In the west, Iktinos' temple of Apollo Epikourios at Bassai (ca. 429) is clearly spectacular for its internal frieze, Corinthian capitals, imported marble, as well as its anti-seismic design and the sophisticated use of local stone.[80] While the exact arrangement of the frieze blocks remains unresolved, the iconography of the sculptural programme as a whole links military episodes (the Heraklean and Trojan Amazonomachies, and the centauromachy), with the return of Apollo from the land of the Hyperboreians, juxtaposing mortality and immortality, violence and civic order, in a way which, while fitting broader fifth-century values, is particularly apposite here.[81] It is the more remarkable for being constructed during a period of Spartan hegemony, rapidly followed by the incursion which resulted in the capture of its patron *polis*, Phigaleia.[82] The symbolic importance of the sanctuary, close to Messenian territory and to key battlefields, is attested by the removal of the statue of Apollo Epikourios to Megalopolis, after which dedications declined markedly (although Phigaleia itself rebuilt its more modest temple of Athena and Zeus Soter late in the fourth century).[83] Megalopolis, at least in its early years, concentrated on the duplication of cults and the acquisition and creation of cult symbols (i.e. statuary) from its

---

[77] Trianti 1985.

[78] See most recently Arapogianni 2002 on Prasidaki, with comparative discussion.

[79] Nakasis 2004 offers the most recent review of the architectural evidence for chronology.

[80] The architecture is fully reviewed in Cooper 1996.

[81] Madigan 1992:esp. 87–90; on the frieze, Jenkins and Williams 1993.

[82] Cooper 1996:50–51, 53–55, which makes the proposed provenance of the marble used for the temple, Cape Tainaron (Cooper 1996:107–114), somewhat curious.

[83] Statue: Cooper 1996:70 (citing Pausanias 8.30.3). Athena temple: *Ergon* 1996:41–47 (X. Arapogianni).

constituent communities, as well as on the "protective" cult of Zeus Soter which acquired an architecturally innovative cult complex from ca. 340.[84] Yet while the foundation of the city did not result in any overall diminution of settlement in its territory (in fact in some places there was a steady increase to a Hellenistic peak, as survey data from Asea well illustrates),[85] temple building outside the city center remained relatively rare and generally later. The Asklepieion at Alipheira is the fourth-century exception, but Alipheira, strategically placed between Megalopolis and Triphylia, remained independent despite its involvement in founding Megalopolis.[86] Its wealth is further shown by its Macedonian-style tomb monuments of the late fourth or early third century which at present have Peloponnesian parallels only at third-century Phigaleia.[87] Throughout Arcadia, religious building remained a city matter. The pan-Arcadian shrine on Mt Lykaion had no securely identified cult building,[88] and the megaron at Lykosoura is only vaguely dated within the fourth to second centuries.[89] The selectivity shown in the pattern of fourth-century building and sculptural elaboration cannot be a matter of chance. The location of the cities involved shows a new dual, eastern and western focus, and as the model of Megalopolis confirms, this was not confined to temple building.

The picture in Achaea is rather different. The fifth-century expansion in the coastal cities surely reflects their ability to mobilise goods along the Gulf, to provide harbour facilities, and to exploit ever-intensifying traffic.[90] This continued through the fourth century, but the kind of monumental development discussed above mostly dates from the third onwards. Detailed reconstruction of the development of coastal cities in particular is complicated by the limitations of rescue excavation and centuries of overbuilding, although it is tempting to suggest from the limited evidence available that there is less obvious evidence of ranking than one finds in Arcadia. Nonetheless, there is clear evidence of fifth-century expansion and the establishment

---

[84] Jost 1985:220–235; Jost 1994; Jost 1996. Sanctuary of Zeus Soter: Gans and Kreilinger 2002.
[85] Megalopolis: Pikoulas 1988. Asea: Forsén and Forsén 2003:260–273.
[86] Orlandos 1967–1968:169–202; Jost 1985:81–82.
[87] Orlandos 1967–1968:203–243; Arapogianni 2001:305.
[88] Jost 1985:180–183 (noting an adjunct building, possibly a xenon, of the end of the fourth century).
[89] Jost 1985:172–178 with previous bibliography.
[90] Hence Thucydides' reports of Phormio's use of Patras as a naval base in 429 (2.83.3–5), and (5.52.2) Alcibiades' attempt to persuade its citizens to construct long walls to the sea in 419. Among material connections, Papapostolou (1990:467–468) emphasizes lingering Attic influence on funerary reliefs of the fourth century from Patras.

of new cemeteries at the two main ports, Aigion (which also acquired its first satellite settlements during the fourth century)[91] and Patras. Similar hints elsewhere include the fragmentary Parian marble temple pedimental group and roof tiles from Keryneia probably after 480—noting the expansion of the settlement at Mamousia in the late fourth to third centuries, after the destruction of Helike.[92] The far south of the *khôrai* of the eastern coastal cities seem (at least on present evidence) to have received less attention: Aigion's inland temple at Ano Mazaraki may not have been rebuilt after the destruction of 373, for example, although dedications continued into the fourth century AD.[93] It should, however, be noted that, unlike western Achaea, these areas have not been surveyed systematically: the results of a recent survey in the Aegialea may alter this picture.[94]

During the fourth century, the most obvious changes in Achaea occurred on the western plains, around Dyme (whose urban center expanded only at this stage), Olenos and Patras.[95] Data from the western Achaea survey confirms the existence of earlier activity—albeit with an Archaic and early Classical dip from hardly impressive Geometric figures—but the late Classical take-off is clear.[96] Within the *khôra* of Patras, rural farmsteads with large storage facilities and associated burials were established in the late fifth or early fourth century, and increased rapidly in number thereafter. The earliest such sites lay furthest from the city center, and the intervening territory slowly filled over subsequent centuries. That the likely commodities produced (oil, grain and wine) were at least in part for export is implied by the popularity initially of Corinthian B amphorae (perhaps of Corfiote manufacture, but likely recycled), followed by the establishment of local amphora production in the third century.[97] Overall, the political and economic pull to the west which began in the fifth century becomes much clearer in the settlement record of the fourth, and on a scale unparalleled since the Late Bronze Age.

Even so, most monumental public buildings are relatively late and often third-century. Temples are the exception, although even these are rarely on

---

[91] Aigion: Papakosta 1991; Morgan and Hall 1996:176–177. Patras: Papapostolou 1990.

[92] Katsonopoulou 2000, with previous bibliography. Anderson 1953.

[93] Petropoulos, Pontrandolfo and Rizakis 2002:155, noting that further research is required into the function of a partially excavated later structure on site.

[94] Petropoulos, Pontrandolfo and Rizakis 2002, 2003, 2004.

[95] Dyme: Lakaki-Marchetti 2000. Patras, see n89.

[96] Petropoulos and Rizakis 1994:esp.197–198, 203–205; Petropoulos 1991.

[97] Petropoulos 1994.

new sites. Admittedly, the lack of evidence from Helike leaves a potentially serious gap,[98] but at present, the picture is one of a longer period of settlement re-organisation and expansion than in Arcadia, followed by the generally later construction of new public buildings at sites of importance under the new order. At Aigeira, for example, the start of a new phase of building, marked by the construction of the Hellenistic theatre and Temple D (ca. 275–250), is often associated with the foundation of the "Second" Achaean League in the fourth year of the twenty-fourth Olympiad (281/0).[99] There is also some evidence for the material ranking of settlements and the political dependency of *poleis*, although the chronology of these changes is generally imprecise. Thus Rhypes became subject to Aigion at some point between the last occurrence of its name late in the fourth century and the appearance of late Hellenistic tile stamps of Aigion on Trapeza hill.[100]

Finally, we should turn to the northeast Peloponnese. In focusing on the new power balance in the central and western Peloponnese, it is easy to overlook the old dominant *poleis*, Corinth and Argos, whose heyday, in terms of monumental urban development and the distribution and likely size of rural population, belongs in the fifth century.[101] Yet here too, the fourth century saw important political developments: indeed, the earliest attested experiment in political union was that between Argos and Corinth, in place by 389 (Xenophon *Hellenica* 4.6.4) although its exact form remains a matter of debate.[102]

A convenient starting point is the physical development of Corinth itself—invaded, politically divided, its territory ravaged, and its western trade severely diminished by a combination of circumstances locally and in the west.[103] The general lack of public building comes as no surprise, but even repairs to prestigious structures took time. The temple of Poseidon at Isthmia lay ruined for most of the fourth century after the fire of 390 (precisely dated from Xenophon *Hellenica* 4.5.4) and there is no evidence for any other major construction project in the sanctuary until the very end of

---

[98] Katsonopoulou 2002; Morgan and Hall 1996:175 with references to previous work in the area.

[99] Gogos 1992: Pt. I and Pt. II ch. 4A on chronology.

[100] Vordos 2002 (and accepting with him the identification of the Trapeza site as Rhypes, which is not uncontroversial).

[101] I thank Agiati Benardou for discussion of fifth-century Corinthian settlement and economy based on her London University doctoral thesis.

[102] Salmon 1984:357–362; Tuplin 1982; Robinson, this volume.

[103] For an overview, see Salmon 1984:354–386; Roberts 1983:64–135. Western trade: Munn 1983:352–363 (departing from a flourishing fifth-century picture: Munn 2003).

the century at the earliest.[104] In the city center, expansion at the sanctuary of Demeter and Kore, where the body politic of Corinth dined in a large complex of dining rooms and represented their youth in large terracotta statues of votaries,[105] was abruptly halted until the end of the century. Dining activity continued, but investment in facilities stopped: when it resumed, the facilities were radically reshaped, with a new formal entrance to the lower terrace and (at least as preserved) a smaller number of dining complexes replacing the old dining rooms.[106] The major fourth-century construction in the city center is the South Stoa, the date of which, while much debated, is likely to fall broadly around 330. With its elaborate commercial and probably also administrative facilities, it may have drawn on outside funds—Broneer linked it with Corinth's role as capital of Philip II's Corinthian League.[107] The sense of a city running on its reserves is clear—and when military success did occur (with an attendant influx of booty), the comparative lavishness of its commemoration is notable. The victories of Timoleon were marked by a quadriga monument in the city center, set up by the Sacred Spring, and by a dedication of Carthaginian arms at Isthmia.[108] This rather bleak picture is, of course, based on investment in monumental construction, and should not be taken to imply more general disruption in other aspects of Corinthian civic and cult life. As noted, dining continued at Demeter and Kore, and at Isthmia, the use of the underground dining caves by an as-yet unidentified civic group, and of the Northeast Altar terrace, continued uninterrupted to the late fourth or early third century.[109]

When Corinth began to revive, late in the fourth century, investment favoured religious facilities, especially at Isthmia, where for two centuries

[104] Gebhard and Hemans 1998:10–15, 17, 41–51, fig. 18: temple fire debris was used in the construction of Road G and Terrace 7 at the very end of the fourth or early third century.

[105] Bookidis 1995:245–246; Bookidis and Stroud 1997:259–260. I am grateful to Nancy Bookidis for information on these pieces in advance of the publication of Bookidis, forthcoming. While their exact meaning (fulfilling cult roles, for example, or celebrating age and/ or social status) and the occasion(s) of their dedication are the subjects of continuing research, we can at least suggest that the vast majority represent real or idealised sub-adult members of Corinthian elite families.

[106] Bookidis and Stroud 1997:171–230 (lower terrace), 231 (middle terrace).

[107] Broneer 1954:94–99; Williams 1978:15–16 with previous bibliography. Austin 1981:no.42 (the League decree = *Staatsverträge* III, 476; Plutarch *Demetrius* 25.2 locates the meeting at the Isthmus).

[108] Williams 1978:145–146, with previous bibliography; Rhodes and Osborne 2003:no.74. Isthmia: Xenophon *Hellenica* 5.1.28–34. On the background to these victories, see Salmon 1984:389–392; Roberts 1983:136–153.

[109] Gebhard 2002; Gebhard and Hemans 1998:21–26.

the festival had been the principal means by which Corinth's external image had been projected. The theatre acquired a new cavea and scene building, the Sacred Glen was established, and the temenos was landscaped with new roads and further terracing.[110] Even during the second half of the century, small changes were made to the stadium: phase IV of the Early Stadium had new statue bases, water channels and a relocated starting line.[111] But the facility was abandoned altogether late in the fourth century, and the stadium moved wholesale to a spacious new site beyond the temenos, an initiative again interpreted by Broneer as reflecting Macedonian influence in the city.[112] Macedonian cultural-political agendas aside, by prioritising investment of this kind Corinth was subscribing to one of the most distinctive aspects of fourth-century construction in the northeast. The main way in which both the old *poleis* and the newly powerful sought to engage with their Peloponnesian peers was by playing on the traditional link between founding or promoting games and political power. It was, after all, barely a century since Pindar had celebrated victors at the Isthmian games, and in doing so, provided detailed evidence of the intensity of competition across what was by then a rapidly growing network of festivals in the north-east Peloponnese and surrounding areas.[113]

The association between major sanctuary-building programmes and the institution of the *theôrodokia* has usefully been characterised as a desire to preserve the traditional networks which linked Greek *poleis* and the panhellenic sanctuaries in a changing world when *proxenia* alone was no longer sufficient.[114] Setting aside what has sometimes (and questionably) been interpreted as a pre-370 list of *theôrodokoi* in Arcadia and Achaea (*Syll.*3 90), the earliest secure evidence for the *theôrodokia* as a discrete institution is a Pisatan decree of 365–363 for Kleandros and Sokles of Sikyon, erected at Olympia. If this Kleandros was indeed the general of the same name, this might imply a Pisatan initiative taken during her period of control of Olympia.[115] The Olympic *theôrodokia* was rapidly followed by those of

[110] Theatre: Gebhard 1973:29–60. Sacred Glen: Gebhard and Hemans 1998:41, with previous bibliography; see also Anderson-Stojanovic 2002.

[111] Gebhard and Hemans 1998:38–40.

[112] Broneer 1973:55–63, 66.

[113] Morgan 2007.

[114] Perlman 2000:18–29.

[115] Perlman 2000:63–65; as she notes, the terms of the mid-fifth century decree at Olympia (B6970), which honours two foreigners who received the sacred embassy, especially the phrase τὰν θε<α>ρίαν δέκεσθαι, plainly imply the immediate precursor of the formal institution. The link between this decree and the institution of the *theôrodokia*

Epidauros and, later in the fourth century, Nemea and the Argive Heraion, with Lousoi (geographically, the exception to the initial cluster) at the very end of the century, and finally, after a long gap, Hermione at the end of the third.[116] In all cases, this initiative followed hard upon the physical redevelopment of the sanctuary in question, and Lousoi apart, the festivals concerned were well-established. At Epidauros, a building programme was inaugurated in the first quarter of the fourth century, with the Temple of Asclepius first to be completed ca. 370.[117] At Nemea, a period of decline through the fourth century was brought to an end by the return of the games from Argos ca. 330, an event accompanied by the redevelopment of athletic and related facilities. In the main sanctuary area, the xenon and bath (probably a functional pair) date around the end of the fourth or early third century.[118] On a nearby site, however, a wholly new complex was created, consisting of a stadium with an innovative vaulted tunnel and an apodyterion, and the stadium area was adorned with bronze statuary.[119] Resemblances between building ensembles in the earliest revival sites are clear and surely not coincidental. The pairing of stadium and apodyterion at Nemea is closely paralleled at Epidauros, and both are chronologically close to (if not modelled on) what is plausibly reconstructed as a similar ensemble at Olympia.[120] At Nemea, however, the revival was rather brief: the return of the games to Argos, perhaps as early as 271, falls close to the archaeological date of ca. 275 for the abandonment of the stadium. It has plausibly been suggested that Argos was simply unable to sustain a festival so far from home in a time of weakness.[121] Recent contributions have discussed in detail the changed political balance in the northeast Peloponnese, noting the changing fortunes of the smaller *poleis* such as Kleonai or Sikyon, previously vulnerable, interstitial communities

---

is fully explored by Siewert 2002:365–368.

[116] Perlman 2000:22–26, fig. 2.

[117] Burford 1969:32–35, 53–81.

[118] Birge *et al.* 1992: ch. 2 on xenon (Kraynak), ch. 3 on bath (Miller).

[119] Miller 2001 (see especially 164–172 for the possibility that the Sosikles whose name is recorded on tile stamps from the apodyterion, was the Sosikles/Sokles recorded at the Argive Heraion, and possibly something akin to "city architect" in Argos at the time); some 200 fragments of bronze likely come from 2 or 3 statues. The presence in the stadium of contingents of spectators from Argos, Sikyon, Phlious and Kleonai, is illustrated by the distribution of coins from these cities: Knapp 2005:22–30.

[120] Miller 2001:177–224 who also presents the less secure case of the Panathenaic stadium at Athens.

[121] Miller 2001:93; Marchand 2002:192–198 offers a persuasive account of the respective roles of Argos and Kleonai in the revival at Nemea.

between (variously) Sparta, Argos and Corinth,[122] and the operation of religious associations in the changing circumstances of the fourth century is discussed elsewhere in this volume.[123] Here I merely note that the pattern of monumental investment by both the old (and now much weakened) powers and the rising smaller and/or previously less conspicuous *poleis* in this area shows particular attention to facilities in sanctuaries which hosted games. It therefore focused on a particular tried and tested form of city self-promotion, following on from the successes of Corinth and Argos in the previous century.

Conclusion

As this brief review has shown, direct material counterparts for the ethnic claims evident in the literary and epigraphical record are few. Many of these claims were short-lived; nonetheless, actions such as the numerous grants of citizenship made by Triphylia could make a real difference to individuals,[124] even though these did not translate into any lasting form of material behaviour. When considering the material record, attention inevitably focuses on the Messenians, but they are far from typical. Indeed, when one sets aside Messenian dedications at Olympia and Delphi, evidence of monumental dedications by *ethnê* is relatively slight and geographically restricted. Private dedications are perhaps truer to the general picture in that they reveal a continuing personal attachment to city and/or sub-regional identity to complement the regional ethnic. The early fourth-century offering made at Delphi by the son of Hetairikhos the Arcadian, of Thisoa of Mainalon, is a case in point.[125] A similar picture emerges from Olympia,[126] as well as from related sources such as personal names, funerary inscriptions, and the way in which foreigners are recorded in catalogue documents (as, for example, the records of contributions to the reconstruction of the Temple of Apollo

---

[122] Kleonai: Marchand 2002: esp.490–500 (ch. 5 offers the fullest account to date of the physical development of the *polis* center). On Sikyon, see also Lolos 1998: esp. 55–59, 78–117 and ch. 5 (on fortification); it is hoped that Lolos' renewed fieldwork on the city plateau (http://extras.ha.uth.gr/sikyon/en—consulted in June 2005) will provide information on the early city, but at present, material evidence becomes plentiful only from the late fifth century onwards, and reveals the extent and wealth of settlement throughout Sikyonian territory.

[123] Robert Parker, this volume.

[124] Rhodes and Osborne 2003: no. 15.

[125] Jacquemin 1999: cat. 467.

[126] Jacquemin 1999: pls 4b and 5b offer instructive comparison, however: a larger number of central Peloponnesian *poleis* are represented at Olympia individually, rather than as part of the combined Arcadian and Achaean offerings made at Delphi.

at Delphi after the Third Sacred War).[127] A brief glance at the Peloponnesian volume of the *Lexicon of Greek Personal Names* (IIIA) shows names constructed from regional ethnics appearing as early as the sixth century, but while the fourth century saw the addition of Argeios, Arkadion, Arkas, and Achaiikos (all attested outside the obvious home region) these are all single instances. And both tombstones and the Delphi records reveal very little consistency even within a single city.[128]

The immediate picture may therefore seem rather unsatisfying. Little seems to have changed in comparison with the fifth century. Yet approaches to reading social relations in the material record of the Archaic and earlier Classical Peloponnese have grown so much more sophisticated in recent years that the background against which we must assess the fourth century is itself one of newly-appreciated complexity—our perception of what constitutes change has shifted. What can be observed, especially from the date and form of building programmes, is the beginning of shifts and dislocations within and between different, but closely connected, parts of the Peloponnese. As emphasized, the built environment has the power to shape the way individuals conducted their lives and thought about themselves and others. This review has shown in outline how new or very recent building forms were introduced, and old mechanisms—temples, festivals, athletic facilities—configured in new ways. Most construction was still conducted by *poleis*; direct responses in the ethnic register were far from inevitable. Interestingly, however, the archaeological record offers some confirmation of the conclusion drawn by other contributors to this volume that there was a contrast between the "city up" construction of Arcadian political identity (with a small number of powerful *poleis* staking claims to wider regional hegemony, whether or not accompanied by explicit reference to Arcadian identity), and the "region down" situation in Achaea, whose long coastal zone was subject to external characterisation, yet whose inland settlements often lay in close proximity to those of other groups or to rare routes through difficult terrain. Other such comparisons could easily be drawn, but the distinctive contribution of the material record here is to force us to focus on the long view. What began slowly with the creation of material symbols (coins and statuary) and the different forms and courses taken by building programmes, with their consequent impact on those who lived around and with them, thus

---

[127] Rhodes and Osborne 2003: no. 66; Bousquet 1988:85–101.
[128] Fraser 2000a and 2000b.

offers an insight into the practical creation of Beck's "federal grammar between *polis* and *ethnos*."

Bibliography

Alcock, S. E. 1993. *Graecia Capta: The Landscapes of Roman Greece*. Cambridge.

Alcock, S. E. 1998. "Power from the Dead: Tomb Cult in Postliberation Messenia." *Sandy Pylos: an Archaeological History from Nestor to Navarino* (ed. J. Davis) 199–204. Austin.

Alcock, S. E. 1999. "The Pseudo-History of Messenia Unplugged." *TAPhA* 129:333–341.

Alcock, S. E. 2002. *Archaeologies of the Greek Past: Landscape, Monuments and Memories*. Cambridge.

Alcock, S. E., and Cherry, J., eds. 2004. *Side-by-Side Survey: Comparative Regional Studies in the Mediterranean World*. Oxford.

Anderson, J. K. 1953. "Excavations near Mamousia in Achaia." *ABSA* 48:154–171.

Anderson-Stojanovic, V. R. 2002. "The Cult of Demeter and Kore at the Isthmus of Corinth." In Hägg 2002:75–83.

Andreou, I. 1998. "Πολεοδομικά της αρχαίας Λευκάδας." *AD* 53:147–186.

Arapogianni, X. 2001. "Ανασκαφές στη Φιγάλεια." In Mitsopoulos-Leon 2001a:299–305.

Arapogianni, X. 2002. "The Doric Temple of Athena at Prasidaki." *Excavating Classical Culture. Recent Archaeological Discoveries in Greece* (eds. M. Stamatopoulou and M. Yeroulanou) 225–228. Studies in Classical Archaeology I. Oxford.

Austin, M. 1981. *The Hellenistic World from Alexander to the Roman Conquest*. Cambridge.

Beck, H. 1997. *Polis und Koinon. Untersuchungen zur Geschichte und Struktur der griechischen Bundesstaaten im 4. Jahrhundert v. Chr.* Stuttgart.

Beck, H. 2003. "New Approaches to Federalism in Ancient Greece: Perceptions and Perspectives." *The Idea of European Community in History II. Aspects of Connecting Poleis and Ethne in Ancient Greece* (eds. K. Bouraselis and K. Zoumboulakis) 177–190. Athens.

Bintliff, J. 1997. "Regional Survey, Demography and the Rise of Complex Societies in the Ancient Aegean: Core-periphery, Neo-Malthusian and Other Interpretative Models." *JFA* 24:1–38.

Bintliff, J. 1999. "Regional Field Surveys and Population Cycles." *Reconstructing Past Population Trends in Mediterranean Europe (3000 BC-AD 1800)* (eds. J. Bintliff and K. Sbonias) 21–33. Oxford.

Birge, D., Kraynak, L. H., and Miller, S. G. 1992. *Excavations at Nemea: Topographical and Architectural Studies: the Sacred Square, the Xenon and the Bath.* Berkeley.

Blum, G., and Plassart, A. 1914. "Orchomène d'Arcadie. Fouilles de 1913. Topographie, architecture, menus objets." *BCH* 38:71–88.

Bommeljé, S., et al. 1987. *Aetolia and the Aetolians: Towards the Interdisciplinary Study of a Greek Region.* Utrecht.

Bookidis, N. 1995. "Archaic Corinthian Sculpture: a Summary." *Corinto e l'Occidente* 233–256. Taranto.

Bookidis, N. Forthcoming. *Corinth XVIII.v: The Sanctuary of Demeter and Kore. Terracotta Sculpture.* Princeton.

Bookidis, N., and Stroud, R. 1997. *Corinth XVIII.iii: The Sanctuary of Demeter and Kore. Topography and Architecture.* Princeton.

Borbein, A. H. 1973. "Die griechische Statue des 4. Jahrhunderts v. Chr." *JDAI* 88:43–212.

Bousquet, J. 1988. *Études sur les comptes de Delphes.* Athens.

Broneer, O. 1954. *Corinth I.iv: The South Stoa and its Roman Successors.* Princeton.

Broneer, O. 1973. *Isthmia II: Topography and Architecture.* Princeton.

Burford, A. 1969. *The Greek Temple Builders at Epidauros.* Liverpool.

Cooper, F. A. 1996. *The Temple of Apollo Bassitas I: The Architecture.* Princeton.

Corsten, T. 1999. *Von Stamm zum Bund. Gründung und territoriale Organisation griechischer Bundesstaaten.* Munich.

Coulton, J. 1977. *Ancient Greek Architects at Work.* Ithaca.

Davies, J. K. 1997. "Sparta e l'area peloponnesiaca. Atene e il dominio del mare." *I Greci. 2. Una storia greca II. Definizione (VI-IV secolo a. C.)* (ed. S. Settis) 109–161. Turin.

Davies, J. K. 2001. "Rebuilding a Temple: the Economic Effects of Piety." *Economies Beyond Agriculture in the Classical World* (eds. D. J. Mattingly and J. Salmon) 209–229. London.

Deshours, N. 1993. "La légende et le culte de Messène ou comment forger l'identité d'une cité." *REG* 106:39–60.

Dietz, S., et al. 1998. "Surveys and Excavations in Chalkis, Aetolias, 1995–1996: First Preliminary Report." *PDIA* 2:233–315.

Dietz, S., et al. 1999. "Greek-Danish Excavations in Aetolian Chalkis 1997–1998: Second Preliminary Report." *PDIA* 3:219–307.

Dietz, S., et al. 2004. "Greek-Danish Excavations in Aetolian Chalkis 1999–2001: Third Preliminary Report." *PDIA* 4:167–258.

Eiring, J, et al. 2004. "Death in Aetolia: the Hellenistic Graves at Aetolian Chalkis." *PDIA* 4:93–166.

Feyel, C. 2006. *Les Artisans dans les sanctuaires grecs aux époques classique et hellénistique.* Athens.

Fiechter, E. 1931. *Das Theater in Megalopolis.* Stuttgart.

Fiedler. M. 1996. "Zur Topographie der polis Leukas." *Akarnanien. Eine Landschaft im antiken Griechenland* (eds. P. Berktold, J. Schmidt and C. Wacker) 157–168. Würzburg.

Fletcher, R. 1995. *The Limits of Settlement Growth: a Theoretical Outline.* Cambridge.

Forsén, J. and Forsén, B. 2003. *The Asea Valley Survey: An Arcadian Mountain Valley from the Palaeolithic Period until Modern Times.* Stockholm.

Fraser, P. 2000a. "Ethnics as Personal Names." *Greek Personal Names: Their Value as Evidence* (eds. S. Hornblower and E. Matthews) 149–158. Proceedings of the British Academy 104. London.

Fraser, P. 2000b. "Delphian Names." *Delphes cent ans après la Grande Fouille* (ed. A. Jacquemin) 141–147.

Frederiksen, R. 2000. "Typology of the Greek Theatre Building in Late Classical and Hellenistic Times." *PDIA* 3:135–175.

Frederiksen, R. 2002. "The Greek Theatre: A Typical Building in the Urban Centre of the Polis?" *Even More Studies in the Ancient Greek Polis* (ed. T. H. Nielsen) 65–124. Stuttgart.

Frietag, K. 2000. *Der Golf von Korinth. Historisch-topographische Untersuchungen von der Archaik bis in das 1. Jh. v. Chr.* Munich.

Freitag, K., Funke, P., and Moustakis, N. 2004. "Aitolia." In Hansen and Nielsen 2004:379–390.

Funke, P. 1987. "Zur Datierung befestiger Stadtanlagen in Aitolien. Historische-philologische Anmerkungen zu einem Wechselverhältnis zwischen Siedlungsstruktur und politischer Organisation." *Boreas* 10:87–96.

Funke, P. 1997. "Polisgenese und Urbanisierung in Aitolien im 5. und 4. Jh. v. Chr." *The Polis as an Urban Centre and as a Political Community* (ed. M. H. Hansen) 145–188. Copenhagen.

Funke, P. 1993. "Stamm und Polis. Überlegungen zur Entstehung der griechischen Staatenwelt in den „Dunklen Jahrhunderten"." *Colloquium aus Anlaß des 80. Geburtstages von Alfred Heuss.* Frankfurter Althistorische Studien 13 (ed. J. Bleicken) 29-48. Kallmünz.

Gans, U.-W., and Kreilinger, U. 2002. "The Sanctuary of Zeus Soter at Megalopolis." In Hägg 2002:187–190.

Gebhard, E. 1973. *The Theater at Isthmia*. Chicago.

Gebhard, E. 2002. "Caves and Cults at the Isthmian Sanctuary of Poseidon." In Hägg 2002:63–74.

Gebhard, E., and Hemans, F. 1998. "University of Chicago Excavations at Isthmia 1989. II." *Hesperia* 67:1–63.

Gerin, D. 1986. "Les statères de la Ligue Arcadienne." *SNR* 65:13–39.

Gneisz, D. 1990. *Das antike Rathaus. Das griechische Bouleuterion und die frührömische Curia*. Vienna.

Gogos, S. 1992. *Das Theater von Aigeira. Ein Beitrag zum antiken Theaterbau*. Vienna.

Grainger, J. D. 1999. *The League of the Aitolians*. Leiden.

Grandjean, C. 2003. *Les Messéniens de 370/369 au 1er siècle de notre ère. Monnayages et histoire*. Athens.

Greco, E., ed. 2002. *Gli Achei e l'identità etnica degli Achei d'Occidente*. Paestum.

Hägg, R, ed. 2002. *Peloponnesian Sanctuaries and Cults*. Stockholm.

Hall, J. M. 2003. "The Dorianization of the Messenians." *Helots and their Masters in Laconia and Messenia* (eds. N. Luraghi and S. E. Alcock) 142–168. Cambridge, MA.

Hansen, M. H., and Fischer-Hansen, T. 1994. "Monumental Political Architecture in Archaic and Classical Greek Poleis: Evidence and Historical Significance." *From Political Architecture to Stephanus Byzantius* (ed. D. Whitehead) 23–90. Stuttgart.

Hansen, M. H., and Nielsen, T. H. 2004. *An Inventory of Archaic and Classical Poleis*. Oxford.

Head, B. V. 1911. Historia Numorum. *A Manual of Greek Numismatics*. Oxford. Second Edition.

Hölscher, T. 1974. "Die Nike der Messenier und Naupaktier in Olympia." *JDAI* 89:70–111.

Hornblower, S. 1991. *A Commentary on Thucydides I*. Oxford.

Ioakimidou, C. 1997. *Die Statuenreihen griechischer Poleis und Bünde aus spätarchaischer und klassischer Zeit*. Munich.

Jacquemin, A. 1999. *Offrandes monumentales à Delphes*. Athens.

Jacquemin, A., and Laroche, D. 1982. "Notes sur trois piliers Delphiques." *BCH* 106:191–218.

Jeffery, L. H. 1990. *The Local Scripts of Archaic Greece*. Oxford. Revised Edition.

Jenkins, I., and Williams, D. 1993. "The Arrangement of the Sculptured Frieze from the Temple of Apollo Epikourios at Bassae." *Sculpture from Arcadia and Laconia* (eds. O. Palagia and W. Coulson) 57–77. Oxford.

Jost. M. 1985. *Sanctuaires et cultes d'Arcadie*. Paris.

Jost, M. 1994. "The Distribution of Sanctuaries in Civic Space in Arkadia." *Placing the Gods: Sanctuaries and Sacred Space in Ancient Greece* (eds. S. E. Alcock and R. Osborne) 217–230. Oxford.

Jost, M. 1996. "Les cultes dans une ville nouvelle d'Arcadie au IVe siècle. Mégalopolis." *Le IVe siècle av. J.-C. Approches historiographiques* (ed. P. Carlier) 103–109. Paris.

Karapanagiotou, A. V. 2001. "Ανασκαφικές εργασίες στο αρχαίο Θεάτρο Μεγαλόπολης 1995–1997. πρωτές εκτιμήσεις." In Mitsopoulos-Leon 2001a:331–342.

Karapanagiotou-Oikonomopoulou, A. V. 2006. "Θέατρο της Μεγαλόπολης 1995: Πρώτα ανασκαφικά στοιχεία." *Α' αρχαιολογική Σύνοδος νότιας και δυτικής Ελλάδος* 441–448. Athens.

Katsonopoulou, D. 2000. "Pedimental Sculptures in Parian Marble from Keryneia of Achaea." *Paria Lithos. Parian Quarries, Marble and Workshops of Sculpture* (eds. D. Schilardi and D. Katsonopoulou) 373–377. Athens.

Katsonopoulou, D. 2002. "Helike and her Territory in the Light of New Discoveries." In Greco 2002:205–216.

Knapp, R. C. 2005. "The Classical, Hellenistic, Roman Provincial and Roman Coins." *Excavations at Nemea III: The Coins* (eds. R. C. Knapp, and J. D. MacIsaac) 3–179. Berkeley.

Kolia, E., and Saranti, E. 2004. "Τα Νεκροταφεία της κλασικής και ελληνιστικής Ναυπάκτου." *Β' διεθνές ιστορικό και αρχαιολογικό Συνεδρίου Αιτωλο-Ακαρνανίας* 231–241. Agrinion.

Kontorli-Papadopoulou, L. 2001. "Αναζητώντας την ομηρική Ιθάκη. Πρόσφατες ανασκαφές στην Ιθάκη." *Ερανος. Πρακτικά του Θ' Συνεδρίου γιά την Οδύσσεια* (ed. M. Paisi-Apostolopoulou) 317–330. Ithaka.

Kraay, C. 1976. *Archaic and Classical Greek Coins*. Berkeley.

Kreilinger, U. 2006. "Οι νεότερες ανασκαφές στην περιοχή της Αγοράς της Μεγαλόπολης." *Α' αρχαιολογική Σύνοδος νότιας και δυτικής Ελλάδος* 434–440. Athens.

Ladstätter, G. 2001. "Der Artemistempel von Lousoi." In Mitsopoulos-Leon 2001a:143–153.

Lakaki-Marchetti, M. 2000. "Σωστικές ανασκαφές στην Κάτω Αχαγιά." *Paysages d'Achaîe II. Dymé et son territoire* (ed. A. D. Rizakis) 113–121. Athens.

Lolos, G. J. 1998. *Studies in the Topography of Sikyonia*. Dissertation, University of California at Berkeley.

Luraghi, N. 2001. "Der Erdbebenaufstand und die Entstehung der messenischen Identität." *Gab es das Griechische Wunder? Griechenland zwischen dem Ende des 6. und der Mitte des 5. Jahrhunderts v. Chr.* (eds. D. Papenfuß, and V. M. Strocka) 279–310. Mainz.

Luraghi, N. 2002. "Becoming Messenian." *JHS* 122:45–69.

Luraghi, N. 2003. "The Imaginary Conquest of the Helots." *Helots and their Masters in Laconia and Messenia* (eds. N. Luraghi, and S. E. Alcock) 109–141. Cambridge, MA.

Luraghi, N. Forthcoming. "Local Scripts from Nature to Culture."

Lynch, K. 1960. *The Image of the City*. Cambridge, MA.

Madigan, B. C. 1992. *The Temple of Apollo Bassitas II: The Sculpture*. Princeton.

Marchand, J. C. 2002. *Well-built Kleonai: A History of the Peloponnesian City Based on a Survey of the Visible Remains and a Study of the Literary and Epigraphic Sources*. Dissertation, University of California at Berkeley.

Martin, T. R. 1985. *Sovereignty and Coinage in Classical Greece*. Princeton.

Martin, T. R. 1995. "Coins, Mints, and the Polis." *Sources for the Ancient Greek City-State* (ed. M. H. Hansen) 257–291. Copenhagen.

Miller, S. G. 2001. *Excavations at Nemea II: The Early Hellenistic Stadium*. Berkeley.

Mitsopoulos-Leon, V., ed. 2001a. *Forschungen in der Peloponnes*. Österreichisches Archäologisches Institut Sonderschriften 38. Athens.

Mitsopoulos-Leon, V. 2001b. "Lousoi nach hundert Jahren." In Mitsopoulos-Leon 2001a:131–142.

Morgan, C. 1999. "Cultural Subzones in Early Iron Age and Archaic Arkadia?" In Nielsen and Roy 1999:382–456.

Morgan, C. 2003. *Early Greek States beyond the Polis*. London.

Morgan, C. 2007. "Debating Patronage: the Cases of Argos and Corinth." *Pindar's Poetry, Patrons and Festivals. From Archaic to Roman Times* (eds. S. Hornblower and C. Morgan) 213–263. Oxford.

Morgan, C., and Coulton, J. J. 1997. "The Polis as a Physical Entity." *The Polis as an Urban Centre and as a Political Community* (ed. M. H. Hansen) 87–144. Copenhagen.

Morgan, C., and Hall, J. M. 1996. "Achaian Poleis and Achaian Colonisation." *Introduction to an Inventory of Poleis* (ed. M. H. Hansen) 164–232. Acts of the Copenhagen Polis Centre 3. Copenhagen.

Morris, S. P. 2001. "The Towers of Ancient Leukas: Results of a Topographic Survey, 1991–1992." *Hesperia* 70:285–347.

Morris, S. P., and Papadopoulos, J. K. 2005. "Greek Towers and Slaves: an Archaeology of Exploitation." *AJA* 109:155–225.

Munn, M. L. Zimmerman 1983. *Corinthian Trade with the West in the Classical Period.* Dissertation, Bryn Mawr College.

Munn, M. L. Zimmerman 2003. "Corinthian Trade with the Punic West in the Classical Period." *Corinth XX. Corinth. The Centenary 1896–1996* (eds. C. K. Williams II and N. Bookidis) 195–217. Princeton.

Nakasis, A. 2004. *Ο ναός της Αθήνας Μακίστου.* Athens.

Neilsen, T. H. 2002. *Arkadia and its Poleis in the Archaic and Classical Periods.* Göttingen.

Nielsen, T. H., and Roy, J. 1998. "The Azanians of Northern Arkadia." *C&M* 49:5–44.

Nielsen, T. H., and Roy, J., eds. 1999. *Defining Ancient Arkadia.* Acts of the Copenhagen Polis Centre 6. Copenhagen.

Norman, N. 1984. "The Temple of Athena Alea at Tegea." *AJA* 88:169–194.

Orlandos, A. 1967–1968. *Η Αρκαδική Αλίφειρα και τα Μνημεία της.* Athens.

Osborne, R. 2004. "Demography and Survey." In Alcock and Cherry 2004:163–172.

Østby, E. 1990–1991. "Templi di Pallantion e dell'Arcadia. Confronti e sviluppi." Scavi di Pallation, *ASAA* 68–69 (ns 51–52):285–391.

Papakosta, L. 1991. "Παρατηρήσεις σχετικά με την τοπογραφία του αρχαίου Αιγίου." In Rizakis 1991:235–240.

Papapostolou, I. 1990. "Ιστόρικες Μαρτυρίες και αρχαιολογικά Ευρήματα της κλασσικής και της πρωιμής ελληνιστικής Πόλης των Πατρών." *Τόμος τιμητικός Κ. Ν. Τριαντάφυλλου Ι.* 465–471. Patras.

Partsch, J. 1890. *Kephallenia und Ithaka.* Gotha.

Pearson, L. 1962. "The Pseudo-history of Messenia and its Authors." *Historia* 11:397–426.

Perlman, P. 2000. *City and Sanctuary in Ancient Greece: The Theorodokia in the Peloponnese.* Göttingen.

Petritaki, M. 2001. "Θεάτρο Κλείτορος· η αναδυόμενη εικόνα του μνημείου μέσα από τα πρώτα ανασκαφικά στοιχεία." In Mitsopoulos-Leon 2001a:117–123.

Petropoulos, M. 1985. "Τορογραφικά βόρεας Αρκαδίας." *HOROS* 3:63–73.

Petropoulos, M. 1991. "Τοπογραφικά της χώρας τών Πατρέων." In Rizakis 1991:249–258.

Petropoulos, M. 1994. "Αγροικίες Πατραϊκής." *Structures Rurales et Sociétés Antiques* (eds. L. Mendoni and P. Doukellis) 405–424. Paris.

Petropoulos, M. 2002. "The Geometric Temple of Ano Mazaraki (Rakita) in Achaia during the Period of Colonisation." In Greco 2002:143–164. Paestum.

Petropoulos, M., and Rizakis, A. D. 1994. "Settlement Patterns and Landscape in the Coastal Area of Patras: Preliminary Report." *JRA* 7:183–207.

Petropoulos, M., Pontrandolfo, A., and Rizakis, A. D. 2002. "Prima campagna di ricognizioni archeologiche in Egialea (settembre-ottobre 2002)." *ASAA* 80:939–965.

Petropoulos, M., Pontrandolfo, A., and Rizakis, A. D. 2003. "Seconda campagna di ricognizioni archeologiche in Egialea (aprile-maggio/settembre/ottobre 2003)." *ASAA* 81:947–962.

Petropoulos, M., Pontrandolfo, A., and Rizakis, A. D. 2004. "Terza campagna di ricognizioni archeologiche in Egialea (ottobre 2004)." *ASAA* 82:783–806.

Pikoulas, Y. 1981–1982. "Η Αρκαδική Αζάνια." *Πρακτικά του Β´ Διεθνούς Συνεδρίου Πελοροννησιακών Σρουδών.* 2:269–281. Athens.

Pikoulas, Y. 1988. *Η νότια Μεγαλοπολιτική Χώρα από τον 8ο π.Χ. ώς τον 4 μ.Χ. αιώνα.* Athens.

Psoma, S. 1999. "Αρκαδικόν." *HOROS* 13:81–96.

Randsborg, K. 2002. *Kephallénia: Archaeology and History. The Ancient Greek Cities.* 2 vols. Copenhagen.

Rhodes, P. J., and Osborne, R. eds. 2003. *Greek Historical Inscriptions 404-303 BC.* Oxford.

Rizakis, A. D., ed. 1991. *Achaia und Elis in der Antike.* Athens.

Roberts, K. L. 1983. *Corinth Following the Peloponnesian War: Success and Stability.* Dissertation, Northwestern University.

Rossetto, P. C., and Sartorio, G. P. 1994. *Teatri greci e romani II.* Rome.

Roy, J. 1999. "The Economies of Arkadia." In Nielsen and Roy 1999:320–381.

Ruggeri, C. 2004. *Gli stati intorno a Olimpia. Storia e costituzione dell'Elide e degli stati formati dai perieci elei (400-362 a.C.).* Historia Einzelschriften 170. Stuttgart.

Saarinen, T. F. 1976. *Environmental Planning: Perception and Behaviour.* Boston.

Salmon, J. 1984. *Wealthy Corinth.* Oxford.

Saranti, E. 2006. "Η αρχαία Ναύπακτος και η ευρύτερη περιοχή της: Τοπογραφικά δεδομένα και πρόσφατες έρευνες." *Α´ αρχαιολογική Σύνοδος νότιας και δυτικής Ελλάδος* 499–510. Athens.

Scholten, J. B. 2000. *The Politics of Plunder: Aitolians and their Koinon in the Early Hellenistic Era, 279-217 BC.* Berkeley.

Schultz, S. 1992. "Die Staterprägung von Pheneos." *SNR* 71:47–74.

Seltman, C. 1955. *Greek Coins.* London.

Shipley, G. 2004. "Messene." In Hansen and Nielsen 2004:547–568.

Siewert, P. 1996. "Votivbarren und das Ende der Waffen- und Geräteweihungen in Olympia." *MDAI(A)* 111:141–148.

Siewert, P. 2002. "Die wissenschaftsgeschichtliche Bedeutung der bronze Urkunden aus Olympia." *Olympia 1875-2000. 125 Jarhe Deutsche Ausgrabungen* (ed. H. Kyrieleis) 359–370. Mainz.

Snodgrass, A. M. 1989-1990. "The Economics of Dedication at Greek Sanctuaries." *Scienze dell'Antichità* 3–4:287–294.

Steinhart, M., and Wirbelauer, E. 2002. *Aus der Heimat des Odysseus. Reisende, Grabungen und Funde auf Ithaka und Kephallenia bis zum ausgehende 19. Jahrhundert.* Mainz.

Symeonoglou, S. 1984. "Ἀνασκαφή Ἰθάκης." PAAH:109–121.

Symeonoglou, S. 1985. "Ἀνασκαφή Ἰθάκης." PAAH:201–215.

Symeonoglou, S. 1986. "Ἀνασκαφή Ἰθάκης." PAAH:234–240.

Tausend, K. ed. 1999. *Pheneos und Lousoi. Untersuchungen zu geschichte und Topographie Nordostarkadiens.* Frankfurt.

Themelis, P. 2003. *Heroes at Ancient Messene.* Athens.

Trianti, A.-I. 1985. *Ο γλυπτός διάκοσμος του ναού στο Μάζι.* Dissertation, Aristotelean University of Thessaloniki.

Tuplin, C. 1982. "The Date of the Union of Corinth and Argos." *CQ* 32:75–83.

Vordos, A. 2002. "Rhypes: à la Recherche de la Métropole." In Greco 2002:217–234. Paestum.

Voyatzis, M. 1999. "The Role of Temple Building in Consolidating Arkadian Communities." In Nielsen and Roy 1999:130–168.

Warren, J. A. W. 2007. *The Bronze Coinage of the Achaian Koinon: The Currency of a Federal Ideal.* London.

Waywell, G. 1993. "The Ada, Zeus and Idrieus Relief from Tegea in the British Museum." *Sculpture from Arcadia and Laconia* (eds. O. Palagia and W. Coulson) 79–86. Oxford.

Williams, C. K. II. 1978. *Pre-Roman Cults in the Area of the Forum of Ancient Corinth.* Dissertation, University of Pennsylvania.

Williams, H. 1983a. "Stymphalos: a Planned City of Ancient Arcadia." *EMC* 27:194–205.

Williams, H. 1983b. "Investigations at Stymphalos, 1984." *EMC* 27:215–224.

Williams, R. 1965. *The Confederate Coinage of the Arcadians in the Fifth Century.* New York.

Williams, R. 1970. "The Archaic Coinage of Arcadian Heraia." *ANSMN* 16:1–12.

Wright, J. 2004. "Comparative Settlement Patterns during the Bronze Age in the Northeastern Peloponnesos, Greece." In Alcock and Cherry 2004:114–131.

X

Subjection, Synoecism and Religious Life
Robert Parker

THE ELEANS HAVE BOUGHT EPEION for thirty talents (Xenophon *Hellenica* 3.2.30); the Eleans refuse to surrender the Marganeis and Skillountians and Triphylians, claiming that "these cities are ours" (6.5.2); the Eleans capture Lasion, which "of old had belonged to them, but at present was enrolled in (συντελεῖν εἰς) the Arkadikon" (7.4.12). The Spartans force the Mantineans to "dioecize their city into four settlements, as they lived in the past" (5.2.7); but after the battle of Leuctra the Mantineans refound their single city (6.5.3). In the same period many communities of southern Arcadia come together to found Megalopolis. Greek history in the fourth century, indeed in all centuries, is full of incidents such as these; and no doubt much of human history is a story of appropriation of territory, coalescence and division of communities. But the intermeshing of religious and political organisation in Greece had as a consequence that religious life was not a timeless backdrop in front of which the play of history took place. Or it was so only in a very broad sense: in the most general terms nothing changed, familiar Greek gods were still worshipped in accord with familiar Greek rituals; but at a more detailed level every re-structuring of the political order required or potentially required the reorganisation of cults, rewriting of sacrificial calendars, re-assignment of priesthoods. These processes have been very little studied, and are indeed often not accessible to detailed investigation. But for a community threatened by subjection, aspiring to liberation or contemplating synoecism the future of ancestral cults must have been one very sensitive issue. In what follows I shall look at the implications for religious life of certain types of political re-ordering, voluntary or involuntary. A comprehensive study would be a large undertaking, and I can do no more than sketch some possibilities. I shall then turn

183

to the specific situations of some Peloponnesian cities or tribes in the fourth century.[1]

Religion in the Dependent *Polis*

Of the 15 different types of Dependent *Polis* recently identified by the Copenhagen Polis Centre,[2] most need not concern us here: membership of a federation or an alliance, for instance, normally had no impact on the cults of a city even when such membership severely restricted its freedom of action in other areas.[3] Again, two cities that were distant in space inevitably conducted largely separate religious lives. But certain types of dependency did potentially have implications for religious activity.

When the Eleans claimed a kind of ownership ("these cities are ours") over Epeion, Lasion and the other communities mentioned above, the general and plausible assumption is that the *poleis* in question (I use the term *polis* here as a shorthand: the exact status of the communities is not important) were internally self-governing but bound to follow the Eleans in foreign policy; the extent to which they were exposed to financial exactions is quite unknown. They were, therefore, the Elean equivalent to the *perioikoi* of Sparta and other Greek cities.[4] Unfortunately, the *perioikoi* even of Sparta, to say nothing of those of Argos or Thessaly, are, as is well known, among the great voiceless groups of Greek society. They must have had their own sanctuaries, festivals and presumably priesthoods too. One ambiguous text may show some Spartan *perioikoi* participating in a festival of Sparta itself, the Promacheia. Conversely, Spartans certainly made dedications in perioikic sanctuaries and competed in their athletic festivals.[5] But it was normal for members of one group to have these two forms of access to the shrines and cults of another group. On an optimistic view, therefore, one might suppose that the *perioikoi* pursued their own religious life free from Spartan interference; that optimistic conclusion would chime with the current under-

---

[1] To familiar abbreviations add RO = Rhodes and Osborne 2003.

[2] Hansen 2004.

[3] Note however IG IV I².73 (LSS 23), a "law" written by the "law-drafters" of the Achaean league for the cult of Hygieia at Epidauros.

[4] For details see Roy in this volume.

[5] See Parker 1989:145, and the references to excavation given by Catling in Cavanagh et al. 2002:238n183. But Catling argues that *perioikoi* residing close to Sparta lacked important shrines of their own: "for these fragmented communities, Spartan festivals and sanctuaries may have provided the main occasions and locations for participation in communal cult activity, and their religious concerns were largely identified with those of the inhabitants of the Spartan plain." (Cavanagh et al. 2002:224).

standing of the *perioikoi* as an integrated rather than an alienated and rebellious element within the Spartan state.[6] As for other *perioikoi* or *perioikoi*-like groups, nothing forbids, though nothing enjoins, the same assumption.

The dealings of Athens with Oropos and Delos, however, show that it was by no means inevitable that a dominant power respected the religious autonomy of cities subordinate to it. In the fourth century, although Delos retained a polity and cults of its own, Athenian pressure on the sanctuary of Apollo was so strong that the Delians appealed to Philip, unsuccessfully, in an effort to recover control; as for Oropos, at all times when the Athenians had possession of the Oropia they treated the cult of Amphiaraos as, in effect, an Athenian cult.[7] In the second half of the fourth century Argos swallowed up Kleonai, which became an Argive deme; the Nemean games, traditionally Kleonai's most precious possession, were henceforth under Argive administration (though the Kleonaians apparently enjoyed a privileged relation to the games for a while), and at an uncertain date (probably in the third century) the ancient festival was even re-located from Nemea to Argos.[8] At the time of the mysterious partial union of Corinth with Argos in the late 390s, enemies of the new arrangements maintained that the Argives had taken over the running of the Isthmian games of 390; and they certainly had some role, if not an exclusive one.[9] Celebrated sanctuaries and festivals such as these are perhaps a special case, a special temptation to a dominant power.[10] On Delos the Athenians had the excuse that they were operating as members of a shadowy Amphictyony. But we cannot necessarily assume that interference occurred in these circumstances alone.

---

[6] See Shipley 1997 passim, who cites earlier studies tending the same way.

[7] On Delos, see Parker 1996:222–225; on Oropos, Parker 1996:148–151, 247, noting, for instance, Athenian occupancy of the priesthood.

[8] See Perlman 2000:131–155; privileged relation: Piérart 1982:138, on IG IV 616; re-location: Plutarch *Aratus* 28.3–4 (where the temporary transfer back to the original site is recorded). Formally perhaps this case belongs in the "synoecism" section below. (Earlier, Mycenae too had aspired to control the Nemean games, Diodorus 11.65.2.) The situation of the Panamareis in Caria in relation to their shrine of Zeus Karios is perhaps another example of a "privileged relation" after absorption: in the second century BCE they still as a *koinon* concerned themselves with the affairs of the shrine even though the priesthood had been assumed by the *polis* Stratoniceia (SEG 45.1556) of which they were probably now a part (van Bremen 2004:227–231); the two demes from which most priests were selected may have been those into which quondam "Panamareis" were absorbed (van Bremen 2004:239).

[9] Xenophon *Hellenica* 4.5.1–2; Plutarch *Agesilaus* 21.3–6; contrast Pausanias 3.10.1; cf. Whitby 1984:297–298.

[10] The theoretical autonomy of Delphi too was constantly infringed, but the issues are too complicated to be discussed here.

Gods whose Worshippers are Expelled

Wholesale expulsion of an existing population is a very different case; but let us note it *en passant* because here too important issues about the maintenance of cults arise. According to an argument attributed to the Athenians in 424 by Thucydides (4.98.2), "the rule among the Greeks is that whatever power controls any territory, great or small, also owns the shrines, which should be tended in such traditional ways as are practicable." The Athenians rather often had the opportunity to apply their principle, when they expelled existing inhabitants and divided territory among cleruchs of their own, and often we duly find them maintaining existing cults (e.g. on Lemnos over a long period, on Aigina in the late fifth century, on Samos in the fourth century);[11] sometimes, as on Delos in the fifth century and at Oropos in the fourth, the desire to establish secure control of the sanctuary may have been a main motive for the expulsion.[12] One showcase exists in which we can observe such a taking-over of cults on a large scale: Delos, handed over to the Athenians by Rome in 166 BCE and at once emptied by the new possessors of its Delian population. The main gods continued to be honoured, but an entirely new set of priesthoods had to be created, which followed the Athenian model of annual tenure, rotating (in some cases at least) between the tribes; and changes of emphasis between cults can be observed.[13] At the organizational level, at least, this "tending in such traditional ways as are practicable" involved extensive change.

A more drastic alternative was annihilation or evacuation of a population and destruction of the city. The best-described case is the destruction of Plataea by the Spartans in 426 BCE (Thucydides 3.68.3): the Spartans built a large temple and pilgrims' hostel beside the existing Heraion, using spoils and building material taken from the city which the goddess had once guarded. The city which most frequently adopted "le modèle de la desertification" was Argos.[14] At Asine, destroyed at a very early date, they left behind a temple of Apollo Pythaeus and there maintained an important cult.[15] But any such gestures made to the gods of Mycenae and Tiryns, over-

---

[11] See Parker 1994:342–346. Melos and Skione were similarly re-settled, though in these cases the male population was massacred, not deported (Thucydides 5.32.1, 5.116.4).

[12] Parker 1996:151.

[13] See Mikalson 1998:208–241.

[14] The phrase is Piérart's, 1997:330.

[15] Pausanias 2.36.5; Bacchylides fr. 4; Thucydides 5.53.1; Kowalzig 2007:132–160.

thrown and left desolate in the mid-fifth century, are not recorded.[16] When Alexander sacked Thebes in 335 he spared the Kadmeia; we are not told what happened to sanctuaries in the lower town, but he exempted sacred properties from the general re-distribution of Theban territory among his allies and we can perhaps conclude that he intended them to be available to finance continued cult (Arrian *Anabasis* 1.9.9). About Colophon and Lebedos, destroyed by Lysimachus between 294 and 287 partly as a punitive measure, partly to gain population for his newly sited Ephesus, little is recorded, but the "sack of Colophon" was a sufficiently terrible event to provoke a lament from the local poet Phoenix.[17] A minimum requirement imposed by piety on the victors was perhaps to attempt to preserve actual sanctuaries, or some among them, from the firebrand and the crowbar.[18] And a festival of Panhellenic standing could not readily be simply abandoned: when the Romans sacked Corinth in 146, the presidency of the Isthmian games was handed over, though perhaps after an interval, to Sikyon.[19]

An expelled population might, like Aeneas, seek to take its gods with it. When the Phocaeans fled their city before the Persian advance, they took with them in the ships "the statues from the shrines and all the dedications except those of bronze or stone, and paintings" (Herodotus 1.164.3). Did the inhabitants of Sicilian cities, so frequently forcibly re-located by tyrants, do something similar?[20] Nothing of the kind is recorded.

Synoecism and Sympolity

The prudent person will not attempt to define, or narrowly distinguish, synoecism and sympolity. The Greeks' own use of these words and their cognates shows a bold disregard for bureaucratic precision, and the variety in what actually occurred is too great for a simple sorting into two heaps, "synoecism" and "sympolity," to be helpful.[21] In broad terms, the phenom-

---

[16] We hear only of the removal of *xoana* from Tiryns to Argive shrines (Pausanias 2.17.5, 8.46.3), and a tithe from the spoils of Mycenae to Delphi (Diodorus 11.65.5)

[17] Pausanias 1.9.7; on these events see Robert and Robert 1989:78–85. Antissa in Lesbos was similarly punitively destroyed by Rome in 167 and its inhabitants transferred to Methymna (Livy 45.31.14).

[18] For the ideal, see e.g. Aeschylus *Agamemnon* 338–42, and *e contrario* Aeschylus *Persians* 809–815.

[19] Pausanias 2.2.2; for the possible interval see Habicht 2006:154–155, citing S. Dow.

[20] Demand 1990: chapters 5 and 8.

[21] See Reger 2004a:148–149 (the whole study, building on many works of L. Robert, is most helpful); Hansen in Hansen and Nielsen 2004:115–119. The only general study I know of the religious consequences of synoecism is the brief one of Nilsson 1951:18–25.

enon that concerns us here is the incorporation of what had been a wholly independent set of cults, or of several such sets, within a larger whole, on the occasion of a political coalescence between two or more communities. For these purposes the question whether the communities in question came together physically, partially or wholly, in an existing *polis* or one newly founded for the purpose, is not crucial, though in practice some population transfer would appear to have been the norm. What is crucial is the necessity that arose to re-write the ritual calendar in the new political circumstances, a necessity brought out in a model way by the opening of a decree from Mykonos to be dated to the last quarter of the third century:[22] "In the archonship of Kratinos, Polyzelos, Philophron, when the *poleis* were synoecized, the Mykonians decided to make the following sacrifices in addition to the existing ones and made the following corrections concerning existing ones." Alas, no sure criterion allows us to distinguish "new" from "corrected" entries in the list that follows;[23] nor have we any evidence either about the independent ritual life of the two *poleis* of the island prior to the synoecism, or about their joint life after it. So the Mykonos decree altogether declines to help in answering the question that it poses so clearly. And among the very many other attested instances of synoecism, sympolity, and the like, many for our purposes do not offer so much as a starting point for enquiry: the union must have entailed changes in the cultic sphere, but we cannot begin to identify them. Synoecism sometimes occurs as an aetiological motif to explain existing cults: the cult of Artemis Triklaria, for instance, had supposedly been shared by the three villages which eventually combined to form Patrai, and a precinct of Dionysus in the same city contained three images named after the three primeval villages.[24] Here the

---

[22] So Reger 2001:159–161. The text is LSCG 96 (*Syll.*[3] 1024).

[23] For some suggestions see Reger 2001:177–178. As he observes, the formulation of the decree implies that the existing calendar of one of the two *poleis* (which will therefore have been already dominant) served as a basis, rather than that two calendars of comparable scale were blended. The old view of von Prott 1896:15 is worth recalling: the text contains rules expressed both in the indicative, usually stipulating sacrifices to be made, and in the imperative, usually regulating details of how the sacrifice is to be performed: the indicative is the traditional mood in such texts, and the imperatives will therefore point to additions; it will follow that few sacrifices are actually added, and the main thrust of the text is to codify and correct.

[24] Pausanias 7.19.1; 7.20.1–2. According to Pausanias, poverty caused Patrai to dissolve again in the third century into the original three villages plus three others, in which condition it remained until re-united by Augustus (7.18.6–7): these later vicissitudes are likely to have influenced the tradition concerning Artemis Triklaria and the cult of Dionysus. On the separate tradition in Strabo (8.3.2, 337) which speaks of synoecism from 7 cities see Moggi

idea of synoecism or of a time prior to synoecism is embodied in a city's folk history and cult practice, as it was also in Athens, where there was even a mysterious festival Synoikia.[25] But such ways of envisaging the past do not help us directly to re-construct actual historical synoecisms.

Unequal Sympolity

Fortunately a modest number of sympolity agreements do mention cultic arrangements; the relevant data are excerpted in an appendix to this paper. And the religious systems of three *poleis* which underwent synoecism in the historical period (Rhodes, Megalopolis, Kos) are known well enough to give speculation at least some basis. A common situation is the "unequal sympolity," which is in effect, whatever name it goes under, the incorporation of a small community into a much larger one.[26] Such mergers often occurred, in Hellenistic Asia Minor, at the instance of a king, but could also be motivated by the ambitions or fears of either party directly involved; the minor partner might be more or less willing. In such a situation the name that persists for the merged entity will obviously be that of the larger *polis*, of which the minor *polis* may now become a deme or something similar (the option of creating greater integration by distributing the new citizens among existing units is less common).[27] The dominant religious calendar will similarly be that of the major partner, and it is often made explicit that the newly incorporated citizens are to participate as equals in its existing rites or simply in everything to which existing citizens are entitled (Heliswasians, Pidaseans, by implication Teans in Lebedos, Magnesians, Medeonians [nos. 1, 3, 4, 5, 9 in the list in the appendix]). A corresponding stipulation whereby members of the major partner may participate fully in the rites of the minor occurs only once (Medeonians and Stirians [no. 9]).[28] More common is a guarantee that rites – some rites at least – of the minor partner shall continue to be performed (Heliswasians, Euaimonians, Pereans [nos. 1, 2, 6]);

1976:92–93. Similar to the Patrai myth is another passage in Pausanias (3.16.9) where he traces the obligatory shedding of human blood on the altar of Artemis Orthia to a bloody conflict between the inhabitants of the four villages of Sparta while celebrating her rites: the implication is that the men of Amyklai did not at that date yet share in the festival.

[25] See Parker 1996:14.

[26] Reger 2004a:145–172.

[27] The Heliswasians and probably the Pereans and Medeonians [numbers 1, 6 and 9 in the list in the appendix] become demes or villages; the Pidaseans in Herakleia under Latmos are distributed [no. 3].

[28] Hypnia and Myania [no. 7] share in at least some sacrifices on a basis of proportional contributions. This might—but need not—entail a generalised sharing of sacrifices.

a special official recruited from the minor partner may be charged with the task (Medeonians [no. 9]), or sums set aside specifically (Pereans, perhaps Medeonians [nos. 6. 9]). Occasionally nothing is said at all about the cults of the minor partner even in a text that is complete (Pidaseans in Herakleia, and in Miletus; Magnesians in Smyrna [nos. 3, 8; 5]). Perhaps it is simply taken for granted that they will be carried on.[29]

Greek religion was both inclusive and exclusive. It was inclusive in the sense that restrictions on who could enter sanctuaries, watch sacrifices or public rites, and make dedications were not very common. On the other hand the right to share in sacrificial meat, to hold priestly office, and to conduct rites in a given cult was strictly controlled; the exclusivity in this sense of a group's cults was integral to its identity.[30] In the case where both parties to a sympolity are admitted reciprocally to each other's rites they both surrender that exclusivity (at least at the level of participation in sacrifice; entitlement to priesthood is not explicitly mentioned). But the loss is unequal: whereas the major partner acquires in effect a new expanded religious identity, the minor partner no longer has anything that is distinctively its own. Such simple absorption of smaller by greater must sometimes have occurred. In little Phygela, for instance, swallowed up by Ephesos perhaps in the first decade of the third century, sacrifices continued to be performed, but they were in the charge of a board of *neopoiai* dispatched from the big city.[31] Again, the rites of Pidasa cannot have been maintained as distinct, if they were retained at all, once its sacred revenues had been pooled with those of Heraklea under Latmos [no. 3]. On the other hand, we noted that, in sympolity agreements where maintenance of the cults of the absorbed city is guaranteed, there is normally no stipulation that these are to be opened to all; the presumption perhaps is that they will remain separate, like the rites of an Attic deme vis-à-vis Athens itself. That such separateness could be an eagerly defended ideal is shown by an inscription from Olymos. It is of the second half of the second century BCE, and thus postdates the political absorption of Olymos within the larger Mylasa by perhaps 75 years.[32] It

---

[29] But Wörrle 2003 may bring this suggestion into doubt, at least in relation to the incorporation of Pidasa into Latmos (cf. n62).

[30] I simplify a little; for a nuanced account see Krauter 2004:53–113.

[31] See Robert 1967 on I. Ephes. 1408. The sacrifices in question are probably those in Phygela's main shrine, that of Artemis Mounichia; what happened to lesser cults of the city we do not know. From the late third century, the Asklepieion of Lebena in Crete seems to have been under Gortynian control: see Melfi 2007:116.

[32] On the political incorporation of Olymos into Mylasa, after 246 BC, see Reger 2004a:164–168.

begins by explaining that a share in the "common *hiera*" of Olymos belongs by descent in the male line to (Olymians and) persons, and descendants of persons, to whom right of participation has been granted by decree.

But, as it is, certain persons who have no right to participate in any of the aforementioned ways are participating in [*hiera* relating to Apollo] and Artemis, gods to whom not only have revenues been consecrated by the people and sacrifices and receptions are held [annually, but also all that relates] and pertains to their honour and reputation is conducted in accord with tradition; in addition, the [*dêmos*] of the Olymians contains [three of what were previously called tribes] and now *sungeneiai*, the Mosseis, Kybimeis and Kandebeloi, and in each of these there are private [sacrifices and rituals] and private revenues: certain persons who have been granted by agreement right of participation in [*hiera*] in the *sungeneiai*, [and now claim that they should also have right of participation in] the meetings of [ ], have ventured to approach the rites conducted by the Olymian *dêmos*, some venturing to [approach just the sacrifices, others also the offices of *hierourgos*] and priest and prophet, and in consequence of their shameless claim to that to which they are not entitled [many impieties have occurred against the rights of the citizens] and against the protection of the gods...

I. Mylasa 861

Doubtless the values of inland Caria cannot simply be transferred to Greece, but the attitude of the Lindians in the synoecized Rhodes of the late fourth century is strikingly similar: they went to court to ensure that "selections in Lindos of priests and *hierothutai* and *hieropoioi* and others with responsibility for communal matters shall be made from the Lindians themselves, as is prescribed in the laws, and persons shall not participate in Lindian sacra who did not participate in them before."[33] The Olymians stress the financial basis of the rights that they are protecting: these cults were supported by specially designated Olymian funds. But priesthood was often a burden rather than an advantage, and the sense of group identity was also and perhaps more strongly at issue. By the agreement between Helisson and Mantinea [no. 1] the little community was to continue to receive sacred

---

Population transfer is not attested, and Olymos retained cults and cult property of "the gods of the deme of Olymos" (I. Mylasa 806.9); it also, remarkably, retained a citizenship of its own which it could confer on Mylasians (Reger 2004a:164–168). Contrast the case of the Panamareis who retained influence over the shrine of Zeus Karios but lost the priesthood (n8 above).

[33] IG XII 1.761 (*Syll.*[3] 340) 38–42: cf. n83 below.

embassies announcing the Panhellenic games. It cost little to the Mantineans to make this concession, which must have helped the Heliswasians to avoid feeling that their ancient city was being wiped off the map.[34] (No actual instance of a sacred embassy visiting Helisson is recorded. Whether the sureties offered to little communities in sympolity agreements proved effective is a different issue, and one usually beyond our reach to enquire into.)

Physical transfer of divine images is only occasionally mentioned as a consequence of sympolity. The misfortune of the Myuntians is a special case: forced by mosquitoes to abandon their city, they took their sacred images and settled in Miletos (to which they were already bound by a much looser sympolity agreement).[35] According to Pausanias, apparently describing events of 362/1, Kyzikos "forced the Prokonnesians by war to become *sunoikoi* with them," and transferred a statue of Meter Dindymene from Prokonnesos to the city. It was probably because the inhabitants of Trapezous fled to avoid incorporation in Megalopolis that some of their statues were transferred thither.[36] Anger at non-compliance probably explains these unusually intrusive measures.

Multi-*Polis* Synoecism

The dynamics of a synoecism involving several *poleis* were very different. Usually, there was no one dominant city to whose practices the others conformed, in religion as in the rest of life; instead, a new start was made with the creation of a new city on a new site (or an existing city was expanded to an extent that constituted a new foundation). Substantial population transfer was necessary if the new capital was to thrive, but the extent to which the old towns out of which it was formed were in fact scaled down was very various. The scope of the initial synoecism of Megalopolis is a matter of controversy, and the variables are large: was the great city's initial catchment area one of c. 1500 square kilometres, or of somewhat less than 500?[37] On a "little Megalopolis" model the population of the *khôra* was

---

[34] *Thearodokia* is often taken as a sign of a community's status as a *polis*. But the case of Helisson shows the criterion to be ambiguous: Helisson is a *polis* in name, a *kômê* in fact.

[35] Pausanias 7.2.11 (date not specified); for the loose third-century sympolity see Herrmann 1965:90–96.

[36] Prokonnesos: Pausanias 8.46.4; for the date, Demosthenes 50.5. Prokonnesos survived, perhaps as a dependent *polis*: Avram 2004:994. Trapezous: Pausanias 8.31.5 with 8.27.5–6.

[37] For an excellent and finally agnostic analysis of the two positions (Roy and Moggi) see Nielsen 2002:413–455. On the religious implications of the synoecism see above all Jost 1992:224–238 (partially translated in Jost 1994:225–228).

largely absorbed in the city, and the sanctuaries of the old communities were kept in use as extra-urban sanctuaries of Megalopolis: Pausanias has several references to sanctuaries that survived, apparently in good repair, in deserted settlements near to the city, and we can imagine that they were sometimes approached by processions from the city.[38] Pausanias speaks also (Pausanias 8.27.5–6) of repentance and resistance to the synoecism by four nearby communities which had initially agreed to it: Lykaia and Trikolonoi were brought in by force; the inhabitants of Trapezous fled; the Lykosourans were spared and apparently allowed to stay where they were "from reverence for Demeter and Despoina," in whose hallowed sanctuary they had taken refuge. On a "great Megalopolis" model the fate of the nearby communities will be the same, but right from the start the new capital will also have controlled quondam *poleis* further away which were now demoted to deme status (Pausanias 8.27.7) but continued as places of habitation (and occasionally re-asserted their independence as cities); like Attic demes, they may have retained effective autonomy in cultic matters, though almost no evidence on organisation is available.[39] Whatever the situation in the 360s, some version of the "great Megalopolis" model will certainly be needed to describe the situation by c. 200 BCE. As for post-synoecism Rhodes and Kos, a thoroughly vigorous municipal life persisted, and religious activity continued to be conducted, and organised, outside the new capital cities with remarkable commitment and vigour; as we have noted, the Lindians on Rhodes were as insistent as the Olymians in Caria on excluding outsiders from their traditional cults.

The new capital cities had to create new religious calendars of their own which were not simply extensions and modifications of one already in existence. The detailed evidence on Kos and Rhodes is presented below in an

---

[38] Pausanias 8.29.5 (sanctuary of Demeter Eleusinia in the ruins of Basilis); 8.35.6 (sanctuary of Poseidon above the quondam *polis* of Trikolonoi); 8.35.7 (temples of Demeter and Artemis in deserted Zoitia); cf. Jost 1992:226. Pausanias 8.38.8 attests a procession from the statue of Apollo Epikourios in the agora to the shrine of Apollo Parrhasios on the slopes of Mt. Lykaion (Jost 1992:234).

[39] See Jost 1992:235f, who wonders whether the scale of construction at Gortys and Lykosoura (the latter, however, not Megalopolitan at all according to Pausanias 8.27.6) in the fourth and third centuries implies the use of Megalopolitan money. Thür and Taeuber 1994: no. 16, lines 18–21 (= IG V 2.344; *Syll.*³ 490, of shortly after 235) is not wholly clear, but seems to show men of Methydrion raising money on the security of a statue belonging to Zeus Hoplosmios (a Methydrian god) and Megalopolis laying claim to that money. On the archaeological evidence for persistence of cults in Megalopolitan territory see Jost 1992:226–227.

appendix. In brief, simple taking-over of existing cults (i.e. existing sanctuaries) seems almost never to have been the procedure.[40] The fate of the great
pan-Arcadian sanctuary of Zeus Lykaios is a kind of counter-case, since it
seems to have passed into the control of Megalopolis; but it may always have
been administered by an amphictyony rather than a single community.[41] In
the main, rather than to take over celebrated cults in the *khôra*, the preferred
option was to create calques of them: the clearest case is the establishment
in Megalopolis of a sanctuary of Zeus Lykaios which echoed, but did not
seek to replace, the god's famous precinct on Mount Lykaion.[42] The cult of
the Great Goddesses in that city was not a calque but a variation, it has been
suggested, on the traditional devotion to deities of that type in the region.[43]
Pan too could not be absent from an Arcadian "great city."[44] A large statue
of Apollo Epikourios was brought "as an adornment" to Megalopolis from
Phigaleia, which is not even in Megalopolitan territory.[45] Similarly, on Kos,
Apollo Delios, always a central figure in the islanders' religious consciousness, continued to be separately honoured in at least one deme but was also
taken up in the city. Gods already popular in the region have found a place
in the city, but in the familiar Greek way a new sanctuary is simply added to
those that already exist.

Any sanctuary established in the capital belonged by definition to
the "whole people," but the foundation in Kos town of a cult of Aphrodite
bearing precisely that title, Pandemos, may indicate a more conscious ideal
of unification, particularly as the same cult seems to have been taken out
into the demes. Zeus Polieus too early acquired a prominent role in the Koan
calendar. On Rhodes the cult of Halios, either non-existent or on a small
scale prior to the synoecism, was built up as a religious centre of the unified
state. New cults, whether of rulers or of rising deities such as Asclepius,

---

[40] Except in the case where sanctuaries of now depopulated settlements were kept in use.

[41] Megalopolitan honours are proclaimed "at the Lykaia and the other crowned *agônes*"
(I cannot suggest what these are) in IG V 2.437.20–21 (second century), and the priests
by whom victor lists in the Lykaia are dated (IG V 2.549–550, late fourth century) are
presumably Megalopolitan. Amphictyony: Nielsen 2002:148–152. Note too p. 210 below on
Alexandreia Troas and the Smintheum.

[42] Pausanias 8.30.2–3, with Jost 1992:229f. Jost sees a temple of Hermes Akakesios built in the
agora (Pausanias 8.30.6) as similarly honouring, not supplanting, the cult at Akakesion
(Pausanias 8.36.10).

[43] Pausanias 8.31.1–8, with Jost 1992:232f.

[44] Pausanias 8.30.2–3; 8.30.6.

[45] Pausanias 8.30.3. According to Schubart-Walz's generally accepted conjecture, the statue
was a "contribution" (συντέλεια): the intriguing idea of such contributions to the new
city's religious culture is unparalleled. On this statue see Cooper 1978:10.

would naturally be attached to the capital and not to one of the old towns. In all these ways a new pantheon could be developed that did not intrude on existing prerogatives.

The argument may seem to have assumed a complacent and anodyne tenor. Nothing, it seems, need be lost: in a synoecism both the new big town and the small old towns can flourish alike. And even in an unequal sympolity the traditions of the minor partner can be respected. It is true that synoecized Rhodes and Kos were, so far as we can judge, unusually successful societies; nor were Megalopolis and Alexandreia Troas failures, though there was some breaking away from both. But the verb συμπολιτεύεσθαι, "to unite politically," has an antonym ἀποπολιτεύεσθαι, "to withdraw from a political union," and such disaggregations were very common, particularly but not exclusively in cases of "unequal sympolity." One inscription even reveals the efforts of a third city acting as a conciliator between two partners thinking about divorce.[46] About the grievances of cities seeking separation we can only speculate, and there were doubtless often concrete economic or political grounds for discontent; simple nostalgia for home among relocated persons must also often have been a factor. But religious factors are surely likely to have played a part: we have seen the fears of the Olymians and Lindians about the preservation of their religious identity; as for persons actually displaced from their homes, their nostalgia must often have distilled around memories of ancestral places of cult.

Back to the Peloponnese

It is time to relate all this to the main themes of this volume. Some connections are obvious: various Arcadian synoecisms and sympolities have already been mentioned above. At other points useful connections decline to be established. Writing a religious calendar for the new state of Messenia was just as challenging an exercise in creating tradition as was writing one for synoecized Rhodes or Megalopolis, but it was an exercise of a different kind. Again, it was neither by forced subjection nor by voluntary sympolity or synoecism that a sense of ethnic identity developed or was maintained in Arcadia and Achaea. But the world of fusion and fission described in this paper was, willy-nilly, very much the world of the communities subject in different ways to the domination of Elis. As the detailed studies elsewhere

---

[46] *Syll.*³ 546b [no. 6 below], with (line 16) the verb ἀποπολιτεύεσθαι. Robert constantly stressed the phenomenon of collapsing synoecisms, e.g. in Robert 1951:5–36; cf. Wörrle 2003:140n94; Reger 2004a:168–172.

show, in the period between 425 and 350 the four *poleis* of the Akroreioi and some other such groups (Marganeis, Amphidoloi, Letrinoi) were at different moments subordinate allies of the Eleans (*perioikoi*), briefly perhaps "Eleans" incorporated into the Elean tribal structure,[47] and independent polities in alliance with Sparta or Arcadia; the *poleis* of Triphylia were initially *perioikoi*, then members of an independent federation allied with Sparta, then incorporated within the Arcadian federation; Lasion was first perioikic (but claimed by Arcadia, Xenophon *Hellenica* 3.2.30), then a free ally of Sparta, then a member of the Arcadian federation; the Pisatans were either discontented "Eleans" or independent, but very subordinate, allies of Arcadia.

Unfortunately the sources largely fail to reveal the differences that these successive metamorphoses may have made to religious life. Two dedications at Olympia, one made by the Amphidoloi, one jointly by the Akroreioi and the obscure Alasyes,[48] have often been taken as evidence of the new sense of freedom experienced by quondam perioikic communities which had thrown off the Elean yoke c. 400 BCE. But epigraphic and archaeological dating criteria for these dedications point rather to the fifth century,[49] and the conclusion to be drawn is therefore reversed: even when under the Elean yoke the perioikic communities were not quite crushed. Some suppose indeed that the dedications (and one by the Letrinoi which is surely archaic) attest the faint survival of an "Olympic amphictyony" like that of Delphi.[50] The great Panhellenic sanctuary must have been a central element in the religious life of the region. What is clear is that, though Elis made use of the sanctuary's prestige in its dealings with its *perioikoi*,[51] it failed to create around it a community of hearts and minds; when the option of secession became available, it was taken. The Pisatans, the people in whose territory the sanctuary lay, certainly found the hand of Elis heavy in religious affairs. By the settlement that ended the Spartan-Elean war c. 400, the Spartans "did not deprive the Eleans of presidency of the shrine of Olympian Zeus, though it was not theirs of old, judging the counter-claimants [the Pisatans, as is universally accepted] to be countrymen and not competent to preside" (Xenophon *Hellenica* 3.2.31). Evidently then the "unequal sympolity"

---

[47] For this explanation of the increase in Elean tribes in 368 (Pausanias 5.9.4–6) see the references in Ruggeri 2004:36.

[48] IvO 257 and 258.

[49] See Siewert 1991 and Ruggeri 2004:152–153.

[50] The amphictyony was first postulated by Kahrstedt 1927: for recent opinions see references in Ruggeri 2004:92n242, 153, and Roy, this volume. Letrinoi: SEG 25.462 (with 1164).

[51] See Roy, this volume.

by which the Pisatans had been incorporated into Elis (as they seem to have been) had done nothing to recognise their ancestral claim on the sanctuary:[52] it is as if the Lindians had been deprived of the control of the temple of Lindian Athena. In 365 the Pisatans became briefly independent with Arcadian aid, and in 364, an Olympic year, "revived the ancient fame of their land and using certain ancient mythical proofs declared that the right of conducting the Olympic *panêguris* was theirs" (Diodorus Siculus 15.78.2; cf. Xenophon *Hellenica* 7.4.28). But the principle noted earlier in relation to really prestigious shrines applied here too: Pisatan independence depended on Arcadian force of arms, and the Arcadians were soon involved in the affairs of the shrine to the extent of using sacred treasure to pay troops (Xenophon *Hellenica* 7.4.33). Whether the Arcadians allowed the Pisatans more ceremonial precedence in 364 than they had enjoyed in Elean-conducted Olympic celebrations is not known, but in the eyes not just of posterity but even of contemporaries Arcadia, not Pisa, could be said to have the presidency of the shrine (Xenophon *Hellenica* 7.4.35).[53]

South of the Alpheus, the cities of the region eventually known as Triphylia, which had been brought under Elean control in Herodotus' time (4.148.4), were liberated by Sparta c. 400 and became an independent federation allied to Sparta.[54] According to Strabo (8.3.13, 343), there had existed in "Triphylia" at Samikon, surely from of old, a "greatly revered" precinct, a grove of wild olives, of "Samian Poseidon"; "the Makistians tended it, and they proclaimed the sacred truce known as Samion. All the Triphylians contribute to the shrine." Strabo must be anachronistic, it has been powerfully argued of late, in implying that this was an ethnic shrine of the "Triphylians": for the grove's standing as a regional religious centre must go back to the archaic period, whereas before c. 400 there was, it is urged, no region known as Triphylia, nor did the peoples inhabiting what later became that region see themselves as an ethnic unity.[55] The Samikon will before 400 have been

---

[52] So Roy, this volume, who now argues that the Pisatans had never been *perioikoi*; but Ruggeri 2004:209 has them first incorporated in Elis in 400.

[53] Cf. Roy, this volume.

[54] See Ruggeri, this volume.

[55] For the non-existence of Triphylia in the fifth century see especially Nielsen 2002:229–269 (for ethnic disunity 234–235); the implications for the Samikon are drawn by Ruggeri 2004:96–108. Herodotus never speaks of Triphylia: according to him, six cities in the region were established by Minyans from Lemnos who expelled Paroreatai and Kaukones (4.148.4); in another passage, however, he speaks of what are evidently the same Paroreatai as being themselves Lemnian (8.73.2). This inconsistency in a prime source may recommend agnosticism about fifth-century understandings of the region. My own guesses are that

a regional shrine but not an ethnic one; or, if ethnic, not of the Triphylians but of one of the sub-groups from which the Triphylians were eventually constituted, probably the Minyans. Whether this case for the "invention of Triphylia" is correct or not, one may wonder what the Elean attitude will have been in the fifth century to what was surely an important cult centre in recently subjected territory. Would they have been happy for business to continue as usual at what could easily have become a focus for resistance? Conversely, after 400 the new Triphylia can scarcely have failed to make use of the hallowed shrine. But let us note in passing that even the new Triphylia was not exempt from interference in its religious affairs, in this case from Sparta.[56] In 370/9 or shortly afterwards the Triphylians joined the Arcadian league, and no more is heard of their own confederacy: to put the matter differently, they now sought to maintain independence from Elis, their central aspiration, as members of the Arcadian league rather than through Spartan-backed independence. In ethnic terms, they either became Arcadians for the first time, or at all events surrendered one of the pair of passports (Minyan and Arcadian) that they had hitherto held.[57] Perhaps the importance of the cult at Samikon will have declined again, now that the Triphylians had definitively turned their eyes to the east.[58] Much of the history of the region may have been reflected in miniature in the history of the Samikon grove.

That micro-history is lost to us, probably irrecoverably: the few phrases of Strabo quoted above are the total of our knowledge. If this paper has achieved anything, it is to have drawn attention to the many such lost histories. In a world where territory was constantly acquired and renounced, where autonomy was lost and recovered and lost again, where communities blended and broke apart, cults could not in any simple way survive through the centuries without disturbance. One can perhaps imagine an ideal, which

---

the term Triphylia existed in the fifth century (so Bölte 1948:186, criticised by Nielsen 2002:250–251), was most commonly understood as referring to Minyans, Paroreatai and Kaukones (so Ruggeri 2004:77–80, with further references), and indicated a certain sense of shared identity even at that date.

[56] See Ruggeri, this volume, on the Spartan intervention that allowed Xenophon to establish his precinct of Artemis Ephesia at Skillous.

[57] For mythological and other links between Triphylia and Arcadia going back to the fifth century see Nielsen 2002:100–105.

[58] Their Arcadian-ness will not have had any necessary impact on their religious arrangements, though it may have encouraged them, e.g., to participate in the Lykaia. Strabo 8.3.25 mentions a sanctuary of Artemis Heleia of which the Arcadians acquired the priesthood. The context in Strabo would suggest a location in Triphylia (so Jost 1985:397f), but the point can be taken no further.

would have been that of the Greeks themselves, whereby cults stood firm amid the ebb and flow of events, maintained by a shared Greek piety that did not need to conflict with particular interests. We saw above that old arrangements did sometimes survive the blending of communities in sympolity and synoecism. To that extent, the claim with which I began—that discontinuity and drastic reorganisation were the inevitable condition of the particular Greek relation between religious and political organisation—may appear exaggerated. Perhaps a different paper could be written about the durability and resilience of cult, its relative imperviousness to political change. But where cult continued it never simply survived, like a venerable ancient tree; it had to be maintained and adapted, like an ancient building. Survival κατὰ τὰ πάτρια could not simply occur but had always to be achieved.

Appendix

A. Specifications Relating to Cult in Sympolity Agreements

(1) Arcadia. Agreement between Mantinea and Helisson.[59] First half of the fourth century, perhaps 390s. Uniquely, a simple translation of the start of this document provides all the relevant information.

> The Heliswasians are to become like and equal Mantineans, sharing in everything to which Mantineans are entitled, incorporating their territory and city into Mantinea into the laws of the Mantineans, but with the city of the Heliswasians surviving as it is for ever, the Heliswasians being a *kome* of the Mantineans. There shall be a *thearos* from Helisson as from the other cities.[60] The sacrifices shall be performed and sacred missions (θεαρίαι) received in Helisson in accord with tradition.

(2) Arcadia. Agreement of "συνοικία on equal and like terms" between Euaimon and Orchomenos, 360–350?[61] Euaimon is incorporated

---

[59] Thür and Taeuber 1994: no. 9. On the date and circumstances see Funke in this volume.

[60] Whether this *thearos* is a member of the board of *thearoi* in Mantinea, i.e. a magistrate, or a sacred *thearos* sent to a Panhellenic shrine is disputed: contrast Thür and Taeuber 1994:103 and Nielsen 2004:513.

[61] Thür and Taeuber 1994: no. 15. That Euaimon (archaeologically unknown) retained some inhabitants has been argued (inconclusively) from the internal evidence of the agreement and from the citation of Theopompus FGH 115 F 61 in Stephenus Byzantinus 283.14–15 (Nielsen 1996:71).

politically into Orchomenos (the continuing citizenship for both groups is that of Orchomenus, 42–43), and some physical relocation is envisaged: the Euaimonians swear "not to revolt" from the Orchomenians, the Orchomenians "not to expel" the Euaimonians (53–90; questions of landholding are also treated earlier). "The *hiera* in Euaimon are to be conducted (?) there for ever monthly as in their present condition" (6–10: τὰ δὲ ἱερὰ τὰ ἰν Εὐαίμονι ἀ[ῒ κ]ὰ μῆν' αὖθι κα[τάπ]ερ ἔχει συντ[ελῆσθαι - - -). Nothing is said in the very incomplete surviving text about rites in Orchomenus.

(3) Caria. Agreement between Herakleia under Latmos and Pidasa, 323–313/2 BCE.[62] The Pidaseans are to be incorporated within an expanded tribal system in Herakleia under Latmos, and provision is made for population transfer from Pidasa to Herakleia (19–20, 27–28); whether the stipulation that "neither city" is to retain any non-shared property (16) can be taken to prove continued subordinate existence of Pidasa is doubtful (the phrase may be retrospective). "The Pidaseans allotted (to tribes and phratries) are to share in all *hiera*" (10–11). Revenues of the two communities, whether sacred or secular, are to be pooled henceforth, and for six years there is to be compulsory intermarriage between the two (13–17, 21–25). Nothing is said about Pidasean sacra (enough survives of the decree to render it certain that nothing was said in a lost portion), and the decree is to be displayed in Mylasa and Herakleia (33–36), not Pidasa.[63]

(4) Ionia. Letters of Antigonos Monophthalmos to Teos concerning the *sunoikismos* of the Lebedians into Teos, c. 303.[64] What the king proposed was complete physical transfer of Lebedos to Teos. The surviving portion of the first letter begins with the ruling that the Lebedian representative at the Panionion should "tent and celebrate" (σκηνοῦν καὶ πανηγυράζειν) with the Teans and be called Tean; detailed religious rules had perhaps preceded.

(5) Ionia. Admission of the inhabitants of Magnesia on the Sipylos and of the fort Palaiomagnesia into Smyrnaian citizenship. Soon (?) after 242.[65] The professed aim is to ensure the loyalty of the new citizens to Seleukos II. Some limited population transfer to Smyrna is envisaged (56–59). The new citizens are to enjoy "like and equal rights" with the other Smyrnaians (44; 53; 77–78). Nothing is said about maintenance of the cults of Magnesia, though

---

[62] SEG 47.1563; cf. Wörrle 2003; Reger 2004a:151–152.
[63] See Wörrle 2003, who sees the treaty as imposed by Asander and designed in effect to obliterate Pidasean identity, and the notes in SEG 47.1563.
[64] *Syll.*³ 344; Welles 1934: nos. 3–4.
[65] OGIS 229; I. Smyrna 573; I. Magnesia am Sipylos 1.

some are alluded to (84–85, cf. 61) and the document survives complete; the assumption evidently is that they will persist.

(6) Thessaly. Aetolia arbitration between Melitea and Perea.[66] 213/2 BCE. Aetolian arbitration has been sought in consequence of disputes that have arisen in a sympolity by which Perea, while remaining physically distinct, has apparently become politically a part of Melitea and under its laws. It emerges that under the sympolity the Meliteans are required to "tend τὰ κοινά in Perea" and pay for certain specific functions there, including the sacrifice of the Soteria (23–28); are other sacrifices in Perea still funded from separate Perean funds?

(7) West Locris. Agreement between Hypnia and Myania.[67] Early second century BCE. The two *poleis* establish a common archon and agree to collaborate in various areas, such as joint embassies; but they retain a separate identity and separate magistracies. Participation in shared activities is to occur κὰτ τὸ μέρος, καθὼς καὶ τᾶν θυσιᾶν μετέχοντι (18–19, 28–29), a phrase which is likely to indicate an uneven proportionality (e.g. one city contributing two victims to the other's one) rather than simple alternation.[68] It does not emerge whether all sacrifices were now joint on this basis or whether the two cities retained some specific to themselves.

(8) Ionia/Caria. Agreement of Miletos and Pidasa. 188/7 or 187/6 BCE?[69] The Pidaseans are to become Milesians (10–12) and to "share in the same *hiera* and magistracies and everything else as other Milesians" (13–15). A fort (at least) at Pidasa will be maintained and the territory will continue to be cultivated (15–25); but "390 beds" are to be provided for Pidaseans re-locating to Miletos (25–28). The Pidaseans are to retain "sacred and public properties," but after a five year period of grace pay normal Milesian taxes on them (28–33). The Pidaseans swear by "the gods who hold their city" (63).

(9) Phocis. Agreement between Stiris and Medeon.[70] Second century BCE. The Medeonians are to become "like and equal" Stirians (10–12). A hierotamias is to be appointed from the Medeonians to sacrifice the ancestral Medeonian sacrifices prescribed in the constitutional law (νόμος πολιτικός, 19–21). Medeonians are to participate in all Stirian sacrifices,

---

[66] *Syll.*³ 546b; IG IX 12.1.188; Ager 1996: no. 56.

[67] IG IX 1².3.748.

[68] So Bousquet 1965:672, citing *FdD* III 4.38.8ff, where Thronion claims a third of the amphictyonic role of the Epiknemidian Locrians just as it has contributed sheep for sacrifice in that proportion.

[69] Milet 1.3.149; for views on the date see Reger 2004a:156n43.

[70] IG IX 1.32; *Syll.*³ 647; Salviat and Vatin 1971:77–80.

and vice versa (51–55). At the end a payment is specified to be made by the Stirians to "the phratry of the Medeonians" (76–82), apparently an indication of the new standing of the Medeonians within Stiris.

B. Religious Implications of the Synoecisms of Rhodes, Kos and Alexandreia Troas

Kos

The *polis* of Kos on the site of the present day town on the north east coast of the island is said to have been founded in 366/5 (Diodorus 15.76.2). The ancient sources (Diodorus 15.76.2, and Strabo 14.2.19) describe the event as a transfer of population to a new site, Strabo speaking more specifically of a transfer away from an existing *polis* Astypalaia; but Thucydides (8.41.2) attests the existence in the fifth century of a second Koan *polis* on the east of the island, Kos Meropis, very probably to be located (on the basis of archaeological evidence antedating 366) on or near the site of the "new" town of Kos. It follows that what happened in 366/5 was, in urbanistic terms, a re-foundation on a greatly enlarged scale, not a new foundation, but in political terms the first unification of an island hitherto divided into at least two *poleis* (since Thucydides and some other sources imply that Kos Meropis no less than Strabo's Astypalaia had been a *polis* prior to 366).[71] There survive extensive fragments, dated palaeographically to the second half of the fourth century, of a calendar of public sacrifices which it is tempting to suppose was produced, after some delay, to meet the needs of the newly unified state (RO 62): the very existence of such a calendar at this date outside Attica and the thoroughness with which it prescribes ritual procedures are both unusual phenomena which invite a specific explanation. A roughly contemporary text which regulates the terms of office of the priest of Zeus Polieus and coordinates the island's cult of Apollo Dalios may have been similarly motivated.[72]

Whatever the immediate impulse for the creation of these texts, the calendar that survives is beyond a doubt that of the synoecized state at a date not long after the synoecism; the prominence in it of an elaborate ritual of Zeus Polieus is very appropriate. But to get behind the calendar to a prior organisation of Koan religion is arduous work. In some cases the calendar that emerged after the coalescence of two *poleis* may have been that of the

---

[71] So Sherwin-White 1978:43–58, powerfully reviving an old view; cf. recently Reger 2001:171–174.

[72] LSCG 156: cf. Parker and Obbink 2000:421.

more dominant of the two, modestly adjusted and supplemented, but a more radical reshaping will certainly have been required here. The dominant *polis* had hitherto, if we believe Strabo, been Astypalaia, but the central focus of religious life was henceforth to be Kos new town; even if we suppose that some "Pankoan" rituals had been celebrated before the synoecism (for we know that on Kos as on other islands common activities such as the issue of common coins could antedate formal political unification), it is not very likely that they took place in Kos old town. The religious life of the island had to be largely relocated, therefore. Again, in the cults of the new state the three Dorian tribes had a very prominent place. Can we suppose that the Dorian tribes had had such an island-wide role before 366, with, say, Dymanes from Astypalaia occasionally meeting with those from Kos Meropis (and whatever other *poleis* may once have existed) to celebrate common rites? Wherever else we meet them, the Dorian tribes are sub-divisions of a unified state, not a form of association transcending political divisions: pandymanian rites bringing together Dymanians from different *poleis* are not known. Or were the individual *poleis* each divided into the three Dorian tribes without any connection being established between those of one *polis* and another? But the deme Isthmiotai of Hellenistic Kos, which is generally accepted to be the old *polis* of Astypalaia under a new name, was divided into three tribes which were not the Dorian ones; and there is evidence for such local non-Dorian tribes elsewhere on the island.[73] It is hard to see why one *polis* should have had both a Dorian and a concurrent non-Dorian tribal structure. Perhaps then the Dorian tribes were first introduced in 366,[74] as a way of replicating at whole-island level the principle of tribal division familiar from the individual *poleis*. This was an altogether new framework for religious life if so, even if one based on more than one familiar template.

Koan religion of the Hellenistic period is very fully documented at several levels, and on the basis of this material one can try to distinguish pre-existing cults incorporated in the state calendar from others newly created for it. But here too it is hard to make sure progress. The idea that it was the synoecism which elevated Asclepius, hitherto a god of Astypalaia alone, to national and then international prominence cannot be sustained:[75]

---

[73] See Parker and Obbink 2001:263–265. Isthmiotai/Astypalaia: the principal argument is the survival of the old place name, in the form Stampalia, in the Isthmos region of Kos: see Bean and Cook 1957:121n244.

[74] So (as a possibility) Sherwin-White 1978:156–158.

[75] An old theory of Pugliese Carratelli still countenanced by Reger 2004b:755 despite the refutation by Sherwin-White 1978:74.

Asclepius has no special connection with Astypalaia, nor does Asclepius' rise to fame occur quite early enough to fit the hypothesis. A more reliable instance of a cult prominent both at Astypalaia and in the calendar of the city is that of Apollo Delios: the local cult was replicated by that at the centre, but not replaced by it.[76] A similar process can be postulated for Zeus Polieus and for Demeter.[77] Another cult found both in the city and in at least two demes is that of Aphrodite Pandemos, but here what happened is perhaps the reverse of the case of Apollo Delios: not adoption by the city of a pre-existent cult, but creation at the centre of a new unifying cult which the demes were then encouraged to take up: Pandemos can be taken to mean "of all the demes," and offerings were made to her on the same day of the year both in the city and in the demes.[78]

The firmest general proposition that can be advanced is that the many cults of new Kos town supplemented and may also have replicated those of the old settlements but did not undermine them. At least two demes of Hellenistic Kos, Isthmiotai and Halasarna (one certainly and one possibly a *polis* under the ancien régime), hosted flourishing locally administered cults: the cult of Apollo and Heracles at Halasarna, for instance, remained much more prominent than, say, any deme-administered cult of Attica.[79]

When Kalymnos was incorporated into Kos at the end of the third century it became, like the old *poleis*, a deme. Even as a deme it appears to have maintained its old tradition of sending dedications to Delos: the deme of the Isthmiotai (quondam city of Astypalaia) did the same.[80]

---

[76] State cult: LSCG 156 B; cult of Isthmiotai: IG XI 2.287 B 45 (an independent *theôria* to Delos c. 250; cf. Bruneau 1970:99). A text regulating the state cult gives a role to Isthmiotai and (?) Halasarnitai (LSCG 156 B 23–25); but we now know that the main festival of Apollo in the great cult at Halasarna, though celebrated in the month Dalios (Sherwin-White 1978:300), was named Pythaia (Kokkorou-Aleura 2004: no. 4).

[77] Zeus Polieus and Athena Polias in the city: RO 62 A; LSCG 156 A (this text too perhaps a product of the synoecism); in Halasarna: Kokkorou-Aleura 2004, no. 6, 20–24. Of course the reverse hypothesis that the deme cult imitates that of the city cannot be refuted. Demeter: LSCG 154 A is a state document prescribing purity rules for priestesses in at least two cults of Demeter, supplemented (but wholly speculatively) by Herzog as "Demeter Olympia [in the city]" (21) and "Demeter [in Isthmos]" (36): the law was to be displayed at Isthmos and Halasarna as well as in the city (14–18). LSCG 175 is a roughly contemporary text found at Antimachia and generally supposed to have been issued by a deme which stipulates terms of office for "priestesses of Demeter." On these texts cf. Parker and Obbink 2000:420–421.

[78] See Parker 2002:152–156, on Segre 1993: ED 178 (A) 26–31; LSCG 169 A 12–13; 172.1–4.

[79] See Kokkorou-Aleura 2004:27–82.

[80] See I. Delos 1432 Bb II, 9–10 (140/39) for a phiale dedicated by "the city of the Kalymnians" to Delian Apollo, but also described as an ἀνάθημα Κώιων: for earlier Kalymnian dedications see Bruneau 1970:96; cf. Hamilton 2000: Apollo, D 8. The formulas used (both "the city" and

Rhodes

In 408/7, according to Diodorus (13.75.1), "the inhabitants of the island Rhodes and of Ialysos, Lindos and Kameiros [the three existing *poleis* on the island] transferred (μετῳκίσθησαν) to one city, what is now called Rhodes." Diodorus is quite wrong to imply that the three old *poleis* were abandoned, though the new capital did quite quickly achieve administrative and military importance.[81] Even before the foundation of Rhodes town, there had been a sense of an island identity (outside the island, for instance, the great athlete Diagoras was a Rhodian, not an Ialysian), a shared mythology, probably some panrhodian cults, and the possibility of collective political action; most scholars suppose that a formal panrhodian political structure was first created in 408, or possibly three years earlier, but an interesting case has recently been made that earlier collective action was already based on a federal structure.[82]

What is universally agreed is that the cults of the new capital were not built around those of one of the old cities or a selection from all of them. The synoecism affected the religious life of the old cities (it can scarcely be coincidence that the list of annual priests in the cult of Athena Lindia, one of many priest lists published on the island, seems to have begun in 406/5, the second year after the synoecism),[83] but not in the sense that they surrendered anything up to Rhodes town. The cult of Athena Lindia was certainly the most prestigious in the island and had a kind of panrhodian role; but neither was the cult opened out to become one in which all Rhodians partic-

---

the co-presence of Kalymnians and Koans) are very unusual (I thank Richard Hamilton for advice on this point). Isthmiotai: see n75 above.

[81] Nielsen and Gabrielsen 2004:1205.

[82] By Gabrielsen 2000, which is now the starting point (summarised in Nielsen and Gabrielsen 2004:1196–1197). Panrhodian cults: on Athena Lindia see Momigliano 1936:49–51; on Zeus Atabyrios the references in Morelli 1959:141, and note the joining of *Tit. Cam.* 280–281 appendix nos. 19–20 to give a list of *theôroi* to the shrine from all three old Rhodian *poleis* (Papachristodoulou 1999:32).

[83] I. Lindos 1, with the calculations of Blinkenberg 1941:90–98; for a list of priest lists see Morricone 1952:360–362. But the argument of Blinkenberg 1937:13–14 for taking back the list of Lindian priests of Poseidon Hippios to the same starting point is unacceptable: one cannot base an exact calculation on a hypothetical average tenure of "permanent" priesthoods. All one can say is that the annual priests in that list begin c. 325 and are preceded by four permanent priests. On the effects of synoecism on the old cities see Dignas 2003:50. An obvious possibility is that the priesthood of Athena Lindia became annual for the first time in 406. Yet annual tenure of a Lindian priesthood (that of Enyalios) appears already in LSS 85 (IKRP 251), usually dated "c. 440–420" (but an extension of the argument of Gabrielsen 2000:185–186 might perhaps allow it to be downdated).

ipated by right, nor was there any attempt to create a new Athena Lindia in the city. The same point can be made about Apollo Erethemios of Ialysos and many other local cults. The emblem of this continuing religious separatism is a Lindian inscription of the 320s, quoted above, which honours a long list of fellow citizens who fought successfully in a court to preserve the exclusivity of Lindian cult.[84] Here Lindian prerogatives are defended by the Lindians themselves; but the original decision not to make the new calendar for the whole island an amalgam of existing rites may rather have been motivated by fears of an individual city acquiring undue prominence.[85]

A paradoxical consequence of the synoecism seems then to have been to make Athena Lindia in some ways less of a panrhodian goddess than she had been before. Priesthood had an unusual prominence in Hellenistic Rhodes, and numerous priesthoods open only to local citizens continued to be eagerly competed for in Lindos and Kameiros (the situation in Ialysos, unexcavated, is less well known). The Lindians even, extraordinarily, had their own "crowned games."[86] Thus the cultic life of the old cities outlived the synoecism in full vigour. They seem to have been the main conduits through which local religious life was organised: a decree of the Kameirians summons together representatives of the various Kameirian κτοιναί (local sub-divisions of mysterious character) to consider (ἀθρεῖν), collectively, (and revise?) the "publicly-financed rites of the Kameirians."[87] The one sense in which the major local cult centres had a panrhodian role is that they hosted games which might, like games organised by Rhodes itself, involve competition between the three tribes, recruited from the

---

[84] IG XII 1.761 (*Syll.*[3] 340) 38–42. For the late-fourth century dating, which is prosopographically assured, see Fraser 1952:194; on the question of the court involved see Gabrielsen 2000:194. Fraser argues that the laws are those of the Lindians, against Blinkenberg's view that they were Rhodian; had Blinkenberg been right, the continuing separate identity of the cults of the three old *poleis* would have been guaranteed by federal law. This situation continued: "Der Staat hatte schon vor Jahrhunderten die Scheidewand zwischen den drei Städten fallen lassen, der Cultus behielt sie ängstlich bei" (van Gelder 1900:305). It is, however, not certain that the threat to Lindian exclusivity came from Ialysians and Kameirians: members of "Lindian" demes in the Rhodian peraea were apparently excluded from tenure of Lindian priesthoods (Fraser and Bean 1954:123).

[85] van Gelder 1900:291; cf. Hornblower 1982:83.

[86] I. Lindos 123; on priesthoods see Dignas 2003.

[87] *Tit. Cam.* 109 (on the date, early third century, see Fraser 1952:194–195). The representatives are to be summoned to the temple of Athena καὶ ἀθρεόντω τὰ ἱερὰ τὰ Καμιρέων [τὰ δαμο] τελῆ πάντα, αἴ τι [- - - -]. Since there is no hint that the representatives are to leave the temple, ἀθρεῖν should refer to consideration of the rites, not to a physical tour of shrines; the αἴ τι clause may have had the sense "in case any change is needed."

whole island.[88] On these and perhaps some other occasions a cult in one of the old towns might play host to all Rhodes; but such an event remained a "*panêguris* of the Lindians" (or Ialysians, or Kameirians), presided over by members of that community.[89]

What of the new capital? The priest of Halios in Rhodes was eventually to become the official who gave his name to the Rhodian year; the post was a pinnacle of prestige to which the ambitious might aspire after, but never before, having held one of the local priesthoods.[90] Halios had always been central to Rhodian mythology but not to cult, and everything commends the widely accepted view that it was the synoecism that first brought Halios to cultic prominence as a unifying symbol of the new state. (Some suppose that the new city was built around a modest existing sanctuary of the god.)[91] The early years of the cult, long obscure, have recently been illuminated by the discovery of a late-fifth century bronze kalpe inscribed "a prize from Rhodes from the Sun" (ἆθλον ἐγ Ῥόδο παρ' Ἀλίο).[92] It looks as if the agonistic Halieia, the island's greatest festival in the hellenistic period, was set up more or less simultaneously with the foundation of the new city; the priesthood of Halios may well date back to the same time.[93] A festival Epitaphia is likely to have honoured the mythical "settler" of the whole island, Tlapolemus; if that identification of the honorand of the Epitaphia is correct, this is the one attested case in which Rhodes town took over a pre-existing festival: Tlapolemeia are already mentioned by Pindar, though

---

[88] This is proved for the Ialysian competition Erethimia by the text published by Kontorini 1975; either tribal competion or, at all events, panrhodian participation is surely likely at other local agonistic festivals, such as the "crowned games" of the Lindians (I. Lindos 123).

[89] The Sminthia in honour of Dionysus Smintheus (Morelli 1959:41–42) may have been such an event: both the "whole people" of Rhodes and the Lindians were involved with it, to judge from IG XII 1.762.

[90] Dignas 2003:38.

[91] Van Gelder 1900:291–292, quoting Dittenberger. The identification of the sanctuary remains controversial: Michalachi-Kollia 1999:73–74. The recent discovery that Kerkaphos, sun of Helios and father of the eponyms of the three old Rhodian cities (Pindar *Olympian* 7.71–74; cf. I. Lindos 57b and 274), was already worshipped in Ialysian territory and perhaps elsewhere in the sixth century (Marankou and Papachristodoulou 1991:484) does not affect the point about Helios himself.

[92] SEG 27.481 (which it is natural to date after and not, with Nielsen and Gabrielsen 2004:1196, before 408 – archaeologically either date seems possible). For fourth century Rhodian amphorae of panathenaic shape, but showing the sun on one side, which also apparently served as prizes see Zervoudaki 1978; LIMC V.I s.v. Helios, 1009, no. 17.

[93] So Morricone 1952, in the first publication of the list of priests of the Sun; the doubts of Gabrielsen 2000:202n49 are not compelling.

we do not know how they were organised.[94] Many further festivals were to follow (Asklapieia, Dionysia, Diosoteria [Maiuri 19], Dioskouria, Dipanamia, Hippokathesia, Poseidania, and eventually Alexandreia and Rhomaia),[95] at many of which teams competed from the three tribes, Lindia, Kameiria and Ialysia, into which, for these purposes, the old cities had mutated; and many individual cults are attested, very prominent among them that of Dionysus in a fine precinct.[96] But fourth-century evidence is too scarce to allow any detailed reconstruction of the growth of the pantheon.

A separate but related question is that of Rhodes' treatment of her overseas possessions. Since most of those communities (the islands, and those of the "incorporated Peraea") constituted or formed parts of demes annexed to the three old Rhodian towns, an obvious possibility is that their rites retained the same independence as those of the Attic demes vis-à-vis those of Athens. And we duly find local priesthoods, ἀγῶνες and πανηγύρεις, subscriptions to build temples, cult regulations, and communal sacrifices and banquets.[97] Two important cults, however, seem to have been administered in some degree from Rhodes itself, that of Poseidon Porthmios on Karpathos, where ἱεραγωγοί were appointed by the Rhodian assembly (IG XII 1 1035.9–11), and that of Hemithea at Kastabos, where the scale of the fourth-century temple implies funding from the centre even if (the point is

---

[94] Pindar *Olympian* 7.80. The Epitaphia are known, as the name of a festival entailing tribal competion, from Pugliese Carratelli 1955: nos. 18 and 19; Maiuri 1925: no. 18; I. Lindos 222 and 707. Pindar *Olympian* 7.36c speaks of an ἀγὼν ἐπιτάφιος in Rhodes town honouring Tlapolemus. Tlapolemeia are still mentioned under that name in an inscription of the second century, *Syll.*³ 1067.8 (IKRP 555); but the festival could perhaps have borne both names. The current explanation of the Epitaphia (see the note to I. Lindos 222) is that, like the Athenian festival of the same name, they honoured the war dead.

[95] See Pugliese Carratelli 1955:250–252. A famous Homeric passage (*Iliad* 2.655f) implies a tribal structure in pre-synoecized Rhodes, perhaps even that those tribes like those after the synoecism were territorially defined. But all in relation to this crucial topic is darkness.

[96] Strabo 14.2.5.

[97] Priesthoods: Bresson 1991: nos. 3, 54, 118, 148; IG XII 1.998; ἀγῶνες: Bresson 1991: no. 4; IG XII 1.1032.23–29; subscriptions: Bresson 1991: no. 122, 149; regulations: Bresson 1991: no. 102; banquets: Bresson 1991: no. 59. The issuing body in most of these cases is not a deme, but the point about local autonomy is unaffected. Bresson 1991: no. 22 (LSCG 143) shows some dependence of Physkos on Lindos, but of a kind to which a deme on Rhodes would very possibily also have been exposed. The issue may be as much financial as religious: the text concerns λογεία, and LSJ s.v. λογεύω shows that the word can refer to a levy of any kind. All Rhodian sub-groups, not just those of the Peraea, were required to seek authorization from the Rhodian assembly to display honorary decrees in sanctuaries: Gabrielsen 1994:130–133.

disputed: see Bresson's commentary on his no. 44) the *dêmos* which issued a decree regulating the cult was that of the Bybassians and not of Rhodes itself.[98] Here then at least a partial "take over" of the most important regional cults seems to have occurred, though we have no reason to believe that it was resented. "Rhodianisation" of a different kind is visible where distinctively Rhodian cults are found in Rhodian overseas territories. It can only have been after the incorporation of Karpathos into Rhodes that the islands' three *poleis*, Brykous, Arceseia, and Karpathos itself, all acquired cults of Athena Lindia.[99] Whether the impulse to introduce these cults came from Rhodes or from Karpathos itself unfortunately cannot be determined. At Thysannous a subscription was launched to build a temple Ἀθάνας [.] αμ[, which by a plausible supplement becomes Ἀθάνας [Κ]αμ[ειράδος] and thus a further example of the same phenomenon.[100] Financing by subscription must imply a certain local receptivity if so. Then there are the cults of Helios, "the Rhodian *dêmos*," and the nymph Rhodos found at scattered places in the subject Peraea, but also e.g. in Kos, an island closely associated with Rhodes but never dependent upon it.[101] A "religious policy" of disseminating Rhodian cults, a rare thing indeed for a Greek city, has accordingly been postulated. But that intriguing issue cannot be pursued further here.

What place, finally, was there for "overseas Rhodians" in the religious life of the island itself? Kameiros summoned representatives of its κτοιναί in the Peraea as well as on Rhodes itself to discuss the Kameirian public cults (but the island Chalke, for reasons which are unclear, was given the option

---

[98] Cf. Cook and Plommer 1966:65: "the sanctuary at Kastabos was by no means an exclusively Bybassian concern. The decree [Bresson 1991: no. 44] is issued by the people of Rhodes; the proposer is a Bybassian, the honorand an Amian, and the original dedicator of the temple [Bresson 1991: no. 38] a Hygassian." Cf. Cook and Plommer 1966:167, "it was evidently under Rhodian patronage that Hemithea and her festival at Kastabos acquired the celebrity that Diodorus describes." But we must I think assume that the cult was already famous by the late fourth century, or why would it have merited such attention? For the importance of Poseidon Porthmios on Karpathos, cf. IG XII 1.1033 (the *koinon* of Potidaieis displays decrees there). IG XII 1.1036 (dedication by a Rhodian general); for archaic finds probably associable with the shrine see Hope Simpson and Lazenby 1962:167.

[99] Arcaseia: *Historia* 7 (1933), 577–579; Brykous: IG XII 1.998; Karpathos IG XII 1.1033.25–26 (at Potidaion; on the relation of Potidaion to Karpathos see Fraser and Bean 1954:142n3). But the argument of Fraser and Bean 1954:147n1—that Telos took its cult of Athana Polieus and Zeus Polieus (SEG III 719) from Kameiros—is fragile, given the ubiquity of that pairing. The island already had an Athanaion while still independent (C. V. Crowther, personal communication on the basis of a text relating to Koan judges [Fraser and Bean 1954:146n3] which he is preparing for publication).

[100] Bresson 1991: no. 122.

[101] Fraser and Bean 1954:130–147.

of not participating).[102] On the other hand, overseas Lindians never held the priesthood of Athena Lindia and must be presumed to have been debarred from it.[103] But overseas Kameirians participated fully in the priesthoods and magistracies of Kameiros; Lindian exclusivity seems to be the exception.[104]

Alexandreia Troas

Alexandreia Troas was a new city synoecized by Antigonos Monophthalmos from at least seven others (of which one, Skepsis, quite soon broke away, as did another, Kebren, later). Few of the "tributary" cities seem to have been completely abandoned, and two (Larisa and Hamaxitos) re-appear as hosts to Delphic *thearoi* c. 230–220; archaeology appears to attest continuing cult activity at another (Neandreia). The new city made use of the ancient sanctuary of Apollo Smintheus, in the territory of Hamaxitos, to display its documents, and building occurred in the sanctuary on a scale which implies the involvement of Alexandreia; whether administrative control was formally taken over is not established.[105]

Bibliography

Ager, S. L. 1996. *Interstate Arbitrations in the Greek World, 337-90 B.C.* Berkeley.

Avram, A. 2004. "The Propontic Coast of Asia Minor." In Hansen and Nielsen 2004:974–999.

Bean, G. E., and Cook, J. M. 1957. "The Carian Coast III." *ABSA* 52:58–146.

Blinkenberg, C. 1937. *Les Prêtres de Poseidon Hippios. Étude sur une inscription Lindienne.* Copenhagen.

Blinkenberg, C. 1941. *Lindos. Fouilles et recherches II: Les inscriptions.* Aarhus.

Bölte, F. 1948. "Triphylia." *RE* VII:186–201.

Bousquet, J. 1965. "Convention entre Myania et Hypnia." *BCH* 89:665–681.

---

[102] *Tit. Cam.* 109 (cf. n87). The point cannot be simply that the Chalketans were geographically shut off from involvement; they were less so than Kameirian demes in the Peraea.

[103] See n83 above.

[104] Rice 1999:50.

[105] For all this see Robert 1951:5–36; Cohen 1995:145–148; Ricl 1997:4–8. Robert 1951:34–35 supposed that Larisa and Hamaxitos had left the synoecism when they received the Delphic *thearoi*. The synoecism of Halicarnassus by Mausolus (see Hornblower 1982:78–105) offers little grist to our mill, but note that the shrine and revenues of Apollo Telmisseus are still precariously in the control of a *koinon* of the Telmissians, heir to one of the tributary communities, in the early second century (Michel 1900: no. 459; cf. Hornblower 1982:94).

van Bremen, R. 2004. "Leon Son of Chrysaor and the Religious Identity of Stratonikeia in Caria." In Colvin 2004:207–244.

Bresson, A. 1991. *Recueil des inscriptions de la pérée rhodienne.* Paris.

Bruneau, P. 1970. *Recherches sur les cultes de Délos à l'époque hellénistique et à l'époque impériale.* Paris.

Cavanagh, W., Crouwel, J., Catling, R. W. V., and Shipley, G. 2002. *The Laconia Survey, I: Methodology and Interpetation.* London.

Cohen, G. M., 1995. *The Hellenistic Settlements in Europe, the Islands and Asia Minor.* Berkeley.

Colvin, S. ed. 2004. *The Greco-Roman East: Politics, Culture, Society.* Cambridge.

Cook, J. M., and Plommer, W. H. 1966. *The Sanctuary of Hemithea at Kastabos.* Cambridge.

Cooper, F. A. 1978. *The Temple of Apollo at Bassai.* New York.

Demand, N. 1990. *Urban Relocation in Archaic and Classical Greece.* Bristol.

Dignas, B. 2003. "Rhodian Priests after the Synoecism." *AncSoc* 33:35–51.

Fraser, P. M., 1952. "Alexander and the Rhodian Constitution." *PP* 7:192–206.

Fraser, P. M., and Bean G. E. 1954. *The Rhodian Peraea and Islands.* London.

Gabrielsen, V. 1994. "Subdivisions of the State and their Decrees in Hellenistic Rhodes." *C&M* 45:117–35.

Gabrielsen, V., Bilde, P., Engberg-Pedersen, T., Hannestad, L., and Zahle, J. eds. 1999. *Hellenistic Rhodes: Politics, Culture and Society.* Studies in Hellenistic Civilization 9. Aarhus.

Gabrielsen, V. 2000. "The Synoikized *Polis* of Rhodes." *Polis and Politics: Studies in Ancient Greek History* (eds. P. Flensted-Jensen, T. H. Nielsen, L. Rubinstein) 177–206. Copenhagen.

van Gelder, H. 1900. *Geschichte der alten Rhodier.* The Hague.

Habicht, C. 2006. "Versäumter Götterdienst." *Historia* 55:153–166.

Hamilton, R. 2000. *Treasure Map: A Guide to the Delian Inventories.* Ann Arbor.

Hansen, M. H. 1997. *The Polis as an Urban Centre and as a Political Community.* Copenhagen.

Hansen, M. H. 2004. "A Typology of Dependent *Poleis.*" In Hansen and Nielsen 2004:87–94.

Hansen, M. H., and Nielsen, T. H. 2004. *An Inventory of Archaic and Classical Poleis.* Oxford.

Herrmann, P. 1965. "Neue Urkunden zur Geschichte von Milet im 2 Jahrhundert v. Chr." *MDAI(I)* 15:71–117.

Hope Simpson, R., and Lazenby, J. F. 1962. "Notes from the Dodecanese." *ABSA* 57:154–75.

Hornblower, S. 1982. *Mausolus.* Oxford.

211

Jost, M. 1985. *Sanctuaires et cultes d' Arcadie.* Paris.

Jost, M. 1992. "Sanctuaires ruraux et sanctuaires urbains dans Arcadie." *Le sanctuaire grec.* 205–238. Entretiens Hardt 37. Vandoeuvres.

Jost, M. 1994. "The Distribution of Sanctuaries in Civic Space in Arcadia." *Placing the Gods. Sanctuaries and Civic Space in Ancient Greece* (eds. S. E. Alcock and R. Osborne) 217–230. Oxford.

Kahrstedt, U. 1927. "Zur Geschichte von Elis und Olympia." *GGA*:157–176.

Kokkorou-Aleura, G. 2004. *Επιγραφές απο τήν αρχαία Αλάσαρνα.* Athens.

Kontorini, V. 1975. "Les concours des Grandes Éréthimia à Rhodes." *BCH* 99:97–117.

Kowalzig, B. 2007. *Singing for the Gods.* Oxford.

Krauter, S. 2004. *Bürgerrecht und Kultteilnahme.* Berlin.

Marankou, L. and Papachristodoulou, I. 1991. "'Ιαλυσία." *AD* 46:479–486.

Maiuri, A. 1925. *Nuova silloge epigrafica di Rodi e Cos.* Florence.

Melfi, M. 2007. *Il santuario di Asclepio a Lebena.* Athens.

Michalachi-Kollia, M. 1999. "Μνημειώδες στωικό οικοδόμημα." *Ρόδος 2.400 Χρόνια* (eds. E. Kypraiou and D. Zapheiropoulou) 73–74. Athens.

Michel, C. 1900. *Recueil d'inscriptions grecques.* Paris.

Mikalson, J. D., 1998. *Religion in Hellenistic Athens.* Berkeley.

Moggi, M. 1976. *I sinecismi interstatali greci.* Pisa.

Momigliano, A. 1936. "Note sulla storia di Rodi." *RFIC* 64:49–63.

Morelli, D. 1959. *I culti in Rodi.* Pisa.

Morricone, I. 1952. "I sacerdoti di Halios." *ASAA* 27–29 (1949–1951):351–380.

Nielsen, T. H. 1996. "A Survey of Dependent *Poleis* in Classical Arcadia." *More Studies in the Ancient Greek* Polis (eds. M. H. Hansen and K. Raaflaub) 63–106. Stuttgart.

Nielsen, T. H. 2002. *Arkadia and its Poleis in the Archaic and Classical Periods.* Göttingen.

Nielsen, T. H. 2004. "Arcadia." In Hansen and Nielsen 2004:505–539.

Nielsen, T. H., and Gabrielsen, V. 2004. "Rhodos." In Hansen and Nielsen 2004:1196–1210.

Nilsson, M. P. 1951. *Cults, Myths, Oracles and Politics in Ancient Greece.* Lund.

Papachristodoulou, I. 1999. "The Rhodian Demes within the Framework of the Function of the Rhodian State." In Gabrielsen et al. 1999:27–44.

Parker, R. 1989. "Spartan Religion." *Classical Sparta: Techniques Behind her Success* (ed. A. Powell) 142–172. London.

Parker, R. 1994. "Athenian Religion Abroad." *Ritual, Finance, Politics: Democratic Accounts Presented to David Lewis* (eds. S. Hornblower and R. Osborne) 339–346. Oxford.

Parker, R. 1996. *Athenian Religion: A History.* Oxford.

Parker, R. 2002. "The cult of Aphrodite Pandamos and Pontia on Cos." *Kykeon* (eds. F. J. Hortsmanshoff et al.) 143–160. Leiden.

Parker, R., and Obbink, D. 2000. "Aus der Arbeit der *Inscriptiones Graecae* VI. Sales of Priesthoods on Cos I." *Chiron* 30:415–449.

Parker, R., and Obbink, D. 2001. "Aus der Arbeit der *Inscriptiones Graecae* VIII. Three Further Inscriptions Concerning Coan Cults." *Chiron* 31:253–275.

Perlman, P. 2000. *City and Sanctuary in Ancient Greece: The Theorodokia in the Peloponnese. Hypomnemata* 121. Göttingen.

Piérart, M. 1982. "Argos, Cléonai, et le koinon des Arcadiens." *BCH* 106:119–138.

Piérart, M. 1997. "L'attitude d'Argos à l'égard des autres cités d'Argolide." In Hansen 1997:321–351.

von Prott, J. 1896. *Leges Graecorum Sacrae e Titulis Collectae i: Fasti Sacri.* Leipzig.

Pugliese Carratelli, G. 1955. "Supplemento epigrafico rhodio. Documenti sulle feste." *ASAA* 30–32 (1952–1954):247–316.

Reger, G. 2001. "The Mykonian Synoikismos." *REA* 103:157–181.

Reger, G. 2004a. "Sympoliteiai in Hellenistic Asia Minor." In Colvin 2004:145–180.

Reger, G. 2004b. "The Aegean." In Hansen and Nielsen 2004:732–793.

Rhodes, P. J., and Osborne, R. 2003. *Greek Historical Inscriptions, 403-323 BC.* Oxford.

Rice, E. E. 1999. "Relations between Rhodes and the Rhodian Peraia." In Gabrielsen et al. 1999:45–54.

Ricl, M. 1997. *The Inscriptions of Alexandreia Troas.* Bonn.

Robert, L. 1951. *Études de numismatique grecque.* Paris.

Robert, L. 1967. "Sur des inscriptions d' Éphèse. 4. Décret pour un officier royal." *RPhil* 41:36–40 (reprinted in his *Opera Minora Selecta* V, Amsterdam 1989:376–380).

Robert, L., and Robert, J. 1989. *Claros I. Décrets hellénistiques.* Paris.

Ruggeri, C. 2004. *Gli stati intorno a Olimpia. Storia e costituzione dell'Elide e degli stati formati dai perieci elei (400-362 a.C.).* Historia Einzelschriften 170. Stuttgart.

Salviat, F., and Vatin, C. 1971. *Inscriptions de Grèce Centrale.* Paris.

Segre, M. 1993. *Iscrizioni di Cos, I .* Rome.

Sherwin-White, S. M. 1978. *Ancient Cos.* Göttingen.

Shipley, G. 1997. "'The Other Lakedaimonians': The Dependent Perioikic *Poleis* of Laconia and Messenia." In Hansen 1997:189–281.

Siewert, P. 1991. "Staatliche Weihungen von Kesseln und anderen Bronzegefässen in Olympia." *MDAI(A)* 106:81–84.

Thür, G., and Taeuber, H. 1994. *Prozessrechtliche Inschriften der griechischen Poleis: Arkadien.* Vienna.

Welles, C. B. 1934. *Royal Correspondence in the Hellenistic Period.* London.

Whitby, M. 1984. "The Union of Corinth and Argos: a Re-consideration." *Historia* 33:295–308.

Wörrle, M. 2003. "Inschriften von Herakleia am Latmos III. Der Synoikismos der Latmioi mit den Pidaseis." *Chiron* 33:121–143.

Zervoudaki, E. 1978. ""Ἥλιος καὶ Ἀλιεῖα." *AD* 30:1–20.

XI

The Development of Greek *Ethnê* and their Ethnicity
An Anthropological Perspective
Christoph Ulf

S TANDARD DEFINITIONS OF *KOINON*/LEAGUE have been, and often still are, based on the assumption of the existence of units that defined themselves in ethnic terms (*ethnê*), which extend far back in time. This tendency is connected with the conviction that all human communities are "ethnic" in that they are founded on biological kinship "from the beginning onwards." Their cultural as well as political cohesion is seen to derive from this biological relationship. This opinion is not abandoned even when one sees not clans or kinship-based states, but the *oikoi* as the smaller units out of which early Greek communities are supposed to have grown. In both views, the *ethnê* coexist with the *polis*. They are viewed as the older political structure, which emerged in an entirely natural manner from the fact of biological relatedness.[1] The foundations of this theory have been seriously shaken in recent times.

The first argument against it runs as follows: there is no such thing as a pre-existing Greek identity; rather, it first began to take shape slowly during the Greek Archaic period. This argument finds important backing in the archaeological record, which demonstrates strong regional variation. This line of reasoning is also supported by the fact that the picture of a league (*koinon*) based on an ethnic foundation originates in a specific period of modern scholarship and bears the hallmarks of projection more than those of scientific analysis.[2]

---

[1] Cf. Beck 1997:10–13, 22–26, and for English-language literature in particular, McInerney 2001:51–54 (with references to contemporary political debates); Morgan 2003:6–7, 12–16; Hall 1997:41.

[2] Comprehensive treatments are Ulf 1996; Hall 1997; Morgan 2001; McInerney 1999:25–35; Siapkas 2003:1–5, 41–59. See also Gehrke 1994.

The second argument consists in the application of the model of ethno-genesis, which was developed by scholars of the Middle Ages. According to this model, ethnic units (e.g. peoples, clans) are by no means "natural" insti-tutions, but rather emerge only under specific historical circumstances. To this process of emergence belongs also the (later) construction of a common ethnic origin.[3]

If one accepts the validity of both arguments, then the question is: What are the reasons or motivations for the consolidation of such units? If it is possible to find an answer to that question, then—one must assume—it must also be possible to find plausible reasons for the development of *ethnê* and their change over time. This conclusion is based on the assumption that the group which appears to be a primordial ethnic unit is in reality only the outcome of a specific form of cohesion within or between socio-polit-ical groups. Such a unit does not exist *a priori* but has to be generated, and is inherently unstable. It presents itself as an ethnic group, and is indicated by the term "ethnicity."[4] If the elements of human behavior and thought that produce or encourage cohesion can be isolated, then the track leading to ethnicity may also be found.

To this end, the present paper has chosen the path of isolating those elements which foster cohesion within and between groups in anthropologi-cally or ethnologically observable societies. This approach proceeds from the conviction that it is possible to construct an analogy between the Greek worlds of the Archaic and Classical periods and ethnological contexts, at least in the sense that the latter provide a useful foil for the ancient processes.[5]

Ethnological Case Studies: Forms of Alliance

The division of forms of human society into "band society," "local society," and "regional polity" provides the point of departure for the following reflections. While the authors of this classification of human societies

---

[3] On the model of ethnogenesis, see Pohl and Reimitz 1998; Pohl 2002; on the parallel studies done by Barth 1969, cf. McInerney 2001:59. Application of the model to the Dark Ages and the Archaic period: Ulf 1990; Ulf 1996; Donlan 1997; Raaflaub 1997; Tandy 1997; van Wees 1998; van Wees 2002; application to the Medians: Rollinger 2003.

[4] The definition of this term adopted here lies between that of an instrumentalist (i.e. ethnicity is used to mask the real purpose) and that of a constructivist (i.e ethnicity is a mere invention). For this and the history of the concept, Sokolovskii and Tishkov 1996; Thompson 1989; Glazer and Moynihan 1975; Sollors 1998. Critical voices about the applicability of the term to ancient societies for different reasons in *Ancient West and East* 4.2 (2005) 409–459.

[5] Cf. Hall 2004; Ulf 2006.

conceive of this differentiation in evolutionary terms, it can nonetheless be interpreted in functional terms.[6] In the following discussion, only the essential factors which give rise to cohesion within and between groups will be briefly treated. Three well-examined examples from the anthropological literature will be introduced briefly, and afterwards those elements which appear applicable to the assessment of cohesion and dispersion in the Greek *ethnê* will be isolated from these examples.

"Band societies" are characterized by a high degree of autonomy of families and kinship groups. This is illustrated in the diagram:

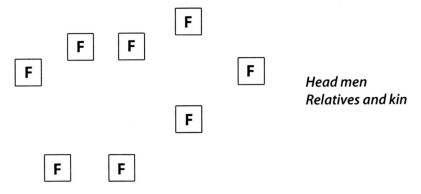

Figure 1. !Kun San. (F= family)

A look at these "family groups" is relevant because the cohesion between them, present only to a limited extent, is reflected in the form of kinship that characterizes it. The individual families are bound to each other through a cognatic kinship system. This provides the opportunity to build up social relationships in all directions, but precisely on account of this openness the relationships remain comparatively weak. Indeed, the groups live alone for the most part, and only in extraordinary circumstances and for a short time does more than one group live in the same place.

Societies categorized as "local groups" or "village societies" behave differently, as two examples show.

The Tsembaga Maring, who live in New Guinea, form one part of altogether some 7000 Maring-speaking Papua. The economic conditions are

---

[6] Johnson and Earle 1987; Plattner 1989. For the history of the evolutionary schema, cf. e.g. Harris 1995; Urry 1997. For the functionalist approach, which can also be connected to an ecological one, cf. Bargatsky 1986 and below, n13.

precarious. They live in a mountainous region of New Guinea's central highlands, cut off from the outside. Their pattern of settlement is characterized by a cycle of aggregation and dispersion. On account of the limited resources, the latent threat of warlike conflicts is present, even if it comes to out-and-out war infrequently. In times of peace, interrelated families live together in hamlets. Whenever war draws near, outbreaks of which are cyclical in nature, the families emigrate to village-like settlements surrounding the traditional ceremonial place of their clan. The families of the clan are closely bound to each other through patrilinear kinship and support each other intensively. The sense of community is visibly expressed by the participation in collective cults. Nonetheless, the bounds of the clan, defined through kinship, are not rigid. Not only individuals, through marriage, but even entire families can be accepted into the clan.

Every clan has at its disposal its own territory, and each family lays claim to a part of it. Moreover, the clan has its own house, where magical objects are kept. When periodic outbreaks of war threaten, at intervals of five to twenty years, the clan-territory is marked off with fences. In war the clan fights as a single combat unit, led by its own ritual chieftain.

The clan interacts with other clans on ceremonial occasions, especially in the *kaiko* ceremony, which stands in close connection to cyclical war.[7] In this ceremony, which extends over a long period of time, a complex process of public exchange of prestige goods (pigs, jewelry) between families and clans takes place. On account of its success in these processes of exchange, which are undertaken in competition, a clan can become so attractive to others that they attach themselves to it. The competition that exists between the clans thus has the goal of strengthening the cohesion of the clans, which are otherwise independent. This intensified cohesion is necessary in order to withstand successfully the conflict that follows the ceremony.

In this way—engineered and strengthened by exogamous marriages and reciprocal relationships among members of different clans—numerous clusters of clans are formed. Such a clan cluster assumes in fact the position of a local group, although it remains "pre-institutional"[8]: it does not have its own name, its own leader, or its own ceremonial house.

---

[7] In addition to the literature cited above, see Rappaport 1967; Peoples 1982.
[8] Cf. Melville 1992 on the concept of the institution.

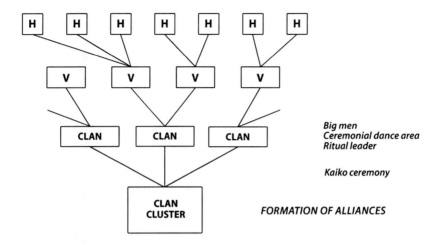

Big men
Ceremonial dance area
Ritual leader

Kaiko ceremony

FORMATION OF ALLIANCES

Figure 2. Tsembaga Maring (New Guinea). (H = hamlet; V = village)

The Enga, who also live in New Guinea, represent another form of socio-political cohesion. They practice intensive agriculture (especially sweet potatoes and yams) in the river valleys of the mountainous region west of Mount Hagen, which are free from the rainforest, but they also cultivate regions of various heights above sea level. Artificial fertilization with compost allows for the constant production of foodstuffs. Since the game animals have been hunted nearly to extinction, the need for protein and fat is satisfied through the energy-intensive breeding of pigs. In addition, stone axes and salt are bartered, as well as prestige goods. The hypothetical population density of 33 to 97 people per square kilometer corresponds to the population density sometimes postulated for Greece in the Dark Ages.

Families live in hamlets, with one house for the men and several for the women in the immediate area of their fields. Each family belongs to a clan-segment, which is determined either by patrilineage or by the somewhat larger sub-clan. Each patrilinear group is named after its progenitor. The sub-clan defines itself by the fictive relationship with a son of the clan's founder. The dance area and the cultic grove form its center. Important external exchange practices are transacted by the sub-clan, as well as matters of public interest (for example, bride-giving), and the compensation payments for those fallen in war are settled. Each sub-clan is led by one man, whose ambition it is to become the leader of the clan and thereby a "big man." Since in this case the status of the sub-clan is enhanced, it is in everyone's interest to increase agricultural productivity. This can be done through raising the work-load of every individual. To this end, the sub-clan leader who aspires to become a "big man" strives to conclude several marriages, because in this way he gains access to a larger productive base. Raising productivity is then the prerequisite for being able to make exchange relationships which are socially successful, that is, based on generosity. These in turn are the prerequisite for rising to the role of "big man." For this reason, constant competition reigns between the sub-clans.

The clan makes use of a territory which is clearly marked off by a fence. Outside of this territory there is the danger of being attacked. The clan is connected to a fictive founder-ancestor. It is visibly defined, as are the sub-clans, by its own dance area, as well as by the ancestral cult house. Here is the center, where the essential rituals are conducted, those which establish a common identity, and where the ceremonial exchanges with other clans also take place. The clan is the largest group which appears as a unit at these types of ceremonies and in war. The "big men" are in this connection the driving force in the creation of an "intergroup collectivity." They have to have at their disposal three capabilities: they must possess an exceptional individual working capacity, they must be extraordinary speakers (with an excellent memory for the various kin relationships and for all earlier collective actions), and they must be superior military commanders.

The same mechanism ensures success here as within the sub-clan. Pressure can be and is exerted on individuals who try to eschew the increased work-load. The outcome of this situation is competition between the clans in the production of goods, which can be presented, mainly at celebrations, as proof of their own excellence and strength. Successful clans tend to become larger, through influx from other clans and—following that—through increased rates of reproduction. The increase of the population promises greater chances of success in war, which threatens in short intervals, every two to three years, on account of the limited area of land available, but it also necessitates intensification of production. Occasion for the conflicts frequently consists of theft of small animals (pigs) and objects of value.

Among the collective ceremonies, the extensive and complex so called "tee ceremony" is of especial significance, because it is the most important medium for the formation of alliances between clans. It consists of a cyclical competition of exchange between clans. The regional exchange from clan to clan, which takes place in a predetermined order and in public, is organized by the "big men."[9] In the course of the ceremony one's exchange partner should be outdone, in order to make him dependent on oneself. This dependence can then be turned into an obligation of support in the case of war.

Thus there exist numerous levels of socio-political solidarity within Enga society. Clan segments and clans represent firm units, formed according to rules that can be recalled, which are supposed to guarantee the successful production of goods above all else. The political level above the clans exists only in the form of agreements based on the principles of gift economy. It requires institutionalized procedures in order to be accomplished, but can also be rescinded by means of those same procedures. The reason to form them consists of the constant threat of war at short notice.

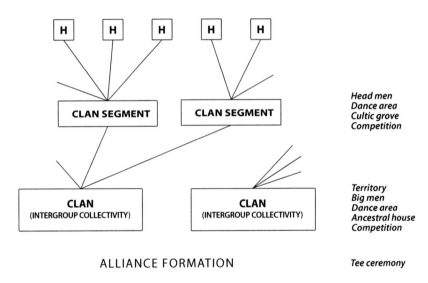

Figure 3. Enga (New Guinea). (H = hamlet)

The "regional polity," represented by the Trobriand Islanders, contrasts with these forms of "local groups," not least on account of its distinct type of cohesion. The Trobriands live in small villages, each led by its own leader (head man). He distributes the land afresh every year to the inhabitants of the village. He is the owner of the sacred objects, which are regarded as essential to the success of agriculture. He initiates the ceremonies at the dance area of the village.

---

[9] Wiessner 2001.

The villages are consolidated into local groups. The links between the villages are maintained through many processes of exchange on the occasion of various celebrations. Thus reciprocal support is assured and the standing ban on warfare between them established. The villages bound together into such a local group stand in a hierarchical relation to each other. The leader of the village with the greatest prestige also holds the leadership of the entire local group. Since the hierarchy of the villages is unalterable, and the leaders inside the villages can come only from certain families, the system includes features of inheritability. In order to fulfill his obligations, the leader marries several women from various villages and then exerts pressure on his in-laws to support him constantly with goods. On ceremonial occasions, he can employ these goods for display and for exchange. In this way a tributary relationship is produced between the leader and the other inhabitants of the villages. Thereby this paramount leader achieves the social status of a "chief." This change in status is mirrored, in turn, by the largely fictitious genealogy which incorporates all the villages within a local group and their leaders' families. For chiefs are set on the top of such genealogies, which are flexible and always illustrate contemporary political relationships.

In one region, several such local groups exist alongside each other. An additional level of cohesion is created above them in the form of a regional unity. The leaders of regional units are selected in the competition which reigns constantly between the leaders of local units. It consists especially of the demonstration of extraordinary economic power and the resulting possibility of the leader's generosity. In order to ensure his success, a chief does not build only on the support of his villages or relations. As chief, he also organizes a far-ranging long-distance trade (the kula trade). In order to do so, he must become involved in a complex pre-existing system of exchange, for which a sufficient number of prestige goods is the prerequisite. The chief's involvement in the kula trade secures privileges for him: clothing and jewelry reserved for him as chief, a special warehouse for his supplies, "magicians" working for him to guarantee the fertility of agriculture, especially the cultivation of yams. These privileges function simultaneously as an ideologically effective safeguard of his position. If by all these means a chief is able to secure a position which appears institutionalized vis-à-vis the other big men in his regional unit, he can nevertheless also be deposed in the case of manifest failure. On the ideological level this is reflected immediately, insofar as new realities are accommodated without difficulty in the flexible and, as far as the hierarchy is concerned, fictitious genealogical system.

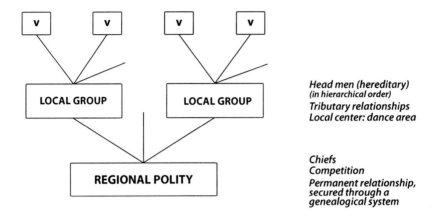

Figure 4. The Trobriand Islanders. (V = village)

Means of Creating Local and Regional Cohesion

In order to be able to draw plausible conclusions for the Greek situation from the case studies briefly described above, it is necessary to sum up their constituent features.

The loose social bonds characteristic of "band societies" correspond to the cognatic system, the widest-ranging way of constructing kinship. The ties which arise out of the cognatic system of relationships and are based on reciprocity are sufficient for overcoming economic and "political" problems. Unlike "band societies," "local group societies" and the societies characterized as "regional polities" live inside the same region in close proximity to each other. The population density is problematically high in comparison to the available resources. The supply of resources cannot simply be increased, since the trade of subsistence goods is only possible to a limited extent.

The limited availability of resources is linked to the tendency not to concentrate in larger settlements, but rather to erect dwellings in the area of the territories to be cultivated. Two factors counteract this tendency. If there is increased pressure to store subsistence goods, or it becomes necessary to gather together against external enemies, then the individual settlements are given up in favor of a central settlement. If this pressure abates, then the central settlement dissolves again. If the pressure does not remain constantly at the same level, then the reaction can be a cycle of aggregation and dispersion. The absence of a consistent settlement center mirrors the absence of a central decision-making authority extending over all the components of the society. The necessary higher cohesion is produced through a unilinear, mainly patrilinear kinship system.[10] In this type of kinship it is possible to construct the sort of genealogies through which socially and politically necessary links and dependencies can be formulated and established.

It seems that political forms of identity require a local point of reference. This receives its attractive quality through symbols of togetherness which are centered here and ideologically enhanced, and which are bound up with the ceremonies and celebrations held here. Celebrations or celebratory meals can be put on with the most varied of intentions. Brian Hayden, who has provided the most comprehensive systematic analysis thus far, differentiates between "diacritical feasts, economic feasts, and alliance and co-operation feasts." Only in the latter case are solidarity, reciprocal relationships, and political and/or economic support the goals to be attained.[11] On these occasions a more or less privileged representative of the group (head man, big man, chief) always appears in the foreground. This is one of the most important occasions on which he can and must display those qualities of his which are necessary for the group's cohesion.

The quality of the leader that is displayed in competition—and thereby also that of his group—is an important means by which successfully to control the pressure which weighs heavily on the groups. For this reason there are attempts to strengthen the group through co-operation. To enter relationships that take precedence over the socio-political unit(s) to which one already belongs means the surrender of a part of one's own decision-making freedom. Therefore the step to production of an "intergroup collectivity" in the form of a clan, a "clan cluster," or an alliance necessitates not only pressure, but also the possibility of perceiving this pressure as an incentive. Limited economic resources and the resulting danger of warlike conflicts produce pressure. So the incentive consists of the chance either to avoid both through the enlargement of the group, or at least to be able to withstand a difficult situation successfully.

However, in the same way as there is an inherent tendency in larger settlements to dissolve, so there also exists a tendency to enter into alliances between groups only when there is an unambiguous—economic or

---

[10] For possible forms of kinship cf. e.g. Vivelo 1988:212–233; Harris 1995; Good 1997.
[11] Hayden 2001:23–64, esp. 55–57. For the applicability to classical studies cf. Ulf 1997b and Ulf 2006.

military—necessity. As a result, while alliances that span socio-political units can certainly be called up in case of need, they nonetheless always remain—if a fixed institutional-legal framework is absent—more or less fragile. This applies to the construction of clusters of clans recognizable in the examples as much as to the temporary and non-institutional alliances between clans.

If one observes these societies from the outside, then it appears that the measure of success is doubtless connected to the degree of organizational tightness. In an evolutionarily-oriented view of human societies, a higher tightness of organization is always linked to a hierarchization, in the sense of stratification or classification by rank. However, the functional interpretation of the various human societies suggested above allows for the possibility that there may be arrangements other than hierarchy capable of producing and guaranteeing the systematic coherence necessary for successful cooperation.

In the "regional polity" as represented by the Trobriand Islanders, the path that leads to hierarchy is documented. The stability of the society is attained not by the introduction of a political level in the narrow sense, but unmistakably by the solidification of influence on the various levels of social solidarity. Here, leadership inside the village community tends to become hereditary. Tributary dependencies develop between the leader of the local group and the village communities that comprise it. The chiefs of the regional unit obtain the resources they need for competition with the other chiefs from the dependence of the leaders of the local groups, but also through the increase of dependencies achievable through marriage to women from local groups belonging to other regional units. Furthermore, the relationships and dependencies are secured on the ideological level through a comprehensive genealogy that takes on a new quality. Since kinship is conceived of taxonomically rather than biologically, the genealogy can confirm the existing network of relationships as much as it can be easily adjusted to suit changing realities. The combination of a tendency to inheritability with a consciously imposed, ideologically usable kinship system offers the possibility of binding social units firmly, and thereby shifts the scope of activity of such chiefs, in comparison to "big men," towards the sort of institutionalized decision-making and leadership which may be termed "political."[12]

[12] Earle 1987.

The possibility of attaining a higher degree of organization that stands in opposition to hierarchization is reflected in the system of the Enga. Here, pressure caused by economic problems and expressing itself in the threat of violence is constantly present to a greater extent than it is with the Tsembaga Maring. But it is never countered with the installation of a fixed hierarchy, but rather solely by alliances that are constantly formed anew. Carole Crumley has construed such relationships as consciously contrary to hierarchical ones and designated them by the term "heterarchy." In such systems, which are no less complex, numerous groups can coexist alongside each other on the same level. Thereby it becomes possible to construct an overarching identity without the necessity of subordinating certain groups to other ones.[13] Of course this "political," i.e. overarching, identity must remain relatively unstable in such a system. But it is precisely this instability that guarantees the possibility of adapting to changing conditions—with the result that such societies can change back and forth from hierarchical to heterarchical forms.

In the case of the Tsembaga Maring, this flexibility is reflected in the fact that the ritual leader is activated, as it were, for the duration of the war, but he is entitled to no real powers, only symbolic ones. The location where the festivals supporting cohesion take place is also furnished with a significant symbol of togetherness in the form of the house of the ancestors. Further, the festivals are organized with an extensive program of ceremonial events (the *kaiko* ceremony, the tee ceremony) so that all subgroups can be included, but also so that they can operate flexibly towards the outside. The resulting alliances are not secured through any institutional foundations. Thus, in the final analysis, how the field of relationships turns out above the level of the clan depends on the quality of the accomplishments of the leaders and their groups. Since this quality can always change in this environment of constant competition—for example, because of the improved performance of a competitor—these connections must remain labile.

The model of heterarchy not only directs attention to the fact that the constructs which impart identity to the local groups and the "regional polity" do not demonstrate primordial "ethnicity," but also indicates that

---

[13] Crumley 1987:158, defines heterarchy as follows: "Structures are heterarchical when each element is either unranked relative to each other element or possesses the potential for being ranked in a number of ways." Crumley 1995. For the various forms of identity, the conflicts that arise from them, and the overlaps, cf. e.g. Müller 1987.

the societies themselves are the engineers of ethnicity with the help of more or less articulated genealogies.

Greek Societies in the Dark Ages and the Archaic Period

None of the case studies mentioned above, nor any other ethnological case study, is to be employed as a direct analogy for Greek relationships. Yet it can be assumed that basic elements abstracted from the case studies and patterns of thought and behavior in socio-political life were also constituent parts of the Greek societies. The plausibility of this assumption has been confirmed by many recent interpretations of the literary sources.[14] The applicability of this model to the constantly growing body of archaeological evidence from the Dark Ages and the Archaic Period is confirmed by the critical synopsis of the current state of research recently provided by Catherine Morgan.[15] For our purposes it can be reduced to the following points.

1. There is no significant difference to be seen between the settlements traditionally regarded as *poleis*, such as Argos, Corinth, or Megara, and other settlements, such as, for example, Pherai or Aigion, which are not counted as *poleis*. The elements brought up as characteristic of a *polis* can also be found in other settlements. The type of identity that is supposed to bond the inhabitants in *poleis* to each other seems not to have been a phenomenon specific to *poleis*, but rather a general phenomenon of all political communities since the eighth century.[16]

2. The units that are generally designated as *ethnê* are not natural or cultural units existing *a priori*. Moreover, the characteristics of the individual Greek "landscapes" are quite variable.[17] Morgan refers to the pronounced landscape profile. Single regions show distinct patterns of settlement and also were not settled in the same way at all times and in all their parts. Also, the settlement duration was not the same everywhere.[18] Further, the idea that an "*ethnos*-landscape" was poor involves obvious reductionism which

---

[14] Cf. e.g. Ulf 1990; Ulf 2008; van Wees 1998; van Wees 2002; Raaflaub 1997; Donlan 1997; Whitley 1991; Morgan 2003.

[15] Morgan 2003; cf. Beck 1997, who places much greater emphasis on the concept of institutions.

[16] Morgan 2003: esp. 45–57, 74–85. For the attempt to determine what a *polis* is, cf. the works of the Copenhagen Polis Center. Especially illuminating for its line of argument is Hansen 2002. Cf. in opposition to this e.g. Murray 2000.

[17] Proceeding from this, Gehrke 1986 has developed a typology of states beyond Athens and Sparta.

[18] Whitley 1991.

does not do justice to the real ecological factors. Considering these factors, it has to be recognized that the relationship between a settlement and its hinterland cannot simply be described according to a single model, and that the various forms of societies and settlements cannot be understood with simple models, such as "simple progression from tribal to federal to *polis* organization" or even with the more complex "central place theory."[19]

3. The assumption of a fixed connection between a given *ethnos* and a landscape is undermined by the essential fact that no region has demonstrated clear borders "from the beginning onwards;" these borders were first drawn parallel to the rise of regional units such as those in Phocis, Locris, Achaea, and also Arcadia.[20]

4. Considering the variety of settlement forms and the absence of regional delimitation, we have to reckon with many sub-regional groupings with different identities. These are recognizable, among other things, in that "ancestry was in some way incorporated into expressions of status and/ or group identity in the mortuary record."[21] However, the relationships in which these identities stood to one another could be very complex. Morgan speaks of "nested tiers of identities" and of "different tiers of political relationships across the landscape."[22] The nature of this complexity can be concretized to a certain degree and at least partially described as "overlapping, rather than nested relations."[23]

5. Doubtless cooperation was necessary in order to build and maintain drainage systems or roads shared by several settlements. Moreover, the landscape profile imposed the necessity of an exchange of goods and of transhumance;[24] both presuppose the cooperation of several groups.

In regions such as the Gulf of Corinth, where communication over the sea is easily possible, there exists the likelihood of a reflective perception of self and other. This can result in cooperation but also in exclusion. Morgan sketches the diversity of such relationships as "complex interconnections

---

[19] Morgan 2003:24, 91, 173, refers to the two models, differentiated by J. Bintliff and A. Snodgrass, of the closed individual settlement with continual growth and the dispersed settlement with a more extensive growth that begins later. It is impossible to observe any unequivocal movement from the country to the city.

[20] Cf. Morgan 2003:24, 28, 31, 38–39, 114.

[21] Morgan 2003:195. The quotation refers to Thessaly, but has a nearly general applicability.

[22] Morgan 2003:42, 113, 168.

[23] Crumley 1987:158 thus characterizes heterarchical as opposed to hierarchical relationships.

[24] Morgan correctly refers to Foxhall 1995, who maintains that evidence of agrarian activities rules out the assumption of a pure pastoralism; for this also Ulf 1999.

of skills, specialization in particular kinds of vessel, access to raw materials and facilities like kilns, mobility of craftsmen, the location of markets and the mechanisms of exchange of finished products."[25]

6. As a primary motivation behind such co-operative relationships, a problem which is named directly in (for example) the Homeric epics can be surmised: hunger, which drives people to steal cattle from their neighbors or to plunder strangers far away.[26] The literary examples do not mention only peaceful cooperation. If a solution to this problem is sought with violence, then cooperation is also necessary, but now in the form that one prepares for war through a closer alliance and/or the search for new partners. In this context, Morgan refers to, among other examples, the latent enmity between Sparta and Tegea, the pressure exerted by Thessaly on Phocis, or the expansion of the Achaean coastal states onto the opposite Aetolia coast. Such a situation leads to the strengthening of internal cohesion, to control of the territory and to demarcation of the borders.[27]

7. The local and regional sanctuaries functioned as places of exchange, both profane and sacred. The search for partners is documented in the comparatively early "elaborate material display," according to Morgan. Such a conclusion is suggested by the well-known fact that "cross-border connections" are produced through the giving of prestige goods. In this way relationships between guests were also created.[28] Besides the wandering artisans, fixed workshops are sometimes documented in the shrines; because of this they also became economically attractive centers.[29]

8. The complex networks which were formed on the basis of various identities and which consisted of cooperation, exchange and obligation, marked the borders of a "region." Since the number and appearance of the participants in such networks changed, the ideologies that developed to reinforce their

---

[25] Morgan 2003:165–171, quotation:167; cf. also 155.

[26] Donlan 1997.

[27] Morgan 2003:132, 165. This gains strong support from social psychology; cf. Brewer 2003:29–33.

[28] Morgan 2003:175, 203. Morgan 2003:107–163, investigates these connections under the heading "communities of cult." This creates the impression that these places were independent of the other settlements and acted of their own accord. On the contrary, it is argued in the present contribution that the special religious character of cult centres should not be taken to imply that they operated as independent, separate communities.

[29] Morgan 2003:72–73, 135. Therein lies probably a distinctive feature of Greece: the artisans themselves and not only their products come from outside. As a result, not only are the needs of the larger units satisfied in these locations, but information is more quickly and more successfully disseminated.

cohesion, as represented by cults and myths, also had to be flexible. They are "open to constant revision and reappraisal." The analyses, repeatedly undertaken in recent times, of "Greek" genealogies and stories about the migrations of ethnic units, come unequivocally to this conclusion.[30]

This picture of ethnicities emerging from a development which is slow, and does not progress in a linear fashion at all, is consistent with the fact that ethnicity can be demonstrated only late: for example, at the end of the sixth century for Arcadia, only after the Persian Wars for Phocis, at the end of the fifth century for Achaea. It also fits into this picture that ethnicity changes and can even disappear altogether. As an example of this, Morgan names the small regions ("marginal areas"), in which no settlement takes shape as a center, such as the valley of the Spercheios in Thessaly or in the valley of Pharai in Achaea; these examples are supplemented by the Azanes, who were known to the authors of the fifth century only as an entity that had existed in the past.[31]

In this synopsis based on Morgan, primarily of the archaeological material, it remains an open question how contact and co-operation within and between various groups emerged, and how it operated in practice. However, if results gained primarily from archaeological material are linked to the ethnological analogies, then a hypothesis, at least, may justifiably be formulated as to how this activity may have arisen. Small family groups, kinship, status competition in the framework of a gift economy and the development of networks; a distinctly ideologically colored linking of groups with the help of display behavior, communal feasts supported by religion, and the formulation of flexible genealogies; finally, too, informal alliances, produced by all these means: there is nothing to prevent our seeing all these elements operating in the Greek societies as well.[32]

---

[30] Cf. Morgan 2003:170, 187–190. For this reason, the conclusion that the consciousness of an ethnically closely related unit of the Greeks in the form of the Hellenic genealogy did not arise before the late sixth or even the fifth century, recently reinforced by thorough investigation, gains importance (Ulf 1996:264–271; Hall 1997:42–44; McInerney 1999:120–153; McInerney 2001; Antonaccio 2001; Hall 2002, esp. ch. 2).

[31] Morgan 2003:176, 186.

[32] F. Bourriot and D. Roussel's demonstration that the origin of tribes and phratries was bound to the *polis* does not mean that kinship played no role. The strongest evidence, rightly cited against such a conclusion, consists of the grave finds which point to family graves and groups of descendants stemming from a common ancestor (Morgan 2003:192–195). The Homeric epics, in which not only the known genealogies are used, but also the groups of descendants become visible in outline, point in the same direction (Ulf 1990:245–250; Raaflaub 1997).

At the outset it was intentionally indicated that the goal is not to discover a direct analogy, but only to point out important elements of thought and action out of which ethnic units can be built. The reason for this lies not least in the fact that the Greek societies in the first half of the first millennium in Greece and on the Mediterranean seaboard were in no way isolated, as the archaeological record has already demonstrated in many cases. It is therefore to be expected that traditions of oriental and Egyptian origin had already begun to affect these Greek societies in the Dark Ages.[33] Moreover, the Greek societies developed in a cultural environment which was not available to the ethnological societies, an environment that included, in particular, the systematic intellectual conceptualization of the world,[34] which was in essence also based on genealogies (such as Hesiod's *Theogony*), and the process by which legal systems came to dominate important aspects of life, as can be seen not only in the earliest laws, but also in the use of contracts.[35] To explicate the process of Greek ethnicization, therefore, demands the consideration of both factors mentioned: the ethnologically documented elements in the formation of ethnic units and the influences stemming from oriental cultures.

Ethnicization on a Super-Regional Level: Dorians and Ionians

Within this complicated topography of diverse societies, political models and divergent influences, the origin of the large units of the Dorians and Ionians, understood as ethnic, is to be re-defined. They can no longer be posited as the sub-units of a primary ethnic unit of "the Greeks." Also, they must be reconsidered from the perspective of their function. This places the connection between the Dorians and the Peloponnesian League, and between the Delian-Attic League and the Ionians, at the center of attention.

The sources point only a few spotlights on the history of the so-called Peloponnesian League. Nevertheless, it is easy to recognize that the attempt to produce a large super-regional alliance of the "Lacedaemonians and their allies" was advanced on three fronts: by violence, by the signing

---

[33] Cf. e.g. West 1997; Rollinger and Ulf 2004b.

[34] Patzek 2004; Bichler 2004.

[35] Hölkeskamp 1992–1995; Rollinger 2004; Gehrke 2000. Morgan 2003:70–71, rightly maintains that it is no "solution" simply to put the origins of the *polis* back into the post-palatial Mycenean times of the late twelfth century. Her position can be strengthened by pointing to the fact that such an argument presupposes the notion of a Greek "people."

of agreements, and on the ideological level by means of genealogy.[36] Dorian ethnicity was derived from the construction of a densely-branching and expansive tree of migratory and genealogical connections. Yet within this structure Sparta, as the leader of the Peloponnesian League, was never rigidly bound to a Dorian ethnicity. Only in the second half of the fifth century does this notion seem to dominate. But it remained perpetually in competition with the assertion of the Achaean origin of the Spartans.[37]

This competitive relationship was possible because "Dorian" was not a stably defined concept from the beginning, under which the Lacedaemonians are to be subsumed next to other groupings. Among the few sources concerning the Dorians, this is shown by the paratactic stringing of Ionians, Aeolians, Dorians and Lacedaemonians in Herodotus. This parallelization of Lacedaemonians and Dorians is all the more note-worthy because in the second half of the seventh century, in the work of Tyrtaeus, one finds neither the names of the Spartan tribes connected with the Heraclids, nor the Lacedaemonians and Spartans equated to the Dorians.[38] It is no less meaningful that the Heraclids are directly linked with the Dorians only in Thucydides at the end of the fifth century. For in the first half of the fifth century, Pindar had to argue that the Lacedaemonians—not the Spartans!—were Dorians: the Heraclids had established themselves in Amyclae as neighbors of the Tyndarids, who resided in Sparta; Aigimios, together with Hyllos, the son of Heracles, had led the Dorians first to Aigina and then to the Peloponnese.[39] First and only in Thucydides is the area of Doris, unknown before Herodotus, linked directly to the Lacedaemonians as their metropolis.[40] The fragility of the Spartan—Dorian connection is again confirmed in that no trace of it is found in the time after Thucydides, in Xenophon or Strabo.

It is evident that the integration of the Lacedaemonians, including the Spartans, into the large unit of the Dorians is an attempt to lay claim to

---

[36] Cf. Cartledge 1979:144–148, Thommen 1996:55–60, Welwei 2004:102–106; also Tausend 1992:167–180.

[37] For a thorough treatment of this point, cf. Ulf 1996: esp. 251–264; somewhat differently Hall 1997:56–65; Hall 2002: esp. 82–89; McInerney 2001:61–62.

[38] Herodotus 1.6; Tyrtaeus F 1 D = 10, 15 G-P; F 2 D = 1a.12ff G-P. The equation of Heraclids with Dorians can be read in this text only based on later sources. The argument derived from the equation is therefore circular; so, e.g. Malkin 1994:33–43.

[39] Pindar *Pythian* 1.61–66; *Isthmian* 9 = F 1.1–4; *Pythian* 5.69–72.

[40] Thucydides 1.107.2–3; 3.91–92. For the strange elements of both passages, which allow them to be seen as an invention of Thucydides, cf. Ulf 1996:262–263. It therefore comes as no surprise that the region Doris does not feature in the Iliad's *Catalog of Ships*.

the leadership among all those who were reckoned to be Dorians. The line of argument built on a common ethnicity can nonetheless change into its opposite. For the incorporation of Sparta into the unit of the Dorians could only be achieved with the help of a genealogical construction. The Spartans had to be integrated into the genealogy on the same level as the other Dorian tribes. From that follows a reduced claim to the right of leadership, for this type of genealogical construction can also easily be interpreted heterarchically. On the other hand, if the genealogical position were changed such that no direct common descent could be inferred, then the Spartans would gain a greater independence vis-à-vis the Dorians. It is surely for this reason that the other genealogical derivation, the descent of the Spartan kings from Achaean roots, remained constantly present. It is documented in the transfer of the bones of Orestes, the derivation of the Spartan kings from Perseus, and in Cleomenes I's claim to be Achaean, not Dorian.[41]

The common intention of these genealogical derivations is to produce an ethnic commonality that reaches far back. Of course, such genealogies must not be confused with historical knowledge about the fate of an ethnic unit. On the contrary, they are easy to identify as a part of the process which is referred to as ethnogenesis. This occurs when the notional possession of a common ethnic history is advanced for the purpose of constructing a political unit.[42] Modern historical analysis has overlooked this intention for a long time and therefore has itself portrayed "a flawed modern construct" in the form of an ethnic unit of the Dorians.[43] If, as demonstrated in this volume by Peter Funke, the Peloponnesian League—not least because of its expansion across numerous regions—was a very complex unit and gains clearer contours only in the sixth century,[44] then one reason for that is exactly the missing ethnic homogeneity.

The "history" of the Ionians, which is bound up with the Delian-Attic League, is no less complex that that of the Dorians. It can be very briefly summarized, because the use of the name in the fifth century has been investigated anew relatively recently.[45]

1. It is more than just problematic to assume the existence of an ancient "tribe" based on the antiquity of a name. The name Iaones is even

---

[41] Herodotus 1.67–68; cf. 9.26; 5.72; 6.53. Cf. also Pretzler in this volume.

[42] Cf. above, n3.

[43] Morgan 2003:187.

[44] Cf. above, p. 20, and Funke 1997; cf. also Funke 1998.

[45] Ulf 1996:250–251; Hall 1997:51–56; Hall 2002; Malkin 2001; Lomas 2004; Vanschoonwinkel 2006.

recorded once in Linear B, but its content is not more precisely identifiable. Additionally, there is the fact that it is used in Assyrian texts of the eighth and seventh centuries as an ethnonym and as a toponym: "the people in the West" with barbarian ways. Thus the word circumscribes only very vaguely people in the West, without making any concrete statements about their origin and internal structure.[46]

2. If the mention of the Ionians in the *Iliad* is an interpolation, then the name appears in a Greek context for the first time in the Homeric Hymn to Apollo.[47] Therein it is stated that the Iaones, men of various languages from the Aegean islands and from Asia Minor, come to Delos for a festival of Apollo.

3. The Ionians are brought into connection with Athens for the first time by Solon.[48] He believes that Attica is the oldest country in Ionia. Whoever uses that text as a starting point is forced to revise Athens' place in the known genealogical accounts. Herodotus and Thucydides know the story that Ion comes to Athens and becomes king there, so that the inhabitants, who were Pelasgian up to this point, become Ionians. Of course, in opposition to the claim that the original Ionians were located in Athens stand other competing accounts. Thus the Ionians are also placed in the northern Peloponnese, in Achaea. On this view, the cult of Poseidon Helikonios in Panionion, in Asia Minor, would be derived from Helike, a place in Achaea; the fact that the participants in this cult number twelve would thus reflect the twelve regions of Achaea. This notion corresponds to the identification of Ion and Achaios as brothers in the genealogy of the Hellenes.

Competition with the Athenian claim is also reflected in the tradition that Miletus and Ephesus were founded once by Athens and then again by the Messenians. Priene, although an Ionian city, would have been founded by the Thebans. And Herodotus also says that the Ionian cities in Asia Minor were an ethnic mix.[49]

In order to satisfy all claims, these competing views of the origin of the Ionians are integrated into a construction of the migration of the Ionians already found in Herodotus. According to this the Ionians came from Achaea; they were driven out by the Achaeans and migrated to Athens. Here

---

[46] For the Near Eastern sources, Rollinger 2001: esp. 236, 248–258; Rollinger 2008.

[47] *Homeric hymns* 3.143–148. This applies only if the text is not taken to refer to the celebration held on Delos by Polycrates of Samos.

[48] Solon F 4 D = 4a W = *Ath. Pol.* 5.2. On the competing stories and subsequent paragraphs cf. esp. Hall 1997:51–56 with full references; Hall 2002:67–71.

[49] McInerney 2001:57–59.

they met fugitives from Pylos. In this way the emigrants from Athens could be simultaneously a combination of different "tribes" and Ionians from Athens. The associations with the name Ionians or Ion, sketched here only briefly, have a single object: through the creation of an "ethnic" past—based on genealogical constructions—community is to be produced.

Jonathan Hall is therefore right to believe that these foundation stories should not be viewed as "reminiscences of genuine population movements," but more plausibly "as an active attempt on the part of the Greek cities of Asia Minor to anchor their origins in the deeper mythical past of mainland Greece."[50] This conclusion is supported by the observation that in Athens in the time after the Persian Wars this type of self-definition was altered. In the face of the need to position itself as a leading power in the Delian-Attic League, a type of self-definition was developed by Athens which Hall calls "oppositional" in contrast to the earlier "aggregate self-definition."[51] In this context value was placed on autochthony. In this tale, the goddess of the city, Athena, who raised Erechtheus, succeeds in the war over the country Attica against the god of the Ionians, Poseidon. The Ionian cities are founded by colonists from Athens.[52] On the basis of a communal origin (*syngeneia*) created in this way, the cities of Asia Minor, for example, after their liberation from the Persians, asked the Athenians whether they would like immediately to replace the Spartans as their leaders, according to Thucydides.[53]

Conclusions are easily drawn from a functional interpretation of the process by which the Dorian and Ionian ethnic units were derived. The term "Dorian" allowed Sparta to build up its area of dominance, which comprised large areas of the Peloponnese. Athens used the name "Ionian" in order to justify its position in the Delian-Attic League, which was ever further-reaching, centrally organized, and aiming to become a super-regional state.[54] However, it is obvious at the same time that these arguments did not remain uncontested, but instead caused problems in establishing the desired dominance. In the realm of concrete power politics, both great Leagues battled with the general problems which arise from domination and subordination, and in particular with two key consequences of the fact that the freedom of

---

[50] Hall 1997:52.
[51] Hall 1997:54; earliest textual evidence: Pindar *Isthmian* 2.19.
[52] Herodotus 7.95; 9.106; Thucydides 1.2.6; 1.12.4.
[53] Thucydides 3.86.3; 6.20.3. On this, Hall 1997:37.
[54] For the Peloponnesian League see above n44; for the Delian-Attic League cf. e.g. Schuller 1974; Welwei 1999:78–79.

League members was mostly theoretical: they were not allowed to leave the League, nor had they full command of their internal affairs.

Local and Regional Ethnicization vs. Hierarchization According to Ethnic Symbols

If one accepts the arguments presented here, then the period of the fifth to the fourth centuries, which stands in the center of this volume, becomes a second phase of ethnicization. Within the framework of centralist "attempts at great power,"[55] which are observable from the sixth century on, one can see the construction of smaller ethnicities being mustered in opposition to the claims of Sparta and Athens.

This policy was not conceived anew by the smaller political units. It had already been suggested, as we have seen, both by the double relationship of the Spartans with the Dorians and the Achaeans, and by the attempt formulated in Athens to make the term "Ionian" the central point of reference in the League, but simultaneously to sever it from its associations within the Hellenic genealogy which had obtained until then. By means of the well-known genealogical argument, as it is used in Euripides' *Ion*,[56] a heterarchical interpretation of the Hellenic genealogy was to be excluded.

In the genealogy presented by Euripides, it is not as usual Xouthos who is the father of Ion, but rather Apollo. The god raped Creusa, the daughter of Erechtheus. Creusa abandoned the newborn child on the Acropolis of Athens, and Hermes brought him to Delphi, where he grew up. Xouthos, descendant of Aeolus, who was settled in Achaea, and savior of Athens in the war against the Euboeans, married Creusa. With this constellation, the self-sufficient, autochthonous "history" of Athens is protected. At the same time, Ion receives a new orientation by having Apollo as his father. For Apollo, linked to Athens through Creusa, positions Ion as the ancestor of the Ionians. The Hellenic genealogy is subordinated to Ion, who stems from a divine father, whereas Doros and Achaios are sons of Xouthos and Creusa, born after him. His independent connection with Athens is extended by his becoming the father of the eponymous heroes of the Ionic tribes. From their sons proceeded the Ionian colonization, through which the Ionian cities were subordinated to Athens. This type of genealogy—regardless of how

---

[55] Cf. Ulf 1993. Beck 1997:253 speaks of a "Fragmentierung und Polyzentrierung des 'internationalen' Systems" ("fragmentation and poly-centralization of the 'international' system").

[56] Cf. Hall 1997:56 (with references to the literature).

seriously it was intended by Euripides—represents an attempt, which can be paralleled by that of the Spartans to claim Achaean origins, to subvert the innate heterarchical tendency of the competing older genealogies. In this way the hierarchical relationship between the Ionian Athenians and the Ionian league members is supposed to be "historically" guaranteed.

This method of exploiting genealogies provides the background against which it is possible properly to evaluate the process of ethnicization by which smaller political units battled against the development of the political hierarchy desired by Sparta and Athens. In these cases ethnicity is used in order to rupture the larger ethnic unit, not in order to establish one. For this purpose a political element is incorporated in the form of a more or less stable alliance underneath the super-regional level. Although there is no clear evidence for it, it has to be assumed that, in practice, the process was set in motion by the means and methods observed in the ethnological case studies: through the activation of reciprocal relationships based on kinship; through the intensification and widening of existing rituals and ceremonies, which strengthen social ties; and, where it appeared possible and necessary, through the safeguarding of new ties with legal agreements.[57] Indeed, it is the conscious and enforced application of these methods that stands behind the "politics of ethnicity," which Morgan was able to describe only generally as a change in equilibrium between the "different registers within the social geography of each group which recognized a common identity."[58] For it would be remarkable indeed if a system of relationships in the form of a comprehensive genealogy appeared in the "political" upper layer, and at the same time such forms of thought had played only a small role or no role at all in the constitution and linkage of smaller units.[59]

These patterns of thought and forms of behavior, which were assumed above to have assisted the creation of societies in the Archaic Period, can now be seen to intensify. Under the new political and economic conditions, this leads to greater cohesion in the "regions" which up until now did not

[57] The sympolity treaty between Mantinea and Helisson discussed by Funke belongs in exactly this context.

[58] Morgan, this volume. With regard to Epirus, Davies 2000:257 speaks of an impulse which was "neither wholly 'top-down' nor wholly 'bottom-up,' but a complex mixture of the two." For Phocis cf. McInerney 1999; an exemplary assessment of the complex relationships inside Arcadia is Nielsen and Roy 1999.

[59] This does not entail any attempt to reinstall a clan-based society ("Geschlechterstaat"). But the creation of phylae and phratries presupposes the reality of—and thought about—structures of kinship, which form the foundations of those social units. This cannot have been a merely aristocratic phenomenon. Cf. also above, n32.

figure in the foreground of the history of events reported in the sources. Everywhere the local and regional networks must have stabilized. Of that there are sufficient indications. But, corresponding to the varying conditions and the resultant varying motivations in the different regions of Greece, this process did not advance in the same way everywhere. Alongside the general drive to orient oneself against the overarching claims to power of Sparta, Athens and then also Thebes, further motives emerge, rooted in local considerations. The motor that tended to push the small units in Arcadia and Messenia towards unity was the will to release themselves from the clutches of Sparta; in Phocis it was the desire to maintain regional self-sufficiency against the pressure of the Thessalians; the aim of Thessaly and Elis was to maintain the dependency of the *perioikoi* and to enlarge their own territory. The consequences of these varying motivations, whose treatment here is in no way comprehensive, may nevertheless be apprehended on the basis a few central parameters.

Among these parameters, Morgan does not count, with good reason, the evidence of archaeologically defined "cultures," because congruencies that are demonstrable only archaeologically cannot be directly equated with a political unity or a "place identity," and also because we must reckon at the same time with "different tiers of political relationship across the landscape." Only concretely demonstrable collective activities present clear indications of a political unit:[60] sanctuaries, the production of genealogies, the formation of quasi-official names for the *ethnê*, the striking of coins, and concrete political actions. All these are described in detail in the contributions in this volume.

It is not a new question whether the celebrations held in cultic locations represent "national meetings."[61] That they may have been—with respectively differing ranges—is suggested by the public ceremonial meals, which are in many cases demonstrable, and by the regional and extra-regional origin of the offerings. Thus, in the contributions to this volume, the dedication of monuments is referred to again and again with the aim of representing regional history in the fourth century. Consider a few examples of this.

According to the evidence of the votives, Enodia, a goddess venerated in Thessalian Pherai, seems not to have been worshipped outside of this shrine until the fifth century. Later, however, her cult spreads out

---

[60] Morgan 2003:164–170, citations: 168.
[61] Morgan 2003:109. Cf. above, n11.

over all of Thessaly and southern Macedonia. The goddess becomes a pan-Thessalian deity.[62] Different in process but analogous in intention is the situation in Corinth. Here, shrines, dedicated to different gods and goddesses, were erected by Corinth at Perachora, Isthmia and Solygeia which are plausibly assumed to have linked the whole Corinthia to the center.[63] The situation in Arcadia offers a contrast. Here the shrines remain sharply separated from each other; they are not (as in the case of Phocis, for instance) integrated into an over-arching regional system. None of the Arcadian cults can ever claim a "national" status.[64] Correlated with this is the fact that a multitude of shrines to heroes is documented, behind which local identities are to be surmised.[65] Similarly in Elis, Samikon for the Triphylians on the one hand, and Olympia for the Pisatans on the other, seem to have functioned as centers for local display before Elis gained control of the sanctuary and Olympia developed into a place for Panhellenic festival.[66]

The varying range of the cults reflects the varying intentions of those who practiced them and also of those who dedicated their votive offerings in the shrines. This conclusion finds striking confirmation when one turns to the second large area open to ideological manipulation: the myths. Myths and the genealogies transported with them are neither fixed once and for all nor limited to an old traditional stock: old stories can be changed, new ones can be invented. In the current context myths serve as means to support and legitimize new "ethnic" identities to counteract the genealogical/mythological rhetoric used by states like Sparta and Athens aiming at regional hegemony.

The (re-)formulation of myths connected to a single location can serve the purpose of discrediting or at least disputing the claim of tales that bind together larger regions. As an answer to Sparta's Dorian rhetoric, the myth of Echemos, who conquered Hyllos, the son of Heracles, was told in Arcadian Tegea. The defeated Hyllos had to leave the Peloponnese and the Heraclids were allowed to return there only three generations later.[67] In Messenia in

---

[62] Morgan 2003:109, 113, 135, 139–140, 149.

[63] Morgan 1994; Morgan 2003:75–60, 150–152.

[64] Morgan 2003:150, 155–161; Voyatzis 1999.

[65] The hero shrines are documented only by Pausanias, but according to him they originated in the classical and Hellenistic period; for this, Morgan 2003:161–162, with reference to Jost 1985.

[66] Roy, this volume; Ruggeri, this volume; Giangiulio, this volume. For the development of inter-regional cults cf. Ulf 1997b.

[67] Pretzler, this volume; Ulf 1996.

the fourth century there was an attempt to communicate a Messenian identity which was independent from Sparta as an ancient identity above the
names of the five Messenian tribes. To that end the "ambivalence between
Heraclids and Dorians" was exploited, which has already been discussed
above. Heracles is presented not as a Peloponnesian but as a Theban hero. He
is not the ancestor of the Heraclids who are related to the Dorians. This story
is obviously an expression of the Messenian ethnogenesis which became
possible after the earthquake of 462. It in no way reflects an "underground
Messenian cultural resistance."[68] Again, the intention to set a new form of
ethnicity against the great myths of the Dorians and Ionians is also unmis-
takable when eponyms for whole regions are incorporated into genealogies
or myths, as, for example, Arkas, Pisos, Eleios or Phokos. Even if these myths
are not always directly documented as narrative accounts, they can often be
inferred indirectly.

Thus, for example, Mantinea was already attempting in the fifth
century to present itself as pan-Arcadian by striking coins with the
"Arcadian" motif of the bear and acorn. It was presumably also during
this period that the bones of Arkas were transported from Mainalos to
Mantinea. The attempt to create commonality in one's own interest that
is obvious in the case of Arkas seems to have been undertaken elsewhere,
too. The coin series which was struck either in the shrine of Zeus Lykaios
or in Tegea, with the head of Zeus Lykaios and the legend "Arkadikon,"
demonstrates this.[69]

The behavior of the Eleans is not much different in this respect. They
traced their ancestry in different variants from Aitolos, who—at least
according to Ephorus—was once driven out of Elis. His descendants, the
Aetolians, nonetheless returned to Elis together with the Heraclids and
took over the administration of the Olympic Games. In a much later addition the eponym Eleios appears as the son of Eurykyde, the daughter of
Epeios. None of these stories can be dated before the beginning of the
fifth century, that is, before Pindar, so the concrete development of Elis
into a fixed political unit might thus belong in this century.[70] The well-
known conflict between Pisa and Elis in the 60s of the fourth century led

---

[68] Luraghi, this volume; Figueira 1999; Siapkas 2003.

[69] Cf. Pretzler in this volume; Morgan 2003:161; Beck 1997:189–190.

[70] Cf. Ulf 1997a:21–22, 26–31. Somewhat differently, Möller 2004:259–260, 264–265. This
assumption is further supported by the fact that the return of the bones of Hippodameia
from Midea to Argolis is to be placed in the context of the alliance of Elis and Argos against
Sparta in 420 BCE; Pausanias 6.20.7; see Möller 2004:265n87.

to a treaty between Pisa and the Arcadians. This was accompanied on the mythological level by the fact that the eponym Pisos became the husband of the daughter of Arkas, Olympia.[71]

The situation in Phocis is similar to what has been observed in Arcadia or Elis. As Morgan is able to show based on the archaeological record, a network arose between the seventh and the sixth centuries that linked the northern and southern parts of Phocis, although a political structure did not yet exist. This process seems to have developed as a reaction against Thessalian pressure which was apparently being exerted as early as the sixth century. However, a common history was created only just before the Persian Wars. Pre-existing local myths, behind which the "individual communities' claims to distinct origins and descent over and above their common Phocian ethnicity" are still recognizable, were now grouped around the eponym Phokos.[72]

Since bonds between communities articulated in newly (re-)formulated myths can, it seems, remain a purely ideological construct, it is in the realm of the history of events where we must seek a more unambiguous demonstration of political ethnicity. In order to create the cohesion necessary for military action, there are no means available other than those described above in connection with the Peloponnesian and the Delian-Attic League. Thus Elis attempted to link the *perioikoi* to itself in various ways, with treaties and with violence. The border between Arcadia and Elis was not significant until the sixth century. This became an important theme in this context.[73] In addition to that, we have conflicts between the Arcadians, between Sparta and the Arcadians, and also between the Thessalians and the Phocians. As early as

---

[71] For this, Möller 2004:258; Ruggeri, this volume; Giangiulio, this volume.

[72] Cf. Herodotus 8.27-28. Morgan 2003:25-27, 113; McInerney 2001:63-67. Numismatic evidence attenuates the problem that these myths are documented only late, but it cannot fully eliminate it. For coins can be struck on account of various interests within the same region by different cities with different meanings; cf. Morgan 2003:26, 84-85, 132; Nielsen 1999:43-46. On the other hand, the personal names of the fifth and fourth centuries demonstrate ethnic coherence. Then again, in conflict with this point is the fact that these names turn up only in the context of an external perspective; Herodotus 6.127; on this, Nielsen 1999:22-32; Freitag, this volume. In the enumeration of the *ethnê* living in the Peloponnese, Herodotus (8.73; cf. also Pausanias 1.17.7) speaks of the Arcadians, who have lived there since ancient times; for this, Morgan 2003:37-38, 196-197. For the epigraphically attested names, Morgan 2003:208-211.

[73] For the relationship of Elis to the *perioikoi*, Roy 2000b, Roy, this volume. An example of this is the conflict over Lasion (Xenophon *Hellenica* 7.4.12): Ruggeri, this volume. Morgan 2003:47.

the sixth century Thessaly had tried repeatedly to gain influence in Phocis.[74] On a larger scale, the threat posed to the Peloponnesians by the Thebans led to the solidarity of the Eleans, Achaeans, Mantineans and other Arcadians. They prepared themselves for the alliance with Athens and Sparta and immediately reached a consensus on the leadership—a consensus, indeed, in accordance with the heterarchical principle, in that the leadership was supposed to change according to the location of each operation.[75]

It is not necessary to describe these conflicts more precisely here. What is essential is that this internal cohesion dissolves again the moment military pressure ceases. The unity of the Arcadians sustained for a short time after the battle of Leuctra also remained unstable, as shown by the immediate resistance of Orchomenos to Mantinea. In this context the short-lived alliance of Akroreia, Pisatis and Arcadia should also be mentioned, as well as the attempt of Triphylia to sever itself from Elis and to link up with Arcadia.[76] This liability becomes especially apparent through the many dedications to Mycenaean tholos graves in the fifth and fourth centuries in the parts of Messenia which freed them from Spartan control; these allow the inference of various local identities. The same holds also for the graves of heroes in the fourth and third centuries in Arcadia.[77] It seems natural to associate the names mentioned in the Homeric *Catalog of Ships*[78] and frequently by later authors with various groups inside the various regions.

The clear tension between the effort to ethnicize entire regions and the tendency towards the maintenance of sub-regional and local identities allows the unsurprising hypothesis to be formulated that larger political units could achieve stability only when they structured themselves hierarchically. This hypothesis is supported by the relative longevity of the Peloponnesian and Attic Leagues.[79] Such relationships also emerge where, as in Elis, a strong central settlement arose. Achaea, too, may already have become a unit in the first decades of the fourth century. This development

---

[74] This can be clearly followed in the archaeological record from the dedications and building activities in the Phocian shrine of Kalapodi; Morgan 2003:24, 131, and Morgan 2001:30–34; Morgan 2003:115–119. Cf. also Beck 1997:87.

[75] Xen. *Hellenica* 7.5.1–2; cf. the situation after Leuctra, which is to a certain degree comparable, Roy 2000a:310.

[76] Cf. Pretzler, this volume; Ruggeri, this volume, Roy, this volume.

[77] Luraghi, this volume.

[78] For the post-Mycenaean origin of the *Catalog of Ships*, see convincingly Eder 2004.

[79] Such types of alliance were not normally long-lived. The reference to alliances in the Lelantine War (of doubtful historicity) cannot be a counter-argument here, as it is certainly a projection backwards from the fifth century.

is presumably related to political activity, especially that on the northern shore of the Corinthian Gulf in the middle of the fifth century.[80] Another aspect of such solidarity is demonstrated by the behavior of Thebes, which used the institutions of *enktêsis* and *epigamia* in order to produce a cohesion that could no longer be dissolved. From these efforts no unified schema can be derived. The situation in Macedonia and Thessaly shows this. Zofia Archibald describes it fittingly as "an overarching regional hierarchy" which did not in either case "properly integrate its constituent parts with the mechanism of government. But despite the self-sufficiency of the individual parts, representation towards the outside is—as in the anthropological analogies—always taken care of by "an intermediary, regional authority."[81]

It seems, then, that the cohesion that emerges in these "micro-states" is not directly correlated to the settlement pattern.[82] As indicators of the degree of cohesion one may propose, with good reason, an "expanding network of sanctuaries,"[83] the creation of a public area, the planning of a settlement or of access to the basic resources of water and land,[84] and, of course, also the legalization of political and social ties. But here the anthropological analogy can sharpen the view further. If it is to be assumed that groups of relatives structured the sub-regional and regional units, as is suggested by genealogies, grave finds and hero graves, then it is to be expected that these means were also used to produce superior, larger units. The advice of Nestor in the *Iliad* (2.362–363), which is clearly to be understood as an innovation, to organize the army into phratries and phylae for the successful completion of the war, reflects an aspect of behavior which should be connected to this process, and which should be expected according to the ethnological analogies. These "institutions" are no more "old" than the Dorian or Ionian phylae, but rather are tools created according to traditional patterns, just like the larger fictive units "Dorians" and "Ionians," in order to create cohesion above the level of local units.[85]

So if it is the case that the cohesion in settlement communities could and did become stronger through the enlargement of kinship groupings and

---

[80] Freitag, this volume.
[81] Archibald 2000:231.
[82] Davies 1997:24–27. Archibald 2000:214, rightly speaks of the opposition of *ethnos* and *polis* not as "alternative modes" but rather as "different levels of social organization."
[83] Morgan 2003:57, 74.
[84] For example, in Larisa from the sixth century onwards in the form of aligned houses, new forms of roof tiles, imported pottery; cf. Morgan 2003:90.
[85] Ulf 1996:271–276; likewise Gehrke 2000.

through their transformation into political institutions, then this also means that the process of ethnicization developing parallel to that on the regional and super-regional levels was not yet concluded in the fourth century. For according to kinship-oriented modes of thought, only the ethnic unit can guarantee a superior cohesiveness. However, by the same modes of thought, that emerging hierarchy can be questioned in order to retain heterarchically oriented structures. Ethnicization was thus no efficient means for achieving the political unity of "the Greeks."

Bibliography

Antonaccio, C. 2001. "Ethnicity and Colonization." In Malkin 2001:113–157.

Archibald, Z. H. 2000. "Space, Hierarchy, and Community in Archaic and Classical Macedonia, Thessaly, and Thrace." In Brock and Hodkinson 2000:212–233.

Bargatzky, T. 1986. *Einführung in die Kulturökologie. Umwelt, Kultur und Gesellschaft.* Berlin.

Barnard, A. and Spencer, J., eds. 1996. *Encyclopedia of Social and Cultural Anthropology.* London and New York.

Barth, F., ed. 1969. *Ethnic Groups and Boundaries: The Social Organization of Culture Difference.* Boston.

Beck, H. 1997. *Polis und Koinon. Untersuchungen zur Geschichte und Struktur der griechischen Bundesstaaten im 4. Jahrhundert v. Chr.* Historia Einzelschriften 114. Stuttgart.

Bichler, R. 2004. "Das chronologische Bild der 'Archaik'." In Rollinger and Ulf 2004b:207–248.

Brewer, M. R. 2003. *Intergroup Relations.* Buckingham. Second Edition.

Brock, R., and Hodkinson, S., eds. 2000. *Alternatives to Athens: Varieties of Political Organization and Community in Ancient Greece.* Oxford.

Burkert, W. 1992. *The Orientalizing Revolution: Near Eastern Influence on Greek Culture in the Early Archaic Age.* Cambridge MA.

Cartledge, P. 1979. *Sparta and Lakonia: A Regional History 1300-362 BC.* London.

Crumley, C. L. 1987. "A Dialectical Critique of Hierarchy." *Power Relations and State Formation* (ed. T. C. Patterson and C. W. Gailey) 155–169. Washington.

Crumley, C. L. 1995. "Heterarchy and the Analysis of Complex Societies." *Heterarchy and the Analysis of Complex Societies* (eds. R. M. Ehrenreich, C. L. Crumley and Janet E. Levy) 1–5. Archeological Papers of the American Anthropological Association 6. Arlington.

Davies, J. K. 1997. "The Origins of the Greek Polis: Where Should We Be Looking?" *The Development of the Polis in Archaic Greece* (ed. L. Mitchell and P. J. Rhodes) 24–38. London.

Davies, J. K. 2000. "A Wholly Non-Aristotelian Universe: The Molossians as Ethnos, State, and Monarchy." In Brock and Hodkinson 2000: 234–258.

Dietler, M. and Hayden, B., eds. 2001. *Feasts: Archaeological and Ethnographic Perspectives on Food, Politics, and Power.* Smithsonian Series in Archaeological Inquiry. Washington and London.

Donlan, W. 1997. "The Homeric Economy." In Morris and Powell 1997:649–667.

Donlan, W. 2002. "Achilles the Ally." *Arethusa* 35:155–172.

Earle, T. 1987. "Chiefdoms in Archaeological and Ethnohistorical Perspective." *Annual Review of Anthropology* 16:279–308.

Earle, T., ed. 1991. *Chiefdoms: Power, Economy and Ideology.* Cambridge.

Eder, B. 2004. "Noch einmal: der homerische Schiffskatalog." *Der neue Streit um Troia. Eine Bilanz* (ed. C. Ulf) 287–308. Munich. Second Edition.

Figueira, T. J. 1999. "The Evolution of the Messenian Identity." *Sparta. New Perspectives* (ed. S. Hodkins and A. Powell) 211–244. London.

Flensted-Jensen, P., Nielsen, T. H., and Rubinstein, L., eds. 2000. *Polis & Politics: Studies in Ancient Greek History.* Copenhagen.

Foxhall, L. 1995. "Bronze to Iron: Agricultural Systems and Political Sturctures in Late Bronze Age and Early Iron Age Greece." *ABSA* 90:239–250.

Funke, P. 1997. "Polisgenese und Urbanisierung in Aitolien im 5. und 4. Jh. v. Chr." *The Polis as an Urban Centre and as a Political Community* (ed. M. H. Hansen) 145–188. Acts of the Copenhagen Polis Centre 4. Copenhagen.

Funke, P. 1998. "Die Bedeutung der griechischen Bundesstaaten in der politischen Theorie und Praxis des 5. und 4. Jh. v. Chr." *Politische Theorie und Praxis im Altertum* (ed. W. Schuller) 59–71. Darmstadt.

Gehrke, H.-J. 1986. *Jenseits von Athen und Sparta. Das Dritte Griechenland und seine Staatenwelt.* Munich.

Gehrke, H.-J. 1994. "Mythos, Geschichte, Politik—antik und modern." *Saeculum* 45:239–264.

Gehrke, H.-J. 2000. "Ethnos, Phyle, Polis. Gemäßigt unorthodoxe Vermutungen." In Flensted-Jensen, Nielsen and Rubinstein 2000:159–176.

Glazer, N. and Moynihan, D. P., eds. 1975. *Ethnicity: Theory and Experience.* Cambridge MA.

Godelier, M. and Strathern, M., eds. 1981. *Big Men and Great Men: Personifications of Power in Melanesia.* Cambridge.

Good, A. 1997. "Kinship." In Barnard and Spencer 1996:311–317.

Hall, J. M. 1997. *Ethnic Identity in Greek Antiquity.* Cambridge.

Hall, J. M. 2002. *Hellenicity between Ethnicity and Culture.* Chicago.

Hall, J. M. 2004. "Culture, Cultures and Acculturation." In Rollinger and Ulf 2004b:35–50.

Hansen, M. H. 2002. "Was the *Polis* a State or a Stateless Society?" In Nielsen 2002:17–47.

Harris, M. 1995. *Cultural Anthropology.* New York.

Hayden, B. 2001. "Fabulous Feasts: A Prolegomenon to the Importance of Feasting." In Dietler and Hayden 2001:23–64.

Hölkeskamp, K.-J. 1992–1995. "Arbitrators, Lawgivers and the 'Codification of Law' in Archaic Greece." *PCPhS n.s.* 38:87–117.

Johnson, A. W. and Earle, T. 1987. *The Evolution of Human Societies: From Foraging Group to Agrarian State.* Stanford.

Jost, M. 1985. *Sanctuaires et cultes d'Arcadie.* Paris.

Lomas, K., ed. 2004. *Greek Identity in the Western Mediterranean.* Leiden.

Malkin, I. 1994. *Myth and Territory in the Spartan Mediterranean.* Cambridge.

Malkin, I., ed. 2001. *Ancient Perceptions of Greek Ethnicity.* Cambridge MA.

McInerney, J. 1999. *The Folds of Parnassos: Land and Ethnicity in Ancient Phokis.* Austin.

McInerney, J. 2001. "Ethnos and Ethnicity in Early Greece." In Malkin 2001:51–73.

Melville, G., ed. 1992. *Institutionen und Geschichte. Theoretische Aspekte und mittelalterliche Befunde.* Cologne.

Möller, A. 2004. "Elis, Olympia und das Jahr 580 v. Chr. Zur Frage der Eroberung der Pisatis." In Rollinger and Ulf 2004b:249–270.

Morgan, C. 1994. "The Evolution of a Sacral 'Landscape': Isthmia, Perachora, and the Early Corinthian State." *Placing the Gods: Sanctuaries and Sacred Space in Ancient Greece* (eds. S. E. Alcock and R. Osborne) 105–142. Oxford.

Morgan, C. 2000. "Politics without the Polis: Cities and Achaean Ethnos, c.800–500." In Brock and Hodkinson 2000:189–211.

Morgan, C. 2001. "Ethne, Ethnicity and Early Greek States, ca. 1200–480: An Archaeological Perspective." In Malkin 2001:75–112.

Morgan, C. 2003. *Early Greek States beyond the Polis.* London.

Müller, K. E. 1987. *Das magische Universum der Identität. Elementarformen sozialen Verhaltens. Ein ethnologischer Grundriß.* Frankfurt.

Murray, O. 2000. "What is Greek about the Polis?" In Flensted-Jensen, Nielsen and Rubinstein 2000:231–244.

Nielsen, T. H. 1999. "The Concept of Arkadia—The People, their Land, and their Organisation." In Nielsen and Roy 1999:16–79.

Nielsen, T. H., ed. 2002. *Even more Studies in the Ancient Greek Polis*. Papers from the Copenhagen Polis Centre 6. Historia Einzelschriften 162. Stuttgart.

Nielsen, T. H., and Roy, J. 1999. *Defining Ancient Arkadia*. Acts of the Copenhagen Polis Centre 6. Copenhagen.

Patzek, B. 2004. "Griechischer Logos und das intellektuelle Handwerk des Vorderen Orients." In Rollinger and Ulf 2004b:427–445.

Peoples, J. G. 1982. "Individual or Group Advantage? A Reinterpretation of the Maring Ritual Cycle." *Current Anthropology* 23:291–310.

Plattner, S., ed. 1989. *Economic Anthropology*. Stanford.

Pohl, W. 2002. "Ethnicity, Theory, and Tradition: A Response." *On Barbarian Identity. Critical Approaches to Ethnicity in the Early Middle Ages* (ed. A. Gillett) 221–239. Turnhout.

Pohl, W. and Reimitz, H., eds. 1998. *Strategies of Distinction: The Construction of Ethnic Communities 300-800*. Leiden.

Raaflaub, K. A. 1997. "Homeric Society." *A New Companion to Homer* (ed. I. Morris and B. Powell) 624–648. Leiden.

Raaflaub, K. A. 2004. "Archaic Greek Aristocrats as Carriers of Cultural Interaction." In Rollinger and Ulf 2004a:197–217.

Rappaport, R. 1967. *Pigs for the Ancestors*. New Haven.

Rollinger, R. 2001. "The Ancient Greeks and the Impact of the Ancient Near East: Textual Evidence and Historical Perspective (ca. 750–650 BC)." *Mythology and Mythologies: Methodological Approaches to Intercultural Influences* (ed. R. M. Whiting) 233–264. Melammu Symposia 2. Helsinki.

Rollinger, R. 2003. "The Western Expansion of the Median 'Empire': A Re-examination." *Continuity of Empire (?). Assyria, Media, Persia* (ed. G. B. Lanfranchi, M. Roaf and R. Rollinger) 289–319. Padua.

Rollinger, R. 2004. "Die Verschriftlichung von Normen: Einflüsse und Elemente orientalischer Kulturtechnik in den homerischen Epen, dargestellt am Beispiel des Vertragswesens." In Rollinger and Ulf 2004b:367–425.

Rollinger, R. 2008. "Near Eastern Perspectives on the Greeks." *Oxford Handbook of Hellenic Studies* (eds. G. Boys-Stones, B. Graziosi and P. Vasunia). In Press. Oxford.

Rollinger, R. and Ulf, C., eds. 2004a. *Commerce and Monetary Systems in the Ancient World: Means of Transmission and Cultural Interaction*. Melammu Symposia 5. Stuttgart.

Rollinger, R. and Ulf, C., eds. 2004b. *Griechische Archaik. Interne Entwicklungen— Externe Impulse*. Berlin.

Roy, J. 2000a. "Problems of Democracy in the Arcadian Confederacy 370–362 BC." In Brock and Hodkinson 2000:308–326.

Roy, J. 2000b. "The Frontier between Arkadia and Elis in Classical Antiquity." In Flensted-Jensen, Nielsen and Rubinstein 2000:133–165.

Schuller, W. 1974. *Die Herrschaft der Athener im Ersten Attischen Seebund*. Berlin.

Siapkas, J. 2003. *Heterological Ethnicity: Conceptualizing Identities in Ancient Greece*. Acta Universitatis Upsaliensis. Uppsala.

Sokolovskii, S. and Tishkov, V. 1996. "Ethnicity." In Barnard and Spencer 1996:190–193.

Sollors, W., ed. 1998. *Theories of Ethnicity: a Classical Reader*. Basingstoke.

Tandy, D. W. 1997. *Warriors into Traders: The Power of the Market in Early Greece*. Berkeley.

Tausend, K. 1992. *Amphiktyonie und Symmachie. Formen zwischenstaatlicher Beziehungen im archaischen Griechenland*. Historia Einzelschriften 73. Stuttgart.

Thommen, L. 1996. *Lakedaimonion Politeia. Die Entstehung der spartanischen Verfassung*. Historia Einzelschriften 103. Stuttgart.

Thompson, R. H. 1989. *Theories of Ethnicity*. New York.

Ulf, C. 1990. *Die homerische Gesellschaft. Materialien zur analytischen Beschreibung und historischen Lokalisierung*. Vestigia 43. Munich.

Ulf, C. 1993. "Tendenzen zur Etablierung von zentraler Macht im archaischen Griechenland." *Bericht über den neunzehnten österreichischen Historikertag in Graz*. Veröffentlichungen des Verbandes Österreichischer Historiker und Geschichtsvereine 28 (ed. L. Mikoletzky) 83–91. Vienna.

Ulf, C. 1996. "Griechische Ethnogenese versus Wanderungen von Stämmen und Stammstaaten." *Wege zur Genese griechischer Identität. Die Bedeutung der fraddress früharchaischen Zeit* (ed. C. Ulf) 240–280. Berlin.

Ulf, C. 1997a. "Die Mythen um Olympia: politischer Gehalt und politische Intention." *Nikephoros* 10:9–51.

Ulf, C. 1997b. "Überlegungen zur Funktion überregionaler Feste in der früh-griechischen Staatenwelt." *Volk und Verfassung im vorhellenistischen Griechenland* (eds. W. Eder and K.-J. Hölkeskamp) 37–61. Stuttgart.

Ulf, C. 1999. Review of B. Eder, *Argolis, Lakonien, Messenien. Vom Ende der mykenischen Palastzeit bis zur Einwanderung der Dorier* (Vienna, 1998). AnzAW 52:45–53.

Ulf, C. 2006. "Anlässe und Formen von Festen mit überlokaler Reichweite in vor- und früharchaischer Zeit. Wozu dient der Blick in ethnologisch-anthropologische Literatur? " *Kult—Politik—Ethnos* (eds. K. Freitag, P. Funke and M. Haake) 17–41. Historia Einzelschriften 189. Stuttgart.

Ulf, C. 2008. "The World of Homer and Hesiod." *Blackwell Companion to Archaic Greece* (ed. K. A. Raaflaub and H. van Wees). In Press. London.

Urry, J. 1997. "History of Anthropology." In Barnard and Spencer 1995:277–279.

Vanschoonwinkel, J. 2006. "Greek Migrations to Aegean Anatolia in the Early Dark Age." *Greek Colonisation: An Account of Greek Colonies and Other Settlements Overseas* (ed. G. R. Tsetskhladze) 1:115–141. Leiden.

Vivelo, F. R. 1988. *Handbuch der Kulturanthropologie. Eine grundlegende Einführung.* Stuttgart.

Voyatzis, M. E. 1999. "The Role of Temple Building in Consolidating Arkadian Communities." In Nielsen and Roy 1999:130–168.

van Wees, H. 1998. "The Law of Gratitude: Reciprocity in Anthropological Theory." *Reciprocity in Ancient Greece* (eds. C. Gill, N. Postlethwaite and R. Seaford) 13–49. Oxford.

van Wees, H. 2002. "Greed, Generosity and Gift-Exchange in Early Greece and the Western Pacific." *After the Past* (ed. W. Jongman and M. Kleijwegt) 341–378. Mnemosyne Supplement 233. Leiden.

Welwei, K.-W. 1999. *Das klassische Athen. Demokratie und Machtpolitik im 5. und 4. Jahrhundert.* Darmstadt.

Welwei, K.-W. 2004. *Sparta. Aufstieg und Niedergang einer antiken Großmacht.* Stuttgart.

Whitley, A. J. M. 1991. "Social Diversity in Dark Age Greece." *ABSA* 86:341–365.

Wiessner, P. 2001. "Of Feasting and Value: Enga Feasts in a Historical Perspective (Papua New Guinea)." In Dietler and Hayden 2001:115–143.

Contributors

KLAUS FREITAG is Professor of Ancient History at the Rheinisch-Westfälische Technische Hochschule in Aachen. The history of the Gulf of Corinth is one of his main areas of specialization, to which he devoted the book *Der Golf von Korinth. Historisch-topographische Untersuchungen von der Archaik bis in das 1. Jh. v. Chr.* (Munich 2000).

PETER FUNKE is Professor of Ancient History at the Westfälische Wilhelms-Universität Münster. He has published broadly on various aspects of Greek history and epigraphy. Most relevant for the themes of the present volume is his book *Homónoia und Arché. Athen und die griechische Staatenwelt vom Ende des Peloponnesischen Krieges bis zum Königsfrieden (404/3 - 387/6 v. Chr.)* (Stuttgart 1980).

MAURIZIO GIANGIULIO is Professor of Greek History at the University of Trento. A specialist of archaic Greek history and culture and of the history and archaeology of Magna Graecia, he has published many articles especially on the foundation and early history of various Greek colonies, and the book *Ricerche su Crotone arcaica* (Pisa 1989).

NINO LURAGHI is Professor of Classics at Princeton University. He has worked mainly on Greek historiography and on tyranny in archaic Greece. His book *The Ancient Messenians: Constructions of Ethnicity and Memory* was published in 2008.

CATHERINE MORGAN is the Director of the British School at Athens. She specializes in the archaeology and history of archaic Greece and is the author of *Athletes and Oracles: The Transformation of Olympia and Delphi in the Eighth Century BC* (Cambridge 1990) and *Early Greek States beyond the Polis* (London 2003), and the co-editor, with S. Hornblower, of *Pindar's Poetry, Patrons, and Festivals: From Archaic Greece to the Roman Empire* (Oxford 2007).

ROBERT PARKER is Wykeham Professor of Ancient History in the University of Oxford. He has written *Miasma: Pollution and Pollution in Early Greek Religion* (Oxford, 1983); *Athenian Religion: A History* (Oxford 1996); *Polytheism and Society at Athens* (Oxford 2005),

MARIA PRETZLER is Lecturer in Ancient History at Swansea University (Wales, UK). Her research in Arcadia started when she was an undergraduate in Graz (Austria) in the early 1990's. In 1999 she completed a DPhil on Pausanias' Arcadia at Oxford, and she has since published a number of articles on Peloponnesian subjects, as well as a monograph *Pausanias: Travel Writing in Ancient Greece* (2007).

ERIC ROBINSON is Associate Professor of Ancient History at the Indiana University at Bloomington. A specialist of ancient democracy, he published *The First Democracies: Early Popular Government outside Athens* (Stuttgart 1997). His book on Greek democracies outside Athens during the Classical Age is forthcoming from Cambridge University Press.

After studies in Edinburgh and Cambridge, JIM ROY taught ancient history in the universities of Sheffield and Nottingham until his retirement in 2004. He has published on various aspects of Greek history, especially concerning Arcadia and Elis, and continues to do so as an Honorary Research Associate of the University of Nottingham.

CLAUDIA RUGGERI graduated in classics from the Catholic University in Milan and continued her studies in Greek history and epigraphy at the University of Vienna, specializing in the history of Elis. Her book *Gli stati intorno a Olimpia. Storia e costituzione dell'Elide e degli stati formati dai perieci elei (400-362 a.C.)*. appeared in 2004. Since 2004 she takes part in the project "The Kerameikos and the north-western part of the city of Athens," funded by the Austrian National Research Fund at the Department of Ancient History of the University of Vienna.

CHRISTOPH ULF is Professor of Ancient History at the Leopold-Franzens-Universität Innsbruck. A specialist of early Greek social and cultural history, he is the author of *Die homerische Gesellschaft. Materialien zur analytischen Beschreibung und historischen Lokalisierung* (Munich 1990), the editor of *Wege zur Genese griechischer Identität. Die Bedeutung der fr/ harchaischen Zeit* (Berlin 1997), and the co-editor (with R. Rollinger) of *Griechische Archaik. Interne Entwicklungen - Externe Impulse* (Berlin 2004)

Index

CPSIA information can be obtained at www.ICGtesting.com
Printed in the USA
BVOW010115300413

319426BV00006B/113/P